HUMAN RIGHTS AMONG INDIAN POPULATIONS

HUMAN RIGHTS AMONG INDIAN POPULATIONS
Knowledge, Awareness and Practice

SHILPY GUPTA
and
A.K. KAPOOR

GYAN

Human Rights Among Indian Populations : Knowledge, Awareness and Practice

Rs. 900

ISBN: 978-81-212-1015-7

Published in 2009 in India by
Gyan Publishing House
23, Ansari Road, Darya Ganj,
New Delhi-110002
Phones : 23282060, 23261060
Fax : 011-23285914
E-mail: books@gyanbooks.com
Website: www.gyanbooks.com

Lasser Type Setting by: Rudra Computer Graphics, Delhi
Printed at : Young Art Press, Delhi - 92

Contents

Abbreviations Used

AD	After Death
ADGP	Additional Director General of Police
AIG	Assistant Inspector General of Police
ASI	Assistant Sub-Inspector of Police
ASP	Assistant Superintendent of Police
BC	Before Christ
BSF	Border Security Force
CBI	Central Bureau of Investigation
CIB	Central Intelligence Bureau
CISF	Central Industrial Security Force
CJM	Chief Judicial Magistrate
CMO	Chief Medical Officer
CPC	Criminal Procedure Code
CRPF	The Central Reserve Police Force
CVC	Chief Vigilance Commissioner
DGP	Director General of Police
DIG	Deputy General of Police
DPO	District Police Officer
DSP	Deputy Superintendent of Police
EHC	Exemptee Head Constable
FGD	Focus Group Discussion
GO	Gazetted Officer
GREF	Ground Reserve Engineering Force
HAP	Haryana Armed Police
HC	Head Constable
IGP	Inspector General of Police
ILO	International Labour Organization
INSP	Inspector of Police
IPC	Indian Penal Code
IRBn	Indian Reserve Battalion

ITBP	Indo-Tibetan Border Police
LPG	Liquid Petroleum Gas
MLCC	Matrilineal Cross Cousin Marriage
NCRB	National Crime Records Bureau
NCSCST	National Commission for Scheduled Caste and Scheduled Tribe
NCT	National Capital Territory
NDPS	Narcotics Drugs and Psychotropic Substances
NGO	Non Gazetted Officer
NHRC	National Human Rights Commission
OAU	Organization of African Unity
OR	Other Ranks
PCR	Police Control System
PHC	Primary Health Centre
PIL	Public Interest Litigation
PLCC	Patrilineal Cross Cousin Marriage
POI	People of India
PWD	Public Works Department
RAF	Rapid Action Force
RPF	Railway Protection Force
SHO	Station House Officer
SI	Sub-Inspector of Police
SLL	Special and Local Laws
SP	Superintendent of Police
SPE	Special Police Establishment
SSP	Senior Superintendent of Police
SVB	State Vigilance Bureau
UGC	Upgraded Constable

Preface

This book endeavours to explain the varied human rights roles played by the tribal, rural to urban Indian populations. Somewhat more specifically it is an attempt to discover the range of knowledge, attitude practice and awareness of human rights among Indian populations.

Although Human Rights is a new field/discipline, it has grown even more rapidly in recent years and it has extended to almost all fields of social sciences, law and human sciences. In fact, the diverse understanding of human rights enable it to occupy at present a unique central position in anthropology in that it ties together different disciplines. This unifying "core" quality of human rights stems from the many levels in which humans operate, from the individuals, to populations to society. It has been observed that the dimensions of human rights from law are discussed and explained when introduced. Here the focus is on the applicability of human rights among tribal, rural and urban populations from the anthropological dimensions. It provides a survey of the important issues and areas of anthropology of human rights at an uncomplicated level, with emphasis on recent and exciting developments.

The role of customary laws, police, and socio-economic and cultural characteristics, that underlie the attitudes and awareness are presented with emphasis on knowledge and practice, in the broader context of the fundamental concepts and issues in human rights and anthropology. It is broader in scope, considerably more researched and anthropologically designed to be maximally useful in teaching and research in law, social sciences and police science. Each chapter is presented not only for the clarity and coverage of appropriate material, but also because it is enjoyable and entertaining discussions of the topic.

Although this book and the Reader can, of course, stand alone, the combination of book, Reader and the research material should provide clear, comprehensive and, we hope, exciting coverage of the field in forms that are most useful to both students and teachers. The subject ultimately of greatest interest to every person is himself and other humans. Anthropology of Human Rights is devoted to an understanding of the basic mechanisms underlying human behaviour with socio-cultural dimensions, experience and awareness. We know far more about the physical universe than about our own brains and minds.

Recent debates in human rights, are numerous and exciting. There are many new and intriguing stories. The recent explosion of interest in the human rights, law and anthropology attests to rapid progress in the find, and to the direct impact it is having on real and practical aspects of human life. Every person should have a voice in the application and control of bio-cultural dynamics and issues in society. The basic information necessary to develop various dimensions on human rights and other relevant topics are presented in this book. We hope you will find it both useful and enjoyable.

A thorough understanding of basic ethnography and methodology is extremely important in enabling students to forge ahead intelligently in areas of their own interest.

It is a great pleasure and privilege for us to express thanks to those who have given precious help, support and guidance without which this work would not have got the present shape.

We wish to express our special gratitude to Prof. Dr. Mool Chand Sharma, Vice-Chairperson, University Grants Commission, New Delhi for providing us constant support and guidance. Being the Professor of law, he gave the suggestions from legal dynamics and he has always been to us a great source of stimulation and advice. An analysis of the underlying meanings and connecting link between the ideas was made possible by his illuminating comments. His detailed theoretical and practical knowledge helped us to develop the concepts most significant to this study, in a comparative paradigm.

We are grateful to Prof. Dr. T.S. Naidu, Dept. of Anthropology, Pondicherry University, Pondicherry; Prof. Dr. Ranjan Gupta, Head, Anthropometry and Human Genetics Unit, Indian Statistical Institute, Kolkata and Prof. Dr. B.G. Banerjee, former Head, Dept. of Anthropology, Panjab University, Chandigarh for giving valuable suggestions.

We are thankful to Prof. Dr. Satwanti Kapoor, Dr. Gautam K. Kshatriya, Dr. V.C. Channa and Dr. K.K. Patnaik, from Dept. of Anthropology, University of Delhi, Delhi and Bhopal for their constant support and encouragement.

We would like to express our gratitude to the Director-General, Bureau of Polic Research and Development, Ministry of Home Affairs, Govt. of India for awarding the research grant under which all the field works have been conducted. Without the grant it would have been very difficult to plan the extended field works.

A part of this research included intensive field work, covering one of the most remote and difficult terrain, the help received from various officials is very valuable. We would like to convey our thanks to the officials of district Lahoul and Spiti and district Rohtak. The SP of District Lahoul and Spiti Mr. Dinesh Yadav; SDM Mrs. Kumud Pathania; Project Officer Mr. Vinay Pathania; Mr. Rakesh Aggarwal, NIC. The cooperation and support of people of Lahoul, Haryana and Delhi have been very vital in the completion of the field work. Without their support, we would not be able to complete the work. We would like to specially thank Mr. Tschering Dorje, Mr. Nawang Norbu, his wife Mrs., Dachen Palmo, Mr. Nawang Gyftsen, his wife Mrs.Shakuntala, Mr. Sungdup Dorje, Mr. Tobdan, Mr. Bir Singh, Ms. Deychen, Mr. Tschering Chawang Tashi, his wife Mrs., Chhering Dolma, Mr. Vikas, Ms. Lammo, Mr. Shayamlal Das Thakur, Mr. Shivlal Guruji, his wife Mrs. Chetan Dolma, Dr. Gaurav, Mr. Bir Chand, Mr. Rameshi Thakur, Ms. Promilla Thakur, Ms. Pushpa Sahani, Mr. Mange Ram, his wife Mrs. Kaushalya Devi and his family Mr. Mukesh and Mr. Dineshi, Ms. Kamlesh, Mr. Ramesh Verma, Mr. Ram Prasad Rohilla, Mr. Daleep Singh Yadav, Mr. L. Shreedhar, Mr. Sudhir and Mr. Rakesh Mangal.

Shilpy Gupta wants to acknowledge her family individually which is as follows:

"Last but not the least, my family and friends have been a constant morale support. During the days of field work, their love, affection and prayers had given me power and strength to keep going. I truly and deeply acknowledge the speechless efforts and concerns of my father, Dr. S.R. Gupta, my mother Mrs. Anita Gupta, my elder brother Shirish and my little sister Ruchika who was always there in my times of hardships. The concerns and constant presence of all those who are close to my heart have always motivated me to complete the work. It would not have been possible without the unstinted boost provided by them. My friends Ms. Abhilash, Mrs. Kajri Trivedi (nee Tandon), Mr. Sumit, Mr. Rahul have always been patient to give me enough space to express my thoughts in front of them and helped me in times of need.

In the end I would like to thank God for giving me such an opportunity in my life and for putting me amid those people who care about me and for protecting me when ever I needed it most."

We are also thankful to Mr. Amit Garg, Director, Publications of Gyan Books Pvt. Ltd. New Delhi for publishing this book within a short time.

Finally, this book is dedicated to all Human Rights activists and anthropologists who want to do something for Human Welfare.

July, 2008
California (USA) **Shiply Gupta**
Gwalior, M.P. (India) **A.K. Kapoor**

1

Introduction

The concept of rights carries a double meaning: that which is universal and alienable, and that which is morally appropriate or just. Human rights refers to those elemental rights which any human deserves to have honored in order to survive, enjoy well-being, and flourish or fulfill him or herself, simply by virtue of being human. The promises and problems of human rights discourse are encapsulated in deceptively simple terms. Although the concept is universal theoretically but not in knowledge and practices among all the population. Although every society embodies the conception of personal dignity, worth and well-being, tribal societies lack the idea of equal and inalienable rights. Human rights are usually framed as the right of the individual in relation to the state; ironically the police authority charged with protecting and promoting human rights, as well as bringing to justice those who violate them, is also the entity that is most often the violator of human rights. This ambiguous position of police is one of the most fundamental dilemmas for human rights.

1.1 Police

The word 'Police', which comes from the Greek 'politeia' meaning 'government', 'citizenship', refers to that phase of government having to do with the protection of life and property, preservation of public tranquility and maintenance of order, and the prevention and control of crime. Among the various agencies of a government, police is the most visible community agency and is often in the 'limelight of community scrutiny and evaluation'. (Troganowicz, 1974)

According to Clift (1970) the term 'police' is relatively new. Taken from the French who, in turn, adopted it from the Latin 'politia', the word literally means 'power of the people'. It has come to have a twofold meaning in modern times. On the one hand it refers to the authority of the people to do whatever they think best for their general welfare and prosperity i.e. the police power of the state, while on the other it pertains to the police functions, especially in the preservation, detection and prosecution of public crimes and nuisances.

The term 'police' broadly connote the purposeful maintenance of public order and protection of persons and property, from the hazards of public accidents and the commission of unlawful acts. It specially applies to the body of civil officers with maintaining public order and safety and enforcing the law including the prevention and detection of crime. (Ghosh and Rustamji, 1993)

1.2 Birth of Concept of Police

The early kings depended on the military for internal government as well as for war and conquest .There were no separate agency for maintaining law and order. However, it was soon apparent that military men were ill-suited to deal with problems of internal security. Their approach to law was inclined to be repressive. It became evident that functionaries for maintenance of law and order have to be different from the military force.

1.3 Development of Police Organization

An "Organization is defined as "the grouping of related activities in a group for efficient operation." Along with this groping there is job of stimulating the will of the employees towards a common objective. (Clift, 1970)

The development of the police idea in society brought to the fore two different concepts. In the first of these, the whole responsibility for maintaining law and order was entrusted to the community itself. The social unit forming the community elected its own police from themselves or sometimes appointed them from outside. The Anglo-Saxon communities in England worked this system with almost perfect efficiency. This type of police is known as the 'Kin Police' or 'Anglo-Saxon Police' system. The Anglo-Saxon period began in the British Isles around the year 600 A.D. and extended to 1066 A.D. It represents basically force exercised indirectly by the people from below upwards.

In the second concept, instead of community appointed police, the ruler appointed officers to deal exclusively with breach of laws and punishment of offenders. The power behind these officers consisted of military type of force through which harsh and vigorous action was provided against law breakers. The origin of the 'Gendarmerie Police System' of the absolute monarchs of Western Europe can be traced to this system, in the beginning of the medieval period. (Misra, 1977)

In the following section a brief of police system of United Kingdom, Unites States of America, Canada and Japan has been given to have a global perspective of various police systems present.

1.3.1 Police of United Kingdom

In the 14th century, William Norman conquered England and first thing he did was to establish a national government. This replaced the purely local government of the natives. This move involved expenditures, so the next thing he did was to institute taxes. Then an account containing the owner's address and the taxable property was maintained in the form of 'Doomsday Book'. This practice of tax collection has come down even to the present day. A constable was appointed to be responsible for the maintenance of peace of the village. (Saksena, 1987)

Before the 19th Century, the Great Britain had no organized police system. Later it evolved the concept of law and order, which really means order according to law and not according to the wishes of any individual. Today, the British Police have come to occupy a unique place among the police forces of the world.

1.3.2 Police of United States of America

The Sheriff and the constable were the first police officers in America. In 1818, town and countries sprinkled throughout the entire North-West territory, there were Sheriffs and constables exercising similar authority. Constitutions ultimately provided for police officers in the various states.

Later state and federal police forces were created. Pennsylvania was the first to create a State Police in 1905. The growth of the law enforcement agencies of the Federal Government was slow. As their utility became apparent, they grew in strength and power.

1.3.3 Police of Canada

The Canadian Police are organized in three categories:

1. The Royal Canadian Mounted Police which is a federal force.
2. Provincial Force
3. Municipal Police

The ultimate responsibility for maintaining peace and order in the country rests with the Central Government.

1.3.4 Police of Japan

The Japanese Police System is a centralized one like the continental system. The Minister of Home Affairs controls all the police agencies in the country. In 1954, the Rural Police and Municipal Police were combined into the Prefectural Police. There is a separate Tokyo Metropolitan Agency for policing of Tokyo and a number of small cities, surrounding the central core of the Metropolis.

1.3.5 Police of India

(A) Police in Ancient India

Knowledge about police administration in early Hindu times in India is rather obscure. Police in ancient India can be known and studied through various scriptures, codes, inscriptions, contemporary works of literature and art etc. The earliest code of human conduct in the world "Manu Samhita" throws ample light on law enforcement in the contemporary society (Srivastava, 1999).

The code of Manu which described the state of society and laid down rules for the conduct of administrations and the general public but made no specific mention of police functionaries. Although according to the code one of the main objects of the institution of the king was to restrain violence and punish evil doers.

(i) ***Administration under the Mauryas*** – The Arthashastra which described the administration arrangements during the reign of the great Hindu sovereign, Chandra Gupta Maurya, mentions an elaborate system of secret and repressive police. A variety of people were used to keep the government informed of all undesirable activities in the state. According to historians, the Mauryan Empire was truly a police state. The smallest administration police unit was the village and village councils were responsible to prevent and detect crime under the supervision of the headman.

(ii) ***Administration under the Guptas*** – During the Gupta period also the administrative institutions as well as the political concepts underwent various important changes. The general administration during the Gupta period was efficient and the governance was without decapitation or other corporal punishments. Criminals were fined lightly or heavily according to the circumstances of each case.

It would thus appear that police functions of the state were discharged by various officers named differently during the different periods. It may, however, be noticed that the basic structure of police has nearly remained the same. The village police, the city police and the palace police were the basic systems which was suitably developed and changed by various kings.

(B) Police in Medieval India

The study of the system of police administration in medieval India under the Mughal and the Maratha governments reveal that neither the Mughals nor the Marathas directly provided for policing rural areas. They merely adopted one of the chief features of the traditional system of the old autonomous village community. Crime was kept under good control by a system of surveillance and espionage. Laws were enforced with rigidity with the help of Kotwal, Faujdar and Kazi.

Dispassionate study reveals that the government under the Mughals was autocratic. It was primarily military in nature and did not undertake wide responsibility or devote itself to manifold functions, as a modern government generally does. Indeed justice and police were two weak points of the Mughal system (Mishra and Mohanty, 1992).

(C) Police During the British Rule

With the decline of the Mughal Empire and the disintegration of the central authority of Mughal rulers, the regular machinery of law and order also broke down. Extortion and oppression flourished unchecked.

This was the State of things when the East India Company acquired Bengal, Bihar and Orissa in 1765. The Zamindars were relieved of their liability. British's introduced the Daroga system for the law and order maintenance. But this system failed badly as there was a marked increase in crime everywhere.

In 1843, Sir Charles Napier realized that only under a recognized organization, the police could function properly and produce desired results. Napier's system was based on two principles: firstly, the police must be completely separated from the military. Secondly, the police must be an independent body to assist the collectors.

This experiment was successful and its broad framework was used to recognize police administration. The main principles of Napier's model were not altered even by the Police Commission of 1860, which designed the present police force for India (Mehra, 1985)

The Police Act of 1861, the Bible of the Indian Police, was the first attempt to introduce a law- enforcing agency with a uniform structure in the greater part of India.

(D) Police Since Independence

A new era began for the police with independence in 1947. The organizational structure of the police continued with the model of 1861, with slight modifications. Numerical strengths have vastly increased. The creation of Central Bureau of Investigation and the expansion of the Intelligence Bureau have greatly enlarged the scope of police work.

1.4 Differing Police Systems

In terms of element of centralization or otherwise, the police in the world have been divided into three main categories:

(A) **Centralized or National Police System:** In this system, the National Government is usually represented by a Minister of the Interior or Home, who exercises more or less complete power upon all matters connected with the police. This system is followed in all countries on the maintained of Europe, most of the newly –Independent Asian and African countries and the Latin –American countrics.

(B) **Partially Centralized System:** In this system the National Government only exercises a check on local police administration which is run by local authorities as in England and India.

(C) **Decentralized System:** In this system, as in United States of America, all Governments whether National, State or local maintain police agencies which are wholly independent of each other. There is however, a visible trend towards centralization of everything.

1.5 Police Administration in India

The organization of police force in a country like India has to be diverse and plural. The Constitution of India deliberately leaves enough scope for the desired plurality. In India police administration is managed at three different levels:

(a) Central Level
(b) State Level
(c) District Level

(a) Central Level: The role of the Central Government in police administration lies in its imparting a uniform pattern to the police organizations in the states and thus towards a centralization in police administration in the country. A host of Union Police Agencies, such as Border Security Forces, Central Bureau of Investigation, Central Reserve Police, Assam Rifles, National Police Academy and Forensic Laboratories and institutes have been created and put under the care of the Central Government to provide support structure to police administrations of the States. The police administrations of Union Territories, is an exclusive and special responsibility of the Union Ministry of Home Affairs which performs numerous police functions, though it shall be erroneous to call it a Ministry for Police Affairs. The indirect but dominant role of the Central Government in police administration of the country, which is symbolized by the Home Affairs, manifests itself as shown in Table 1.1 (Sharma, 1999):

Table 1.1: Role of Central Government in Police Administration

S.No.	*Parliament*	*S.No*	*Ministry of Home Affairs*
1.	Law-making on subjects in the Union and the Concurrent Lists.	1.	Administration of All–India Statutes.
2.	Amendments in Basic Police Acts.	2.	Administration of Union Territories.
3.	Special measures during emergencies.	3.	Personnel Management of the I.P.S.
		4.	Police Co-ordination.
		5.	Supply and Control of arms and equipment.
		6.	Operations of Home Guards and Civil Defense.
		7.	Operations through a network of staff agencies and auxiliary units of Central Police Organization Services.

Source: Singh, 2002

Bayley (1969) has very aptly pointed out the three major characteristics of the Police System in India. These are –

(i) The State Based Police Organization.

(ii) The Armed and Unarmed Police Constabulary.

(iii) The Horizontal Stratification.

The Union Ministry of Home Affairs, Government of India, also owes it to the state to come to their assistance and rescue, in case the police administration in the states needs its specialized help and guidance. To discharge this function the Ministry maintains an extensive network of auxiliary agencies and reserve units spread all over the country. There are Staff Units, Mixed Units and Line Units. Table 1.2 can present this classification as under:

Table 1.2: Central Police Organization

S.No	*Staff Units*	*S.No*	*Mixed Units*	*S.No.*	*Line Units*
1.	Central Forensic Institutes	1.	Central Intelligence Bureau (C.I.B.)	1.	The Central Reserve Police Force (C.R.P.F.)
(a)	Central Forensic Science Laboratory and Intelligence Bureau	2.	Central Bureau of Investigation (C.B.I.)	2.	Border Security Force (B.S.F.)
(b)	Serologist Office			3.	The Assam Rifles
(c)	Central Finger Print Bureau Central	3.	Special Police Establishment	4.	Railway Protection Force (R.P.F.)
(d)	Detective Training School	4.	C.V.C. (Chief Vigilance Commissioner)	5.	Central Industrial Security Force (C.I.S.F.)
(e)	Central Institute of Criminology and Forensic Science			6.	India Reserves
(f)	Examiner of Questioned Documents			(a)	Indo – Tibetan Border Police (I.T.B.P.)
(g)	India Security Printing			(b)	National Crime Records Bureau (N.C.R.B.)
(h)	Inspector of Explosives			7.	National Security Guards
2.	Sardar Vallabh Bhai Patel Police Academy			8.	Rapid Action Force (R.A.F.)
3.	Internal Security Academy				
4.	Directorate of Police Wireless				

Source: Sen, 2000

(b) State Level: Unlike the British and the American System of Police, the Indian Police System does not fall into any neat category of a Unitary or Federal Police .The organization and the administration of police force in a country like India has to be diverse and plural. The Constitution of India deliberately leaves enough scope for the desired plurality. The Union Government, though not directly involved in the Police administration of the country very significantly retains and administers a number of sensitive and critical areas that have their direct bearing on the function of policing.

The police organization in Indian States is primarily governed by the Police Act of 1861, which was based on the recommendations of the Police Commission of 1860. Section 4 of this Statute lays down the principles, on which the organization of the police force rests till today (Sharma, 1981). The section inter alia states:

"The Administration of the police throughout a general police district (now called States). State shall be vested in an officer to be styled the Inspector General of Police and in such Deputy Inspectors General and Assistant Inspectors General as the State Government shall deem fit."

The police organization at the state level distinctively staff –cum-line functions .Most of these line and staff functions are performed simultaneously. Some of the staff agencies operate from the state head quarters and may or may not have field units.The line functions of the State level police administration include implementation of policies pertaining to law and order and detection and investigation of crimes with the help of district units. The Home Minister, the Home Commissioner and their Home Department constitute the civilian wing of the State police .The professional wing has its unarmed and armed wings.

The professional wing of the State police works under the overall command and supervision of the I.G.P. of the state. He has a couple of Special, Additional and Assistant Inspectors General of Police to aid and advise him at the police head – quarters. They may also administer some of the specialized police functions, like anti corruption, vigilance, civil defense and traffic etc. at the State level. The IGP is the Chief of the State police and the Police Act assigns specific responsibilities to him in the area of police policy formulations and line operations involved in the execution of the policy. He is the chief personnel officer of his department and has wide powers and discretion with regard to financial management and disciplinary matters in his organization. As an administrative leader of his team, he functions through a number of Deputy Inspectors General of Police working on territorial or functional basis.

The DIG in charge of police range supervises the work of 4–6 administrative districts, which constitutes the intermediary level in the

Table 1.3: State Police Organization I.G.P.

Spl. I.G.P. Vigilance /Anti corruption ↓ *Homeguards / Civil Defense Commissioner of Police*				*Addl. I.G. P.*			
↓ DIG Range	↓ DIG/AIG Rly. Police	↓ DIG/ Training	↓ DIG H.Qr.	↓ DIG/SP Wireless	↓ DIG CID	↓ DIG Spl.Br.	↓ DIG Armed Po
↓ S.P. District	↓ Rly. Police Sub-div.	↓ P.T.C.	↓ Motor Transport		↓ Criminal Branch	↓ Spl.Br. Security Branch	↓ Commdt /SP
	↓ Rly. Police Circles	↓ A.T.C.	↓ Fire Services		↓ Finger Print Branch		↓ Dy. Comm
	↓ Rly. Police Stations	↓ R.T.C.			↓ Dog Squad		↓ Coy co
	↓ Rly. Police Outposts	↓ A.T.C.			↓ Forensic Science Lab		↓ Platoon Comm.
							↓ Hd. C
							↓ Constable

Source: Sen, 2000

administrative hierarchy , just below the State and above the District. The functional DIGs at the State level take care of auxiliary units, such as CID, the Intelligence Department, the Railway Police, the Police Training Institutions, the Police Head Quarters and the armed battalions at the State level. There is no uniform pattern about the number and work of the DIGs in various States of the Union.

The organizational chart of the State Police as given in Table 1.3:

(c) District Level: The District has been the most primary and basic unit of administration in India since medieval times. The police administration is built around police districts. Each police range comprises of four or more police districts, which coincide with the boundaries of the revenue districts.

Organizationally, the district is further sub-divided into police circles and police stations. The Police circles are placed under the control of circle inspectors, while the police stations are administratively managed by the Superintendent Inspector of Police. Some police stations have their police out posts or '*chowkis*' within territorial jurisdiction; which are usually under the charge of head constables or Assistant SIs of police depending on the importance of the place where an out- post is located.

For organizational purpose, a police station is the smallest field unit of police administration. The Superintendent of Police (SP), who heads the district police office, also coordinates the functions of the heads of the district police lines, district crime bureau, district special branch, district traffic branch and the district prosecution branch.

The District Police Organization is represented by its chief, the S.P. Working under the overall supervision of DM, he looks after the problems of law and order and that of the administration of crime and vice in the district . The Superintendent of Police, who presides over this organization is the key functionary through whom the State Government operates and the police stations below look to him for command, guidance and action. As the chief intelligence officer of the district he collects information from the lower levels and communicates his assessment of the same to his superiors of the district police personnel system. In districts which territorially include big cities, the SPs have additional and special responsibilities such as regulation and control of traffic, collection of special intelligence and handling of political and communal conflicts of violent nature.

Hierarchically speaking, the district police in the most of the state stands organized in two police sub-divisions and police circles, which comprise a cluster of police stations. The Additional or Deputy Superintendents of Police look after the work of police subdivisions, while the Circle Inspectors deal

Table 1.4: District Police Organization

↓

S.P.
(Incharge – District HQ)

↓

↓	↓	↓
Confidential Office / Spl. Branch Under Addl. S.P.	Addl. SP	A.S.P. /Dy. S.P. of Sub – Division (Incharge-Subdivision)
↓	↓	↓
Dist. Crime Branch Under Inspector	A.S.P./Dy.S.P. Incharge (H.Q.) Home Inspector (Incharge - DPO)	Circle Inspector
↓		↓
Spl. Investigating Agency under Inspector /S.I.	District Police Office	Sub Inspector / Inspector S.H.O. Police Station
↓		↓
Reserve Line under Reserve Inspector		Head Constable / S.As.
↓		↓
Traffic Police under Dy.S.P. / Inspector		I/c Police Post
↓		
Spl. Squads		
↓		
Prosecuting Branch Office		

Source: Sen, 2000

with the supervisory work of police stations falling within their respective circles. A number of staff agencies such as crime bureau , special branch and special investigation agency etc. stand converged into the office of the District SP, who in turn , operates through a network of a line units, such as police stations, special squads, prosecuting branch, traffic police and reserve police. The organizational profile of the District police is presented in Table 1.4 below:

1.5.1 Role of Police

The police are the central agency of the criminal justice system. The police means a civil force of a State, which is entrusted with the duty of:

- Maintaining public order and enforcing regulations for the prevention and detection of crime ;
- Preserving essential tranquility;
- Security of its citizens;
- Security of vital installations;
- Suppression of noise and disorder;
- Regulation of locomotion and traffic;
- Prevention of indecency;
- Control of numerous types of nuisance ; and
- Rendering assistance in relief and rescue operations.

While the legal functions of the police are very sharply defined in various acts and statutes, the role of police as a social service agency has been left vague and undefined to include anything and everything, which other agencies may not perform or may fail to perform (Aujla, 1998)

Police has existed in one or the other form in India since time immemorial. Police, as a distinct set-up in India, is a legacy of the British rule. Indigenous system of policing in India was enforced through the headman who was assisted by one or more village watchman. On the break up of the Hindu kingdoms, the Afghan and Mughal rulers came to power in most of India. The domain of a king or a '*sultan*' was divided into territorial areas each under a dignitary, generally known as a '*faujdar*'. The '*faujdar*', who was principally a military officer, functioned as Chief of Police in rural areas. In smaller towns, the police was under the revenue officer, subject to overall supervision of '*faujdar*'. In large towns, the police administration was under the '*Kotwal*'.

1.5.2 Studies on Indian Police

There is a considerable body of officials and non-official literature on the history and contemporary situation of the Indian police. The works of Majumdar, 1960; Gupta, 1974; IIPA, 1978; Khan, 1983; Chaturvedi, 1988 and

Kant, 1996 gives an excellent account of the development of the police organization and administration in India. Much of this work has been carefully examined by Bayley (1969), a landmark study. It provides many empirically grounded insights in diverse areas of police organization and operations including attitudes of the community towards the police, student-police relations and rural police. Sharma (1977) extends the analysis of Bayley in some respects. Baxi (1982) analyses the legal framework of the Indian police organization and the status of a colonial minority it creates. Baxi contrasts the existing para-military model of police organization with models of participative management and argues that police accountability and efficiency can be maximized by the latter model. A special feature of his analysis is the examination of institutionalized recourse to torture as way of policing; he examines the diverse political contexts which creates this situation and examines the diverse political contexts which create this situation and examines some of its underlying 'justification'. Dhillon (2005) has talked about the nexus of Indian police and politics, focusing on the colonial concepts and democratic compulsions. Verma (2005) has undertaken the historical and organizational analyses of the structure and culture of Indian police. He has outlined a reform process in which technology plays a vital role. He has also talked of crime as a 'phenomenon', the problem in its measurement and the use and misuse of crime statistics. Chaturvedi (2006) has also talked about the administration of police and their *modus operandi* adopted in investigation of the crime. Kumar (2006) has talked about the history and heritage of Delhi Police. He has highlighted the role of Delhi police in Indian history.

Many scholars have worked on the aspects of dilemmas and challenges involved with the job of policing (Sharma, 1985; Dhillon, 1989; Mathur, 1994 and Dixshit, 2000). Work has also been done focusing on the aspect of police – public relationship, expectations of the public from the police (Diaz, 1983; Chaturvedi, 1984; Das, 1987; Diaz, 1989; Shah, 1993; Dikshit and Shah; 1993 and Kohli; 2005). Scholars have written about the aspects of justice administration and police (Rao, 1974 and Sharma, 1985).

Mishra(2005b) advocates that the protection of human right is fundamental to genuine and lasting law and order. As law enforcers, police are the first line of defense for human rights. They are the guardians of the law, including human rights law. In order to protect human rights, police must first know and understand them. Furthermore, police officers must be familiar with the various international guidelines and bodies of principles, and be able to use them as tools in their everyday work. He says that they must understand that international human rights standards concerning their work were developed to provide invaluable guidance for the performance of their crucial functions in a democratic society.

Mathur (1991) examines how the police developed in various societies, what role it is expected to play in a pluralistic developing society and many such critical issues which provide proper perspectives to the police. The scholar has provided a penetrating study about police culture, police leadership, police moral and police training in the context of changing perspectives. The extent and scope of the complexity and intensity of the police have been ably delineated with a view to shed adequate light on the organizational nexus and social identities of mass pluralities in the context of democratic system. He has dealt complex subjects such as collective violence, terrorism and growing agrarian unrest. Reasons for erosion in police morale have been analyzed in our changing society.

Vadackumchery(2001) introduced a new concept of 'enforcement crime' which means 'the crimes committed by enforcement officers during the course of law enforcement or on the pretext of law enforcement or on the pretext of law enforcement'. He feels that the enforcement crimes must be treated just like any other crime and dealt with accordingly. Indian police have entered the third millennium and the challenges for them are many. They have to work in a legal framework which recognizes victim justice, gender justice, human rights justice, social justice, enforcement justice, just justice, total justice etc. under an equal justice system which stands for distributive justice to criminals, to the victims, to the victims of power and authority, to the society and to the justice system itself.

Police and human rights have a very close relation. They go hand in hand either as a control body for executing human rights or as a promoting body for violating human rights. Various authors have written about police and human rights focusing on the role of police in maintaining the human rights balance in the state. Many scholars have worked on the historical aspect of police, their origin, and their formation. Work has been done to elaborate about the police organizational set up, law and order in the police society, relation of police and political development, police with reference to social change, human rights, ethical dilemmas within the complicated criminal justice system. Many Indian and internationally acknowledged experts of policing and representatives of human-rights organizations have written about police in transition which deals with the questions of transition, European trends in the governance of the police, the relationship between police and criminality, the role of the police in the constitutional framework, the limits of policing, police brutality, civilian oversight of the police and the possibilities of a democratic reform of police forces in Central and Eastern Europe, Asia and India (Mullik, 1969; Clift, 1970; Troganowicz, 1974; Misra, 1977; Triloknath, 1978; Sharma, 1981;Alderson, 1984; Pike, 1985; Mehra, 1985; Mccabe and Wallington,1988; Mishra and Mohanty, 1992; Ghosh and Rustamji, 1993; Amnesty International, 1994; Crawshaw, 1998; Crawshaw and Williamson, 1998; Sharma, 1999; Crawshaw, 1999; Mawby, 1999; Srivastava, 1999; Sen, 2000; Kadar, 2001; Mallick, 2002; Singh, 2002; Pollock, 2003; Mishra, 2005a and Biju, 2005.)

1.6 Concept of Crime

Crime is a very complex phenomenon which is an individualistic behaviour. Originally crimes were private matters. Individuals who were wronged would seek retribution against the wrongdoer or the wrongdoer's family. Crime is one such important word, which signifies different meanings to many different people and is always straining at the boundaries of its currently assigned meaning. The earliest reference to the word 'crime' in the English vocabulary can be traced to 14th Century, according to the Oxford English Dictionary. Contrary to this, the term is traced to have been created as early as 614 A.D. in the verdict of the Merovingian King Chlotar. Crime had existed as a concept in the early formalized codes of law. It also appears in Babylonian Code of Hammurabi of about 2270 B.C. in the Law Codes of ancient Palestine in the Twelve Tables of Roman Law and in German Law. (Bloch, 1962)

The concept of crime, like all other concepts is essentially dependent upon the perception, rationality and interest of those who are constantly after constructing such concepts. The various conceptions of crime differ from one another primarily in the extent to which they refer to the criminal law i.e. to the extent to which they conform to the State's definition of crime. There is lego -socio- psycho -bio conception of the term crime (Ansari, 1987). Social scientists tend to equate the term crime with all behaviour that is injurious to society. Others view crime as those acts that deviate greatly from the accepted norms of the society (Sinha, 1981 and Sahay, 1981). Few scholars have also talked about the 'criminal tribes'. The term 'criminal tribes' was coined by the British administrators in 1871 on the supposition that the crime in India is a hereditary profession.(Elwin, 1943; Bhargava, 1949; Biswas, 1960; Bhowmick, 1980; Ali, 1990). Deogaonkar (1990) had studied tribes as the victims of crime and bondedness. Religious people regard crime as belonging to the genre of sin .Others whose personal code emphasizes truth as the ultimate value, equate falsehood with crime.

Sutherland and Cressey (1978), defined crime as 'the behaviour in violation of criminal law, no matter what the degree of immorality, reprehensibility or indecency of an act, it is not crime unless it is prohibited by the criminal law'.

Sutherland (1960), proposed the definition of crime, 'the essential characteristic of crime is that it is behaviour which is prohibited by the State as an injury to the State and against which the State may react at least as last resort by punishment.'

Koran and Corkle (1959), define crime as, 'an act or omission ascribed to a person when he is punished by the authorities in continuous political control over the territory in which he is.'

Reid (1976) defined crime, 'as an act, commission or omission, sinful or non-sinful which a society or State has thought fit to punish under its laws for the time being in force.'

Schur (1969), defined crime from the legal point , 'any act by which any omission or commission run counter to the criminal law would be defined as a crime or criminal behaviour in the legal sense .

".......according to Osborn, crime is an act or default, which tends to the prejudice of the community and is forbidden by law on pain of punishment, inflicted at the suit of the State. In other words, there is nothing, which by itself is a crime. Only such acts or omissions are crimes, which are made punishable by the legislature. For example, the consumption and sale of liquor are offences in Gujarat, but not in adjoining Rajasthan. The acts and omissions mentioned above are called crimes / offences. It does not follow that an act or omission, which is not punishable, is innocent. The rich man who refuses a morsel to save a fellow creature is far worse than the starving wretch who snatches and devours a loaf from a bakery. Yet the law punishes the latter and not the former for cruelty". (c.f. Pound, 1963)

In the words of Darrow (1934), 'crime is an act forbidden by the law of the land and for which penalty is prescribed.'

Tappan (1960), defined crime in a very comprehensive way 'crime is an intentional act in violation of criminal law committed without justification and penalized by the State.' Out of all the legal definitions of crime mentioned here this legal definition of crime of Tappan is regarded as the closest approximation to clear definition given by law. This definition of crime says:

(a) there is no crime without law and without a state to punish the breach of law,

(b) there is no crime where an act that would otherwise be offensive is justified by law,

(c) there is no crime without intention and ,

(d) there is no crime where the offender is deemed incompetent.

Anthropologists define 'crime' as a 'violation of criminal law that is a breach of contract code specially sanctioned by the state which through its legislature agency defines crimes and their penalties and through its administrative agencies, prosecutes offender and imposes and administers punishment. (Evans-Pritchard, 1940; Elwin, 1943 and Sahay, 1981). The sociological aspect of crime is more comprehensive than the legal one. All the definitions of crime offered from the sociological angle, view crime as an act violative of social norms. Deviance is universally found but whether an act deserves to be called 'crime' depends on the sanctions attached to norms.

Sutherland (1960) says that, 'crimes are the acts or omissions violative of the social norms, acts which are always approved by the society even though these are not prohibited by law'.

Akers (1965) defines that, 'crime is a violation of the prevalent sentiments of pity and probity.'

Elliot and Merrill (1950) says that 'a crime is *ipso facto* implies a disturbance in a social relationship and a social definition as to what such a disturbance is crime may be defined as anti-social behaviour which the groups rejects and to which it attaches penalties'.

The sociological concept of crime as explained however is not also wholly acceptable. **First**, every antisocial and deviant behaviour cannot be termed as crime. **Secondly**, set of values of the world community does not have a universal amity and consensus differs from place to place and from society to society and from time to time. The meaning of 'good' or 'bad' does not have the universal application , and also the meaning of these words conveying the moral approval and disapproval respectively, is circumscribed by the norms of each society changing from time to time because of which the concepts of crime also varies from society to society. **Thirdly**, human actions are broadly divided into two categories – a) those which conform to norms of society and; b) those which deviate from norms of society. **Fourth**, according to the anthropological thought, the crimes are the violation of the rules of the conduct. What is collective conscience is crux of the whole problem which differs from society to society, segment to segment, hence no uniformity to reach the definition of crime to be universally accepted anthropologically.

"Crime as legally defined concept is violation of legal norms, but in the social sense, it is regarded as deviant behaviour which consists of the commission of an act prohibited by social scientists. Keeping this fact in view Durkheim defines crime as 'an act that offends certain very strong collective sentiments. The only common characteristic of all crime is that they consist ... in acts universally disapproved of by members of each society .... Crime shocks sentiments which for a given system, are found in all healthy consciences.' (c.f. Ansari, 1987)

1.6.1 Other Important Concepts

According to Constitution of India, 'Crime' is defined as one of the following:

1. An act committed or omitted in violation of a law forbidding or commanding it and for which punishment is imposed upon conviction.
2. Unlawful activity.
3. A serious offense, especially one in violation of morality.
4. An unjust, senseless, or disgraceful act or condition

All the categories of crimes committed in India are classified under the Criminal Procedure Code (Cr.P.C.) for ensuring punishment through law. This divides all the crimes into two categories.

(a) Cognizable Crime (Sec. 2(c) Cr.P.C.)

(b) Non- Cognizable Offence (Sec. 2(1) Cr.P.C.)

(a) Cognizable Crime : All cognizable crimes reported in the country are dealt by the police in which, a police officer may arrest a person without a warrant. In such crimes, the police has a direct responsibility to take immediate action on receipt of a complaint or of credible information, visit the scene of the crime, investigate that facts, apprehend the offender and arraign him before a court of law having jurisdiction over the matter. Cognizable crimes are broadly categorized as those falling either under the 'Indian Penal Code (IPC)' or under the 'Special and Local Laws (SLL)'.

(b) Non-Cognizable Offence: These crimes are generally left to be pursued by the affected parties themselves in Courts. Police does not initiate investigation in non-cognizable crimes.

Classification of crimes under the Indian Penal Code (IPC):

(i) **Crimes Against Body :** Murder, Its attempt, Culpable Homicide not amounting to Murder, Kidnapping and Abduction, Hurt ,Causing Death by Negligence.

(ii) **Crimes against Property:** Dacoity, Its Preparation and assembly, Robbery, Burglary, Theft.

(iii) **Crimes Against Public Order:** Riots, Arson

(iv) **Economic Crimes:** Criminal Breach of Trust, Cheating, Counterfeiting

(v) **Crimes Against Women:** Rape, Dowry Death, Cruelty by Husband and Relatives, Molestation, Sexual Harassment and Importation of Girls

(vi) **Crimes Against Children:** Child Rape, Kidnapping and Abduction of Children, Procuration of minor girls, selling/buying of girls for Prostitution, abetment of Suicide, Exposure and Abandonment, Infanticide, Foeticide

vii) Other IPC crimes.

(c) Special and Local Laws (SLL) : The Indian Penal Code, 1860 (IPC) enumerates the acts of commission and omissions that constitutes crimes (offences) and specific punishments for them . Since 1860 many new forms of crime have come into existence. Several new laws have been enacted, from time to time, with the creation of new offences, which are not punishable under the IPC. These laws are called, 'special laws' and 'local laws'. A special law applies to a particular subject such as excise, gambling, essential commodities etc. A local law applies to a particular area such as Calcutta Port .The police on its own initiative may register offences under SLL provided that they are cognizable. A viewpoint is that action of police in detecting and registering SLL cases has sobering effect on the society. The other view is that vigorous enforcement of SLL diverts the world be offenders to more serious IPC crimes (Banerjea, 2005) . Various crimes which have been grouped under the Special and Local Laws are:

(i) Arms Act
(ii) Narcotic Drugs and Psychotropic Substances Act
(iii) Gambling Act
(iv) Excise Act
(v) Prohibition Act
(vi) Explosives and Explosive Substances Act
(vii) Immoral traffic (Prevention) Act
(viii) Indian Railways Act
(ix) Registration of Foreigners Act
(x) Protection of Civil Rights Act
(xi) Indian Passport Act
(xii) Essential Commodities Act
(xiii) Terrorist and Disruptive Activities Act
(xiv) Antiquity and Art treasure Act
(xv) Dowry Prohibition Act
(xvi) Child Marriage restraint Act
(xvii) Indecent Representation of Women Act
(xviii) Copyright Act
(xix) Sati Prevention Act
(xx) SC/ST (Prevention of Atrocities) Act

(xxi) Forest Act

(xxii) Other Crimes (not specified above) under Special and Local Laws including Cyber Laws under Information Technology Act (IT), 2000.

(d) Crime Rate : The rate of crime, being the incidence (Total number of cases) of crime per lakh of population . Many factors influence incidence of crime of an area. Of these, population is the principal factor.

1.6.2 Crimes in Indian Population

In India numberless criminal incidents are happing every minute. Even though Indian constitution ensures protection of citizens from crime and legislative measures are established by the government to prohibit criminal activities, crime trends are increasing day-by day in every walks of life. For a country of such enormous size, social diversity and strife, the crime situation in India prevailing today is a cause for anxiety. Singh (2006) provides an in-depth analysis of various facets of crime in India like violent crimes, organized crimes, economic offences, patterns of crime against women and children, crime against dalits and backward classes and cyber crimes. He has argued that to protect people from anti-social forces the government has to ensure more effective policing with a firm application of the law.

(A) Crime Statistics under Indian Penal Code (IPC)

Crimes vary markedly from one state to another in India. Crime rates also vary considerably within urban, rural and tribal areas. On an average 3 IPC crimes are reported every minute in the country. Among the states, in the year, 2002 Uttar Pradesh reported a decline of 18.00 percent while Jharkhand and Mizoram reported an increase of 23.50 percent and 25.60 percent respectively over the previous year. Madhya Pradesh contributed more than 10 percent of crimes closely followed by Tamil Nadu, 9.4 percent (Crime in India, 2002).

Bangalore Commissionerate of Karnataka State reported the highest incidence of IPC crimes during 2002. Crimes head-wise analysis for districts reveal that Patna City of Bihar State reported the highest number of murders (472), their attempts (682) and robberies (491). Hoshangabad district of Madhya Pradesh reported the highest number of culpable homicide not amounting to murder cases. The highest incidence of kidnapping and abduction were reported from the North-West district of N.C.T. of Delhi. Comparatively, Mumbai city reported the highest incidence of burglary, theft (including auto theft) and criminal breach of trust while Bangalore commissionerate reported the highest number of cheating, counterfeiting and hurt cases. The highest number of dacoity cases were reported from Ahmedabad , Gujarat. Maximum rape cases were reported from Raipur, Chhattisgarh. Jaipur in Rajasthan reported highest incidents of causing deaths by negligence. Vijayawada district reported highest incidents of cruelty by husband and his relatives. Sitapur district of Uttar Pradesh reported highest incidents of dowry deaths. Sagar district of Madhya Pradesh reported the highest number of molestation cases. Faridabad district of Haryana reported the highest number of sexual harassment cases while Palamu district of Jharkhand reported the highest number of importation of girls (Crime in India, 2002).

(B) Crime Statistics under Special and Local Laws (SLL)

Cases under these Acts represent preventive policing i.e. reporting of crime indicates better policing efforts. Mostly the Central Acts on special subjects which are applicable in the whole country are considered for the purpose of crimes reported under Local Acts is clubbed together in 'Other SLL' crimes due to their disparity from one place to other. On an average 7 SLL crimes are reported per minute in the country. The highest rate of crime under Arms Act is reported from Delhi. Punjab reports the highest crime rate under Narcotics Drugs and Psychotropic Substances Act (NDPS). Under Gambling Act , Goa reports the highest crime rate. Kerala reports the maximum crime rate under Explosives and Explosive Substances Act. Under the Immoral Traffic (Prevention) Act, Chhattisgarh reported the highest crime rate. Under the Indian Railways Act, Madhya Pradesh reported the highest crime rate. Mizoram reports the highest crime rate under Registration of Foreigners Act. Himachal Pradesh recorded the highest crime rate under the Forest Act. Under the SC/ST (Prevention of Atrocities) Act, highest percent of crime against Scheduled Castes are reported from Uttar Pradesh and highest percent of crime against Scheduled Tribes are reported from Madhya Pradesh. Where as the highest crime rate for crimes against Scheduled Castes is reported from Madhya Pradesh and against Scheduled Tribes is reported from Nagaland (Crime in India, 2002).

1.7 Population

The word 'Population' as is explained in the Oxford English Dictionary is 'the total number of its inhabitants or the degree in which a place is populated or inhabited. It is also defined as 'the action or process of peopling a place or region.' (Little et al, 1958).

The word 'Population' as used in several disciplines has somewhat different meanings. Statisticians use it to designate an empirical total as distinguished from a 'universe', a theoretical total. For them it is 'the total number of cases with a given characteristic (or characteristics), or all members of a given set or class. A population may be an existing finite number of cases, as all the possible tosses of a coin. Whether the population is finite or infinite, it is from this totality of cases that a 'sample' is drawn. A population is sometimes referred to as a 'utlivese', because it includes the entire existence of a specific characteristics.

Geneticists conceive of a 'population' as one of the sub-units of a totality that has been classified according to the distribution of its genes. Somewhat similarly, zoologists and other scientists of life sciences understand the word to mean a breeding group more or less isolated from other members of the species. Ecologists define population as all the organisms that constitute a specific group or occur in a specific habitat. Demographers define 'population' of a particular area, as the number of persons who, by one criterion or another, are there on a particular date.

In the country the members of a nation, state, or whatever, one can enumerate either all that in some sense 'belong' there whether or not they are currently resident or all who are physically present whether or not they belong there makes population of that place. (Peterson and Peterson, 1986)

Anthropologists and other social scientists also work with populations that vary enormously. They define 'population' as 'the people or individual families or households or bands of foragers, or members of ethnic units having a common culture, or the citizens of a state, who live within the confines of a village or a region'. (Barfield, 1997)

The members of an ethnic group refer to all the people presumed to belong to the same society and who share the same culture and language and which had been transmitted uncharged from generation to generation.

According to Burman (1994) 'Population' means an aggregate of persons with or without structure binding them together .The word 'population' should not be replaced with 'peoples' or 'people'.

When the members having a common or distinct 'culture' occupy a particular territorial area , having a feeling of unity and regard themselves as a distinguishable entity , then that group of people forms a 'society'. A society is a special type of group with a comprehensive social system that includes all the basic social institutions required to meet basic human needs.

1.7.1 Indian Population

The Indian population is divided into a large number of endogamous groups consisting of different castes, tribes, religions, minorities, scheduled castes etc. The basis of the isolation of these populations is varied, but it is mainly geographic, religious, ethnic or occupational. (Singh et al, 1994)

Populations of India can be broadly classified under three categories:-

1. Urban Population
2. Rural Population
3. Tribal Population

1.7.2 Urban Population

Population living in the urban areas is urban population. The definition of urban areas adopted in Census 2001 is as follows –

(a) All statutory places with a municipality, corporation, cantonment board or notified town area committee, etc.

(b) A place satisfying the following three criteria simultaneously :

(i) a minimum population of 5000;

(ii) at least 75 percent of male working population engaged in non-agricultural pursuits ; and

(iii) a density of population of atleast 400 persons per sq.km. (1000 per sq. mile)

Apart from these , the outgrowths (OGs) of cities and towns have also been treated as urban under 'Urban Agglomerations' like railway colonies, university campuses, port areas , military camps etc. According to the Census of India definitions, the unit of classification for urban area is 'town'. Towns with population of 1, 00,000 and above are called cities.

Population of various states of India is declared 'urban' according to the definition given by census of India. For the present study the urban population of Delhi was selected because, Delhi not only has urban population, it is also a metropolitan city, with a cosmopolitan (multi-ethnic) environment. Multinational corporations, metro rail, fat salaries, snazzy eateries, swanky cars, neon signs, highways, flyovers, trendy apparel, vast multi-storeyed markets, wide roads, sub-ways, indoor stadiums and multiplex cinema halls and many more which makes it Metropolitan zone. (Kapoor and Kapoor, 2001)

Work Done in Urban Population

Much of India's increasing urban population comprises migrants from rural areas. The earlier works of scholars discusses the evolution of urban society, concept of 'urban' in Indian context, trends of urban development in India since independence. Anthropologists have also conducted study in cities in the rubric of urban anthropology.(Adams, 1966; Bose, 1970; Mitra,1970; Loewenstein, 1971; Blanton, 1976; Rao, 1977; Fox, 1977; Bose,

1978; Nath, 1986; Eisenstadt & Shachar,1987 and Desai , 1990). Scholars have studied aspects of change with urbanization, experiences of people who have migrated to an urban space, urbanization in third world countries. (Beshers, 1962; Morris, 1968; Gore, 1968; Singh, 1976; Castells, 1976; Saunders, 1981 and Haider, 2000).

1.7.3 Rural Population

The population living in areas defined as rural in the census of a particular country is known as rural population. In India the smallest unit of area for which the census data is presented may be a village or town. The definition of a village in the 1921 census of the then Punjab was identical with that of an estate under section 3 (I) of the Punjab Revenue Act , which stated that an estate means any area for which a separate record of rights has been maintained and is also of assessed for land revenue or would have been assessed, if the land revenue had not been released, compounded for or redeemed or which the local government may be general rule or special order, declare to be an Estate 'village' , is the basic unit of rural area .

A century ago, the term 'village' was used in most parts of India to denote the smallest unit of administration of land revenue and this also included congregation of the inhabitants on a fixed site , with occasionally some outlying hamlets.

A village may not be a mere cluster of houses with local name. It may be made up of chief areas of habitation and the surrounding areas falling within certain demarcated boundaries with a distinct hadbast number allotted to a revenue village after settlement. During 2001 census, 'village' has been taken as the basic unit for the purpose of data tabulation. A revenue village is a cadastrally surveyed area having definite boundaries and could consist of one or more hamlets.

Various criteria are used and it is not possible to give a single definition of the term 'rural population'. The underlying concepts used in definitions are fivefold:

1. National administrative divisions, based on historical, political or administrative, rather than statistical concepts.
2. Population size
3. Local administrative areas
4. Specific rural characteristics
5. Predominant economic activities

Most censuses employ combinations of all the above five (Wilson, 1985). Sorokin and Zimmerman (1929) consider the principal criterion of

Table 1.5: Characteristics of Rural and Urban Population

S.No.	*Factor*	*Rural*	*Urban*
1.	**Occupation**	Totality of cultivators and their families. In the community are usually few representatives of several non – agricultural pursuits.	Totality of people engaged principally in manufacturing, mechanical pursuits, trade, commerce, professions, governing and other non- agricultural occupations.
2.	**Environment**	Predominance of nature over anthropo–social environment. Direct relationship to nature.	Greater isolation from nature. Predominance of man-made environment over natural. Poorer air. Stone and iron.
3.	**Size of Community**	Open farms or small communities: 'agriculturalism' and size of community are negatively correlated.	As a rule in the same country and at the same period, the size of urban community is much larger than rural community . In order words, urbanity and size of community are positively correlated.
4.	**Density of Population**	In the same country and at the same period the density is lower than in urban community. Generally density and rurality are negatively correlated.	Greater than in rural communities. Urbanity and density are positively correlated.

(Contd.)

(Contd. Table 1.5)

S.No.	*Factor*	*Rural*	*Urban*
5.	**Homogeneity and Heterogeneity of the Population**	Compared with urban population, the population of the rural communities is more homogeneity in racial and psycho- social traits.	More heterogeneity than rural communities (in the same country and at the same time).
6.	**Social Differentiation and Stratification**	Rural differentiation and stratification less than urban.	Differentiation and stratification show positive correlation with urbanity.
7.	**Mobility**	Territorial, occupational and other forms of social mobility of the population are comparatively less intense. Normally the migration current carried more individuals from the country to the city.	More intensive. Urbanity and mobility are positively correlated. Only in the periods of social catastrophe is the migration from the city to the country greater than from the country to the city.
8.	**System of Interaction**	Less numerous contacts per man. Narrower area of the interaction system of its members and the whole aggregate. More prominent part is occupied by primary contacts. Predominance of personal and relatively durable relations. Comparative simplicity and sincerity of relations. 'Man is interacted as a human person'.	More numerous contacts. Wider area of interaction system per man and per aggregate. Predominance of impersonal, causal and short-lived relations. Greater complexity, many fold superficiality and standardized formality of relations. Man is interacted as a 'number' and as 'address.

difference between rural and urban society to be occupational. From this basic difference, other characteristics are developed. Table 1.5 shows eight characteristics in all which are used as a means for comparing the 'urban' and 'rural' populations (Mann, 1965). Following are the characteristics:

(i) Occupation
(ii) Environment
(iii) Size of Community
(iv) Density of Population
(v) Heterogeneity and Homogeneity of Population
(vi) Social Differentiation and Stratification
(vii) Mobility
(viii) System of Interaction

Hence, keeping the above characteristics in mind, the term 'rural population' and 'urban population' has been taken into consideration for the present study.

Rural and Urban Population Statistics

India is one of the developing countries of the world and the bulk of its population reside in villages .The population of India in 1961 was 439.2 million, of whom 360.7 million or 82 percent lived in villages and 78.5 million or 18 percent in cities or towns (Madan and Madan , 1983) . Although there has been, between 1961 and 2001, a slow but steady shift towards urbanization, yet, as stated above a large majority of the people still reside in villages, as shown in Table 1.6

Table 1.6: Rural and Urban Population Statistics

S.No.	*Type of Population*	*Percentage of Total Population (Year Wise)*				
		1961	*1971*	*1981*	*1991*	*2001*
1.	**Rural**	82.0	80.1	76.6	74.3	72.2
2.	**Urban**	18.0	19.9	23.4	25.7	27.8

Source: Rural Development Statistics, 2001

Work Done in Rural Population

The works among the rural population of India has always attracted the attention of many scholars of various fields. Earliest reference of the work of

Maine (1889), Baden-Powelt (1896), in the village committees produced gigantic reports dealing with rural conditions in India. The Famine Commission reports are probably the best known nineteenth-century examples and the Royal Commission on Agriculture, one of the most important since the turn of the century. There are the massive statistical series of all India coverage of rural population. Various scholars like Gait, 1902; Dube, 1955; Majumdar, 1958; Kessinger, 1974; Arora, 1978; Sarkar, 1985 and Prasad, 1991) had written about numerous aspects of life of rural population of India. The scholars had seen the rural set up from the perspective of concept of rural population, aspects of rural development and change, villages of east and west, India as a village community, social and economic aspects of rural population. Works on the rural population of regional villages like North India, South India, Rajasthan, Bihar, Bengal, Gujarat, and Southeast India had also come up in the form of monographs. Lately, the aspects of rural life, reproductive behaviour, cults and traditions could also be seen in the works of scholars. (Hunter,1868 ; Krishnaswamy, 1947; Lewis, 1958; Culshaw, 1961; Chauhan, 1967; Iswaran, 1968; Singh, 1980; Anker and Anker 1981 and Gough, 1981).

Scholars have also related the problems of poverty with rural population. The extent of rural poverty needs no elaboration. Rural poverty is variously and to varying degrees attributed to a continuing condition of under-development, to active process of under-development, to ill-health poor nutrition etc. Works showing the impact of these and many others factors on poverty had been conducted in past. (Panikar, 1970 ; Mellor, 1972; Behari, 1976; Shah, 1977; Longhurst & Pacey, 1981; Jones et al, 1982; Bardhan, 1984 and Prasad, 1991).

In another concept, social scientists have talked of rural population with reference to stratification, transformation, development and mobility. Since independence, the theme of rural social transformation has become the major issue for the social scientists. Social stratification has various aspects like mobility, changing indices of status determination, class structure and caste structure. The scholars have shown the impact of social transformation on health behaviour, occupational diversification, mass participation in development programmes, politico-economic changes in the rural population. (Desai, 1959; Sharma, 1974; Deb,1975; Narain et al, 1976; Sharda,1977; Dube, 1992; Joshi,1992; Joshi,1992; Vyas,1992; Sharma, 1992; Sachchidananda, 1992; Sharma,1992 and Banerji, 1992).

Many scholars had focused on rural women as the concept of rural population would be incomplete without discussing the role of rural women, impact of social transformation on women, development of rural women etc. (Awasty, 1982 and Sethi, 1992).

1.7.4 Tribal Population

India as a country, mothers 8.43 crores of tribal population, which constitutes 8.2% of the total population .The term 'tribe' originated around the time of the Greek city – States and the early formation of the Roman empire. The Latin term, 'tribus', has since been transformed to mean, 'a group of persons forming a community and claiming descent from a common ancestor' (Gregory, 2003). According to Morris (1980), a tribe is a 'group of persons with a common occupation, interest, or habit,' and 'a large family'.

The layman's understanding of the word 'tribe' is invariably synonymous with primitiveness, savagery and wildness. The origin of it as concept is modern. With the rise of colonialism it has been used politically. The tribes or aborigines were ascribed the lowest position in the human civilization of which the highest level was said to have been achieved by the white men in the west. In other words, the tribes became the conceptual opposite of the westerners.

In modern India, the term 'tribe' came in vogue first when the British penetrated interior areas at the beginning of their rule. The early military campaigners, administrators and Christian missionaries were stuck by the quaintness of the certain people in terms of their social behavior and practices and at times also physical features. They were taken as 'cultural enclaves' (Bara, 2002). Convinced by these broad features , the early British aptly , found in these unusual humans the Indian 'tribe', as counter parts of these indigenous people , whom they encountered in Africa , America and Australia

There are many ways in which the tribes can be described as given by many anthropologists:

1. By region
2. By language
3. By race
4. By their level of integration with rural folk to which they are connected
5. By their economy
6. By their cultural pattern as a whole
7. By their level of education

(A) Distribution of Tribes

The tribal communities live in about 15% of the country's areas, in various ecological and geo-climatic conditions ranging from plains, forest, hills and inaccessible areas. The life style of the tribal people is conditioned by the eco –system and is in tune with nature and natural resources. Tribal people, being essentially ecosystem people, the country's wide ranging diversity in nature and natural resources present a varied tribal population throughout India's length and breadth. In general, most tribal populations' inhabit under-developed areas of the country which are remote, having low density of population and lacking in adequate access to basic amenities, education, employment opportunities and affordable health care services.

Most of the tribal areas are the undulating plateau lands coinciding with the forest areas in the country having much less density of population. It is because of these reasons that creation of critical infrastructure in the tribal areas in the sectors of roads , communication , health , education , drinking water etc. has always been left out by development agencies on one pretext or the other like economic non-viability , high cost , etc. As a result, the physical infrastructure in the tribal areas is inadequate and at a much lower footing than the rest of the areas.

While some communities have adopted a mainstream way of life at one end of the spectrum, and on the other, there are Primitive Tribes. The word **'Primitive Tribe'** in Indian setting was first of all conceived in 1931 by J.J. Hutton. Later he was joined by W.V. Grigson (1938) in the framing of the guidelines for the welfare of the tribes. The word 'tribe' has not been defined anywhere in the constitution of India. It is a matter of great debate among the academicians, administrators, and development planners throughout the country regarding the concept of 'tribe' and 'primitive tribe'. But it states in Article 342 that the scheduled tribes are "tribes or the tribal communities or parts of or groups within tribes or tribal communities" which the president may specify from time to time by public notification. As these communities are presumed to constitute the oldest ethnological segment of the Indian society, the term 'Adivasi' ('Adi' means 'oldest' and 'Vasi' means 'inhabitant) is commonly used to designate them. The International Labour Organization Convention 107 held at Geneva on 5th June 1957, classified these people as indigenous.

The term 'primitive' has a double meaning. It applies to both bodily forms and culture (Boas, 1911). There are 75 Primitive Tribal Groups (PTGs), who are characterized by:-

(a) a pre-agriculture level of technology
(b) a stagnant or declining population
(c) extremely low literacy, and
(d) a subsistence level of economy

(B) Scheduled Tribe

The term 'Scheduled Tribes' first appeared in the Constitution of India. Article 366 (25) defines Scheduled tribes as "such tribes or tribal communities or parts of or groups within such tribes or tribal communities as are deemed under Article 342 to be scheduled tribes for the purpose of this Constitution". (Ghurye, 1959)

This Article says that only those communities who have been declared as such by the President through an initial public notification will be considered as Scheduled Tribes. Any further amendment in the list is through an Act of Parliament. The list of Scheduled tribes is State – specific and a community declared as Scheduled tribe in a state need not be so in another state. The essential characteristics were first laid down by the Lokur Committee. The criteria followed for specification of a community as a Scheduled Tribe is not spelt out in the constitution but has become well established. It takes into account the definitions in the 1931 Census, the reports of the First Backward Classes Commission (Kalelkar Committee), 1955; the Advisory Committee Report on Revision of SC/ST Lists (Lokur Committee), 1965; Backward Classes Commission Report (Mandal Committee), 1980; Backward Classes Commission Report (N.K. Muralidhara Rao Committee), 1982 .

From a study of the available clues, views and definitions, having a bearing on the subject and of the pragmatic selections of tribes actually made so far for the Presidential orders and the parliamentary legislation, the following criteria may be taken for identifying a tribe to be scheduled:

1. Autochthony
2. Groupism or a very strong community-fellowship, if not descent from a common ancestor or loyalty to a common headman or chief.
3. A principal, if not an exclusive, territorial habitat.
4. A distinctive way of life, primitive or backward by modern standards, and apart and aside from the main current of culture.
5. Economic, political and social backwardness.

The list of Scheduled Castes and Scheduled Tribes were notified for the first time under the constitution Order1950. These lists have been amended or supplemented from time to time. On reorganization of the states the Scheduled Tribes (modification) and Scheduled Castes came into force from October 1956. The first order affecting the Himachal Pradesh has been the Scheduled Castes and Scheduled Tribes Order (amendment). The main objective of this Act was to remove the area restrictions in respect of scheduled castes and most of the scheduled tribes. With the result most of the Scheduled castes and scheduled tribes are not notified as such throughout the state, unlike in the 1956 order these were notified in relation to different regions the state registering area restrictions.

There are 573 scheduled tribes as notified under Article 342 of the constitution of India (Kshatriya & Kapoor, 2003) , spread over different states and Union Territories of the country , the largest number being in the state of Orissa , i.e. 62 .The main concentration of tribal population is in Central India and in the North –eastern States . However, they have their presence in all the States and Union Territories except Haryana, Punjab, Delhi, Pondicherry and Chandigarh. The predominant tribal populated States of the country (tribal population more than 50 percent of the Total population) are – Arunachal Pradesh, Meghalaya, Mizoram and Nagaland, Union Territories of Dadra and Nagar Haveli and Lakshadweep. (Annual Report, Ministry of Tribal Affairs, 2004-05)

The population of scheduled tribes has been on the increase since 1961. With the growth rate of the population of Scheduled Tribes at 24.45 percent during the period 1991-2001, more than half the scheduled tribes population is concentrated in the states of Madhya Pradesh, Chhattisgarh, Maharashtra, Orissa, Jharkhand and Gujarat.

The Schedule Tribe population in the state of Karnataka has witnessed highest growth rate of 80.82 percent followed by Nagaland (67.23 percent). The lowest growth rate in respect of Schedule Tribe population as per the 2001 census was recorded in Andaman and Nicobar Islands (10.08 percent) followed by Himachal Pradesh (12.02 percent) (ibid)

(C) Major Studies Conducted on Tribes

As early as in 1901, Census Organization of India under the stewardship of Sir Herbert Risley has done some pioneering work on the tribal communities. In 1931, Hutton, the then Census Commissioner of India resolved to continue and extent the Anthropological investigations which were initiated by Risley. He was the first one, who made serious attempt to list the primitive tribes at the census of 1931 (Gupta, 2005).

Tribal research in India started as early as in 1784 when the Asiatic Society of Bengal was established by Sir William Jones to study 'nature and man'(Kapoor, 1996). Various works focusing on the ethnographic life styles of the members of the tribal society had come up. Their cosmology, religious practices, belief system , rites and rituals, marriage pattern language, dress pattern, festivals, village set up etc had always been different from the main stream of life, thus attracting more and more anthropologists. (Dalton, 1872; Crooke, 1896; Seligmann, 1911; Elwin, 1939; Furer-Haimendorf, 1943; Roy, 1961; Berreman, 1962; Vidyarthi, 1963; Bhowmick,1963; Bose,1964; Chandra,1972; Vidyarthi, 1971; Mann, 1973; Tiwari,1984 ; Rizvi, 1987; Setty, 1988 ;Chakraborty,1990; Hodson, 1989; Bhowmick, 1994; Sharma, 1994; Sahu, 1995; Som, 1995; Sharma, 1996 and Sahu, 1998). All these authors have focused on ethnographic phases of the lives of the tribes.

The writings of Rivers (1906) and Radcliffe-Brown (1922) began the tradition of writing full length monographs. Roy (1921) reviewed such studies by these scholars in the first issue of 'Man in India'. First Indian anthropologist S.C. Roy in 1912 wrote the full length monograph on Munda, which was followed by a series of five monographs (1915, 1925, 1928, 1935 and 1937) on different tribes of Chotanagpur. With the entry of Verrier Elwin (1947, 1955, 1958 and 1964) and Furer –Haimdendorf (1945, 1962 and 1969) the tribal studies in India received a fresh jump and several monographs on the tribes of Madhya Pradesh, Andhra Pradesh and later north east India were written by them.

Soon the trend of the literature produced by scholars changed from pure ethnographic accounts to the study of demographic account, process of social change, transformation, development, relation between environment and economic structure, literacy, poverty, psycho-social perspective, genetics, gender, tourism, non-government organization and tribes, management of health, disaster, resources, intellectual property rights, economic policy and impact on tribals and human rights etc. (Chandra, 1969; Mohan,1975; Roy,1981;Prasad & Kapoor, 1982; Benerjee,1988; Kapoor, 1990; Bairathi,1991; Dange,1991; Vithal,1992; Sastry,1993; Aparajita,1994; Chandra,1994; Burman,1994; Kapoor, 1996; Fernandes and Raj, 1996; Patra et al, 1997; Soni,1998; Kapoor, 1998; Sharma & Sharma, 1999; Danda,2000; Kapoor, 2000 a, b, c; Heredia, 2002; Ramaswamy, 2002; Sarangi, 2003; Baraik & Lakra, 2003; Biswas and Kapoor, 2003; Kshatriya & Kapoor 2003; Shah, 2003; Gupta, 2005; Vashum, 2005; Gupta and Kapoor, 2005;2006;2007; Gupta and Gupta, 2005; Shukla, 2005; Dixit, 2006.

1.8 Customary Laws

In all societies relationships among individuals are regulated by a corpus of norms, customs, taboos, traditions, values and moral standards and certain laws (Sinha, 2003).

There are various types of laws in a society

1. Enacted Law – This law is based on legislation.
2. Conventional Law – This law is based on agreement.
3. Case Law – This law is based on precedent.
4. Customary Law – This law is based on customs.

Customs reflect norms and values of the society. Customary laws in society in general and traditional society in particular are of great significance to any society. The term 'Customary Law' has two essential components or concepts – 'Custom' and 'law'

'Custom' is the oldest form of law-making. Briefly speaking, custom is a continuing course of conduct observed by the community. "The word custom is used to apply to the totality of behavior patterns which are carried by tradition and lodged in the group, as contrasted with the more random personal activities of the individual." (Sapir, 1954)

1.8.1 Origin of Custom

Precise origin of custom is almost impossible to ascertain .It is the high antiquity of the custom which gives it validity. A rule of human conduct by continual observance by the people for some period of time with the common sanction of the people gets the status of a custom .The birth and growth of the custom is the natural consequence of the organized living of people and the progress of human society. With the growth and progress of human society, the rules of human conduct go on multiplying; still a stage reaches when they become a well recognized and well established body of rules. These rules are compendiously called 'customs'. These rules of conduct must be obviously, arisen and followed on account of their utility or necessity (Diwan, 1978).

1.8.2 Types of Customs

1. Custom of caste or tribe
2. Local custom
3. Family custom
4. International custom

A local custom is the one which operates in a locality, in a particular geographical area, not necessarily in conformity with the administrative divisions, and is usually, binding on all persons living in that area. It is different from a class or tribal custom.

A caste custom or tribal custom is one which is binding on all the members of the entire class or entire tribe where ever they may be.

A family custom is one which is binding on the members of a family. Impartible estate and succession by the rule of primogeniture are two important examples.

International customs are followed by one country and the other. Source of these customs have been codified by the United Nations. (Diwan, 1985)

Customs cannot be extended by analogy. There are some customs of which the court takes judicial notice when a custom is repeatedly brought to the notice of the court, the court may treat the custom proved without any evidence. With the exception of these customs of which the court takes judicial notice, all customs must be proved by evidence. Usually customs are proved by instances. It may also be proved on the basis of the conduct of members of the tribe or locality. Record of customs, such as riwaz-i-am may be used for proving a custom.

The second concept of the word 'Customary Law' i.e. 'law' is a subject which can be treated in more than one context. Custom relates to society and law is concerned with state. Pospisil (1972) points out that 'law in contrast to what is nearly customary i.e. internalized norm of the society everybody obeys, is a relative phenomenon. Even what is custom at societal level, may be law at a group level (clan, lineage etc.). Khare (1972) shows that indigenous culture and lawyer's law go hand in hand in the Indian context

Pospisil (1974) defines law as 'rules or modes of conduct made obligatory by some sanction imposed and enforced for their violation by a controlling authority'. He points to four basic characteristics of law:

(i) The existence of authority
(ii) The principle of universal application
(iii) The principle of *obligatio, under* which a decision or statement becomes a law in as much as it implies rights and duties.
(iv) The existence of sanctions , which may be physical or moral (ostracism, ridicule, and so on) (Seymour-Smith, 1993)

1.8.3 Essentials of Valid Custom

The following are the essentials of a valid custom:

(a) **Antiquity** – Section 3 (a) of the Hindu Marriage Act, 1955, provides that custom should be observed for a long time. It should be ancient. The court has time and again held that if a custom is established to be 100 years old or more it is of sufficient antiquity.
(b) **Continuity** – Continuity is as essential as antiquity. Discontinuity will destroy a custom. An absolute law can be repeated but there is no method of repeating custom except by abandonment.
(c) **Certainty** – Custom must be certain, and clear not vague. One has to prove what exactly the custom is and how far it is applicable with a reasonable amount of certainty.
(d) **Reasonability** – It should not be unreasonable. An unreasonable custom is void, although custom may not always be founded on reason.
(e) **Morality** – Any moral custom is void. Like the standard of reasonability, the standard of morality may differ from time to time and from society to society.
(f) It should not be opposed to public policy.
(g) It should not be opposed to law.

Thus Customary law can be understood in a collective manner, as a set of norms of any society, in its traditionally upheld wisdom to prescribe a code of conduct for the members of the society. Another expression to it may be in terms, that customary laws is not law by any stretch of imagination but in reality it mode of being collective. The rules though unwritten are taken seriously as binding on the members and are transmitted from generation to generation without any distortion to it, just by oral communication. In fact customary law acts as measures of informal social control over people as it includes methods of reward and punishment developed by them. At the conceptual level, customary laws are static and society being dynamic, more often than not; there appears some void between the customary laws and its acceptance and adherence (Chandra, 1996).

1.8.4 Why is Customary Law Obeyed?

According to Malinowski (1926), no society can work in an efficient manner unless laws are obeyed 'willingly and spontaneously'. The threat of coercion and the fear of punishment cannot be the permanent force for the members of society to follow laws. People obey laws because of interdependence and mutual obligation. If one does not do one's duty by others, one cannot expect them to do anything for one's own sake. And neither individual nor an individual family is a unit self sufficient by itself. The force of habit, awe of traditional commands and a sentimental attachment to it, the desire to satisfy public opinion –all combine to make custom be obeyed for its own sake.

1.8.5 Customary Laws vs. Social Scientist

Many social scientists had conducted legal studies, which were focused mainly to differentiate customs, rules, norms, and sanctions that subsequently developed into customary laws. The socio-legal scientist, as they may be called, tries to focus on the sociological aspects of law, such as, the influence of family and kinspersons in the dispute settlement, the role of the judge and the process of law in the absence of written code. Besides the attitude of the litigants, the reaction of the society towards the erring person and his family are also studied. The socio- legal scientist covers those aspects which are not taken up by the lawyers and legal scientists, who mainly carry out studies of judgment delivered in accordance with the statutory legislation of the state. The legal scientist usually follows a particular code of conduct that has already been written down. The mode of dispute settlement is usually based on the written codes. (Maine, 1861; Pospisil, 1971; Sharma, 1979; War, 1994; Chandra, 1996; Singh, 1996; Pathak, 2005)

1.8.6 Global View on Customary Laws

Custom is one of the oldest institutions of the world. Each and every country of the East and West has its own customary laws like Babylonian, Chinese, German, Athenian, Roman, Irish laws etc. In Roman, Corpus juris Civills (body of civil law), a plethora of customary laws are found. The Twelve Tables of Roman Law codified Roman Customary Laws. Hamurabi's code of Babylon is based upon the preceding customary law. Chinese customary law antedates a period of Hamurabi. The customary laws of Australian and African tribes can be compared to our tribal customary laws. The customary laws of medieval Germany grew from the findings of the lay judges, doubtful cases were resolved by the adoption of a declaration as to the nature of the rule of customary law, after an official inquiry by the local law finders. (Bandyopadhyay, 1994)

The common law of England in its classical period well illustrates the conception of customary laws. The English common law grew originally from the collections of tribal customary law. Ancient Irish law also clearly shows its customary nature. It lays down tribal and primitive forms of rules and remedies (ibid)

1.8.7 Hindu Law and Social Legislation

"Hindu Law has always been to a great extent customary". "The Code of Manu" was in force in India, Burma and Siam. 'Sruti', i.e. what was heard, was source of law par excellence and may be referred to as formal source of law. Smriti, i.e. the recollections stand next in order. Custom follows the next. Parishads, Puranas etc come after them (Sengupta, 1914; Ram, 2005).

Hence custom was an important source of law in ancient India. To quote Manu, 'the custom which has come down by immemorial tradition and obtains among the castes is called approved usage'. Hence, in certain cases the weight of customary law was found more than the written text of smritis, the formal law. The Hindu Law of succession and inheritance which ultimately got codified in the form of Hindu Succession Act was based on the customary law. In the constitutional schemes, Articles 244, 244 A, 371 A, Fifth and Sixth schedules clearly indicates the concern of the makers of the constitution to preserve and maintain the customary laws of the tribes.

1.8.8 Customary Laws among Tribes in India

It is observed that the works on the customary laws focuses the tribal society only. There is no work on the customary laws aspect, in the rural and urban society of India. Anthropologists are always attracted by the fact of the coexistence of customary laws with the state laws. Pathak (1991) on the Adis of Arunachal Pradesh found that the elite section were of opinion that codification of customary laws shall not take away its originality and charm. Ramachandran (2005) had studied the Adiyan of Kerala in the light of customary laws and constitutional laws.

Vijayakumar (2006) in this study on the native community of India's Lakshadweep islands, though predominantly Muslim, which is organized around the matrilineal joint family highlights various aspects of customary laws of the society. Under the customary matrilineal law of succession evolved in the islands and followed for centuries, joint family property devolves from mothers to daughters. After marriage women continue to live with their maternal joint family, as do their children. Husbands are normally resident in their own maternal homes and visit their wives regularly. He examines the salient features of social organization in the islands and its relationship with the legal system in different historical periods from antiquity to the present day. The scholar points out that traditional matrilineal Lakshadweep society has succeeded in providing dignity and all social rights to women and also security for children in case of divorce. He goes on to examine the changes currently taking place which may bring to an end the entire social system built up over hundreds of years. He provides rich empirical evidence as well as a description of the syncretic religious-cultural framework of the islands. The analysis highlights the fact that customary law there is very different from the mainland's legal system and practice. It then examines how developments in the mainland have influenced the thinking of the people. During the same period certain court cases and judgments have resulted in some uncertainty as to the status of customary law. The author contends that the major socio-legal changes currently taking place may prove to be detrimental to the interests of women and children.

Prasad and Chakraborty (2006) have talked of justice as a dynamic and changing state. In aligns with morality and proper distribution of favours and losses. This is possible by a democratic social order. Both the scholars have highlighted two systems of justice viz., custom based justice and modern legal justice based on the rule of law, operating side by side. The custom based justice is un-codified. The modern legal as per the justice rules of 1937 framed by the colonial rulers. Crime had previously been almost absent in the Mizo society. Presently, crimes of different nature, (criminal and civil) are increasing owing to the enlarging money economy, the loosening of social bonds, the emergence of classes of the neo-middle rich and the poor and the concentration of wealth at the top and poverty at the bottom of the social hierarchy. Authors emphasize more thrust on legislation and trail of cases by the State Courts rather than the District Councils' Courts, trying cases by un-codified customary laws and also suggest streamlining the existing judicial administration in order to have a uniform and impartial justice. The complete separation of executive and judiciary to achieve the objective of justice is suggested.

Pathak (2005) shares her views on the Adis tribe of Arunachal Pradesh. The system of law in the state possesses many significant and interesting features deserving attention and scrutiny not only from an anthropological point of view but also from a legal perspective. There are some twenty major tribes in the state with each having diverse customs and cultures. The scholar had endeavored to study the administrative and legal development in the state of Arunachal Pradesh with special reference to the Adi Tribe. The Adis are sensitive by nature and proud of their heritage. They have a rich culture and an age-old set of customary laws. An objective approach towards their lifestyle, custom, culture, religion and belief throws new light on their inner world. with an analytical analysis of the legal aspects of these tribes.

Narwani (2004) has studied the laws applicable to tribal communities in different parts of India. Tribal communities have been obeying customary laws through their traditional Panchayats since long. Vast literature is available on religion, culture, marriage and family traditions of tribal communities living in the Fifth Schedule states or in autonomous hill districts of the north-east covered by the Sixth Schedule of the Indian Constitution. It was only in 1996 that Panchayats (Extension to Scheduled Areas) Act was enacted by Parliament and it was enjoined upon the states having scheduled areas therein to adopt it within one year. Perhaps no exercise has yet been made to analyze in details the codified law as being implemented in the Fifth Schedule states till date and difficulties encountered in its implementation in the light of recommendations of the Bhuria Committee.

Vitso (2003) seeks to show how and to what extent do customary laws define the status of women in general and the Chakhesang women of Khezhakeno village in particular. This village is regarded by several Naga tribes as the village of their origin.

1.9 Anthropology of Law

The association of law and anthropology began towards the end of the 19th century, when European colonial powers decided to recognize the indigenous laws of their colonies. Anthropology has several advantages over the other disciplines like political science, sociology, jurisprudence, economics etc.

First, it is not culture bound. It studies societies comparatively, no matter how "primitive" or "civilized" it is. It does not discriminate qualitatively in one type of human society against another.

Second, anthropologists study law in any community as an integral part of the cultural whole, not regarded as an autonomous institution.

Third, modern anthropology does not concentrate on the study of 'Social Forces' and the 'Superorganic' to the exclusion of the role of the individual.

Fourth, society is viewed as a dynamic phenomenon so that the social role of law is not limited solely to maintaining the status quo.

Fifth, anthropology of law is a science of law and therefore empirical.

1.10 Human Rights

Human rights are universal standards and refers to those elemental rights which any human deserves to have honored in order to survive, enjoy, well being and flourish or fulfill him or herself, simply by virtue of being human. They are the internationally agreed values, regulating the conduct of states towards their own citizens and towards non-citizens. Human rights are, in words of Preamble of the Universal Declaration of Human Rights: "a common standard of achievement for all peoples and all nations" (Barfield, 1997).

The term 'Human Rights' was introduced in 1776 in US Declaration of Independence. The dictionary meaning of the expression would be:

"Human" means "pertaining to mankind"

"Right" means "according to truth"

So it means dealing with the mankind according to truth and justice (c.f. Batra, 1979)

1.10.1 Origin of Cõncept of Human Rights

All human rights are derived from the dignity and worth inherent in the human person and that the human person is the central subject of Human Rights. In simple terms, whatever adds to the dignified and free existence of a human being should be regarded as Human Rights.

Early men were existing in the conditions which were devoid of rules and regulations. The stronger human being use to dominate over the weaker. In the drive for dominance over others with sheer superior muscle power, three very distinctive institutions viz the family, slavery and the state were developed. The family system was experimented upon and developed. The head of the family was burdened with the duty to ensure security and in return the individuals living under him had to surrender their individuality. The head has the authority over the family property, children, wives etc. The women have no independent status. Manu Samhita says "A women is never independent. She has male for her masters. A women or wife is subservient to her lord. She should never supersede him. With this abject subservience to the husband, she was denied any right to property".

Living in family gave man security & happiness. It made him sly. He started occupying lands belonging to others, who were physically and mentally inferior to him. To secure continued enjoyment of luxurious living he started the institution of slavery. Slaves were either purchased in the open markets on captured in war. They were treated as property and not as human beings. These were a general belief that some were to rule and other to be ruled.

Earlier the patriarchal joint families were groups round the chieftain hill fort. This attitude ultimately crystallized into the much-derided caste system encoded by Manu in which the intelligent, the strong and the powerful were categorized for a higher status. The myth that it was the fruit of there past deeds, that they were born in the class Sudras was based on the idea that specific duties were assigned to specific castes. The Brahman was to speak the truth and represent the body politic as the tongue does for the human body; he was to stand between the ruler (the lion) and the ruled (the lambs); the Kshatriya was to protect the body politic from attacks by others and keep it clean as is the function of arms for the body; the Vaishya was to trade and to assimilate his earnings for the benefit of the entire body politic as the stomach does for the body; the Sudra was to work in the fields, in the industries, in fact everywhere to bring prosperity to the entire body politic as is done by the feet to the body, without them body cannot move.

In order to protect this universe, said Manu, the most resplendent one, assigned separate duties to those who sprang from his mouth, arms, thighs, and feet. Brahmans were endowed with intellect. They were to study the scriptures carefully and to instruct their pupils. In additions to the studying of the scriptures, the Kshatriyas were commanded to protect the people. The Vaisyas were to tend cattle, to bestow gifts, to study the scriptures, to trade, to lend money to cultivate land. The Sudras were to serve all others. It could be said the people could not speak of rights, not to speak of equality.

When living in family, man had learnt to enjoy gains from the labour of others. In order to perpetuate his gains the family developed into a clan, a clan into a village; villages into a single community. Eventually the state came into existence. It came into being as the enlargement of families. The nature of man to acquire more & more wealth resulted in war. With frequent wars taking place, the condition of man become, highly deplorable.

Under such circumstances, thoughtful men all over the world spoke of "rights" which men has in common and which were inherent rights in the sense they were based on man's "rational and social nature". These rights, they said were the natural rights. They were called natural rights because they could not be taken away by man who so ever he may be since they were the rules of life created by nature itself. This was natural law. It was developed to counter man- made laws. These laws have its basis in man's natural inclination to right reason implanted in him by nature. From time to time contents of natural law changed. The earlier stress was on religion and morality. The later on right reason and the nature of mankind. The law of nature was based on what right is called as moral thinking of man and second, that it was not man-made law.

The natural law doctrine mitigated the sufferings of man-kind a bit. Masters were forbidden to kill their slaves. Equally important part was played by religion in lessening the suffering of mankind, as there was reduction in war. (Gupta, 2005)

Then, first Magna Carta i.e. the Great Charter was written in 1215 A.D. It was a petition urging the king to concede certain rights to particular sections of the people. Its contents neither have the universality of application nor direct relevance to common man's basic freedoms. So it was not observed and was frequently violated. Yet, it has set a trend. The struggle continued. Common man had learned the way to secure his freedom and right. It further got spurred with the enlightenment of Renaissance. So there were rights. These were basic norms for enjoyment of life. The government was to force them. Ideas about universal rights for all people developed during the enlightenment in Europe, were codified in International conventions following world wide concern over NAZI GENOCIDE and other horrors of worlds war II, and have increasingly become a central concern in modern political theory and legal practice. Earlier, the term 'Human Rights' was coined in 1776 in US declaration of independence. It is said that all men are created equal. That they are endowed, by their creator, with certain unalienable rights; that among these are life, liberty and the pursuit of happiness, that to secure these rights, governments are instituted (Batra, 1979).

Later there were substantial international conventions on human rights, such as the International Bill on Human Rights of the UN, which includes the Universal Declaration of Human Rights, announced in 1948 and two covenants encompassing the Political, Civil, Economics, Social and Cultural rights (Pathy, 1992).

1.10.2 Classification of Human Rights

The sweep of the Human Rights concept expanded day by day broadly they fall in four generations (Messer, 1993 a) :-

1. First Generation Rights Include.

(a) Political Rights

(b) Civil Rights

These protect the basic security of persons. Socialists and welfare state concepts and nations added the second generation of rights.

2. Second Generation Rights Include

(a) Socio-economic rights

(b) Cultural rights

These include rights to employment and fair working conditions, rights to standard of living that ensures health and well being, right to social security, education and right to participation in cultural life of the community and special rights for women and children.

3. Third Generation Rights

Third world nations, especially in Africa, added 'third generation' rights. It includes:-

(a) Solidarity or development rights to peace, a more equitable socio economic order, and a sustainable environment.

4. Fourth Generation Rights

Indigenous people added a "fourth generation" of indigenous rights, which will protect their rights to political self-determination and control over socio-economic development.

Human rights and fundamental rights are the two faces of a coin. The end of the boundary of fundamental rights marks the beginning of the domain of Human rights. Fundamental rights enumerated from article 14 to 32 in Part III of the Indian constitution, whenever violated seeks help of human rights for enforcement. But merely providing "rights" in the constitution did not guarantee their existence in practice. It remained a mere 'declaration' of common standard of achievement to promote respect for human rights and freedom. No legal obligation was created. The implementation and enforcement are very difficult. Human rights are usually framed as the rights of individual in relation to the state. Ironically, these political authorities charge with bringing justice are those who most often are the violators of human rights. Apart from the political authorities, cases of violation of Human Rights had emerged, where violators were the non-tribal groups residing in the tribal vicinity (Baehr, 2000,).

In the empirical situation, violators of human rights often target individuals, and groups, based at least in part, on their apparent biological, social, cultural, or linguistic differences. Indigenous people or ethnic minorities are the groups of people who are subjected to ethnocide, genocide and human rights abuses, as they are usually the least powerful and vocal group within a country. Development of such group is, therefore, necessary to alleviate their backward socio economic conditions from the holistic point of view (Subramanian, 1997).

Centuries of social repression have engendered in them a feeling of inferiority and thus it is not surprising that they have lost all confidence in themselves. Such category of people can only be developed; if awareness is inhabited about those aspects which they are entitled to deserve merely by virtue of being human, in order to survive and not to exist.

Development does not merely imply 'economic growth' it also denotes 'social development'. In the context of tribal communities development has to strike a balance between economic and social domains and it has to be 'culture' and 'region' specific. Development should cultivate the ability in the individual to voice his grievance in the proper forum so as to seek redress and to extricate them from massive exploitation (Behura, 1996).

1.11 Human Rights: An Overview

As the human beings are ubiquitous, so is the issue of human rights. All the societies and communities of the world have to deal with the concept of human rights. With the expanding number of categories, and more specific content of human rights, both experts and policy makers now accept the idea that human rights concepts are culturally relative.

1.11.1 Anthropology and Human Rights

For the development of the sense of self-esteem and to be free from servitude, awareness has to be generated. They need to be enlightened on the basic aspects of human rights, about the legal aspects of rights being violated. At this juncture of law and tribal people, anthropologists can act as an inter-phase; as they have tended to advocate rights of collectivities especially indigenous people. Advocacy for human rights is by now part of a boarder applied anthropological agenda.

Anthropologists are in a unique strategic position to deal with human rights for the following reasons (Levinson & Ember, 1997):-

1. Human Rights are predicated on a theory of human nature. Anthropology is a science of human kind that documents and celebrates the biological and cultural aspects of the unity and diversity of the human species.
2. Anthropologists not only study, but as a practice seek to apply their knowledge (of bases and forms of human diversity and unity) to the solution of human problems.
3. Anthropology is the most appropriate profession to grapple with the matter, of culture, culture diversity, relativism, human nature, cultural universals, both in theory and practice.
4. Above all, unfortunately, the human rights situations is likely to become worse rather than better in the near future, since the growing levels of population and economic consumption will put more pressure on the land and resources of indigenous people.
5. They contribute to establishing standards and methods of measurements and monitoring that might involve giving people not only participation but also a voice.

Anthropological study of human rights and laws in a tribal community could be very varied as the concept of human rights is culturally relative. Related to specific requirement of the tribal people and sometimes the lexi local (customary laws or traditional laws) and sub-cultural norms come in conflict with the development programs and the framed human rights (Pandey, 2001).

Since 1948 the United Nations (UN) has aspired to create a global community, based on human rights, "a common standard of achievement for all people and nations" (the UN Universal Declaration of Human Rights), anthropologists have contributed to the study of human rights all over the world (Herskovits,1947; Messer, 1993; Downing and Kushner, 1988; Unesco, 1987; Wright, 1988; Preis, 1996; Moran, 1996 and Eberhard, 2002). Anthropologists have contributed to these efforts in two critical ways: first, by providing cross-cultural research on the questions of "what are rights?" and "who is counted as a full 'person' or 'human being' eligible to enjoy them?" Second by monitoring compliance with human rights standards and by criticizing human rights violations or abuses.

It has been observed that anthropologists have been largely uninvolved in human rights formulations. There are five basic reasons for this distant and impassive behaviour:

1. Anthropologist's insistence that human rights concepts are culturally relative, in opposite to universal formulations (Executive Board, 1947; Renteln, 1988 and Cohen, 1989).
2. Anthropologist's advocacy of collective and indigenous rights over and against the universal formulations framed in terms of the individual's rights.
3. Anthropologist's commitment to applied anthropology and political economic action over human rights approaches to overcoming oppression and inequality.
4. The political sensitivities of doing field work (Downing, 1988).
5. Anthropologist's involvement with small-scale socio-cultural analysis and comparative moral systems, based on duties, gift-giving, culture, religion, festivals, cosmology rather than with sovereign state-level societies and legal systems based on rights.

Over the due course of time anthropologists have prevailed in broadening the international discourse on human rights, which now includes collective and indigenous rights and details more specific content for social, economic, and cultural rights. Because of anthropologists involvement, the human rights perspective has broadened in terms of social transformation and development of society.

1.11.2 Global Scenario of Human Rights

The UN has been promoting and codifying human rights for 45 years through the Universal Declaration of Human Rights and associated resolutions, covenants, fact-finding commissions etc (Luard, 1967). There are almost as many theories of rights as there are rights theorists. Scholars have argued for a broader view of rights which would encompass moral rights as well (Hart, 1979). Western nations after the atrocities of World War II, have dominated the drafting of the Human Rights. This is the reason of the dominance of foreign authors in this field.

Scholars all over the world have worked and are working on the topic of human rights. The scholars have written about the historical survey of human rights followed by the various theoretical approaches and a broad classification of human rights. Many authors have also defended the accounts of human rights saying that it is compatible with the universal moral rights and thus does not require the acceptance of claims of cultural relativism. Many leading scholars and activists in their mature and an insightful works have explored the principle issues and developments in international human rights and then compared the concepts and conditions of rights in various parts of the world. Literature is also available on balancing new technology practices with human rights. Such works have viewed freedom and well being as the necessary conditions of human actions. The issues of contradiction between the theory of universal human rights and the everyday practice of human wrongs had attracted the attention of numerous scholars all over the world. The contributors ask whether human rights abuses are a result of failure of governments to live up to a universal human rights standard, or whether the search for moral universals is a fundamentally flawed enterprise. Work has been done on the philosophical basis of human rights, and reflects on the structures that affect the development of a global human rights culture (Bilder, 1969; Cranston, 1973; Dinstein, 1976; Dworkin,1977; Laqueur, 1979; Donnelly, 1985; Donnelly, 1989; Henkin, 1990; Meron, 1991; Claude, 1992; Davidson, 1993; Moran, 1996; Dunne & Nicholas, 1999; Walters, 2002 and Fields, 2003).

(A) Regional Perspective

There is debate in the scholarly world regarding the issue of the concept of human rights. It is argued that the concept is western and not universal. The international document is not sufficient to resolve the question of whether the human rights are western or universal. It is believed that these documents contain some rights which are universal and some which are not. To decide which rights are truly universal, an attempt has been made in to characterize the concept of human rights according to various geographical, cultural, religious, and ideological perspectives. It is important, however, to be aware of the limitations of this literature:-

(a) First, there do not even exist articles on the concept of human rights in all societies.

(b) Second, the articles that do exist tend to focus on what is distinctive about the concept in the country or religion in question. Thus, emphasizing on what is distinctive rather than what is common.

(c) Third, we cannot tell whether or not to rely on the characterization provided. Analysts have spoken of the same culture, sometimes giving the radically different interpretations to the concept and often formulating conclusions on the basis of misleading evidence. Discussions of human rights in China, for example, tend to focus on what rights Chinese officials have granted rather than on what the traditional values are.

(d) Fourth, no systematic comparative analyses of human rights have ever been undertaken.

The following is a representative selection of the kinds of articles on non-western conceptions of human rights which are available:

(B) Africa

In Africa, debate has raged over whether Human Rights are individual or collective and whether the rights to development and to freedom from hunger take precedence over Western political emphasis on individual civil-political freedoms. Scholars from anthropology, political science, economics, and other disciplines have turned their critical gaze towards the ideologies, policies and practices of human rights including international human rights. African political leaders, challenged by ethnic conflict and deteriorating ecological and economic conditions, have produced their own regional African Charter on Human Rights, and assert that in African societies 'peoples', not individuals, have rights and that individual freedoms may have to be sacrificed, at least in the short term , to support subsistence and development rights. Studies have focused on how societies ascribe and individuals achieve human dignity, how can human rights be promoted in Africa. Authors have also explored the sociological dimensions of human rights in Africa from historical, socio-economic and political perspectives. Important Conventions, Resolutions, Declarations and Recommendations of both international (the U.N. and I.L.O.) and regional (Organization of African Unity {OAU}, Southern African Studies) institutions have been focused on also. Issues of genocide, apartheid, indigenous rights etc has also been reviewed.(Adegbite, 1968; Wai,1979; Bello,1981; Howard, 1984; Marasinghe, 1984; Welch & Meltzer, 1984; Howard, 1986; Cobbah, 1987; Hamalengwa, 1988; Shivji, 1989; Totten, 2000; Gray, 2002; Henrard, 2002; Aluko, 2003 and Murray, 2004).

(C) Asia

In Asia, as in Africa, human rights questions of cultural relativism have centered around which rights take precedence:-

(a) subsistence and development freedoms or,

(b) political freedoms

Scholars have worked on the aspects whether the cultural and religious language of duties and obligations can be translated or reconciled with universal human rights notions. Human rights of various countries in Asia like China, Japan, Taiwan, and North Korea have been reviewed (Sutter, 1978; Khushalani, 1983; Appadurai, 1984; Burks, 1985; Hsiung, 1985; Lee, 1985; Tai, 1985; Wilson, 1985 and Inagaki, 1986).

(D) Latin America

Latin America has been the focal point for organizing indigenous rights, documenting abuses by states against native peoples and pressing for rights to land, culture, and self determination in development. Continuing a long history of debate over 'who is a human being' with full rights before the law, the contradiction between constitutional guarantees to citizen and abuses against indigenous peoples highlights the continuing gap between citizenship and protections. The injustices of poverty and the failure to meet basic needs expressed as human rights to subsistence, health, and education are also major themes that have been developed (Crahan, 1982; Davis, 1984; Quesada, 1986 and Doughty, 1988).

1.11.3 Indian Scenario of Human Rights

In this section, the focus is on the works of Indian scholars on various issues and concepts of human rights.

(A) Concept of Human Rights

The concept of rights carries a double meaning: that which is universal and inalienable, and that which is morally appropriate or just. 'Human rights' refers to those elemental rights which any human deserves to have honored in order to survive, enjoy well being , and flourish or fulfill him or herself , simply by virtue of being human. Various Scholars from different backgrounds like law, political scientists, economists, police personnel, administrators or activists have written about the Hindu concept of human rights, philosophy of human rights, their evolution, issues, challenges, implementation and violation (Puntambekar, 1948; Sinha, 1978; Bajwa, 1995; Subramanyam, 2001; Biju, 2002; Misra and Misra, 2003; Sharma, 2003 and Kaarthikeyan, 2005). Scholars have also argued if human right is a western concept and have discussed it in the Indian perspective (Panikkar, 1982 and Pandeya, 1986). The concept of human rights have been revisited by many scholars, sometimes with a critical lens also focusing on the need of human rights in the society, role of state in the proper implementation and enforcement of human rights (Batra, 1979; Trivedi, 2004 and Sharma, 2005).

(B) Types of Human Rights

The Indian Constitution was drafted in 1949 at a time when the Universal Declaration of Human Rights was to be framed. The framers of Indian Constitution were influenced by the concept of human rights. It guaranteed various human rights to its people. When human rights are guaranteed by a written Constitution they are called 'Fundamental Rights' because a written Constitution is the fundamental law of the State.' Numerous scholars have written about various human rights granted by the constitution. They include the right to life and freedom , freedom from arbitrary arrest and imprisonment, the right to a fair trial, freedom from slavery and genocide, the right to nationality, freedom of movement, right to privacy and ownership to property, freedom of speech, religion and assembly, the rights of people to self – determination, culture, right to adequate food ,shelter, health care and education; right of infants to mother's milk, security, development. (Thapar, 1978; Khare,1991; Pal, 2001; Gupta, 2001; Sengupta, 2001; Mishra,2002; Singh, 2002; Das, 2003; Kaur, 2003; Padhy and Choudhury, 2004 and Noorani, 2005)

(C) Human Rights and Ethnic Minorities

The term '*ethnic group*' has been used by social scientists in two different senses, one narrow and one broad. In the broad definition, an ethnic group is a social group distinguished by race, religion, or national origin. In the narrow definition, ethnic definition is defined as a single family of social identities- a family which, in addition to races and ethnic groups, includes religions, language groups and all of which can be included in the most general term, ethnic groups, defined by descent, real or mythical and sharing a common history and experience. Sometimes ethnic groups are subject to prejudicial attitudes and actions by the state or its constituents. (Gupt, 1997)

An '*ethnic group*' is a minority human group bound together by ties of cultural homogeneity. There prevail a high degree of loyalty and adherence to certain basic institutions such as family patterns, religion and language for example a tribal group of any state, people of Jammu and Kashmir etc. It has been increasingly realized that some of the ethnic groups in India comprises the over exploited segment of humanity and face the formidable worldwide phenomenon of erosion of their collective survival rights. There is a conspicuous neglect of the collective and communal rights, which are most crucial for the survival and advancement of tribal peoples. There is no reference to the collective and communal rights of ethnic groups in the Universal Declaration of Human Rights, as it is deeply rooted in the western individualistic milieu. The declaration has evinced faith in the eventual socio-cultural homogeneity of the people belonging to respective member states and becoming oblivious of the fact that they should simultaneously include a statement about the rights of minorities. The only worthwhile collective right recognized in declaration is through its Article 17 which provides that 'everyone has the right to own property alone as well as in association with others and that no one shall be deprived of his property'. Later in 1966, Article 27 of the International Covenant of Civil and Political Rights was the first meaningful declaration safeguarding the minority rights. It states, 'in those States in which ethnic, religious or linguistic minorities exist, persons belonging to such minorities shall not be denied the right, in community with other members of the group, to enjoy their own culture, to profess and practice their own religion, or to use their language.' The object is cultural protection as against the common stress on assimilation. This article does not impose on states any obligation to actively support the rights of the minorities. In short, towards the most disadvantaged peoples of the world, the concern of the UN system has been scanty and insignificant. Few of the studies have been conducted on the minorities groups of muslims, dalits, religious groups etc. (Mitra,1982; Kumar,1988; Pathy, 1992; Burman,1994; Mendelsohn & Baxi,1994; Khan,1995; Dalvi and Bokil, 2000; Subramanian,2001; Chenoy, 2001; Pandey, 2001; Mrunalini, 2002; Noorani, 2002; Srivastava, 2003; Rao, 2003; Mathew, 2003; Upadhyay, 2003 and Dev, 2004; Rawat, 2005; Rajawat, 2005)

Shhabir (2005) has highlighted numerous burning issues, concerning the protection and promotion of human rights. These are related to individual, groups, society, law and Constitutions providing deep insight into the concept of social justice affecting scheduled castes, weaker sections, subjugated segments and minorities. It also focuses on poverty jurisprudence highlighting the problems of backward classes, weaker sections and minorities searching the ideal solution of their problems, and also suggesting acceptable and practical ways and means for tackling them successfully. He has also aimed to provide visionary light on law, minority's educational rights, reservation in public and private sectors, human rights of oppressed segments, the issue of conversion within the framework of the Constitution of India and torture as a challenge to the national human rights institutions with special reference to the role of National Human Rights Commission of India are examined logically (Shabbir, 2005).

Srivastav (2006) has talked of safeguarding human rights as an essential part of responding effectively to the AIDS epidemic at individual, national and global levels. HIV strikes hardest where human rights are least protected, particularly among people and communities on the margins of the society including sex workers, injecting drug users and men who have sex with men. Across the globe more than 40 million people live with HIV, half of whom are women. Human rights violations, including stigma and discrimination faced by people living with or affected by HIV/AIDS, still constitute a major barrier both to prevention efforts and access to care.

(D) Human Rights and Development

Human rights, social development and social justice are the outcomes of the social welfarist approach which emerged after the World War II (1939-45). The member states were called upon to protect and promote the interest of the weaker section of society and elevate their socio economic deprivations, illiteracy, exploitation, health hazards and morbidity so that they may be brought into the main stream of national and international development. The right to development was adopted by UN in 1986. Right to development states that, 'it is an inalienable human right by virtue of which every human person and all peoples are entitled to participate in and contribute to and enjoy economic, social, cultural and political development in which all human rights and fundamental freedoms can be fully realized'. By virtue of this right all people are entitled to participate in, contribute to and enjoy that process of development. It is assumed that right to development helps in the process of development. In other words there is a value addition in looking at programmes for development as a process of realization of human rights. When development is seen as a human right, it obligates the authorities, both nationally and internationally, to fulfill their duties in delivering that right in a country. Nationally, the government must do everything, or must be seen as doing everything to fulfill the claims of human right. If the right to food, education, and health are regarded as components of a human right to development, the state has to accept the primary responsibility of delivering the right either on its own or in collaboration with others. It has to adopt the appropriate policies and provide for the required resources to facilitate such delivery because meeting the obligation of human rights would have a primary claim on all its resources (Kumar, 1981; Sen, 1998; Pandey, 1993; Sharma, 2002; Sengupta, 2003 and Rai, 2006).

(E) Human Rights and Law

Human rights have always been the realm of law makers and law keepers. There is no dearth of literature, articles and books written by lawyers, policy makers etc. These authors have mainly focused on the Universal Declaration of Human Rights (1948), The International Covenant on Civil and Political Rights (1966), International Covenant on Economic, Social and Cultural Rights (1966) and various other international and national laws and policies which are incorporated in the constitution. (Baxi,1978; Khanna, 1978; Ramcharan, 1983; Tripathi, 1992; Gupta, 1994; Subramanian,1997; Kapoor,1999; Baxi, 1999; Parekh, 1999; Banerjee, 2000; Iyer, 2002; Kapoor, 2002 and Singh, 2006).

(F) Human Rights and Gender

The very notion of human rights implies universal application to both women and men; however, the development of human rights law has been partial and androcentric, privileging a masculine world view. For most women in the world, reality is long work hours in agriculture or the home, with little or no remuneration, while faced with political and legal processes that ignore their contribution to society and accord little recognition of their particular needs (Cook, 1994; Kaul, 2006)

The 1948 United Nations Universal Declaration of Human Rights expresses the credo that all human beings are created free and equal. But not until 1995 did the United Nations declare women's rights to be human rights, and bring gender issues into the global arena for the first time. The subordination of indigenous and minority women, ethnic cleansing, and the struggle for reproductive rights are some of the most pressing issues facing women worldwide. (Marjorie, 2001; Knop, 2004)

Women and Human Rights encompass a global/ Indian perspective on women and a wide range of issues, including political and domestic violence, education, literacy, and reproductive rights. Many scholars from the field of bioethics, medicine, public affairs, literature, history, anthropology, law, and psychology have worked on the aspect of gender and human rights. (Malyneux, 2003; Ram, 2005)

Mathur (2004) in her book provides a theoretical framework by analyzing gender violence in the changing perspectives of development, health and human rights; examines the ways in which violence against women as been studied, and draws links between gender violence and power relations; analyzes the state's response to countering gender violence; discusses institutional measures and policy initiatives as mechanisms for redress and protection; provides case studies to illustrate these initiatives; and highlights the role of the three key Non-Government Organizations (NGO's) in the state of Rajasthan, and their changing approaches over time to deal with the growing issues of gender violence.

1.11.4 Cross-Cultural Perspective

Any study that compares the cultures of two or more societies may be said to be a cross-cultural study. Anthropologically cross –cultural studies are valuable as they give a complete comparative picture of all the populations under study on a single platform, thus expediting the process of making generalizations. Cross-cultural comparisons were well launched by the second half of the nineteenth century. The classic objection to this method is that one is counting a mixed assemblage of cherries, olives, apples, oranges, papayas and watermelon. A common answer to this criticism is that all the things counted are plant foods and comparable enough on this general level. However, this cavalier attitude does not always satisfy all the social scientists. Many cross-cultural studies have been conducted till date on the various aspects of social structure, child training, socio-cultural development, sampling methods, ethnography, kin avoidances, drunkenness, in-laws avoidances etc (Eggan,1954; Apple,1956; Barry,1959;Field,1962; Brown,1963;Colby, 1966; Driver, 1966; Bowden, 1969; Chaney, 1969 and Driver, 1970). Till today none of the study has been conducted on the aspects of human rights and police in the cross-cultural perspective, among three different populations in the Indian scenario. This itself makes the study a pioneering effort as, it is an inter-disciplinary approach with a cross-cultural perspective.

1.12 Rationale of the study

In view of the above review of literature, it can be claimed that till today no work has been done in the field of anthropology which relates police with population with reference to human rights in a cross cultural perspective and having an interface dimension. No work has ever been reported which had been conducted in three different populations, focusing on tribal, rural and urban population at a point of time. The present study becomes more meaningful especially in the dearth of the relevant literature. The major motivating factor before embarking for this major project was the totality of the study. Judging the importance of the document which would be generated, it was decided to carry out the work on this interdisciplinary field.

1.13 Significance of the Study

The combination of the present work i.e. an interdisciplinary approach, a cross cultural perspective and an interface dimension makes the present work all the more significant. There is an urgent need to look at the comparative account of human rights among the Indian population. Field work being the most important tool of anthropology adds to the significance of the study, as there are very less studies which are based on empirical data collected. The field work for the present study has been conducted among the tribal population of Lahoul Spiti District, Himachal Pradesh; rural population of Rohtak District, Haryana and finally urban population of National Capital Region of Delhi. The present work explores the penetration of the knowledge, attitude and practice of the human rights from the top constitutional level till the grass root level. The document thus produced would act as insinuation for the activists, social workers, planners, development experts and scholars, who aspire to work in the field of human rights.

1.14 Hypothesis to be tested

Following hypothesis is to be tested in the field:

1. Are knowledge, attitude and practice of human rights affected by ecological settings?
2. Does education plays a role in deciding the level of awareness about human rights?
3. Does exposure to the outer environment reduces the level of unawareness about crime, human rights violation?
4. Does police plays a role in spreading the awareness about human rights as well as in violating them?
5. Does living near or in the vicinity of the police station affects the awareness of the human rights?
6. Do all the customary laws comply with the state laws?
7. Are customary laws followed by those who are educationally backward?

1.15 Objectives

Following are the objectives of the present study:

1. To explore the knowledge, attitude and practice of three different populations about crime and human rights.
2. To study various socio-cultural variables with reference to awareness about human rights and crime awareness of three populations.
3. To study the role and interaction of police personnel from people's (population) point of view and their attitude towards police, in the present scenario.
4. To study the detailed ethnographic account of the populations under study.
5. To study the customary laws, if any, with reference to human rights in cross-cultural perspective.
6. To know about the factors and situations which may exacerbate the whole process of violation of various human rights.

•

2

Area and People

Map 1: Map of India

The present study was conducted in three different geographical areas of the Indian region :

Area 1. Himachal Pradesh
Area 2. Haryana
Area 3. Delhi

Area 1

2.1 State : Himachal Pradesh

2.1.1 Location

India has 28 states and 7 Union Territories. Himachal Pradesh is one of these states. It acquired the full –fledged status of a state on 25th January 1971 and earned the 'eighteenth' rank in the Schedule of the States. The name 'Himachal Pradesh' was inserted into the Schedule I under the head 'States' by an Act of the Parliament (53 of 1970). The state lies in the western Himalayas. It extends between

30° 22′ 40" and 33° 12′ 44" North Latitudes and 75° 45′ 55" to 79° 4′ 20" East Longitudes. It is bounded by Jammu and Kashmir in north, Punjab in the west and southwest, Haryana in the south, Uttaranchal in the south east and by Tibet (China) in the east. The area of the state is 55,673 square kilometers.

2.1.2. Administrative Divisions

Table 2.1 : Administrative Divisions of Himachal Pradesh

Administrative Divisions	*Number*
Revenue Divisions	3
Districts	12
Sub-Divisions	52
Development Blocks	75
Tehsils	75
Gram Panchayats	3,037
Villages	20,118

Source : Census of India, 2001, Series 3, Himachal Pradesh.

2.1.3. Demographic Profile

According to the Census of India, 2001, total population of Himachal Pradesh is 60.77 lac. The population of the State amounts to 0.59 percent of total population of the country. In terms of population size Himachal Pradesh ranks 21st. The population of the state grew by 1.62 percent per annum during the year 1991-2001. The State have 12 districts. About half of the population is concentrated in three districts, namely, Kangra, Mandi and Shimla. The State has 90.21 percent of the rural population and only 9.79 percent of the urban population, which is lowest among the states and UTs in India. Density of population per square kilometer is 109 persons. The sex ratio of the state is 970 females per 1000 males. The state has 56 Scheduled Castes and 8 Scheduled Tribes.

2.1.4 Police in Himachal Pradesh State

(A) History of Himachal Pradesh Police

In the exercise of the powers vested by the Police Act 1861, the Government of Punjab in 1914 framed Punjab Police Rules. Subsequently, in 1934 new rules, which were more exhaustive, were promulgated. In 1959 an updated version of the rules of 1934 was published. As Himachal Pradesh was primarily a part a Punjab, so it adopted Punjab Police Rules, in July 1951. These rules of 1934 continue to apply to Himachal Pradesh. From time to time, the Government of Himachal Pradesh has amended these rules. While the basic structure of these rules is essentially sound, yet in many respects they have become obsolete. As such, there is strong case for thorough revision of these rules. So far, there is no proposal in Himachal Pradesh either to revise these rules or to prepare Himachal Pradesh's own police rules.

(B) Composition and Hierarchy

The police of Himachal Pradesh consists of two main branches – civil police and armed police. The civil police includes mainly the district police force, supervisory echelons at the range / zone / police headquarter and personnel of the specialized branches that deal with crime, intelligence, traffic, vigilance and enforcement matters. The district police forces have armed reserves, which are mainly used to meet the requirement of force for providing guards and escorts. An armed reserve is deemed as a part of civil force. The armed police is in the form of battalions, which are meant for law and order situation beyond the means of district police.

The posts in Table 2.2 are listed in the hierarchical order, the post of constable being at the bottom and that of DGP being at the top of the

Table 2.2 : Composition and Hierarchy of Himachal Pradesh Police

Designation	*Civil Police*	*Armed Police*	*Total Posts*
Director General of Police (DGP)	2	-	2
Additional Director General of Police (ADGP)	6	-	6
Inspector General of Police (IGP)	13	1	14
Deputy General of Police (DIG)	11	2	13
Assistant Inspector General of Police (AIG) / Superintendent of Police (SP)	38	5	43
Deputy Superintendent of Police (DSP)	93	32	125
Inspector of Police (INSP)	156	44	200
Sub-Inspector of Police (SI)	368	162	530
Assistant Sub-Inspector of Police (ASI)	730	62	792
Head Constable (HC)	1399	890	2289
Constable (Const)	6006	4040	10046
Total	8822	5238	14060

Source: Data on Police Organizations, Criminal Justice India Series, Vol. 14(1), 2005.

hierarchy. Officers of Indian Police Service (IPS), when posted against junior posts, are designated as Assistant Superintendent of Police (ASP). An ASP is superior to a DSP in status, though their functions are identical. Officers of and above the rank of DSP are called gazetted officers (GOs). Inspectors, SIs and ASIs are known as upper subordinates. They are also called non-gazetted officers (NGOs). Officers of and below the rank of head constable (HC) are known as lower subordinates. They are also called other ranks (ORs). The upper and lower subordinate officers are also called enrolled officers and they are appointed under section 7 of the Police Act, 1861. Term 'policemen' refers to constables, HCs, ASIs, and SIs. They constitute the majority in a police force. More importantly, they are the cutting edge of police administration and are the prime determinants of police image.

(C) Police, Area and Population Ratio

Area : Himachal Pradesh have 15.85 civil and 25.25 policemen of all categories (civil and armed) per 100 square km, as against all India averages of 36.20 civil and 47.16 policemen of all categories. (Banerjea, 2005)

Population : Himachal Pradesh have 14.52 civil and 23.14 policemen of all categories per 10,000 population. All India averages on that date are 11.16 civil and 14.54 policemen of all categories. (ibid)

(d) Administrative Divisions

For the purpose of administration, the state is divided into 12 districts, 3 ranges, 84 police stations, 104 permanent police posts and 25 temporary

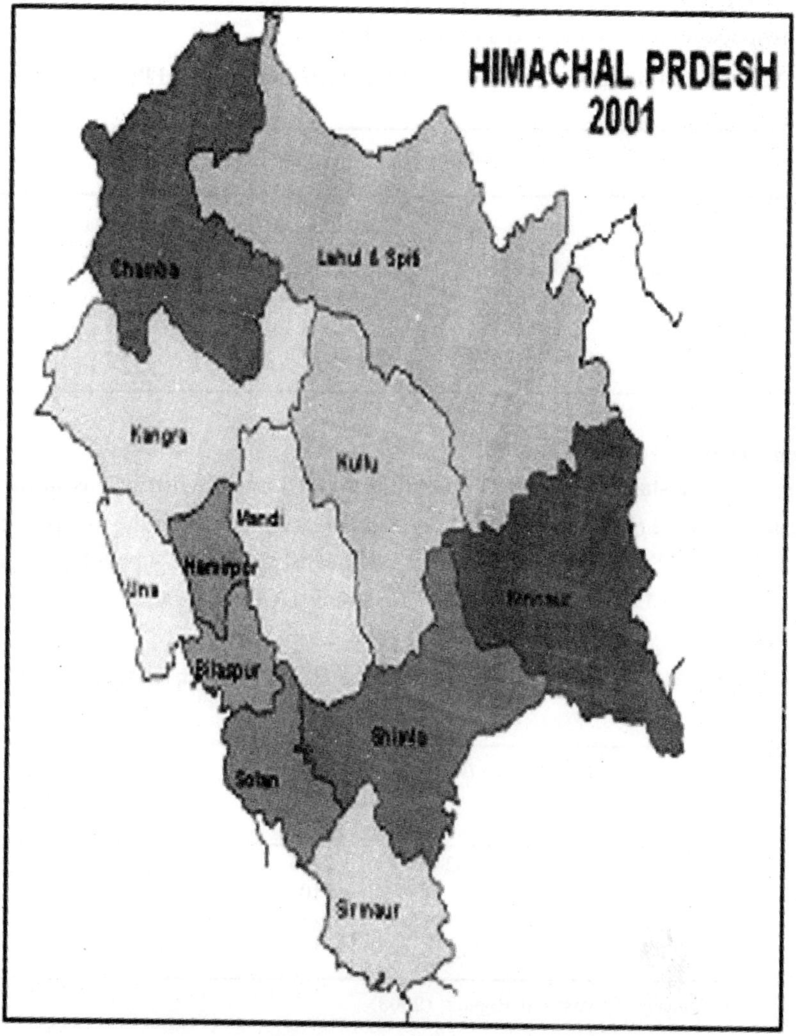

Map 2 : District Map of Himachal Pradesh

police posts. The districts are grouped in ranges. The administration of police within range is vested in a Deputy Inspector General of Police (DIG). There was only one range in Himachal Pradesh. Its headquarter was Shimla. All the districts of the state were in solitary range. On 16 February 1974, another range (the northern range), with headquarter at Dharamshala was created. Consequently, range at Shimla was re-designated as southern range. On 24 April 1986, third range (central range) with headquarter at Mandi was created (ibid). Thus Himachal Pradesh now has three ranges and their respective jurisdictions as shown in Table 2.3.

Table 2.3 : Police Ranges and Their Districts in Himachal Pradesh State

Range	*Headquarter*	*Districts in the Range*
Southern Range	Shimla	Shimla, Solan, Sirmaur and Kinnaur
Central Range	Mandi	Mandi, Hamirpur, Bilaspur, Kullu, and Lahoul and Spiti
Northern Range	Dharamshala	Kangra, Una, Chamba

2.2 District : Lahoul and Spiti

The state of Himachal Pradesh is divided into 12 districts, as shown in the Map 2. For the present study, work was conducted in the District of Lahoul and Spiti. The total population of the district is 33,224 people, out of which 18,413 are males and 14,811 are females (Census, 2001), as shown in Table 2.4.

Table 2.4 : Population Details of the District Lahoul and Spiti

S.No.	*Tehsil*	*Area (sq.km.)*	*Total Rural Population*		
			Male	*Female*	*Total*
1.	Lahoul	6244	7455	5649	13,104
2.	Udaipur		5105	4340	9445
3.	Spiti	7591	5853	4822	10,675
	Total	13,835	18,413	14,811	33,224

Source: District Statistical Report, (2003)

The entire population of the district is rural as there is no town. The average density of population of the district is 2 (Lahoul – 4 ; Spiti – 1) persons / sq. km. Sex ratio is 804 women per 1000 men (Lahoul – 795 ; Spiti – 824) (Census, 2001).

2.2.1 Location

The district of Lahoul and Spiti lies between East longitude 76' 29" and 78' 41' 34" and North Latitude 31' 4' 57" and 32' 59' 57" at an average altitude of 10,050 ft ranging between 5480 m and 6400 m above sea level. The total geographical area of the district is 13,835 sq. km. The district of Lahoul and Spiti is rent asunder in the north from Ladakh region of Jammu and Kashmir by the Baralachala range which has a towering height of 5500 m and in east is situated the Tibet region. In the southeast the district is separated from Kinnaur district by a lofty mountain with an average height of 5000 m. In the south- west and west, the district is dissociated from Kulu and Chamba districts by the majestic range with an average elevation of 4500 m. The access to Lahoul and Spiti is through one of the passes only Rohtang Pass adjoining Kullu at 3915m altitude; or Baralachala adjoining Ladakh at 5500 m or Kugti pass adjoining Chamba at 4500. Spiti is separated from Lahoul by a mountain rib. The two valleys of Lahoul and Spiti have a tenuous link over the Kunzom pass (4500m).

2.2.2 Administrative Set –up

The district has three sub- divisions. One each in Keylong, Kaza, Udaipur ; two tehsils – Lahoul at Keylong and Spiti at Kaza ; two development blocks – one each at Lahoul and Spiti.There are 521 villages in the district. Out of this 249 are uninhabited and 272 are inhabited. Out of 272 villages ; 213 are in Lahoul tehsil and 59 are in Spiti tehsil. There are 41 panchayats – 20 in Lahoul, 8 in Udaipur and 13 in Spiti. There are two panchayats samitis in the district – one in Lahoul and other in Spiti.

2.2.3 History of the District as an Administrative Unit

The district of Lahoul finds historic mention as early as the seventh century of our era, being alluded to as a district to the north- east of Kulu by the Chinese pilgrim Hwen Tsang under the name of Lo-hu-lo, which is clearly the Lho-yul of the Tibetans and the Lahoul of the people of Kulu and other neighboring states. It is probable that the country was from the earliest times a dependency of Tibet, its population being mainly of Tibetan origin and its name 'southern district'; affording in itself a clear indication of its subjection in early times to a northern power. When the Tibetan Empire was broken up in the tenth century, Lahoul was probably included in the kingdom of Ladakh formed out of the wreck by a chieftain. In what manner and at what time its separation from Ladakh took place before, it is impossible to ascertain, but the traditions of Lahoul goes to show that the separation is of long standing and it took place before the second consolidation of the Ladakh kingdom which took place in AD 1580 or 1600. It is probable that in the confusion preceding the re-consolidation of the Ladakh kigdom, Lahoul became independent, and remained for a short time governed by '*Thakurs*' or petty barons of small clusters of villages (Gazetteer of Kangra District, 1897). However, this period of perfect independence was not a long one. In the second half of the seventeenth century with the disintegration of Ladakh kingdom ; Lahoul passed into hands of the Kulu chief. In 1840, Maharaja Ranjit Singh took over Lahoul along with Kulu and ruled over it till 1846 when the area came under the sway of the British. From 1846 to 1940, Lahoul formed part of the Kulu sub-division of Kangra district and was administered through the local '*Jagirdars*'/'*Thakurs*'. One of the '*Thakurs*' was designated as Wizier (headman) of Lahoul and was invested with judicial and executive powers. Another '*Thakur*' was given the powers of a revenue officer. These functionaries exercised traditional as well as other power conferred by the Government. The Assistant Commissioner, Kulu used to visit the area once a year for a month or so. In the late thirties the unprecedented prosperity of the people through growing Kuth and their consequent awakening created a formidable challenge to the power and influence of the Wizier of Lahoul, which gradually started declining. The inadequacy was soon noticed by the Government which considered the extension of the regular system of administration. (Himachal District Gazetteer, 1975). Accordingly in 1941, a separate sub-tehsil comprising Lahoul and Spiti was formed and a Naib- tehsildar was posted at Keylong, thereby divesting the '*Thakurs*' of their powers. The system remains in vogue till June 1960, when Lahoul and Spiti district came into being. Simultaneously, Lahoul was constituted into a separate tehsil and later on, it was formed into a sub-division (Bajpai, 1987).

As has been noticed earlier, the birth of Spiti may also have taken place on the decline of central power in India. The Nonos of Spiti were the rulers there during the Ladakhi rule. It is said that the title of 'Nono' is derived from the Greek. It seems that during the strong rule of Ladakh; Spiti was an integral part of Ladakh and during the weak rule it was an autonomous body until nominally attached to Ladakh. The Spitians send tribute or price of peace to Ladakh, Kulu and Chamba periodically. After the Tibetan- Ladakhi war of 1681-83 Spiti was practically free but was only nominally under Ladakh.Later Raja Man Singh of Kulu invaded Spiti and ruled over it from 1688 till 1719 (Wilson, 1837).

The middle of 19th century, Spiti changed hands between Ladakh and Kulu. Then the East India Company took over the possession of the Spiti portion in the year 1846 after the Anglo- Sikh war. Before that it formed apart of Ladakh, a subsidiary of Jammu and Kashmir. Because of remoteness and poverty of natural resources, the British following the example of the Ladakhi rules, did not introduce any substantial changes in the administration set- up of the territory. The Nono of Kyuling was recognized as the hereditary Wizier of Spiti and was suppose to represent the British India Government. He collected the land revenue for the Government, his judicial jurisdiction included trial of all criminal cases, except cases of murder ; and he performed all the functions and enjoyed all necessary powers for the fulfillment of his tasks and duties ; as laid down in the regulations of 1883. In 1941; a sub-tehsil of Lahoul and Spiti was created with head quarters at Keylong (Bajpai,1987). After independence in 1947 a proper attention was paid to the development of Spiti for bringing it at par with Punjab of which Lahoul –Spiti was a part. A Development Council directly under the Chief Minister of composite Punjab was constituted. With a view to developing the area more rapidly the Government of Punjab in 1960 converted Lahoul and Spiti area into an district with head quarters at Keylong. Spiti area was constituted in a sub- division with head quarters at Kaza. The area was termed as 'excluded' and the Government of India subsequently declared as ' Scheduled Area'. On 1st November, 1966 the hill regions of Punjab was merged with Himachal Pradesh and thus Lahoul and Spiti district is now a part of Himachal Pradesh.

2.2.4 Development of the District

With the formation of the district several offices at Keylong were established. Thus the region became the hub of development activities, which were accelerated by the unexpected Chinese aggression in 1962. The development of agriculture, animal husbandry and cottage industries, communication, education, medical facilities and community development, power generation were some of the activities of the state in that area.

(A) Communication

Lahoul and Spiti, a territory on our international border with Tibet, in the past had never attracted the attention of the rulers. The result was that no communication worth the name ever developed here. Only the narrow tracks which had been carved by the herds of sheep and goats were available and few adventurers had discovered the paths themselves. An extremely different trade route was in existence. It passed through high Rohtang Pass and went up to Leh in Ladakh and beyond to Yarkand.

With change of international situation beyond our borders and disappearance of Tibet, an effective administration was the first priority of the Government. Road construction began in a massive way. Chinese aggression of 1962 had hastened the pace of construction for the military movement. While an all weather road National Highway Number 22 was development from Shimla to Kaurik via Puh and Sumdo, another National Highway Number 21 was developed from Manali to Leh via Rohtang Pass and Keylong. This is not an all weather road as the Rohtang Pass closes in the winter. This is the highest mountain road and is fit for vehicular traffic during the summer season. Now tunnel under the Rohtang Pass is being made, which will be an all weather road. Besides this main road, a road from Tandi to Thirot was constructed first of all. Now this road extends till Tindi which further connects Pangi valley of Chamba district with Lahoul. Towards the sTod valley, on one side the road is extended beyond Baralacha Pass connecting Ladakh and on the other it extends till Chikka. The GREF (Ground Engineering Reserve Force) army are now constructing road beyond Chhika to extend it till Zanskar in Jammu and Kashmir.

Towards Spiti from National Highway at Gramphoo near Khoksar, a road extends up to Kaza, the sub- divisional head quarters. From Kaza another road extends to Sumdo in Kinnaur district and connects it to the National Highway Number 22 which is an all weather road leads to Kalka and the plains of Punjab. There are many inter- villages and inter- valley roads and paths through which the movement of men and material goes on. The bridge over the rivers and nullahs are changed into regular bridges.

The progress of the road construction can be judged from the fact that around late 1960s, the total length of the road was 348 km which include the motorable road, single lane motorable road, jeepable and less jeepable road. Than in late 1970s, the total network of the road was extended to 733 km. and still growing.

(B) Post and Telegraph

The regular postal service, perhaps, was never in existence in the early years of the British occupation. It was probably after the establishment of Moravian mission in 1853 that some kind of postal work started in summers only. A school teacher used to officiate as Deputy Postmaster as long as there was any work to be done. The mail was sent from Sultanpur to Kulu to Keylong thrice a week. In 1869 a branch office was opened at Keylong for summer seasons only (Harcourt, 1874). From 1917 the exchange of letters was alternate day and as long as the satisfactory weather conditions was obtained. In 1935 a second post office was opened at Lote in Patan valley. Similarly a branch post office was opened at Kaza in 1939. After independence the postal services were extended to various centers in the district and a daily postal service was provided. Now there are 27 post offices in Lahoul and 20 in Spiti area. The mail service is operated from Manali and Kinnaur, one via Rohtang Pass and the other via Puh Sumdo to Kaza. This service continues as long as the passes are operative. During winters once a fortnight mail reaches Keylong and Kaza by helicopter. Table 2.7 shows the number of post offices the district has.

(C) Agriculture and Irrigation

Table 2.5 : Land Under Cultivation in the District Lahoul and Spiti

Development Block	*Percentage of Land in Hectares*			
	Potato	*Peas*	*Hops*	*Barley*
Lahoul	35.89	45.68	1.34	3.84
Spiti	2.09	51.09	-	44.19

Source : Deputy Commissioner's Office, Keylong, (2003)

Several steps were taken to increase the agriculture production. Though the mechanized farming is not yet being practiced by the farmers but some progressive ones have purchased some tractors. Besides providing improved implements and seeds, Government has also encouraged the use of insecticides and artificial manure also. Table 2.5 shows the land under cultivation for various crops.

Irrigation: All the villages in the district are irrigated through kuhls (canals). Almost all the villages have been covered by the potable drinking water.

(D) Education

There was no provision for any formal education in this district except the Buddhist monasteries where monks and nuns used to impart basic alphabetical education and religious teaching. The Moravian Mission made a beginning by establishing the just primary school at Keylong and a branch school at Tholang in the Patan valley in 1861. In the beginning missionaries tried to teach the youngsters Bhoti language. Their religious teachings mainly at spreading Christianity. In course of time mission people opened a series of schools but due to lack of students, they had to close down, except one at Keylong. The first regular school was started by the District Board Kangra in 1919 with Urdu as a medium. Spiti region had no school till the one was established at Kaza in 1932. The educational facilities within the district remained restricted to the primary school level only prior to the independence.

After independence the growth of education has been very rapid. By about 1950, the number of schools went to twenty nine, of which twenty three were primary, five middle and one high school. Besides these schools there were about 10 adult education centers functioning. Spitian students were less educated as compared to Lahoulis students.

Today the educational facilities have expanded remarkably. There are 12 Senior Secondary Schools, 13 Secondary Schools, 30 Middle Schools, and 202 Primary Schools. There are several *balwadis* established by Bhartiya Grameen Mahila Sangh in 1964, for the benefit of small children in the district. Table 2.6 shows the total school structure present in the district.

There is one college also in the district. The nearest university to the district is Shimla university.There are no professional colleges in the district.

There are above dozen officers in the Indian Administrative Services, Indian Police Services from this district. A large number of people are also in

Table 2.6 : Structure of Education in the District Lahoul and Spiti

Development Block	*Number of Schools*				
	Primary	*Middle*	*Secondary*	*Sr. Sec.*	*College*
Lahoul	140	19	9	8	1
Spiti	62	11	4	4	-
Total	202	30	13	12	1

Source: District Education Officer, Keylong, (2003)

Central Services and the State Administrative services. The district had also produced a number of doctors, teachers, engineers and scientists. The average literacy rate of the district is 73.14%. Males contribute for 82.76% of literacy and females for 60.94% (Census, 2001).

(E) Health Set –Up

Difficult terrain with extreme climate in complete isolation away from the main national life led people to believe more in the supernatural and depend more upon on priests and lamas. Some indigenous medicinal herbs and plants were used for the treatment of ailments and diseases. People's faith in charms and incantations as cure for various ailments was prevalent until very recently. Even now this faith is traceable in the more interior and remote regions. In course of time some private practitioners trained in Tibet went village to village to provide medical relief to the sick. But along with them people's belief in *Tana – Mana, Mit – Shale* and crude acupuncture by *Amchis* (hereditary Tibetan village doctors) had not shaken for a very long time. The modern allopathic system of medicine and treatment was introduced by the Moravian Mission at Keylong with their arrival in the region in 1853. District Board, Kangra had opened a dispensary at Keylong in 1929 which functioned till 1943 when it was taken over by the Government. By the forties sanitary teams started touring Lahoul during summer months. After independence these teams were accompanied by a doctor for touring the remote places of Lahoul valleys. But in Spiti region dispensary was opened in 1958 and prior to that people were to depend upon primitive medicines, magic and sorcery.

After the formation of the district in 1960, the civil dispensary at Keylong was raised to the civil hospital under a Chief Medical Officer–cum–District Medical officer. Civil dispensaries and primary health centers were opened gradually. In 1969 Ayurvedic system of medicine was also introduced. The district hospital was opened at Keylong in 1976. Table 2.7 shows the growth in the health set up of the district.

Table 2.7 : Health Setup of the District Lahoul and Spiti

Year	*Hospital / Community Health Center*		*Dispensary*		*Primary Health Center*	*Sub - Center*
	Allopathic	*Ayurvedic*	*Allopathic*	*Ayurvedic*		
1998	3	1	5	18	8	32
1999	4	1	5	21	10	35
2000	4	1	5	21	9	35
2001	4	1	5	21	9	35
2002	4	1	5	21	9	35
2003	4	1	5	22	9	35

Source: Office of Chief Medical Officer; Keylong, (2003).
Office of District Ayurvedic Officer; Keylong, (2003).

Table 2.8 : Block wise Health Centers in District Lahoul and Spiti

Development Block	*Community Health Center*		*Dispensary*		*Primary Health Center*	*Sub-Center*
	Allopathic	*Ayurvedic*	*Allopathic*	*Ayurvedic*		
Lahoul	3	1	2	15	6	25
Spiti	1	1	3	7	3	10

Source: District Statistical Report, (2003)

Now the medical facilities to the people are provided by four allopathic community health centers, one Ayurvedic community health center, five allopathic civil dispensaries, twenty two Ayurvedic civil dispensaries, nine primary health centers, thirty five sub-centers. Table 2.8 shows the block wise division of the health centers of the district.

In addition to this there are 14 hospitals for animals; 36 dispensaries and a mobile unit in the district.

(F) Social Welfare and Block Development

Social Service Organizations and Community Development work began in this tribal district soon after it was taken by the Government of the Himachal Pradesh. Voluntary Social Service Organizations had made their beginning in the forms of *Parvatiya Adim Sewak Sangh* and *Bharat Sevak Samaj* earlier, before these were taken over by the Government in a very large scale.

The Social Welfare Board of Himachal Pradesh has a Project Implementation Committee at Keylong.Under it came several extension centers.In every center, there use to be a craft teacher, a mid-wife and a Gram Sevika, who was to conduct adult education classes, look after balwadis. Now, these functions are distributed to various people who would come under different organizations. Craft teacher has a place in school and mid-wife in the hospital.

For recreation, information and to some extent education, Government had provided to people radio sets. Mobile cinema units use to tour the district showing documentary to the people, through information centers at Keylong and Kaza. An evaluation study conducted by the Director of Economics and Statistics of Himachal Pradesh Government in 1974, reveals that the general prosperity of the people has increased (Directorate of Economics and Statistics, 1974)

The Block Development carries the work of providing drinking water, construction and repairs of the kuhls, inter- village paths, school buildings and hospital construction through panchayats, construction of public latrines, play grounds of the school, distribution of seeds, insecticides, implements, fertilizers etc. Presently various development programs are running in the area, which have been discussed under the section of 'Lahoul Block'.

2.2.5 Democratization

There has always been some degree of democracy prevailing in Lahoul and Spiti. The village head men were elected by the people. The unofficial panchayats have always been there and the people used to get their problems settled with the help of the elders or Siyanas.In this system, the accused party was required to tender an apology and also compensate the aggrieved party. Some time in late forties or early fifties some official panchayats were formed.Thus there has been people's participation in the democratic process, first unofficial in Siyanas system and later in the panchayat raj elections.After changing hands with Kulu, Chamba ; this district is finally a part of Himachal assembly.

2.2.6 Crime and Punishment

Since the very beginning of the human civilization, in these areas the basic cause of the human crimes were absent. The people were poor and had few belongings to loose, steal or snatch. The society has been polyandrous and hence the possibility of sex crimes was negligible. Yet the society which has been organized must be having some method of setting disputes amongst the people. Five wise men or Panchas have been in existence all over India prior to the advent of modern western civilization. Paanch system of Kulu must have influenced this region and there may have been panchas to decide the petty quarrels amongst the people.

Captain Harcourt observes ' .... it may be deemed that the people of the country are singularly free from the majority of the vices that are common else where.' This was the situation in the nineteenth century. Till the first half of the twentieth century the position was not very different. Dr. Van Dar Sleen who had spent four months in the Himalayas, observed about the crime and character of he people : '....... There are no cases of theft of women, and as every one knows, all is fair in love and war. The penalty for such misdemeanor is always decided by the votes of the neighbors, and is as a rule, paid promptly. Neither are there any murderers because if you happen to kill to anybody in fit of temper or drunkenness, this is mis- fortune, not a crime. One source of frequent squabbles is the right to land and crops. Water rights too are a special bone of contentions; such as who may or may not tap the supplies of certain springs. Lucky mortals who are troubled neither with the existence of the legal code nor with the lawyers. Here law is simply law, and swift at that whether it be always justice I have my doubts'. (c.f. Sahani, 1994)

With the increase of affluence in Lahoul the crime also began to grow.Harcourt reports that in 1869 few people ripped open the bales of the traders at Rohtang pass and extracted goods from them. The culprits were severely punished and the case was publicized in every kothi of the area, which served as deterrent for the recurrence of the similar crimes for long time to come. In twentieth century, the only reported murder was in 1935, of a man attached to Moravian Mission. Thus, the complainants were the people of missionary. But due to the absence of evidence crime could not be proved and the case was dropped on tendering the written apology by the complainants.

2.2.7 Police and Courts

With the advancement of modern western civilization in the area, the crime rate has also increased ; which in turn required a police force to trace and tackle the problem, and courts to pass order on them.Though a seasonal police post was established in Lahoul prior to independence, its real organization began much later.

(A) Police: After the appointment of tehsildar in Lahoul in 1941 a seasonal police post was also created in 1943 at Keylong. Till 1948 this police post was functioning only in summer for the six months. The post was headed by a sub – inspector and six constables and was a part of the police establishment of Kangra district with its head quarters at Dharamshala. In 1948 the seasonal police post was made permanent and it worked round the year. This system continued till the formation of the district in 1960. In 1963, this post was upgraded and a Superintendent of Police was posted in the district. Today, there are two Police stations at Keylong and Udaipur, four police posts at Tindi, Jahalman, Khoksar and Sumdo.

(B) Courts: After the formation of the district, five criminal courts were created at Tehsil level.

The courts of Sub- Divisional Magistrate with the powers of Class I Magistrate.

The court of Tehsildar with powers of Class I Magistrate Both these courts are present at Keylong for Lahoul and at Kaza for Spiti.Over and above these four courts, the district Magistrate Ist Class at Keylong was also established. In matter of disputes of civil nature Deputy Commissioner of Lahoul and Spiti was given the powers of sub-ordinate Judge of Class II. Now in the open season, the court of Chief Judicial Magistrate sits at Keylong and otherwise in Kulu.

2.2.8 Visit to Police Station

There are two police stations in Lahoul Block. One is at Udaipur Sub-division and other at Keylong Sub-division. Other than this, there are two police postings - one at Khoksar and second at Jahalman. Two traffic check post are installed at Sarchu and Darcha.

Keylong police station was visited, as this is the head quarters of Lahoul Block. S.P. of the district D.K. Yadav (at that time) was very supportive. The total staff of the police station is 21. There is a line office also in this police station. Villages are clubbed according to *kothi* or *panchayat*. There are 14 *kothis* and 23 *panchayats* under Keylong police station. Area from Rohtang pass to Sarchu is under its vigilance.

2.2.9 General

The whole district is 100% electrified. In the year 2003 mobile phone facility was also launched in the district.Although the network is viable only in the radius of three to four kilometers from the district head quarter Keylong. In the year 2004, five more towers for the amplification of the mobile signal have been constructed in the area. Now it is claimed that the whole valley has the signals of mobile phones. There are eight Nationalized Bank branches and three co-operative bank branches. The lèad bank in the area is State Bank of India. Nearest railway station is in Shimla. Nearest airport is in Bhuntar which is near Kullu for Lahoul and Shimla airport is for people of Spiti.

Due to heavy snowfall in winters, the Lahoul block of this district remains cut off from the rest of world for about six–seven months from November–April / May in a year. Therefore this pocket is only an area in the country which becomes totally inaccessible. The helicopter service is started during winters for 3-4 months to provide mobility and avoid isolation of employees and local people during prolonged winter. However, the availability of the service to all and sundry is not cent – percent ; as there are lot of formalities to be done before embarking the flight. Moreover, at times the commencement of copter services is delayed because of lack of funds.There are six helipads in Lahoul Block – Stingri, Udaipur, Tingret, Sissu, Jhalaman, Palchan.

The Spiti block does not remain cut off or isolated during the winters. However, the motorable road from Gramphoo to Spiti is in a very bad condition, thus making the access, all the more difficult. There are just two petrol pumps in the area of 13,835 sq. km of the district. One is at Tandi, Lahoul ; 105 km away from Manali and other is at Kaza, Spiti ; 421 km away from Shimla.

2.3 Block : Lahoul

There is a confusion prevailing in the literary world, regarding the spelling of the area under consideration. Various authors have spelled it in different ways - LAHAUL ; LAHOUL ; LAHUL. The earliest references to the area in recorded history appear in the writings of a Chinese pilgrim. The most famous of these, Huan Tsang, who came to India about 640 A.D. and named it as " La - hu- la" and Kullu as "Kiu - lo- to".

Then, as early as 1819, two British, William Moorcroft and George Trebeck went on exploring the Himalayan provinces. After so many centuries, they again explored the hilly tracts of the district Lahoul - Spiti. In their travelogue they spelled the area as "LAHOUL" (Wilson, 1837). Since then, this spelling was used. Later in 1853, when the Moravian missionaries came in the valley, they also practiced using the same word. These missionaries who settled in Keylong (now the district head quarters) introduced in the region some vegetables like potatoes, cabbage, tomatoes etc. They also helped imparting education to the locals by opening schools at Keylong and Tholong. The missionaries gave much to the area - smokeless iron stoves for internal heating, ventilation with window and glass panes, growing of vegetables and knitting of socks and pullovers (Gill, 1972). The Moravians have left their mark on the valley and the people. The Christian missionaries made their impact on people not through their theology, but through medical aid and education (Randhawa, 1974).

It is to be mentioned here that Government of India while declaring the Lahoulis as Scheduled Tribe have used the spelling as "Lahaula" (List of Scheduled Tribes, Government of India).But with the passing time, as more and more authors wrote about the area adulteration crept in and the real old spelling was lost in due course of time. Thus, in order to revivify the old spelling of the area i.e. LAHOUL will be used throughout the text.

2.3.1 River System and Water Resources

Lahoul is a very narrow valley and is a collection of three separate valleys formed roughly in 'Y' shape. The river Chandra forms the right branch of the 'Y' which is called as Chandra Valley. This is also called as

Map 3: Map of District Lahoul and Spiti

Tinan Valley. The Bhaga river forms the left branch and is called Bhaga Valley or sTod Valley or Gahar Valley as shown in Map 3.

Together, their combined waters constitute the Chandra bhaga, after their confluence at Tandi, thus forming the lower stem of the 'Y' including the Patan Valley. Thus, Chandra and Bhaga are the main drainage lines of Lahoul.

2.3.2. Climate

The season here follows more like that of temperate zone. The winter season is from November till April followed by the spring which lasts up to the end of May. The next four months may be termed the summer season. October and first half of November constitute the transition season. Since the valley is situated in rain shadow area, north of the Pir Panjal ranges the weather remains pleasant and quite comfortable during summers i.e. from May to mid Oct. This is the best season to visit this valley. It seldom rains and the mercury level does not exceed 30ÚC and never falls below 15ÚC through out the period mentioned above. During winters, because of western disturbances it snows heavily and the temperature goes down by 15 – 20Ú C below Zero. There is an average snow fall of 7 ft.

2.3.3. Physical Regions

Lahoul can be divided into five distinct physical regions:

1. ***The Chandra Valley*:** The valley is named after the river 'Chandra' which flows through it. The valley starts from the snow bed on the south-eastern foot of the Baralacha Pass. For the first 72 km the valley is barren and uninhabited with high peaks and large glaciers tapering downwards from snow fields on the top of ridges. The slopes are characteristically stony and bare. Pastures exist in patches only along the valley where the Gaddis camp during the summer. The Chandra valley has five panchayats, covering 32 villages out of a total of 213 villages in the whole block. Names of Panchayats are Sissu, Gondhla, Khangsar, Khoksar, Mooling. Out of these Sissu is the biggest panchayat with 10 villages. From the village Sissu to village Tandi, it is called Tinan Valley. Above Sissu is called as Rangloi Valley. Together they make Chandra Valley. Khoksar is the first village in the valley. From there on scenery becomes greener and less oppressive. The valley on the right bank broadens out; villages are more frequent and cultivated area more widespread, flanking both sides of the road which runs through the middle of the valley. On the left is a sheer mountain wall from the river bed to the rugged crest. Beyond Gondhla, however, the topography

to the left also becomes less rugged and the mountain slopes are gentler, with terraced fields sloping down to the river.

2. ***The Bhaga Valley:*** This valley starts from the south-western foot of the Baralacha Pass. It is barren, rocky and uninhabited up to Darcha. However, there are two small satellite villages towards the Zanskar side, near Shingola Pass -Rarik and Chikka. Another satellite village, called Yoche lies 10 km in the interiors from Darcha. Thus, Darcha lies at the junction of Rarik Nallah and Yoche Nallah with the main Bhaga river. The valley broadens out from here onwards. The right bank has large tracts of level and cultivable land. Every seven or eight kilometers comes across a small village. This valley has six panchayats – Yurnath, Barbog, Keylong, Kolong, Darcha and Kardang. A total of 42 villages are covered in these Panchayats. Out of these Yurnath is the biggest panchayat with 12 villages. From Chikka till Quaring is called sTod Valley and away from Quaring till Billing is called Punan Valley. Together it is called Gahar Valley. 'Gahar' in Sanskrit means 'High interior land'. Keylong which is the district head quarters is also the largest village in this valley and lies on the right bank of Bhaga river. There are precipitous cliffs on the left bank also. Kardang, the one time capital of Lahoul and the seat of the famous monastery, lies on a commanding spot opposite to Keylong.

3. ***Patan Valley*** : The valley of the combined Chandra and Bhaga rivers, is called Patan Valley. 'Patan' in Sanskrit means 'low and flat land'. It is also called Manchat Valley on the basis of dialect spoken here. This is the longest valley of the block as it extends from Tandi, where the Chandra and Bhaga rivers meet till Tindi, on the boundary with Chamba. It is a broader, more fertile and thickly populated valley. This valley has 14 panchayats, which cover 113 villages of the block. Names of panchayats are Tandi, Ranika, Shansha, Jobrang, Gohram, Jahalman, Nalda, Bhuring, Thirot, Trilokinath, Udaipur, Tindi, Gushal and Warpa. Of these Bhuring is the biggest panchayat, having 16 villages.

4. ***Mayard Valley*** – The river in the valley flows downs, to join the Chandra-Bhaga river at Udaipur. The valley has 3 panchayats, covering a total of 26 villages. Names of panchayats are – Shakoli, Chimrat and Tingret. Out of these three, Tingret is the biggest Panchayat with 10 villages.

5. Across the Baralacha Pass, towards the north is a vast tract of land some 260 sq. km in are known as the lingti maiden. This tract is uncultivated and uninhabited and has a minimum elevation of about 4,270 m. The plain is

a good grazing ground and Gaddis move in during the summer. The plain is dissected by the Lingti which meets the Yunan river and the combined stream runs north-east to meet the Tsarab river, before flowing north into Zanskar.

2.3.4 Development Programs and Projects

Following development programs are running in the area at present :

(A) Education

Under District Primary Education Program (DPEP) total allocated amount is 11 crores 47 lacs, in which the amount of 8 crores 60 lacs are for Lahoul valley and 2 crores 87 lacs for Spiti valley have to be spent. Under this program 16 new schools have been constructed and 35 schools are repaired in which electricity, water and toilet amenities have been provided. Under Sarswati Bal Vidya Sankalp Yojna, in each primary school the provision of three rooms is ensured. From this scheme the H.P. Government has already spent Rs. 98 lacs & 50 thousand in which 60 rooms have been constructed and 9 are under construction. Under Yashwant Gurukul Awas Yojna, in each primary school the budget of Rs.60 lacs has been allocated for Lahoul valley. From this scheme construction of 24 sets have been completed. The Himachal Pradesh Government have started a novel Thakur Sen Negi Meritorious Student Scholarship Scheme for tribal areas, under this scheme 100 male students and 100 female students on the basis of merit in tenth class, Rs. 11,000 per year for each student as a scholarship is awarded for their 11th and 12th classes.

(B) Desert Development

In the district Lahoul and Spiti, Desert Development Project Program has been started in the year 1995 –96. The main purpose of this Development Project was to:

- to maintain ecological balance
- to prevent ecological degradation by optimum utilization of natural resources like land, water and forests.
- to generate employment and extra income to the inhabitants of the project area.

Under this project 181 watersheds development projects are already functioning, in which 94 watersheds in Lahoul block and 87 watersheds in

Spiti block. To complete the projects, maximum time of five years have been fixed. In this period there is a provision of Rs. 25 lacs in each water shed project. In the sixth step 20 water sheds for Lahoul block and 20 water sheds for Spiti block have been approved. In the last three years priority has been given for the construction of roads and bridges in the Lahoul valley. Recently 13 km Motorable road has been constructed in the Lahoul valley and Primary Health Center, Tingret has been constructed in the Mayard valley by the PWD. To uplift the horticulture in this area, on the basis of 50% subsidy 20 thousand different variety of plants of apple and other fruits had been distributed.

(C) Welfare

The State Welfare Department is committed for the upliftment of the unprivileged and the poor people in the tribal areas. Housing subsidy is given to people under the Indra Awas Yojna (IAY), started in the year 1993-94. Under this scheme, an amount of Rs.22,000 is given to the houseless people who are below poverty line (BPL). Preference is given to poorest of poor. As amount of Rs.10,000 is given to houseless persons from BPL to convert the kuccha house to pucca house. Priorities of the scheme are to allot new houses and to complete the pending houses.

(D) Integrated Child Development Services (ICDS)

This program was started in 1990 –91 and presently 43 *anganwadis* are functional in Lahoul block and mobile *anganwadis* are rendering benefits to the far flung areas. The different schemes of this department are as under:

1. Complementary Nutrition Scheme : The beneficiaries of this scheme are pregnant women / mothers and children between the age of months to six years and are provided with nutritional food as well as eatables.
2. Pre-school Education for Children between the age of 3 to 6 years.
3. Self Help Group: These are small groups of 8-20 members, who get together and decide to form a group. Saving is made by the members of the groups, by contributing equal amount on monthly basis through a consensus. The saved money is not kept in the bank. Saved money is circulated among the group members so that members can start some economic activities which are suitable to them. The ultimate aim of SHG scheme is to enable the poor and rural women to generate additional income to their families so that their economic, social and personal status can be improved.

4. Immunization

(E) Employment

Various schemes have been launched by the Government in the area, to provide employment to the unemployed people.

1. *Swaranjayanti Gram Swarozgar Yojna (SGSY)* : This is a centrally sponsored scheme, launched in 1999 in the area. It was started to provide economic assistance to BPL families, to cross the poverty line. Under this programme, emphasis is to be laid on development in rural area through SHGs.
2. *Jawahar Gram Samridhi Yojna (JGSY)* : It was started in 1999. The main objectives of this yojna was to provide additional employment for the unemployed poor in the rural areas. Later JGSY merged with SGSY. The priorities of the scheme were to release the funds to the panchayats immediately.
3. *Employment Assurance Scheme (EAS)* : This scheme was started in 1993, to create the additional wage employment opportunities during the period of acute shortage of wage employment through manual work for the rural poor living below the poverty line.
4. *Sampoorna Grameen Rozgar Yojna (SGRY)* : This Yojna was started in the year 2001 with the main objectives of providing wage employment, food security and creation of infrastructure and permanent assets in the rural areas.

The target group for this scheme is those either from BPL or APL families who are in need of wage employment and are willing to take up manual works in and around his or her village and habitation preference is given to the poorest of poor.

(F) Integrated Tribal Development Project (ITDP)

The state Government is committed for the overall development of the state. Special attention is being paid by the Government for the development of Tribal areas. The strategy of sub-plan for areas having tribal concentration was evolved in the sixth Five Year Plan beginning from 1974 –75. For this purpose, single line administration was introduced in this district. In this district, two ITDPs are functioning viz. Lahoul and Spiti at Keylong and Spiti under Additional Deputy Commissioner, Spiti at Kaza.

Following programs are categorized under ITDP:

1. *National Social Assistance Program (NSAP)* : This program was started in the year 1995 – 96. Under this, three schemes are categorized:
   (i) *National Old Age Pension Scheme (NOAP)* : An amount of Rs.150 per month is paid to helpless persons from BPL, if they are aged above 60 years.
   (ii) *National Family Benefit Scheme (NFBS)* : An amount of Rs.10,000 is paid to the next of kith and kin of the deceased head of BPL family as interim relief.
   (iii) *National Maternity Benefit Scheme (NMBS)* : An amount of Rs.500 is given to the pregnant ladies from BPL families for pre-natal and ante-natal care. The beneficiaries should be at least 19 years old.

2. *Credit Cum Subsidy Rural Housing Scheme* : This scheme started in the year 1999-2000, to provide housing loan and subsidy to the BPL families of rural areas. Total subsidy to be paid is Rs.10,000 and the rest is credit from the bank.

3. *Food for Work Program* : This program was launched in Lahoul and Spiti in the year 2001. Main features of the program are –
   - To provide food grains to laborers at concessional rate so that their families don't face the scarcity of food grains.
   - The food grains under the scheme are in terms of money @ Rs.7 per kg for rice and Rs. 5 per kg for wheat. Rice is provide only in Himachal Pradesh. This rate will be uniform for both BPL and APL.
   - The wage rate per day in Lahoul and Spiti is a total of Rs.65 per day. Out of which Rs.40 is being paid in terms of cash and Rs. 25 in the terms of food grains to be lifted from fair price shops.

4. *Natural Calamity Scheme* : The main features of this scheme are :
   - To execute repair works and renovation works on the basis of total damages done during natural calamities.
   - The repair and renovation of following structures can be done under this program-
     (a) Banks, wells and other drinking water sources
     (b) Ponds and Kuhl
     (c) Building of school and communities centers.

2.3.5 Administrative and Political Organization

In the formation of the district on 14 July 1960; the usual set of district administration was established gradually. The chief administrative authority within the district vests in the Deputy Commissioner who were due to single line administration is not only District Magistrate and Collector but for all intents and purposes is also the head of all the district level officers. In addition to the usual and traditional role as Deputy Commissioner, he has multifarious duties. As Deputy Commissioner, is the executive head of the district looking after development of panchayats, local bodies and civil administration. As District Magistrate, he is responsible for the maintenance of law and order and is the head of police and prosecuting agency in the district. As Collector, he is at the apex of the revenue administration and is responsible for the collection of land revenue and all dues recoverable as arrears of land revenue. He is also revenue – judicial authority. He is responsible for the co-ordination of functions of all district level departments. In face of topographical conditions of the conditions of the district, he is vested with special and enhanced powers for speedy execution of development work. He is authorized to effect transfers of non-gazetted staff within district and take appropriate disciplinary action if need be. He can order any punishment, short dismissal and removal from service. Lahoul and Spiti has two sub-divisions under sub-divisional officers. Under him are tehsildars, who are assisted by *Kanungos* and *Patwaries* etc.

There are two tehsils and two sub-divisions in the district namely Lahoul and Spiti which are conterminous. The Deputy Commissioner in the district is assisted by the usual compliment of ministerial and executive staff. But due to scarce and migratory population the work load is rather light and the employees comparatively are few in every department as compared to other districts. Three sub-divisional each posted at Keylong, Udaipur and Kaza are vested with powers of Magistrate Ist Class and Collector Ist grade. Two tehsildars are posted in Keylong tehsil and Kaza tehsil have the powers of the Magistrate second class and Assistant Collectors. They have to assist the Sub- divisional officers both in magisterial and in revenue work. Tehsildars in turn are assisted in the revenue work by the field revenue staff. The following district level officers, as shown in Table 2.9 are the in-charge of their respective departments, and work under the supervision and direction of the Deputy Commissioner.

There are several other departments of the Government of India which are also present in the district. They are postal department, Intelligence Bureau and Indo – Tibetan Border Police.

For the administrative purpose, the district Lahoul and Spiti is divided into two Sub-divisions – Lahoul and Spiti. Each of these sub-divisions has one tehsil each – Lahoul and Spiti respectively. Since Lahoul is a big tehsil so it is divided into has two blocks – Udaipur and Keylong, having the head quarters at Keylong. Spiti tehsil had one block – Kaza, which is also the

Table 2.9: Departments in District Head Quarter, Keylong

Department	*Designation*	*Headquarters*
Police	Superintendent of Police	Keylong
Medical	Chief Medical Officer	Keylong
Forest	Divisional Forest Officer	Keylong
Development	Block Development Officer	Keylong, Kaza
	Project Officer, ITDP	Keylong, Kaza
	Project Officer, DRDA	Keylong, Kaza
Panchayat	District Panchayat Officer	Keylong
Education	Deputy Director Education	Keylong
Public Relations	District Public Relations Officer	Keylong
Public Works	Executive Engineer	Keylong
Industries	GM, District Industries Corp.	Keylong
Veterinary	Assistant Director	Keylong
Co-operation	Assistant Registrar	Keylong
Irrigation and Public Health	Executive Engineer	Keylong
Agriculture	District Agriculture Officer	Keylong
Horticulture	District Horticulture Officer	Keylong

head quarters of the sub-division. Lahoul tehsil has 22,549 souls, covered in 28 panchayats and 213 villages.Spiti tehsil has 10,675 population, covered in 13 panchayats and 52 villages. For judicial administration there are three police stations – one each at Udaipur, Keylong and Kaza. There are four police postings : three in Lahoul tehsil – Tindi, Jahalman and Khoksar and one in Spiti tehsil at Sumdo. There are two check posts for controlling and checking the vehicular traffic. One at Sarchu and other at Darcha.

In the local governing or administrative bodies, there are panchayat system, *Mahila Mandals, Yuva Mandals, Vaan Sanrakshan Mandal.* The panchayat system is operative at the village level. The paanch from each village is the representative of the people of the village. Paanch is the lowest member of the rung of the panchayat system. Above him /her is Up-pradhan, then Pradhan or Sarpaanch. This hierarchy runs at the Panchayat level. Then at the Block level, highest in the hierarchy is the chairperson of the Panchayat Samiti, then the vice – chairman and then members. At the district level, highest authority lies with the chairperson of Zila Parishad and then members of the parishad.

2.4 People of Lahoul

According to the Surveyor General of India, the total area of Himachal Pradesh is 55,673 sq. Km. which is divided into 12 administrative districts. The total population of the Himachal Pradesh according to 2001 Census was 6,077,248 and a density of population in Himachal Pradesh is 109 persons per square km. According to 1991 Census, the total scheduled castes population of the state is 13,10,296 and scheduled tribes population is 2,18,398. The scheduled tribes population are concentrated in districts of Kinnaur and Lahoul and Spiti, parts of Chamba district and scattered in other districts. There are 11 scheduled tribes in the state- Beda or Beta ; Bodh; Chan; Domba or Gara or Zeba; Jad or Khampa or Lamba; Kanaura (including Chamand and Damang); Kanet or Seok (in Chhota and Bara Banghal); Kolta; Lahaula or Lahoulis ; Pangwala and Swangla. For the present study, work has been conducted on the Lahoulis, a scheduled tribe of District Lahoul and Spiti, Himachal Pradesh.

2.4.1 Work Done on People of Lahoul

The earliest reference of the area Lahoul and Spiti and the tribe Lahoulis is seen in the work of Murray, 1882; Wilson,1837; Cunningham,1854 and Harcourt, 1874 which are all travel monologues detailing about the geographical and topographical features of the area. The first official document of Punjab Government (1897) had the reference of Lahoul, was also an ethnographic account of the area. First reference of Lahoul in the beginning of 20th century was seen in the work of Grenard, 1904; Oakley, 1905; Shering, 1906 ; Imperial Gazetteer, 1908; Wilson, 1914; Himachal Academy of Arts, Culture and Language,1917. In the beginning of the second decade of the twentieth century, first work was of Sleen (1929). Before this no work on Lahoul has been reported. Beginning from 1930s onwards, the literature on the Lahoul grew exponentially. Various scholars have highlighted the area of Lahoul focusing on the topography, glaciers, trekking paths, rivers, religion, language, people, history as an administrative division etc. The works of the scholars which are predominantly the travelogues or monologues of the expeditions have been written by Hutchinson,1933; Brunton,1937; Douglas,1952; Khosla,1956; Smyth,1956; Dunsheat,1957; Holms,1958; Jones,1958; Lynam,1958; Solari,1958; Davies,1960; Lynam,1961; Scarr,1961; Shivananda,1962; Agarwala,1963; Cunningham,1963; Fisher,1963; Gadbole,1963; Minh,1963; Cunningham,1967; Kaushal,1967; Grierson,1968; Evans,1970; Sengupta,1970; Moorcraft,1971; Chetwood,1972; Francke,1972;Gill,1972; Atkinson,1973; Datta,1973; The Himalayan Club, 1973; Miller, 1973; Dasgupta,1974; Sircar,1974; Woodroffe,1974; Directorate of Economics and Statistics, 1974; Bailey, 1975; Cunningham,1975; Lama,1975; Guenther,1977; Lama, 1977; Vairagi, 1978; Bajpai, 1987; Tobdan, 1993; Sahani, 1994 and District Statistical Office, 2003). In the beginning of the twenty first century the scheduled tribe of Lahoul and Spiti has been seen with many different perspectives other than ethnographic accounts. Very few scholars have worked in the tribes from the dimension of human rights, globalization, ethnicity and social variability, development, social transformation etc. (Gupta and Kapoor, 2003; Gupta and Kapoor, 2004; Gupta, 2005; Gupta and Kapoor, 2005 and Gupta and Kapoor, 2006).

Area 2

State : Haryana

2.5.1 Location

Haryana is situated in the North –western part of India between 27°39′ and 30°55′ north latitudes and between 74°28′ and 77°36′ east longitude. It has Uttar Pradesh in the east, Punjab and Chandigarh in the west, Himachal Pradesh in the north and Rajasthan in the south. Delhi, the capital of India, stands conspicuously its south eastern extremity on the bank of the river Yamuna. Haryana abuts Delhi on three sides. With the Shivalik Hills in the north, the river Yamuna in the east, the range of Aravalli Hills in the south west and the river Ghaggar in the west, Haryana is distinctly demarcated from the surrounding states. These natural boundaries have produced conditions for a distinct culture, special mode of living and a different

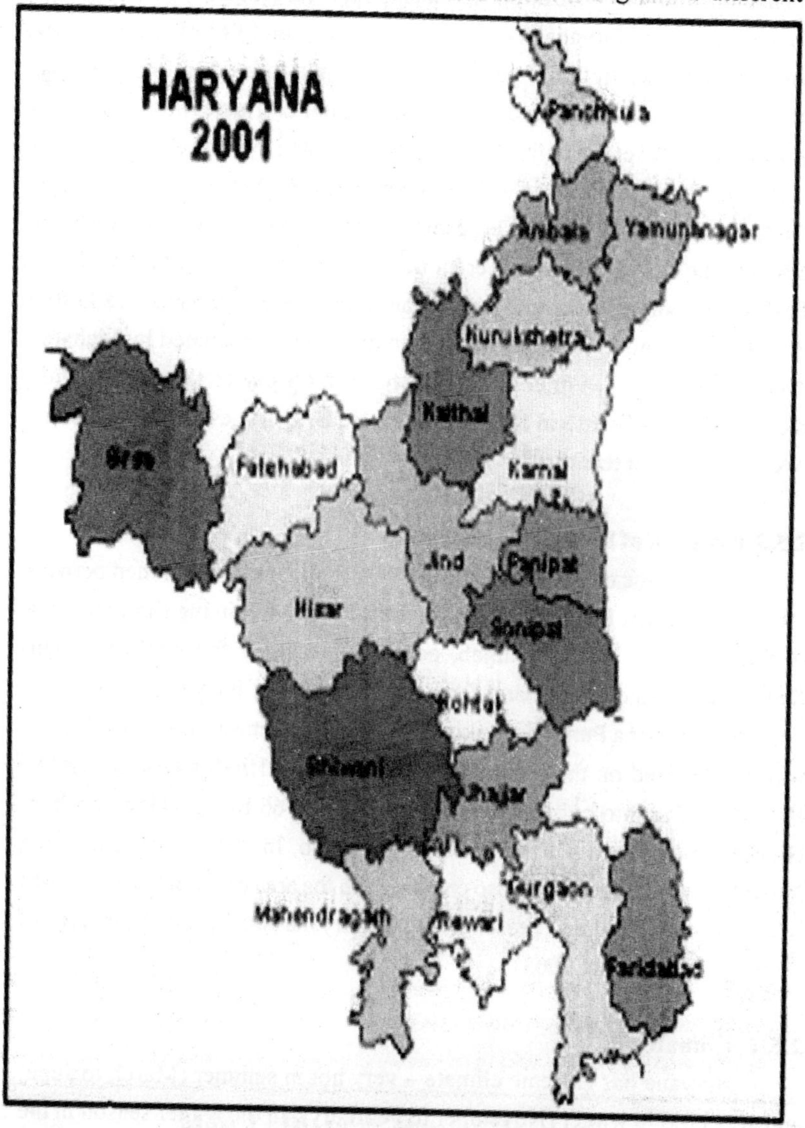

Map 4 : District Map of Haryana

linguistic pattern giving a sort of individuality to the region (Singh, 1994). The area of the State is 44,212 square kilometer (Statistical Abstracts of Haryana, 2002). Map 4 shows all the districts present in state of Haryana.

2.5.2 Historical Background

Haryana literally means 'the green country'. It is known as the cradle of ancient Indian civilization. Kurukshetra, where battle of Mahabharata was fought is in Haryana. The State saw the rise and fall of many empires through centuries.In the 7th century AD, Haryana formed an important part of the empire of Harshavardhan with its capital at Thaneswar, adjacent to Kurukshetra. After the defeat of Prithviraj Chauhan by Mohammed Ghori in 1192 AD, the region passed through several hands. During the period of the Delhi Sultanate and Mughal Empire all decisive battles, which profoundly affected the destiny of India, were fought in Haryana at Panipat. The British East India Company acquired the Haryana region on 30 December 1803 from the Marathas under the treaty of Sirijianjan Goan. Threatened by Maharaja Ranjit Singh, the then ruler of Punjab, these chiefs placed themselves under the protection of British in 1809. This enabled British to establish full control over the Haryana territory by 1809.

2.5.3 Creation of Present Day Haryana

At the time of Independence in 1947, Punjab was partitioned between the newly created Pakistan and India. East Punjab fell in the share of India. In the new state of East Punjab, people of Haryana felt neglected. This feeling reinforced the demand for a separate State of Haryana. At the same time, demand for a Punjabi speaking state gained momentum.Finally, Punjab was reorganized on the basis of language and the Hindi speaking state of Haryana came into existence on 1 November 1966 by speaking non-hilly Hindi speaking areas of the territory of Punjab. In this process the union territory of Chandigarh was also created from the area of Punjab. Chandigarh is the common capital of present Punjab, Haryana and the union territory of Chandigarh. (Menon, 2003)

2.5.4 Climate

Haryana has extreme climate – very hot in summer (March to June) and very cold in winter (November to February). In the winter season in the month of January, the mercury dips down to the freezing point. In summer season, heat of May and June makes the temperature rise between 48° C to 50°C. The annual rainfall varies from 25 cms in the western part of Hisar district to 110 cms in the eastern part of Ambala district. The months from July to September mark the peak precipitation period and account for over 80 percent of the annual rainfall. There is also a little rain during the winter season due to cyclones. Most of the winter rainfall is received in the month of January.

2.5.5 Natural Resources

(A) Land

Land is the main resource, which is controlled by individual proprietors belonging to the upper classes. The soil of Haryana is fertile and, given enough water, can yield rich harvest. About 80.70 percent of total geographical area of Haryana is cultivated area. (ibid, 2003)

(B) Forests

As per India's national forest policy, 33 percent of total land area of the country should be under the forest. As against this, the forest covers only 19 percent of land area of the country. In Haryana, only 3.51 percent of the total area was under forest in 2000-2001. Forest produce includes timber, firewood, bamboos, fodder, gum, resin and grass. Currently schemes are being implemented in the State for planting of trees, environmental protection and social forestry.

Administrative Structure

Table 2.10 shows the administrative divisions of Haryana

Table 2.10 : Administrative Divisions of Haryana

Administrative Divisions	*Number*
Divisions	4
Districts	19
Sub-Divisions	47
Tehsils	67
Sub-Tehsils	45
Blocks	116
Villages	6,955
Town	106
Panchayat	6,032

Source : Statistical Abstracts of Haryana, 2000-01.

2.5.7 Demographic Profile

According to Census of India (2001), total population of Haryana is 210.83 Lac. This means that Haryana, which comprises 1.44 percent area of India, sustains 2.05 percent of the population of the country. Among the states and union territories in the country, Haryana ranks 16th in terms of population size. The population of the State during 1991-2001 grew by 2.47 percent per annum (Census of India, 2001). Haryana as a state has 71.00 percent of rural population and 29.00 percent of urban population. 53.73 percent of the population is male and 46.27 percent is female. Density of the population per square kilometer is 477 persons.

The sex ratio of Haryana has declined continuously since 1981. In 1981, it was 870:1000, in 1991 it became 865:1000 and in 2001 it was 861:1000. Immediate fallout of the decline in sex ratio will be a significant decrease in the marriageable age of women, which is already quite low in Haryana. This, in turn, will push up fertility and negate all the achievements of family planning / welfare. At the same time, it may lead towards a trend in androgyny, a situation that privately people acknowledge even today in Haryana. Some areas, it is understood, already have a large presence of 'imported wives', mainly from Bengal, Assam and Jharkhand. The Census authorities of Haryana tried to study and plot the crime against women per thousand population in various districts against the sex ratio. They found that districts with higher sex ratio are lesser prone to crime against women (Census of India, 2001). All India Literacy rate is 65.38 percent. The literacy rate of Haryana is 68.59 percent.Haryana ranks 20th in this regard. 31.41 percent is illiterate. The literacy rate of males in Haryana is 79.25 percent and females is 56.31 percent, gap being 22.94 percent (Census of India, 2001). Haryana has no Scheduled Tribes. It has 37 Scheduled Castes.

2.6 Police in Haryana State

(A) History of Haryana Police

The state of Haryana was created on 1st November 1966 on reorganization of the erstwhile state of Punjab on lingual basis. Haryana police came into existence on allocation of 40 percent of the police force to it, like other assets of the composite state of Punjab, on 1st November 1966. Hence, any effort at attempting to record the history of Haryana police would be considered incomplete if it does not explore the evolution and development of Punjab Police.

(B) Composition and Hierarchy

A police force consists of two main branches – civil police and armed police. Personnel of battalions of Haryana Armed Police (HAP), Haryana Commando Battalion and Haryana Indian Reserve Battalion (IRBn) constitute the armed police of Haryana. The sanctioned strength of officers of and below the rank of Inspector of Haryana Armed Police is 6217. The sanctioned strength of Haryana Civil Police is 33,193.This is exclusively of the sanctioned strength for bodies like the State Vigilance Bureau (SVB), Enforcement Wing of Excise and Taxation Department and National highway patrol and road safety organization, which operate independently of the control of the Director General of Police, Haryana.

The posts in Table 2.11 are listed in hierarchical order, the post of constable being at the bottom and that of Director General of Police being at the top of the hierarchy. The post of ASP, which is held by an officer of Indian Police Service, is considered superior to the post of DSP, which is held by an officer of State Police Service, though the functions of the incumbents of these two posts are identical. Officers of and above the rank of DSP are called Gazetted Officers (GOs). Inspectors, Sub-Inspectors and Assistant Sub-Inspectors are known as upper subordinates. They are also called non-gazetted officers (NGOs). Officers of and below the rank of Head Constable are known as lower subordinates. They are also called other ranks (ORs).

(C) Police, Area and Population Ratio

Area : In Haryana the area per policeman is one square kilometer and the corresponding India figure is 2.12 square kilometer per policemen.(Menon, 2003)

Population : Population per policeman in Haryana is 477.41 persons and the corresponding India figure is 687.74 persons.(ibid)

(D) Administrative Divisions

Haryana has 4 police ranges, 19 police districts, 47 police sub-divisions, 206 police stations and 321 police posts. Like other states, in Haryana also the police range is headed by a DIG. Each district is headed by a Superintendent of Police (SP), who is generally known as Senior Superintendent of Police (SSP). Each district has a number police sub-divisions and a number of police stations. Each sub-division is headed by a

Table 2.11 : Composition and Hierarchy of Haryana Police

Designation	*Strength*
Director General of Police (DGP)	4
Additional Director General of Police (ADGP)	3
Inspector General of Police (IGP)	13
Deputy General of Police (DIG)	10
Assistant General of Police (AIG)	3
Superintendent of Police (SP)	28
Addl. SP	26
Assistant Superintendent of Police (ASP)	18
Deputy Superintendent of Police (DSP)	138
Inspector	382
Sub-Inspector of Police (SI)	1325
Assistant Sub-Inspector of Police (ASI)	3343
Head Constable (HC)	6437
Upgraded Constable (UGC)	2185
Exemptee Head Constable (EHC)	3066
Constable	22429
Total	39410

Source: Data on Police Organizations, Criminal Justice India Series, Vol. 10, 2005

sub-divisional police officer, who is a Deputy Superintendent of Police (DSP) or an Assistant Superintendent of Police (ASP). An Inspector of police heads a police station in urban areas and a Sub-Inspector of Police (SI) heads a police station in rural areas. The officer in charge of a police station is called Station House Officer (SHO). Some police stations have police outposts. Each police outpost is headed by an Assistant Sub-Inspector (ASI) or SI

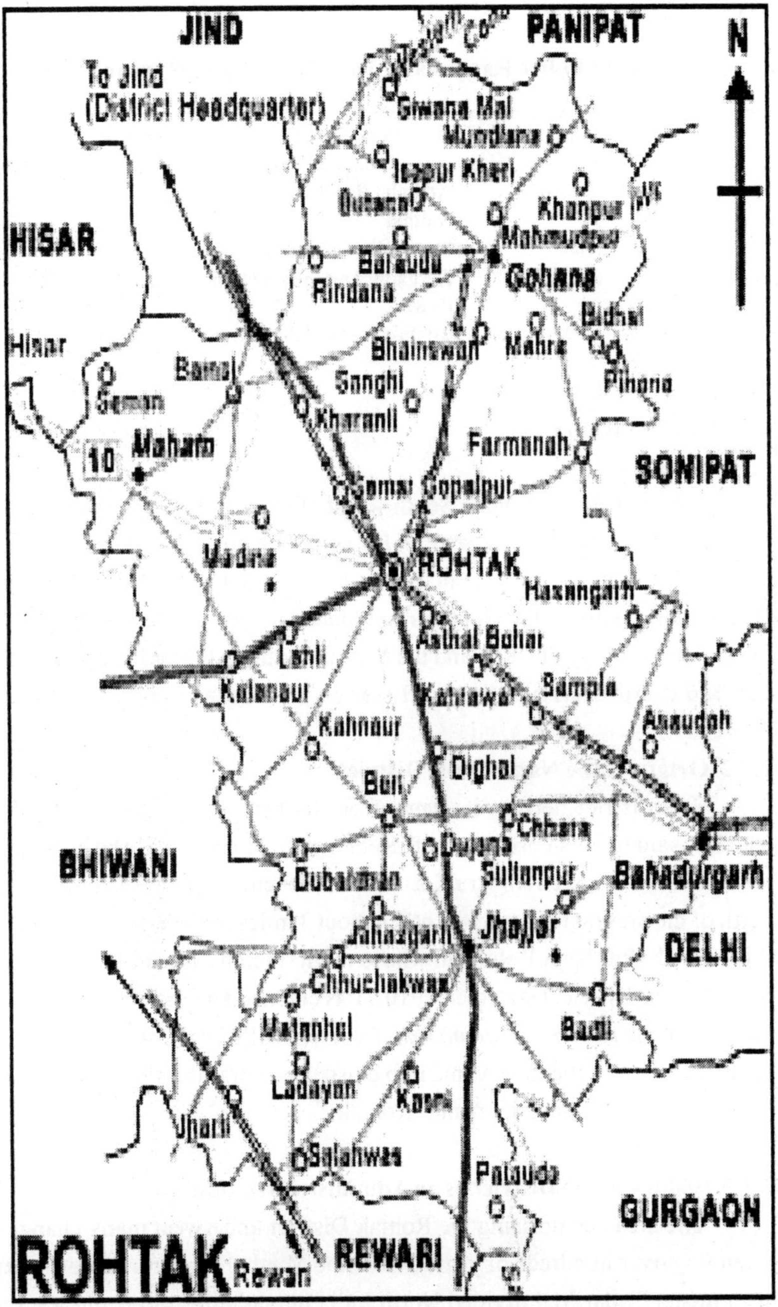

• **Map 5: Map of District Rohtak**

(ibid). Table 2.12 shows the range with its head quarters and districts in Haryana state.

Table 2.12 : Police Ranges and Their Districts in Haryana State

Range	*Headquarter*	*Districts in the Range*
Ambala	Ambala	Ambala, Panchkula, Yamunanagar, Kurukshetra, Kaithal
Hisar	Hisar	Hisar, Bhiwani, Sirsa, Jind, Fatehabad
Gurgaon	Gurgaon	Gurgaon, Faridabad, Narnaul (Mahendragarh), Rewari
Rohtak	Rohtak	Rohtak, Karnal, Panipat, Sonepat, Jhajjar

2.7 District : Rohtak

2.7.1 Location

The districts lies in the South – east of Haryana State with an area of 1668 sq. km. between 28°19′ and 29°18′ north latitude and 76°13′ and 77°13′ east longitude and is compact in shape. It is bounded by the Jind and Karnal Districts on the north, the Gurgoan and Mahendragarh districts on the south, the Union Territory of Delhi and the Meerut Districts (Uttar Pradesh) on the east and the districts of Jind and Hissar on the west as shown in Map 5.

2.7.2 Origin of the Name of the District

The district derives its name from its head quarters town Rohtak, which is said to be a corruption of 'Rohtasgarh', a name still applied to the ruined sites (also called Khokra Kot) of two older cities, one lying immediately north of the present town and the other about 3 miles to the east. Traditionally it is named after Raja Rohtas in whose reign the city is said to have been built (Punjab District Gazetteer, 1910). It is claimed that the town derives its name from the *roherra* (*Tecoma undulate*) tree called *rohitak* in sanskrit. It is said that before the town came into existence, it was the site of a forest of *rohitak* trees and hence its name 'Rohtak'.

2.7.3 History of the District as an Administrative Unit

The areas comprising the Rohtak District underwent many changes, extending over hundreds of years before the Mughal Emperor Akbar, when his minister Todar Mal divided North India into administrative circles, the areas of Rohtak fell within the sarkars of Delhi and Hissar.

On the death of Bahadur Shah I (1707 –12), the successor of Aurangzeb, the Mughal empire began to decide rapidly. The area in which Rohtak lay frequently experienced a change of masters. The claims of the Imperial grantees were contested sometimes by the Rajputs, Jat and Sikhs and often by the Marathas. By the treaty of Suji Arjungaon, signed on December 30, 1803, the Rohtak area, along with the other possessions of Sindhia situated to the west of the Yamuna, passed to the British and came under the administrator of the North – Western Provinces.

The formation of the present day Rohtak District began when the gift was abandoned by the Dujana Chief. The Gohana and Kharkhauda – Mandothi estates lapsed to the British Government on the deaths of Lal Singh in AD 1818 and Bhag Singh in 1820. In 1824, the Rohtak District was formed as a separate unit consisting of Gohana, Kharkhauda- Mandothi, Rohtak-Beri and Maham Bhiwani tehsils. The Bahadurgarh territory formed its eastern and Jhajjar, its southern boundary. Until AD 1832, the whole area, including Rohtak, was under the resident at Delhi, but when in that year it was brought under the same regulations as the rest of North India, the resident became commissioner. The district was abolished in AD 1841, Gohana going to Panipat and the rest of the tehsils to Delhi, but in the very next year it was created again. The two districts of Rohtak and Jhajjar together with the rest of the Delhi and Hissar divisions were detached from North – Western Provinces after 1857 and passed to the Punjab by the Notification No.606 of the 13th April, 1858.The Rohtak district remained a part of the Hissar division until 1884.

After its transfer to the Punjab, the Rohtak district experienced several changes before assuming its final form. On the abolition of the Hissar Division in 1884, the Rohtak District was transferred to the Delhi divisions. It consisted of 4 tehsils – Rohtak, Gohana, Jhajjar and Sampla but in April 1910, the last named tehsil was abolished for reasons of administrative economy, and its area was divided between the Rohtak and Jhajjar tehsils. The Sonepat tehsil, which had remained attached to the Delhi District since the year 1861, was added to the Rohtak district in September 1912, on the separation of Delhi territory from the Punjab.The district was than attached to the Ambala division.

In 1948, Dujana State was merged in Jhajjar tehsil and a new Sub-tehsil of Nahar was created. In 1970, the district was sub-divided into four tehsils namely Rohtak, Sonepat, Jhajjar and Gohana and a Sub-tehsil of

Nahar. Later Jhajjar was made a separate district. At present the district is sub-divided into two tehsils – Mahem and Rohtak.

2.7.4 Administrative Structure

Table 2.13 shows the divisions in district Rohtak. District Rohtak which comes under Division Rohtak of the state Haryana has 5 Blocks :

Table 2.13: Administrative Divisions of District Rohtak

Block	*Panchayats*	*Villages*
Rohtak	55	57
Lakhan Majra	13	13
Meham	34	24
Kalanaur	24	28
Sampla	25	24
Total	151	146

Out of these 5 Blocks, Rohtak is the biggest block with 56 panchayat and Lakhan Majara is the smallest block with only 13 panchayat. In total there are 157 panchayats in the District Rohtak. Sampla block has 25 panchayats and 24 villages.

2.7.5 Demographic Profile

The state of Haryana is divided into 19 districts. For the present study, work was conducted in the District of Rohtak. The total population of the district is 940301 people, out of which 50,8200 are males and 43,1101 are females (Census, 2001). The Rohtak District contributes 4.46 percent of the state population. This districts stands at 13th position in growth of population. The average density of population in Rohtak was 445 in 1991 which increased to 539 in 2001. The Rohtak district stands 8th in the state. Sex Ratio is at 847 in the district which is a declined ratio when compared to 1991 census. In the year 1991, the sex ratio was 865. The reason for decreasing sex ratio is National Capital Delhi which is situated near by. In terms of sex ratio, the rank of Rohtak in the state is 15th The literacy rate of the district is 74.56 percent of which 84.29 percent are males and 63.19 females. The district stands at 4th position in literacy in the state.

2.7.6 Climate

'Rohtak' enjoys a semi arid monsoon type of climate, owing to a long distance from the sea region. The region fails to get the full benefit from monsoon current. Hot summer and evaporation more especially in the southern parts exhibit a whole transition between the arid desert of Rajasthan and the moderately humid upper Ganga plain. It experiences the usual three seasons – winter, summer and rainy. Both, heat in summer and cold in winter are extreme. Moreover, there is not only considerable difference in the weather from season to season but also from year to year.

2.7.7 Agriculture

Very little or negligible percentages of forest is present, infact in the real sense it is not a true forest. Great part of land is under the agricultural use i.e. farming.The main crops of the area are wheat, mustard, sugarcane, bajra, jowar and cotton.

2.8 Block : Sampla

2.8.1 Location

Sampla block lies in the Rohtak District of the State Haryana. It is situated in south of the Rohtak. It lies between 76°10′ N to 76°50′ N longitudes and 28°10′ W to 28°50′ W latitude. It makes 17 percent of the district Rohtak.

2.8.2 Village Boundary

The village Sampla is surrounded by small neighboring villages. In the east there is Godh and Rohtak; in west there is Kultana and Ismaila ; in north there is Nayabans, Gijji and in the south there is Asauda village.

2.8.3 Origin of the Name

The history of Sampla does not contain much of the information as most of the inhabitants of Sampla have migrated from the nearby areas i.e. Rajasthan, Delhi and even some parts of Uttar Pradesh and Punjab. Regarding the name of block, there are more than one views. Initially lot of snakes were found over here so the name of the place is 'Sampla'. 'Sampla' in Hindi means 'snakes'. Sampla is a multi-caste village and multi religious village. Majority of people are Hindus, Sikhs are also found. Initially the whole area was called by the name 'Sampla' but later on it was divided into small segments based on the locality and the development as initially this area was totally occupied by Jat and Chamars. Although this place gave a number of freedom fighters but most famous person of this area is 'Choudhary Chotu Ram' who was the agricultural minister before independence. His eminent work during British time included the starting of various polytechnics, schools and also a number of agricultural projects which are mainly concerned with the development of farmers.

2.8.4 Family System

Families in the area are patriarchal, patrilineal and patrilocal. Society is male dominated. Head of the household who is generally either the father or the husband is the key member in decision making. Females mostly occupy the back stage in the family matters and decision making process. They are dependent on their male counterparts for any decision to be done. Rule of inheritance is on the basis of equigeniture. Land and all movable property is equally divided among the sons of the family. Daughters, however, have no right in the property. They are entitled to dowry at the time of their marriage.

2.8.5 Visit to Police Station

There is only one police station in the Sampla Block, located in village Sampla. There are 6 police stations in the district Rohtak. One each in Meham, Kalanaur, Sadar Rohtak, City Rohtak, Civil Lines and Sampla. Sampla Block which has 25 panchayats and 24 villages comes in the custody of Sampla police station.

2.9 People of Haryana

According to Census of India (2001), 28.92 percent of the population is urban and 71.08 percent is rural. The Anthropological Survey of India launched the People of India project on 2 October 1985 to generate an anthropological profile of all communities of India. "As part of this all-India project, the ethnographic survey of all the 82 communities of Haryana was taken up in a collaboration with local scholars. Religion has always provided the main basis for the structure of the Haryana society. In ancient times, Aryan people followed the Vedic religion. Later on Buddhism, Jainism, Islam and Sikhism influenced the people. Swami Dayanand's teachings greatly impressed the people and the Arya Samaj has a large following among Hindus of Haryana. In present day Haryana, Hindus are about 90% of the population, Sikhs 6.2%, Muslims 4.05% and Christians 0.10%. Hindus are divided into a number of castes like Jat, Brahmin, Ahirs, Gujars, Aggarwals, Arora Khatris, Sainis, Rajputs and Rors. Among them all, the Jat occupy a preeminent position in Haryana, being the largest group in the state. The artisan castes such as Telis (oil traders), Sunars (goldsmith), Lohars (blacksmiths), dhobis (launderers) and Nais (barbers) are found throughout the state, especially in villages (Singh, 1994)

The Jat are spread throughout Haryana. The origin of Jat is shrouded in mystery. Harijans constitute about one fifth of the population. As a result of various facilities and privileges provided by the Government, the Harijans are now taking an active part in all the activities. The Muslims in the state are mostly Meos and are concentrated in the Mewat region. There are Muslim Rajputs as well as converted Muslims. The Sikhs generally live in Ambala, Kurukshetra and Karnal districts. Sikhs too have their own castes like Jat, Sikhs, Aroras etc.

Jat is a heterogeneous group which occupy a preeminent position in Haryana. They are divided into 12 clans and about 300 *gotras*. Though the origin of Jat is shrouded in mystery, they are believed to be an Indo-Aryan tribe, connected to the Vedic civilization (4500 BC - 2500 BC) that existed along the Saraswati river. Even today, the highest density of Jat population is along the dried bed of Saraswati, starting from Haryana, going on to Punjab and ending up in Rajasthan. They play a predominant role in this region. Agriculture, soldiering and cattle rearing have been the main occupation of the Jat, but now they are branching out in other fields like military and police. They are also well represented in Government civil services.

Ahirs, Yadavs or Yadavas are to be met with throughout the country especially in Haryana. Although the Ahirs and Yadavas form one group, the former (the Ahiras or Abhiras) are an important community of Haryana, but numerically they constitute less than 10 % of the total population. Most of them live in the region around Rewari and Narnaul which is therefore known as Ahirwal or the abode of Ahirs.

Gurjars or Gujjars are settled in Faridabad and Panchkula districts and the Samalkha segment of Panipat district. They are simple, thrifty and industrious. The Gujars are cultivators only in the plains but in the hills they are more given to keeping cattle than following the plough.

The Brahmin of Haryana are divided into four main groups: Gaurs, Saraswats, Khandelwals and Dhima. The Gaurs claim that they come originally from Bengal. But it is believed they came as *Purohitas* of the various immigrant farming tribes. The Saraswats are original settlers of this region, taking their name from the Saraswati river. The Khandelwals and Dhima came into this region later, most probably from neighboring Rajasthan. The Brahmin themselves had a ranking system between them with the Gaurs being on the top followed by the Saraswats, the Khandelwals and the Dhima. The Gaurs used to consider themselves to be superior to the other Brahmin and neither ate, drank nor intermarried with them.

In the present study, work has been conducted on the Jat and Brahmin of Block Sampla, District Rohtak and both of them represent rural population on the basis of characteristics which have been discussed earlier.

2.9.1 Work Done on People of Haryana

Haryana came into existence in 1966, prior to this it was a part of Punjab province. The earliest reference of Haryana is seen in the works of Sherring (1879) and Crooke (1896) and Elliot (1896). The official mention of the area is in the gazetteer by Hunter (1908). After this there was a series of work by various scholars of different fields highlighting the tribes, race, castes, language, origin of the nation, battle fought etc. (Russell and Hiralal,1916; Grierson, 1916; Ibbeston, 1916; Cunninghan,1918 and Rose, 1919). After this period of the second decade of twentieth century, there was a lull in the literature of Haryana. Again in 1950s with the work of Giri (1950) on the dress pattern, there the literature could be seen. Scholars had written about the farmers of Haryana, Mewat, histories of various castes and communities like – Saini, Meo, Rajputana, Sikhs and Jain, glossary of tribes and caste (Randhawa, 1959; Gahlot, 1966; Ali, 1967; Blunt, 1969; Saini, 1970; Maheswari, 1970; Majumdar, 1972; Fyzee, 1974; Yadav, 1977 ; Dahia, 1980 Sangave,1980; Bingley, 1984; Sethi, 1985; Datta & Phadke, 1985; Bishnoi, 1986 and Singh,1986). Works on the development aspects are also viewed (Malhotra, 1981 and Mann, 1992). Tewari et al (1996) have done the KAP study regarding the Oral health of rural communities of Haryana.

Various ethnographic accounts of the area have also been written (Munilal, 1974; Baines, 1976; Shams, 1981; Singh, 1989; Singh & Mann, 1993 and Singh, 1994). Gazetteer organizations have also conducted work from time to time for collecting the ethnographic data from the area (Prem,1970; Rohtak District Gazetteers, 1970; Karnal District Gazetteers, 1976; Bhiwani District Gazetteers, 1982 and Gurgaon District Gazetteers, 1983).

Many anthropologists have also conducted the research on the aspects like dental traits among Jat of Haryana, skin pigmentation and tanning, blood group polymorphic systems etc. (Bhalla & Singh, 1979 and Joshi et al.,1985).

In view of above review of literature, it can be claimed that the focus of the present work is a pioneering effort as till date none of the scholars have carried out the study from the perspective of police and human rights in the rural population.

Area 3

2.10 National Capital Territory: Delhi

2.10.1 Location

Delhi is situated on the right bank of the river Yamuna at the periphery of the Gangetic plains. It lies a little north of 28 N latitude and a little to the west of 78 Longitude. To the west and the south- west is the great Indian Thar desert of Rajasthan state, formerly known as Rajputana and, to the east lies the river Yamuna across which has spread the greater Delhi of today. The ridges of the Aravalli range extend right into the Delhi proper, towards the western side of the city, and this has given an undulating character to some parts of Delhi. The meandering course of the river Yamuna meets the ridge at Wazirabad to the north, while to the south, the ridge branches off from Mehrauli. The main city is situated on the west bank of the river. Map 6 shows the districts of Delhi.

2.10.2 Historical Background

The earliest known city of Delhi is Indraprastha, which is associated with the Pandavas. It is said to have been situated on a huge mound on the western bank of the river Yamuna, now occupied by the Purana Qila. In the first century BC, Raja Dillu is believed to have built another city on the site where the Qutab Minar now stands and named it Dilli. The next city was Suraj Kund, built by a Tomar Rajput in AD 1020. The main city was subsequently moved to the old site of Delhi. Later it was converted into the fine walled city called Lal Kot. The famous iron pillar is associated with this dynasty. The city was expanded four times by the last Hindu ruler of Delhi Prithvi Raj in 1170. The end of his reign saw the Muslim invasion in 1191 and his defeat in the battle of Panipat. Later Ala-ud-Din Khilji, successor of Mohammed Ghori, built a new city at Siri, about three miles north east of Delhi. Than in 1321, city was of Tughlakabad was completed with fortress and walls. The Lodis who reigned the capital in the fifteenth

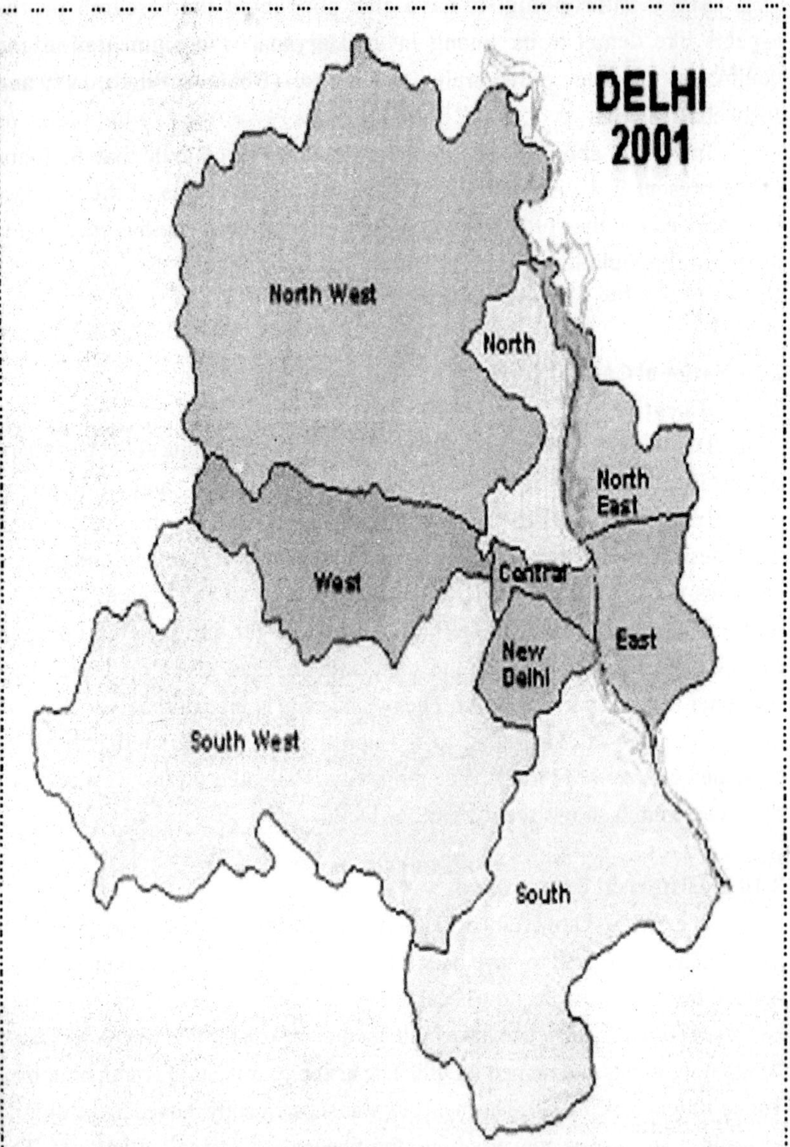

Map 6 : District Map of Delhi

century, transferred the capital to Agra. Akbar reigned from Agra, but his grandson, Shah Jahan, built a new city two miles north of Firuzabad between 1638 and 1658. The city survives to this day, although with changes, as the walled city of Delhi.

In 1804, the city and its surrounding areas came under the sway of the British. The imperial capital of British India was established at Calcutta, and remained there till 1911. In 1912, this capital was shifted to the plains of Delhi. A new city, the city of New Delhi was planned and built. This new city has continued to be the national capital of India since 1947 when India attained independence from the British. Ever since, the city has spread out far and wide, though mainly southwards, incorporating all the earlier cities of the Delhi plains.

2.10.3 Political Organization

One of the seven Union Territories, Delhi enjoys the privilege of being the capital of the Indian 'Union of States'. Delhi is unique in several respects in India's history of politics and governance. Besides being a metropolitan city with a cosmopolitan population, it is seat of power of the Republic with the Central Government, The Indian Parliament and the Supreme Court located in its territory. It is also the seat of several other apex institutions such as the Supreme Court of India, the National Human Rights Commission, the National Commission for Scheduled Castes and Scheduled Tribes, the National Commission for Women, the National Commission for Minorities, the National Legal Service Authority and the Communal Harmony Foundation.

After Independence and till 1956, Delhi was constituted as a uni-district State headed by a Chief Minister. In 1956 Delhi was designated a Union Territory comprising three municipal areas, namely (I) the Municipal Corporation of Delhi, (ii) the New Delhi Municipal Corporation, (iii) the Delhi Cantonment. Hereafter, as a sequel to the 69th Constitutional Amendment Act, the passage of the National Capital Territory Act in 1991 the state was redesignated as the National Capital Territory (NCT) of Delhi.

For the political and the social control, the uni- district of Delhi was divided into nine revenue or administrative districts in 1990. Similarly, for the purpose of policing also the single district State was first divided into six districts, and later further divided into nine police districts, which are coterminous with the administrative districts. Delhi being both the capital of the Union Government as well as the seat of the NCT of Delhi, has distinct features in matters of political control of some of the agencies of criminal justice administration. Thus, while prosecution, courts, prisons and correctional services are under the political control of the Delhi Government, the police and the Central Police Organization are under the direct control of the Ministry of Home Affairs, Government of India.

2.10.4 Demographic Profile

The Provisional Population of NCT of Delhi is 13.78 million, consisting of 7.57 million males and 6.21 million females. The population of Delhi accounts for 1.34 percent of the total population of the country and ranks 18th amongst all the States and Union Territories. Out of the nine districts, the North-west District with 2.85 million population constitutes 20.66 percent of the population of Delhi and is thus the most populated district. New Delhi District with 1.72 million population shares only 1.25 percent of Delhi's area and is thus ranked last. The sex ratio of Delhi as a whole has been recorded at 821 in the 2001 census, which is lower when compared to the all India sex ratio of 933. The highest sex ratio is recorded in North-east district i.e. 851 whereas it is least at 783 in the south –west district. The density of population of Delhi in 2001 is 9,294 as against 6,352 in 1991. The highest density i.e. 29,295 has been recorded in North-east district. Literacy rate of Delhi is 81.70 percent. Males are at 87.30 percent of literacy and females are at 74.7 percent. (Census, 2001)

2.10.5 Police in National Capital Territory of Delhi

(A) History of Delhi Police

The present system of administration in Delhi can be traced back to 1803. The Delhi Police which had been in existence since Mughal period was reconstituted under the Police Act, 1861 by the British. It then came under the British protection and eventually became a part of the British Punjab. The first major re-organization of this force took place in 1946. On 16th February 1948, the Delhi Police was placed under the charge of an IGP exclusively responsible for maintenance of law and order in the city. In 1978, the Delhi Police Act was promulgated, by which Delhi came under the Commissioner of Police system. Almost all powers of the District Magistrates as per the Criminal Procedure Court (Cr. P.C.) were vested in the Police Commissioner. Since than, the Commissioner of Police, Delhi has been heading the Delhi Police.

The Delhi Police is the only organization of its kind which is not controlled by the Government of National Capital Territory (NCT) of Delhi.

Instead it is controlled and regulated by the Ministry of Home Affairs, Government of India. In this way this organization was designed to enjoy more autonomy than its counterparts in other states.

(B) Police, Area and Population Ratio

Area : Delhi have 3140.46 civil and 3843.76 policemen of all categories (civil and armed) per 100 square km, as against all India averages of 36.20 civil and 47.16 policemen of all categories. (Menon, 2002)

Population : Delhi have 33.79 civil and 41.36 policemen of all categories per 10,000 population. All India averages on that date are 11.16 civil and 14.54 policemen of all categories (ibid).

(C) Administrative Division

Delhi has been under commissionerate system of policing. The Police commissionerate of Delhi is divided into 3 ranges –

1. Southern Range
2. Northern Range
3. New Delhi Range

Each Range is headed by an officer of the rank of the Joint Commissioner of Police (Jt. CP). These ranges are further divided in 9 Police Districts as shown in Figure 1 –

1. New Delhi
2. South Delhi
3. South – West Delhi
4. East Delhi
5. North Delhi
6. North-east Delhi
7. North-west Delhi
8. West Delhi
9. Central Delhi

Each of these Police Districts are headed by an officer of the rank of Deputy Commissioner of Police (DCP) and these districts are further divided into 36 Police Sub –Divisions headed by an officer of the rank of Assistant Commissioner of Police (ACP) with a total of about 123 regular police stations headed by a Station House Officer (SHO), who is drawn from amongst Inspectors of Police (ibid).

(D) Police Station System

The task of policing in Delhi has been achieved by blending the traditional Police Station System with the modern idea of Police Control Room (PCR) System. Thus, the system of policing has tried to secure the benefits of both the systems with a view to making the policing most effective and democratic.

Every Police Station is headed by a SHO of the rank of Inspector of Police. One Additional SHO (of Inspector Rank) and several Sub – Inspectors (S Is), Assistant Sub – Inspectors (ASIs), Head Constables (HCs) and Constables to assist him. A staff strength of various police stations varies from 70 to 200 personnel per police station. The geographical and functional division of a police station in various sub – units can be represented as :

(i) **Police Station (headed by SHO) :** Every police station is manned round the clock by a duty officer, of the rank of Head Constable working in eight hourly shifts. Duty officers are the true representatives of the Station House Officer as he receives information or direction regarding any event first.

(ii) **Division (Police Post) :** Each Division is headed by a Sub – Inspector with a manpower of 2 Head Constables, and 3 or 4 Constables. Police stations are divided in various divisions under the control of Sub – inspector of police to monitor the functioning of every beat and picket (check –post)of his area. It is the functional unit of the police station from where police –surveillance is maintained and BCs (Bad Characters) are monitored. Generally the role of Division Officers becomes significant in the maintenance of law and order and investigation of crime.

(iii) **Beat :** A Beat is manned by one Head Constable and assisted by 1 or 2 Constables.

As a smallest functional unit of Delhi Police every Beat officer represents the SHO of his area, a person who is supposed to have knowledge of each and everything pertaining to his beat (Menon, 2002).

Police Stations have three types of static manpower to respond to every situation arising within the jurisdiction of the police station (PS).

(a) **Duty Officer (8 hourly shift)** – to receive and process the communication.

(b) **Emergency Officers (12 hourly shift)** – Every police station has a strength of 4 to 6 police officials (drawn from the rank of SI to HCs)

Figure 1 : Organizational Chart of Delhi Police

Organization Chart of Delhi Police

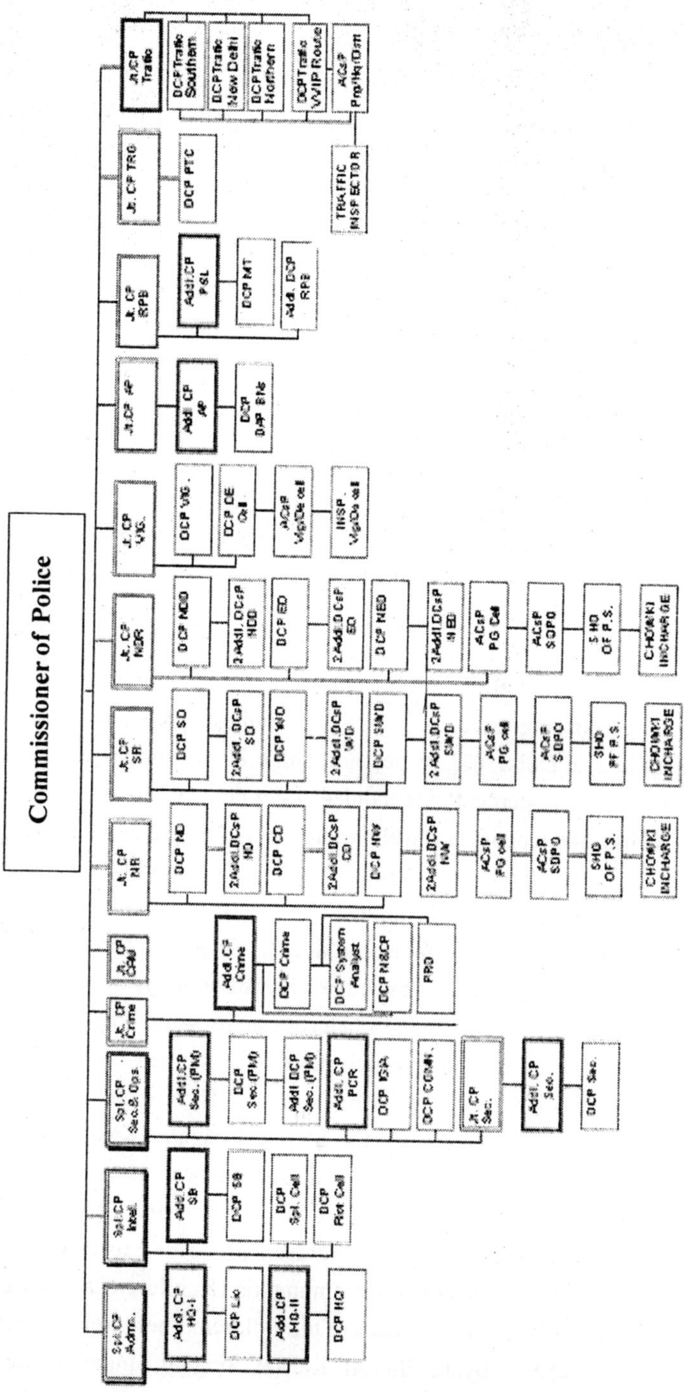

who on receipt of any complaint /information rush to the sight of action and take necessary steps with the aid of PS Reserve.

(c) **PS Reserve (12 hourly shift)** – Every police station has a contingent of Constables and HCs who aid the Emergency Officer in controlling the situations.

Every police station has various separate functional wings such as :

(a) Investigation wing

(b) Law and order wing

(c) Intelligence wing

(d) Administrative staff

(e) *Pairuvi* officer for courts (officer responsible for putting across the police viewpoint before the courts).

(f) *Malkhana* (Armory or police safe –deposit)

But these functional divisions hardly exists as practically same manpower has to work as Beat / Division Officer, Emergency Officer /PS Reserve

2.11 People of Delhi

According to Census (2001), the highest percent of urban population in India is in Delhi (93.18 percent) and 6.82 percent are rural population. Delhi has 16.92 percent of scheduled castes population. As a national capital, Delhi has drawn people from all the parts of India. The communities identified for study under the People of India Project (POI) stood 147 and 28 scheduled tribes (Singh, 1996). The communities identified under the POI project are Hindus, Muslims, Sikhs, Jains, Buddhists, Christians, Zoroastrians, Sindhis. People from various states have been identified in Delhi.

For the present study, a heterogeneous sample has been taken. All the various ethnic groups which have been studied in the present study have been pooled for the purpose of analysis. The sample from communities like Agarwal, Punjabis, Brahmin, Sindhi, Bengalis, Kashmiri Pandits and heterogeneous sample of South Indians have been accrued for the study.

Agarwals claim themselves to be the followers of Maharaja Agarsen, the King of Agroha. Maharaja Agrasen proceeded to conduct 18 Maha Yagnas. He divided his kingdom among his 18 children and established the 18 gotras after the guru's of each of his children. These were: Garg, Mangal, Goyal, Kucchal, Goyan, Bansal, Kansal, Singhal, Jindal, Thingal, Airan, Dharan, Madhukul, Bindal, Mittal, Tayal, Bhandal, and Naagal. Today, these people are known as Agarwals, Guptas or Banias. They still have the same 18 gotras that were given to them by their gurus and they carry on the fame of Maharaja Agrasen. As per Maharaja Agrasen's guidance, the Aggarwals are in the forefront of social service. Agroha temple Complex and Agroha Medical College are being build near Agroha (Hissar), with generous donations from whole of the Agarwal community. Agarwals are the top business and trading community today (ibid).

The Punjabis of Delhi are mainly immigrants from the Punjab. The majority of Delhi Punjabis had migrated from west Punjab and its neighbouring states that fell in Paksitan at the time of the partition in 1947. Punjabis also known as Khatris are divided into several subcastes. Within Khatris, too, there was a distinct hierarchy. On the top of the pyramid sat *dhai-gharais* (two and a half houses), consisting of three subcastes - Kapoor, Malhotra and Khanna. The reference to two and a half is because of the Khatri superstition of the number three. Below them were *bara-gharais* (twelve houses) including such castes as Gujral, Marwaha, Tandon, Chopra and Wahi. Further lower in the order were *bawinja-gharais* (fifty-two houses). Distinct from these *"ghars"* were the *"Khukhrain biradri"* consisting of eight subcastes - Kohli, Sethi, Anand, Bhasin, Sahni, Suri, Sabharwal and Chadha. Khukhrains are very proud of their biradari, some claim that Porus was a Khukhrain and that Sahni is a mutation of the Hindi word, Sainani, which means a soldier (ibid).

The Sindhi in Delhi migrated in large numbers after the partition of the country to their present habitat in the national capital. The identity of Sindhi is defined, inter alia, by their language (Sindhi), their history, their cuisine, form of religion, structure of their name (suffix *ani*). They are mainly an urban community, engaged in trade and business and Government service. Sindhi is a scheduled language, written in Perso-Arabic script. The Sindhis are differentiated at many levels, the territorial, i.e. the place of their origin (Mirpuri, Hyderabadi, Saiti, Sakhru, Ghotki, Shikarpuri and Chappru)- people hailing from different territories enjoy different degrees of prestige in the Sindhi community; occupational(priesthood Brahmans, Amils in Government service and Bhaibandhs in business); the religious (Hindu and Sikh). The Hindu Sindhi are further divided along the *varna* order, the Brahmans (Pandit, Maharaj), Kshatriya and the Vaishyas artisans. There are a number of clans/ gotras. Some of the surnames are Advani, Jethmalani, Dubyani, Harisinghani, Varjani, Israni, Lalchandani. (ibid)

A fair number of Bengalis, comprising mostly of immigrants, have settled in Delhi and its surrounding areas. The community is a composite one consisting of innumerable castes, subgroups, gotras ,sects, religious groups etc. Bengalis incorporate Hindus, Christians, Brahmans, Muslims and Buddhists among its members.

Kashmiri Pandits are considered a territorial segment of the Saraswat Brahman. Delhi is the largest concentration of the Kashmiri Pandits after Jammu. The Kashmiri Pandits in Delhi are divided into two groups, the Purana Kashmiri Pandits and the Taza Kashmiri Pandits. Those who migrated before independence are now called the Purana Kashmiri Pandits while others who migrated to Delhi after 1950 in search of jobs, education or trade are called the Taza Kashmiri Pandits (ibid).

South Indian group of population has many other ethnic groups- Malayali, Tamil, Kannad. The Malayalees also known as Keralite or Keralians are Malayalam speaking group of people. The Keralites are divided into religious groups like Hindu and the Christians. Hindu Keralites follow hierarchy. There are Brahmans like Nambudiri, Kshatriyas like Tampi, Vaishyas like Moosad, and the warrior but presently agricultural castes like the Nair, Menon and Pillai. Christian Keralites have no hierarchy. The group of Tamil speaking people is divided into two major groups – the Brahmans and Non-Brahmans. Each of these groups is further subdivided into Shaivite (Iyer), and Vaishnavite (Iyenger) and the latter is divided into castes like the Mudaliar, Chettiar etc. (ibid)

2.11.1 Work Done in Delhi

Delhi has been changing hands from one emperor to another, thus creating a history of its own. Earlier writings on Delhi has been predominantly done by scholars from Urdu stream (Hasan, 1978; Anjum, 1986; Dehlvi, 1986; Saboohi ,1989 and Dehlvi, 1991). The earliest reference of 'Dilli' can be traced to Crooke (1896), Elliot (1896), Gazetteer of Delhi District (1912), Dayal (1978), Goel (1991).

Delhi has been right from its beginning the melting pot of various populations of numerous castes. Lot of literature is available related to the various castes present in Delhi. The scholars have studied the caste population like Anglo-Indians, Kayasthas, Jat, Gujars, Kashmiri Pandits, Parsees, Tamils, Khatris, Tibetans. (Bingley,1904; Hutton, 1946; Gaikward,1963; Sastri,1963; Kulke,1974; Drummond,1980; Kolenda,1984; Saklani, 1984; Pillai, 1984; Bhatnagar, 1986; Puri, 1988; Jain ,1994 and Singh, 1996).

Many others scholars have written about Delhi as an urban city, as an political centre, as an urbanized place, about its neighborhood, as the capital city. (Bopemagage, 1957; Rao,1965;Chandra, 1969; Mitra, 1970; Sharma, 1992 and Frykenberg, 1993).

Anthropologists have worked among the population of Delhi from the perspective of their smelling ability, blood groups, enzyme studies etc. (Anand, 1957; Bali & Murti, 1965; Mukherjee et al, 1975; Channa, 1975; Channa, 1979; and Banerjee, 1985).

3

Methodology and Inter-cultural Communication

Research is a systematic and careful study and investigation in some field of knowledge, undertaken to establish facts or theories. It is scientific and systematic search for pertinent information on a specific subject. It inculcates scientific and inductive thinking (Kumar, 1997; Kothari, 2004). Social research is somewhat different from the general research. According to Young, (1988), social research is a systematic method of exploring, analyzing and conceptualizing social life in order to 'extend, correct or verify knowledge, whether that knowledge aid in the construction of a theory or in the practice of an art.'

The focus of this chapter is on the various research methods that were chosen for collecting data during the progress of the research. It also delineates the rational behind the selection of those methods or techniques. It further deals with the rationale of the research study which has been undertaken in three different geographical settings in the State of Himachal Pradesh, State of Haryana and National Capital Region of Delhi. The chapter also highlights the reasons for taking up these three areas of study, defining research problem, sample size. It further discusses various aspects of data collection, like methods employed in data collection, reasons for selecting particular method, and their significance in the present study. Focus is also done on the varied types of field work experiences in all the three areas of study.

3.1 The Locale for the Study or Universe of Study

1A. Tribal Area

As the students of anthropology, field work has always fascinated the researchers. Working and learning the tribal ways of life had always been a desire. The best way to feel and experience this is by conducting field work among these people.

We decided that the present work would be a comparative and a cross-cultural account, so it was planned to take up two more areas along with a tribal area – Rural and Urban Areas.

1B. Rural Area

Rural areas of Haryana have been selected for the purpose of conducting field work in a rural set up. Since, the state of Haryana lies in the closest vicinity of the National Capital Territory of Delhi, so it was decided to work in this State. There are 19 districts in Haryana. For the present study, work has been done in District Rohtak as among all the nineteen districts, it is the closest district from Delhi, thus receiving the maximum influence of the neighborhood of the metropolitan city. The District Rohtak has five blocks – Sampla, Rohtak, Kalanaur, Maham and Lakhan Majara . Out of these five, only Rohtak Block and Sampla Block are on the main railway track .According to the Census of India, 2001 Rohtak Block has more urban population, so it was not taken as the field area . Sampla Block, as compared, has more of rural population .Thus Sampla Block of Rohtak District of the State Haryana was selected as the field area for collecting the data from the rural population . The villages which were covered for the present study are – Sampla, Naya Bans, Khedi and Gadi Gaon.

1C. Urban Area

Urban area of Delhi have been selected for the purpose of conducting field work. Delhi being the National Capital of India is considered to be the place of many opportunities. So general awareness of the population here is expected to be more than other population. The residential colonies which were covered for the present study are- Najafgarh, Jain Nagar, Rohini, Vasundhara Enclave, Mayur Vihar, Vipin Garden, Dilsahd Garden, Pamposh Enclave, Inderpuri and Shakti Nagar.

3.2 Research Design

Research design involves combining the essential elements of investigations into an affective problem solving sequences. It is usually an idealized blue print or road map that help the researcher to conceptualize the work. The research design is made in such a way so that the methods adopted for collecting the relevant data and techniques are planned in advance. For the present work a well planned strategic research design was prepared with focus from hypothesis formulation to data analysis. So that the research could be conducted within a particular time frame with enhance efficiency.

3A. Schedule

After the review of literature, keeping the objective of the study in mind, an elaborate interview schedule was designed to elicit the information from the respondents. The schedule, thus made, has two important parts – Household Schedule and the Topic Related Schedule.

(i)Household Schedule: It was prepared to elucidate the information from each household regarding-

- Family Size
- Head of Household
- Economy
- Habitation Pattern
- Demography
- Occupation

(ii) Topic Related Schedule: This part of schedule fulfills all the objectives defined for the study including the knowledge, attitude and practice of Human Rights. Questions pertaining to various different human rights have been asked. Semi-Structured Schedules had been developed with closed, open and multiple response questions for the collection of data. To confirm the responses in the schedule, the same question was asked in different ways two or three times during the interview (triangulation). The responses which were found to be consistent were considered reliable. Various rights, as framed by the constitution were asked from the respondents in all the three areas:

(i) Right to Life
(ii) Freedom from Torture
(iii) Freedom from Slavery
(iv) Freedom from Arbitrary Arrest and Detention
(v) Freedom of Movement
(vi) Equality before Courts
(vii) Equal Protection of Law
(viii) Freedom of Thought
(ix) Freedom of Religion
(x) Freedom of Expression
(xi) Freedom to Seek, Receive and Impart Information

(xii) Right to Peaceful Assembly
(xiii) Right to Marry
(xiv) Right of Minorities to Enjoy their own Culture, Religion and Language
(xv) Right to Work
(xvi) Right to Social Security
(xvii) Right to an Adequate Standard of Living
(xviii) Right of Everyone to Education
(xix) Right to take part in Cultural Life

Interview schedule was the basic and the most important instrument used during the data collection. The major advantage of using an interview schedule during this study was its adaptability. It helped in meeting and talking to respondents, reading their facial expressions, probing responses, investigating motives and feelings, following up ideas, which would not have been possible in a questionnaire.

Questionnaires could have concealed a lot of information, as the responses would have to be taken at face value. The responses during the interviews were developed and clarified at the site itself. The shape of the informal interview conducted was determined by the individual respondents themselves and these helped in yielding a rich and valuable data. Though interviews were not completely rigid, they were also not unstructured. A guided frame work has been established, which was always available to ensure that all the areas crucial to study were covered. Though the conversations about many topics were interesting and could have produced useful insights into many problems, it had to be remembered that this was an interview and not just an interesting conversation. Thus, the respondent was allowed a considerable degree of latitude within the established frame work. During all the interviews the researcher's main aim was to be completely objective, and thus avoid any kind of bias.

3B. Methodology

Various tools of data collection have been used during the pilot work and main field work. Tools like – Interview Schedule, Observation, Case Study Method, In-Depth Interview, Focus Group Discussion have been employed. Collection of secondary data has also been done from various offices in each area.

3C. Sample

Data from the three geographically different field settings were collected as mentioned earlier. A total sample of 900 households – 300 each from Tribal, Rural and Urban settings were collected.

In **Tribal Population,** the total sample of 300 households has been divided on the basis of education. A sample of 150 is covered from those who are educationally advanced and rest from those who are less educated or illiterate. The reason for dividing the sample on the basis of education is that Lahoul is a remote hilly area. Here, because of difficult topography equal educational opportunities is not availed by everybody, thus affecting their awareness. Villages have been covered in such a way so that they cover the entire block of Lahoul. This includes those villages which are near and far from the police station. Among the tribal population, two ethnic groups namely, Bodhs (following Buddhism) and Swanglas (following Hinduism), declared as Scheduled Tribe under the Article 342 of the constitution have been taken as 'tribal population'

In **Rural Population,** out of 300 households data from 150 houses near the police station and 150 away from police station have been collected. This would give us a relative picture about the impact on the awareness of the population of having police station in the vicinity of the households. Here also uniformity had been maintained in terms of education. Among the rural population, two ethnic groups comprising of Jat and Brahmin have been taken into consideration, on the basis of the criteria laid down for the rural characterization. Hence, these two groups have been referred to as 'rural population'.

In **Urban Population,** sample at a specific socio-economic level and educationally empowered had been contemplated to maintain the homogeneity in data. However, ethnically data is heterogeneous as mono-cultural samples has been difficult to gather. Here also sample had been collected, keeping in mind the relative position of police station. In case of urban population which constitutes six ethnic groups on the broader framework, who are living in the metropolitan and modernized city of Delhi as characterized in the Census, 2001 and Kapoor and Kapoor (2001) have been taken as the 'urban population'.

It is to be mentioned here that these ethnic groups or population residing in the tribal, rural and urban areas were taken as tribal, rural and urban populations.

3D. Field Work

Field works in the tribal, rural and urban areas have been completed from the year 2003 till year 2005. Following is the time chart of conducting all the field work:

(a) Tribal Area

(i) Pilot Survey: June 2003 – July 2003

(ii) Main Field Work :(1) September 2003–November 2003 (Till Valley closes) (2) April 2004 (as soon as Valley opens) – June 2004

(b) Urban Area

November 2004 – February 2005

(c) Rural Area

May 2005 – July 2005

3E Pattern of Field Work

The following some field work pattern were followed in three different geological areas for the present study :-

1. Pilot Survey
2. Correction of Schedule
3. Main Field work.
4. Rapport establishment
5. Interview of Respondents.
6. Focus Group Discussion (FGD)
7. Observation
8. Case Studies.

3.5 Barriers / Limitations of the Research

In all the three field areas, the barriers were of different types. Research in the Himalayan Region requires certain intensive efforts. Conducting a research among unfamiliar people and hostile environmental conditions needed prior groundwork. In order to avoid the danger of bias creeping in, the continuous, intentional efforts had to be made, to be with the people and learn as much as possible about them. Various ethnic groups and communities are available in District Rohtak and Delhi. In the present study two ethnic groups of the rural area-Jat and Brahmin have been grouped together and referred as 'rural population' and six ethnic groups of the urban population- Agarwals, Punjabis, Brahmins, Sindhis, Kashmiri Pandits, Bengalis and heterogeneous sample of South Indians have been clubbed together to name as 'urban population' for the purpose of the analysis. Because of time limitation, the sample from all the ethnic groups could not be collected. Moreover the households are widely spread out in Delhi area.

3.5.1 Vastness of the Topic

Human rights is a very oceanic topic. There are numerous articles elaborated in various covenants and charters. Study of all these articles is not possible in a stipulated time frame of research work. Moreover for the present work, three populations have been considered, so it was all the more complicated to do such an over elaborate study, which would have infact lost its significance at one point of time.

3.5.2 Language

One of the most critical means of gaining acceptance into a culture is mastering the language of that culture. Although, the second language of the Lahouli is Hindi. To conduct a successful research, rapport formation with the interviewees' language is very essential. An unknown Lahouli language was the first important obstacle because many a times respondents in groups use to talk in their own language.

3.5.3 *Review of Literature*

Till date, no such anthropological research on human rights dimension in the cross-cultural perspective is conducted, therefore, not much data is available. It was beneficial to review the other general information available on the Lahouli tribe, works done in the rural and urban population. An insight into general published documents/ books/ articles was of great help to the researchers, in finalizing the objectives and in conduction of this research.

3.5.4 Bias

The danger of bias creeping in during the interviews is always there, mainly because the persons interviewing are human beings and not robots. The interviews would invariably result in the researchers getting emotionally involved during the discussions. Yet, the researchers tried to be mainly objective and consistent in all the interviews. The awareness to avoid bias during the interviews was a constant self-control on the researcher.

3.5.5 Time Span

The field area of Lahoul and Spiti is not accessible throughout the year. The culture in the open season is absolutely different from the culture in winters, when the valley is closed. Researchers could not stay in the valley for seeing winter there.

3.5.6 Disinterest of Respondents

Disinterest of respondents to participate was a major barrier, especially among the rural and urban population. Even after kind persuation some of the respondants refused bluntly, thus wasting the researchers time and spoiling the mood as well.

4

Ethnographic Live

The experience of writing about the ethnographic life of the people is like "living the field work again". The details of their minute culture and day to life has been incorporated. This chapter focuses on the ethnographic life of Lahoulis of Lahoul Block of District Lahoul and Spiti, Himachal Pradesh as tribal area, rural population which comprised of Jat and Brahmin of Sampla Block, District Rohtak, Haryana as rural area, and population of the metropolitan capital of India, Delhi representing heterogeneous ethnic groups or communities as urban areas separately.

4.1 Ethnographic Live of Lahoulis

The word 'Lahouli' is a blanket term. It is a broad generic term, including anybody who is a permanent denizen of this area. The people such as the Brahmin, Ranas, Thakurs (Rajputs, Kanets or Bhots and the schedule castes like Lohars (iron smiths); Dagis or Shipps (carpenters) are all broadly classified as Lahoulis. Anybody living in this geographical territory will enjoy a tribal status (Gupta and Kapoor, 2004).

Tribals living in the Patan valley tract along the Chandra- Bhaga, are exclusively called as Swanglas. While doing the literature review it was found that these people have been categorized separately in the constitutional list, other than Lahoulis. Thus, 'constitutionally' there are two tribal groups in the Lahoul valley - Lahoulis and Swanglas. The criteria of categorizing separately is the religion. Lahoulis are Buddhists whereas Swanglas are Hindus.

It was found, during the field work that although two tribal groups are demarcated in that area, but people call themselves as 'Lahouli'. Even the Swanglas say that they are Lahoulis. There is no difference in the benefits extended to both the groups They inter marry also. Both have same dress pattern and festivals. Even the birth, marriage and death rituals are majorly similar, with few distinctions. They are Swanglas, by virtue of religion, otherwise they are Lahoulis, as they live in Lahoul. This is a major indication of the ethnicity among Lahouli tribe. Keeping all these features in mind, it was found that in Lahoul there are several sporadic ethnic groups forming one larger group which is known as Lahoulis. Thus, making it a mixed race. In their features, a combination of Mongolian and Aryan traits is observed. Their slightly high cheek bones and almond like eyes are the indications of a Mongolian origin where as their straight noses are an index of Aryan blood (Randhawa, 1974).

Other than facial features, people of Lahoul valley are also categorized according to the area they live in. As detailed earlier, Lahoul block is majorly divided into three valleys - Chandra valley, Bhaga valley and Chandra - Bhaga valley. These are further divided into small valleys. The various ethnic groups living in these areas, hail from different historical backgrounds, speaking a distinct dialect, following varied religion, changed socio-economic profiles, various levels of awareness and knowledge, having different somatometric and somatoscopic characteristics etc. In order to highlight the ethnic variability the following group of people have been taken into consideration :-

1. The People of Chamba - Lahoul
2. The People of STod valley
3. The People of Ranglo
4. The People of Gahar valley
5. The People of Gondhla valley
6. The People of Patan valley

The People of Chamba - Lahoul that is around Triloknath are said to be either the original inhabitants or the earliest settlers in this valley. The people here are mostly Hindus and speak *Reunpa* dialect. Locally they call themselves as 'we the people of Chamba- lahoul' to differentiate from other geographical areas.

The People of STod valley, has majorly come from Tibet. Besides there features and general looks, the language is more than 90 % Tibetan perhaps closer to the one spoken in the southern part of Tibet. This area has usually been, directly or indirectly dominated by Ladakh. Therefore the mass religion of the people is Buddhism, who have a *sTod* dialect. Being in the closest vicinity of Ladakh, sTod valley has the largest number of migrants, as compared to any other village in Lahoul valley. William Moorcroft has written, later friendly relations were established with Ladakh, which might have given more freedom for migration (Wilson,1837). Even now the Thakurs of this valley have marriage relationship with the Raja of Ladakh. People of sTod valley are less aware of their environment, various development programmes run by the government etc as compared to those living in and around the district head quarters; thus creating a gorge like concept of 'we' and 'they'. This internal differentiation among the people of Lahoul is not a one day process. It has happened because of gradual accumulation of differences among them. It is quite evident from the talks of people of other valleys, that they think people of sTod valley are under-developed, less aware as they live in interior, thus feeling superior to them. It was observed during the field work, as according to the general unwritten rule -

"lesser the technology and awareness, more is the innocence, rawness, and hospitality".

People of Ranglo is important for their origin pattern. A majority of people of this area also are of Tibetan origin. A different area, from where many tradesmen came to conduct business between India and Tibet. Later they intermixed with people already settled there. Thus resulting in a mixture of culture and dialect. They speak *Ranglo- Khoksar* dialect.

People of Gahar Valley, have mostly come from Baltistan. The original people of Baltistan were Buddhists. Most of those who left that area, either came to Lahoul and settled in Gahar valley or had gone to the Sugnam valley in Spiti. From the point of view of language, the dialect of Gahar valley i.e. Bunnan is somewhat similar to that of Sugnam valley. There are few scheduled castes houses also in this valley.

The People of Gondhla Valley, seems to be a mixture of the people from Malana (a tiny ravine in the Kullu valley at the back of Nagar), Busher, Zanskar and perhaps some from Ladakh as well (c.f. Sahni,1994). Since this valley in Lahoul block lies first while entering the district from Rohtang Pass, i.e. on the Manali - Leh National Highway, the people here are more aware and professional in terms of extending hospitality as compared to those of sTod, Mayard or Tindi.Also known as Tinan valley, it is the only valley in Lahoul block, which has complete villages occupied by scheduled castes; villages which have both the tribal and the scheduled caste population co-existing in large number, unlike other villages where just few scheduled caste families live.

Figure 2 : Hierarchical Chart Showing Various Castes Groups In Lahoul

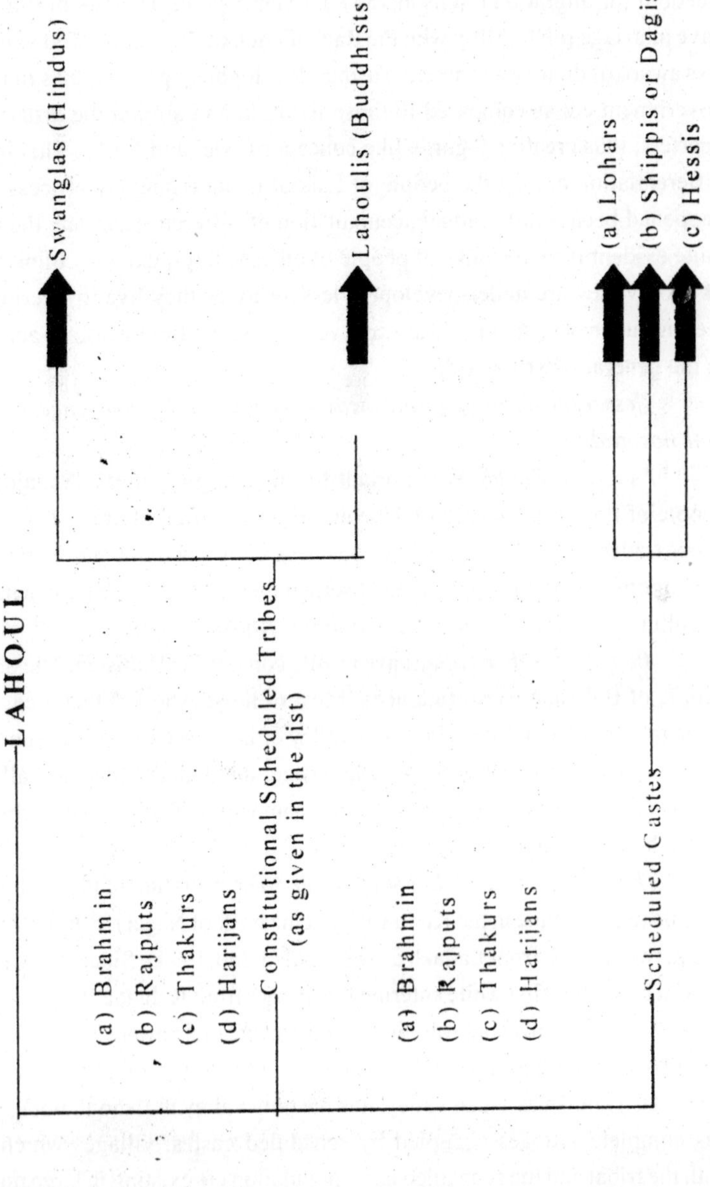

The People of Patan Valley, of Lahoul has the maximum mixture of people. The major reason is that this area has been most vulnerable, as it has been occupied by various groups of people of different kingdoms at different times, each leaving its own mark and its own group of settlers. Another reason for its being tossed around was the climate and the altitude. Availability of agricultural land here is more as compared to any other far valley of Lahoul. 'Patan' in Urdu means a 'flat land'. This valley is slightly flatter than the rest of the valleys. People here are able to grow two crops per year, unlike those of Mayard or sTod who are able to yield just one crop every year.

'Swangla' like 'Lahouli' is a generic term which includes Brahmans, Rajput groups and Harijans which has also been reported by Singh (1996). The caste system in the Patan valley certainly sheds some light on different groups of people with different background. There is no inter-dinning of Brahmin and Harijans or Kshtriyas. The language spoken by these people is in *Manchat or Patani dialect.*

In Lahoul inter community relations are based on caste hierarchy and several restrictions in marriages and eating together are observed. Scheduled castes such as Shippis, Lohars, Hessis etc. have no inter-marital or inter-dinning relations with Swanglas and Bodhs. In the caste hierarchy Brahmin are at the top (Figure 2). However, Thakurs in the area are in the higher economic strata thus are considered above Brahmin. Swangla Thakurs are hierarchically considered above the Buddhist Thakurs. Earlier Swanglas used to observe a social distinctions by refraining from taking cooked food from Buddhists and others but now this is dwindling. But in case of scheduled castes, this distance is still maintained and Swanglas particularly, have no social contacts with them.

The scheduled castes are never discriminated against high caste people in the matter of entering into the temples and monasteries. There is no restriction either on drawing water from the same sources from which high castes take it. Upper caste people such as Swanglas, Thakurs and Bodhs marry their daughters in their own group generally, when the patriclan should differ in each case. Now, love marriage between Swanglas and Bodhs are taking place frequently. The offspring's of the inter-group marriages are called *Garu.* In matters of inter-dinning the upper caste people do not observe any rigid restrictions.

There are many other factors which indicate towards the social variability among Lahoulis. Socio-economic profile being one of these. There is vast difference in the economic and the social profile of Lahoulis. On one hand selected few are Thakurs and Ranas, who claim to be a part of the royal genealogy and on the other there are those Lahoulis who are categorized below poverty line. Although it is said that no body in Lahoul is poor and will die of hunger. Everybody at least have subsistence economy. Even then government has categorized few people as poor, keeping certain basic criteria in mind.

Education and occupation are two major factors which may change the society type in due course of time. Families in which most of there members are educated are gradually losing their working hands. Those who are educated, are not interested in coming back in the village scenario and be a part of agricultural set-up. They infact look upon to settle outside the valley and do a job. On the other hand, a completely illiterate family, will continue doing agriculture for their sustenance.This way gradually, over the period of time, vast differences are perceptible, thus creating two different types of groups, which are basically one.

4.1.1 Language and Dialect

It might sound fantastic that in the tiny valley of Lahoul with a population of 22,674, ten distinct dialects are spoken. The dialect has a direct bearing on the history or the origin of the people, thus implying at the social variability and varied ethnicity of Lahoul. Harrcourt (1972) also named four dialects, namely, *Boonan, Teenan, Manchat, and Tibetan.*

It is said that dialect changes in Lahoul, after every few kilometers or after every few villages. The dialect of two extremes are so unique in each other and different, that there is no commonality. Even people of one valley are unable to comprehend the dialect of another valley. Very few people can understand or speak more than two of dialects. Only a few rare individuals can speak or understand all the ten.

Following are the various dialects spoken in Lahoul:-

Gahar or Bhaga valley has following two dialects:-

1. *STod dialect* :- This is of Tibetan origin.
2. *Bunnan dialect* :- This is of Tibeto - Burmese origin.

Chandra valley has two dialects :-

3. *Ranglo - Khoksar dialect*:- This is of Tibetan origin.
4. *Tinnan dialect* :- This is of Tibeto - Burmese origin

Chandra - Bhaga valley or Patan valley has following two dialects:-

5. *Manchat or Patani dialect*:- This is of Tibeto - Burmese origin.
6. *Reunpa or Triloknath dialect or Chamba - Lahoul dialect*:-This is of Tibeto - Burmese origin.
7. Mayard valley has *Patnam Kad dialect or Myardi dialect.* This is of Tibetan origin.

8. Tindi area, near Pangi district has *Pangwal or Tindiali dialect.*
9. *Chenali dialect* :- This is the dialect spoken by scheduled castes of Lahoul valley. Lahoulis call these scheduled castes as Shippis. They are the occupational class like wood or stone masons, agricultural labourers, community musicians etc. They call themselves as Chenals.
10. *Dhombeyali dialect* :- This is spoken by the scheduled caste community. Lahoulis call them as Dhombha or Dhomb caste. These are either black smiths or musicians of the society.

All the ten dialects are spoken languages only. None of them has a script of its own and so do not enjoy the status of true languages.

4.1.2 Dress and Ornaments

The main dress of Lahoul region is made out of woolen cloths which could be used around the year being suitable for the cold climate of the region. Men generally wear loose trousers made of dark thick cloth and a woolen coat. The head cap is similar to the one used in Kinnaur. *Pula* or straw shoes with locally made socks with charming and colorful designs are commonly used. Now *pula* is replaced by shoes. A marked change is visible in men's dresses with advancement of time and means of communication. They now use imported clothes from plains. Women's dress in Lahoul consists of a tight fitting *pajma* and long robes or coats with sleeves, made of a thick dark wool along with a jacket. This is called *Chholu-basket* and shirt like Punjabi *kurta* is worn as an under-cloth beneath the *chholu.* A sash is worn round the waist over the *chholu.* Woman cover their head with scarf locally called as *Gundu.* Lamas have usually mehrun dress.

Ornaments and jewelry are the most prized possession of women the world over. Here also most of the women wear ornaments. They are made of gold and silver. Men wear gold rings, ear rings called *Murki* and *Kyanti* or neck ring. Females generally wear ear ring called a*long,* necklaces of various types made of turquoise coral and pearl. *Phuli* is nose ornament and is made of gold. *Nyagtheng* is a chained silver ornament, studded with precious and semi-precious stones. Among the young ladies, chains with pendent of gold and pearl beads are also common now. Silver bangles are also used by Lahouli females. Other ornaments like *Poshel, Kirkisti* etc. are worn occasionally only. For instance during the celebrations of *Gotsi* the celebration related to the birth of first male child, mother of the baby is supposed to wear all these ornaments. Also, the girl who performs all rituals on occasions like marriage, *gotsi,* particularly in Garh valley also wears all these ornaments. *Kirkisti* is an ornament made for forehead. A pair of round ambers is fixed in the middle of the forehead with small gold buttons of stars. It is tied with a thread on both sides of the forehead.

4.1.3 Food Habits

Lahouli people are generally non-vegetarian. Wheat, barley, rice, buckwheat *(Kathu)* and pulses like *Masur, Moong* and beans constitute the staple food of the people of Lahoul. Amongst the vegetables- potato, cabbage, green vegetable etc has become the main vegetable at least in the summer season. People in Lahoul relish meat. And its preparations, like *Thugpa* which is their favorite in winters when the availability of fresh vegetables is scanty. Millet baked bread called *chilra* is their favourite in winters. A recent trend is their inclination towards eating rice, which is purchased. Salted butter tea is very popular and is often taken at regular intervals. *Chhang,* a mild intoxicant beverage, *arak* (local distilled liquor) is also drunk occasionally. Smoking of tobacco is very common among the men folk. People in Lahoul usually take three meals a day. The morning meal consists of bread made up buckwheat or wheat or barley served with vegetables or *dal* and *Tsampa* (roasted barley flour).

In summer's variety of vegetables are grown by them in their gardens and for winters these vegetables are dried and stored. People generally dry cabbage, carrot, green vegetables, *paneer*, meat, garlic. Midday meal usually consists of rice along with *dal.* Dinner consists of vegetable stew, boiled potato and *Tsampa*. Sweet dishes are not common but milk and curd are sweetened and consumed by the people. Tea is always the favorite of the people of this cold region.

4.1.4 Religion

In Lahoul, there is a mixture of Hinduism and Buddhism, the former is prevalent in the villages of the Chandra–Bhaga valley and the later one in the villages of the Chandra and the Bhaga valleys. Out of the total sample of 300 collected, 42.67% are Swanglas and 57.33% are Buddhist. Both males and females gods i.e. Shiva and Durga are worshipped by the people of the Patan valley primarily. Lord Buddha is worshipped by the Buddhists of Lahoul. Besides, there are many animistic deities in the shape of boulders, caves, trees and bushes. The tribal deities Gyepang and Dabla are most popular. Apart from these, almost every home possesses its own family –deity represented by a stone slab or pillar, and on each slab or pillar boughs of juniper leaves are placed. People tie small colorful flags, with the names of their ancestors written on it, on their roofs. It is believed that, more the fluttering of the flags, more is the prosperity of the house or to keep away the bad/evil eyes.

4.1.5 Village Settlements

Villages are predominantly located on the sun-facing side of river. Availability of land for cultivation, sun rays, regular source of water for irrigation and drinking purposes were perhaps the main criteria for the choice of sites for initial settlement. Selection of spot for construction of house is, however an arduous task. Whole of the territory is prone to devastating avalanche and snow slide which can raze any structure to the ground and carry away leaving not even a trace of it. Therefore locations for construction of house are selected with utmost care, examining the spot through observations for long periods and inquiry from the aged people. Initial choice appears to have been on the ridges where ruins of ancient structures can still be found. Such places may be advantageous from one angle, but they are open to fierce icy winds from all directions. In such a condition living both for men and animals is difficult. Hence, people will attempt to search a suitable place on or near the plains or an umbrageous point on the sides of ridges which should be protected from snow slide. That search has not yet stopped completely. The experiment that has been going on ever since the first settlement of the people in this region, is continuing till today. People plant trees near the villages as fortification, particularly on the sides exposed to dangers of any such calamity.

4.1.6 Housing Pattern

Houses in Lahoul are usually situated in very small clusters. The houses here are built in such a way so that living in them is not difficult even in severe winters when temperature reaches much below minus.

The roofs which are generally flat are composed of rafters laid closely. Across these, junipers or pine is laid, of any length, obtainable and split up in thickness of 3 or 4 inches, the pieces touch each other and put on loose. Birch is also used. These are covered with a thick layers of earth on top. The roof is edged with flat stones which keep out the weather very well. All roofs are cleared of snow immediately after every fall in the winter. In the villages of Lahoul, the houses are predominantly kuccha in which the material used in the construction of buildings are stone, wood and mud. Walls are plastered with a mixture of clay and straw both from inside and outside, and are painted with yellowish day or white earth. Floors of the room are coated by a mixture of clay and cattle dung. Thick walls of stone and floors give good protections against the bitter cold. But with the time changing, people have started constructing cemented houses with asbestos or tin roof.

Houses are generally two or three storey high. Ground floor is used as a vivarium as it is used for keeping cattle, the middle are for living purposes, since it is warmer than both the ground and the top floors, and the uppermost floor for other purposes. Grass is stored on the roof tops in big stocks. The second floor of the house consists ordinarily of an interior or winter room (*gunsa or chagsthab*) which is well protected from the direct blow of wind and an outer or summer room (*yarsa*) which is comparatively large and airy. In the middle of the room there is an oven like fire place made up of thick iron sheet, called *Tandoor.* Smoke is discharged through an iron pipe projecting out from a hole in the roof. But in some remote villages of Lahoul like Tindi, a large open hearth is used instead of *tandoor.* The wood burning in it serves the purpose both of cooking food as well as heating the room. The fuel, used for cooking in Lahoul is thus wood and coal, nevertheless the use of LPG cylinders as the main fuel for cooking food is not very prevalent here. It is however used as a subsidiary fuel in the kitchen, except for few pockets, where there is no road.

Kitchens are usually maintained in one corner of a room.Store rooms (*gyags khang)* and beer room *(chhang khang)* are other important rooms. Worship room in the top floor also serves as prayer hall and guest room at important occasions. In the mud houses, generally dry pits toilets are seen. A touch of modernity is, however, felt when flush toilets are also seen in the houses. The dry pits are made available on the first or second floors and the wastes are collected in the ground floor, which is used as manures in the fields.

Doors of the rooms are generally kept small in order to restrict the entry of cold wind. This has a religious sanction too. It is a common belief among the people that a dead body may sometimes rise up and start moving. This phenomenon is called *rolangs.* Anybody touched by *rolangs* acquire a similar character. It can create chaos if somehow it is able to get out of the room. It is believed that it can walk erect and cannot bend down. In order to prevent its exit from the room, people keep doors small.

As such the sizes of the rooms are measured according to the number of pillars like two pillared room (*ka-nyima*), four pillared room (*ka-zhima*) etc. Rooms are decorated with beautiful coloured Tibetan woolen carpets and a small wooden table having eastern dragons painted on it called *soltakh.* The use of cots is restricted to few well to do and modernized people of the region. Thus, necessitated by the climatic conditions, people in Lahoul have commodious houses. People generally maintain the stock of ration which could last at least for a year or so, and articles of household goods support to cater to the need of the gatherings of the whole economy. Also they rear large number of livestock and as the winters are long, adequate stock of fodder for cattle, firewood etc have to be maintained which require considerable covered space. Social system is another factor compelling people for building houses considerably larger than they ordinarily need for their own use, as the social functions like marriage, *gotsi* etc. and other social gatherings are organized at the houses. Each house tries to be self sufficient as it counts in their social status.

4.1.7 Rites de Passage

Rites de passage, also known by the term, 'life-crisis rituals', are rituals which mark the passing of one stage of life and entry into another e.g. Birth, puberty, marriage, initiation to the priesthood, or death. The concept was first brought to attention by the Belgian scholar Arnold Van Gennep. Van Gennep distinguished three kinds of rites of passage: rites of separation, transition rites, and rites of incorporation or aggregation. He noted that rites of separation often take prominence in funeral ceremonies that transition rites may be important in pregnancy, betrothal, or initiation, and that rites of incorporation, one often highly developed in marriage ceremonies. However, it is more usual to think of three elements in a single rule, which includes each form- separation, transition, and incorporation as a separate phase (c.f. Honigmann, 1973).

The variation in culture in the five different valleys of Lahoul leaves one amused. Apart from the fact that dialects spoken in these valleys are different from each other, there are also certain practices which are also unique to each valley. For instance, Patan valley being more developed as compared to the others as it has gone more changes in terms of the practice of old customs. In this valley, one finds a greater influence of Hindu culture from the northern plains. Mayard and Gahar valleys are considered different from Patan but similar to each other, the rituals performed during various occasions are slightly different. The religious ceremony in Lahoul consists in almost all the cases among Bodhs, in the simple reading of prayers or passages from the holy books by a lama while the whole company of men and women sit around with clasped hands. The social celebrations of these events is mainly in the form of feasts in which much *chhang* (local liquor) is served and drunk.

(A) Birth Rituals

(i) Gotsi

This festival celebrated mainly in the Bhaga (STod and Punan) valleys, marks the celebration of the birth of all the male children in the proceeding year.It falls in the month of February and is celebrated mainly in those families in whose houses a baby boy was born in the previous year. In the morning all the villagers gather at the house where a male child is born during the proceeding year and take *chhang*. A dough of *sattu is* made and kept in a big wooden plate. This dough is then lifted by four men and carried to the place where Keylong deity is supposed to reside. A young girl in her best clothes and decorated with all kinds of ornaments accompanies this dough. This girl carries a pot decorated with butter and containing *chhang*. She is followed by two men, one carrying a burning stick of pencil cedar and the other bearing pencil cedar leaves tied in lamb's skin.

The dough of *sattu* (roasted barley flour) is than distributed among the villagers who all pray god to bless the village with a male child in the coming year. All families organize feasts for their relatives and friends. The party is organized in the name of the male child and a lot of *chhang*.

All women blessed with male children in the proceeding year, march in a procession, dressed in the traditional attire, singing and dancing to the sound of drums and flute. Each of them carrying her baby and accompanied by other villagers, march to a place where the village deity is believed to reside. *Gotsi* is a day devoted to the worship of Keylong deity and the local deity of Gahar valley. The Keylong *devta* has no temple devoted to him but is believed to reside in a deodar shrub in lower Keylong, as in a field in Keylong. The *devta* is offered *sattu, ghee, chhang* and juniper tree twigs. *Ghee* is used to make the dummy of sheep's head which is then placed on the pile of *sattu*. Green stems of deodar are used to make incense (*dhoop*)which is also offered to *devta*. Than the village *lohars* plays *nagara* and the priests recites holy verses and perform rituals.

An interesting ritual by the village priest, *labdagpa*, involves the shooting of nine arrows into a stuffed lamb shire dummy ; the number of times the arrow hitting the target symbolizing the number of male children that would be born in the following year. In some villages the arrows are aimed at birch leaves on which the figure of a yak is drawn. The villagers than go from house to house where sons have been born, drinking *chhang* and spend the whole night dancing.

(ii) Raldex

Raldex is a festival similar to the above described Gotsi but is observed on a larger scale where not only the villagers but also all relatives gather to celebrate with the families who are blessed with male children in the preceding year.

(iii) Mundan

When the child attains the age of one or two years, his or her *mundan* (shaving of the head) ceremony takes place as an auspicious day in consultation with lama or priests. The relatives and other friends are invited to this occasion and they are served *chhang* and food.On the appointed day the maternal uncle or in his absence some other persons whose mother and father are alive, cuts the hair of the child with a pair of scissors.The invitees bless the child and present clothes and cash to the parents.All the invites bring with them a pot full of *chhang*.Then the hair of the child are buried in their own field, as it is considered auspicious for the yield of the year.

(B) Marriage Rituals

In Lahoul, there are generally three different types of marriage prevalent

1. The *Tabaghston* or *Mothebiah* or *Moubiah* is the form where parents settle the marriage and perform it with great pomp and show.
2. The *Kowanchi biah* is a marriage which is performed very briefly lasting just a day or two.
3. The *Kummai baghston* or *Kunchi biah* is the marriage by elopement (Bajpai, 1987)

Tabaghston is the arranged form of marriage and are big marriages in which the ceremony of betrothal is conducted. Negotiations for betrothal is conducted by the father and maternal uncle of the boy. They along with two or three elderly persons go to the parents of the girls, taking with them a pot of *chhang* or a bottle of *arak*. The bottle containing *arak* is tied with flowers generally of marigold and a small quantity of butter is also put in the bottle as an auspicious sign. The decisive point in the negotiations for a betrothal is the acceptance or refusal of a pot of *chhang* sent to the father of the girl. The girl's consent is also taken into consideration while accepting the proposal. In the case of acceptance of the proposal, the *arak* is sprinkled with a juniper twig accompanied by the chanting of mantras as ritual performance. After that, liquor is distributed among all family members.

In the valleys of Gahar and Tinan, the dates for solemnizing the marriage is fixed by a lama whereas in the Patan valley the date and time of the marriage is fixed by the respective parents. The marriage function begins when the marriage party starts from the bridegroom's house for the bride's house. Unlike in Tinan and Patan valley, in Gahar and Mayard valleys bridegroom does not accompany the marriage party. On reaching the bride's house, a member from the bridegroom's side gives some money outside the door, to a person from the bride's side as entry fee, which is settled after much bargain between the two sides. The marriage party takes with them *chhang*, butter, dried meat etc. to the girls house. The marriage party is given a warm welcome from the members of the bride side. The attraction of marriage in Lahoul is the custom in which all rituals are performed by *bagme yato* (bride companion), a girl who is dressed in traditional, colorful attire, wearing all jewelry and ornaments. The girl selected for the purpose should have both her parents alive. This tradition is most prevalent in Gahar valley.

Bagme Yato from bride's side welcome the marriage party by sprinkling *chhang* with juniper leaves and then applying butter on the head of all the members. But those who had death in the family in the preceding year politely refuse the *shagun* of offering butter on the head. After this guests are served food along with lot of *chhang*. On the same evening, the bride is taken to the groom's house. She is accompanied by the friends, family members and relatives. After a warm welcome and all rituals performed, feast is organized on behalf of bridegroom's side for the members of bride's side. Delicacies like *Marchu* are offered to the guests along with *chhang* and *arak*. After two three days of festivity, everyone departs to his or her respective home. The bride after few days goes to her parents home along with the groom.This is known as *Feronee* or return visit.

Kowanchi Biah : This form of marriage is not as elaborate as that of *Tabhagstan* type. In this type, marriage party consists of very few people. The whole celebrations concludes in just a day or two.

Kunmai baghston or kunch biah : This is also known as *Shorde Baghston* in sTod valley. This is marriage by elopement, when boys and girls are at liberty to choose their life partners. The selection is made by frequent meetings of boys and girls. After a period of courtship, the boy gives some money or an ornament to the girl, which is called *Nya* or *Niys* as a token of formal proposal and acceptance. If the girl accepts this *Nya,* the matter is favourably settled, but, if she refuses it, the implication is that she is not willing. After the acceptance of *Nya* by the girl, the boy fixes the date and time of elopement with the girl. The boy and some of his friends reach the spot and the girl elopes with them to the boys house but she makes a show of hue and cry and of her efforts to get rid of their hold. Cases of theft of girls without consulting them are not very common these days and are on gradual decline. After theft, the bride reaches the grooms place where feast is organized.

Then elderly persons from boys side go to the girl's house with a bottle of *arak* to apologize for the misbehavior of the boy and request for the approval of the marriage. After a little protest and show of resentment, approval is granted, by accepting the bottle of *arak* brought by the boy's side. In some cases, parents then go to the bridegroom's house and inquire from the girl about her consent. Then bride and bridegroom are invited by the girl's parents.Such a way of acquiring mate is common among those people who prefer a less expensive marriage.

(C) Customary Laws of Divorce

Divorce in Lahoul is conducted by seeking a ritual called '*Kupachacha*' or '*Tshud-Thwagsti*'. Here a simple woolen thread is tied in the little fingers of both the companions and is pulled apart in the presence of some elderly persons. Sometimes, a light flame is also used to separate the woolen thread from the middle. If both husband and wife agree to separate, a meeting of the prominent and respectable villagers is called and the facts of separations declared. Either husband or wife may obtain a divorce under conditions laid in the customary laws of Lahoul. Divorce is allowed on several conditions or any of these such as barrenness, adultery, illness, incompatibility, negligence, habit of gambling and opium eating etc. A husband can obtain a divorce by providing a proof of unfaithfulness of his wife, before the meeting. Similarly, a wife may also obtain a divorce if the meeting holds that the husband has grossly neglected her and he has involved himself in the activities like gambling etc. The seeker of divorce has to pay the other party some compensation.

(D) Funeral Rites

Since Lahoul has two different religions prevailing in the area, so the death rituals are also different.

(i) *Ceremony of Bodhs*

The Buddhist funeral ceremony is adopted not only by those who are currently Buddhists, but also by those who are in the category of Bodhs or Rajputs of the Patan and Tinan valleys. In other words it is common among all non- Brahmin and non-Harijans. When somebody dies, the corpse is covered with some piece of cloth and let to lie till the lama of that area arrives. He, and any others who may accompany him, bring several Tibetan Buddhist scriptures and instruments such as *gNah* (drum), *bugjal* (cymbel) and *drillu* (bell) along with them. According to Tibetan Buddhism, the soul ordinarily takes three and a half to four days, from the time the symptoms of death appear, to be freed from the mortal physical body. Soon after the death, the body is removed from the bed and is laid on the floor with his head towards the temple of Trilokinath. An butter lamp is lit near the head. The dead body is not cremated on the day of death.The cremation takes place on the second day. In Gahar valley this is conducted as instructed by the scriptures. They keep the lamp lit for three and a half to four days, if they are not sure that the soul has been released properly. In the Patan valley the corpse is cremated as soon as the lama arrives and performs the funeral rites. Until than nobody eats or drinks anything.

In this ceremony the corpse, after clearing, is wrapped in colorful clothes and is laid on a carrier. In some cases they prefer to carry the body in a seated position, in which case a chair may be tied to the carrier.The lama chants the *mantras* from the holy book, *Bardo Thodol*, and goes round the corpse seven times chanting and playing the instruments. Also he performs a ceremony called *Yangkhug*, in which an effigy of the deceased is drawn on a piece of paper, which is later burnt.Besides helping the dead, the *yangkhug*, is meant to protect the family's fortune and keep its luck from being swept away along with the deceased. When the lama finishes his rituals, the corpse is carried to the funeral pyre. The pyre is lit with the fire of birch bark brought from the deceased's house. Normally it is lit by a member of the family. Butter, grains and incense are offered to the fire by the lamas. The corpse is generally cremated in the family field. After burning the corpse, the persons who attend the funeral ceremony gather in the deceased's house and take their food and disperse. Besides the ceremony performed by the lama, the '*Chinal*' or the Harijans also provide their own funeral music.There are ragas dedicated for such occasions, which are played on the flute, *nyishan* or *nagara* (pair of drums) and also a *poun* (a different type of drum with a humming sound) are available on the morning after the cremation, the *astu* (remaining bones) from the funeral pyre are collected, by a lama along with few persons, wrapped in clothes and made to look like an effigy. After this it is taken to the river nearby and scattered there. Few people of the area also take the ashes to Haridwar for immersion there. The *puja* from the day of death performed by the lamas continues for three to nine days depending upon the financial conditions of the family for the peace of the departed soul. This *puja* is called *chhoga.* After forty nine days, another ceremonial worship is performed and the villagers are invited to a meal. In some cases death anniversaries are also held. The dead infants, however are either thrown in the river or buried. To commemorate the dead, a '*chorten*' or stupa is sometimes constructed by the well –to – do ones and the people pay reverence by going round it clockwise.

(ii) Ceremony of Swanglas

Among the Brahmin and the Harijans, the funeral ceremony is performed by a medium called the '*Bhata*' (as is *Chandal* in Hindu religion). Unlike the Buddhist lama, a *Bhata* does not possess any books or scriptures from which to read.In this ceremony, a cow or a calf is taken three times round the corpse, or the effigy, while the *Bhata* chants the mantras. The cow is then donated to the *Bhata* himself. There is no waiting period, unlike in the Tibetan Buddhist ritual, and the corpse is cremated as soon as the *Bhata* has completed his rituals.The *Chinals* or the Harijans also provide the funeral music.The son of the deceased lights the pyre. Next morning the relatives and the *Bhata* goes to the cremation ground, collect the ashes and consign these to the river.

4.1.8 Festivals

(i) Halda : Halda signifies the advent of the new year, the casting away of all evils. The festivals of light known as Diwali which signifies the close of a year and the beginning of the next is celebrated all over India each year in the month of October or November. A similar festival might be called the 'festivals of lights of Lahoul' is observed as *Khogla* in the Patan valley and Halda in the Tinan and Gahar valley around the end of the January or early February each year. In sTod it is celebrated as *Losar.* Though known by different names in different valleys, festival is celebrated in the same way in all the five valleys of Lahoul.

Legend is that in the past during the war with Ladakh, the king of Lahoul not being sure of his return from the battle field ordered people to celebrate *Halda*, before he embarked on his assault on the enemy. Generally held in the month of January the dates vary from valley to valley and year to year. In Gahar valleys it is celebrated ahead of the other valleys. The Buddhist lama residing in the Guru Ghantal monastery consults the lunar calendar to fix the date of *Kofla* each year to coincide with the full moon. But the preparations begin much earlier. In every house cedar wood is split into fine strips and then tied together into bundles to make a torch called *Halda.* The torches are then piled up to form a bundle which is decorated with dry flowers. Incense and oil lamps are placed beneath this pile, along with sweetmeals and fried bread and *Marchu* (local bread) to worship the local village deity.

The next morning a congregations of representatives from each household visits each home in turn where they are invited to share a simple feast. In the evening, the *Haldas* for each house are lit and brought together at a central square, This is repeated four or five times each, in honor of a different deity. When the ceremony is over, the villagers return home to the most sumptuous dinner, they can afford. The round of visits to each others houses usually continues for two or three days.

(ii) Phagli : Another important festival of Lahoul is the *Phagli* or *Khun*, celebrated mainly in the Patan valley. Since *Phagli* immediately follows *Halda,* the two are often considered synonymous. The festivals heralds the beginning of the new year of the traditional calendar and is significantly for the worship of lord Shiva, since Patan valley belongs to the Hindu faith and Himachal is considered the land of Lord Shiva. On the first day *(kuhunyet)*, the rituals begin at mid- night. A *Shivalinga* (idol of Lord Shiva) is made with ice, on the roof of the house either by using an upturned basket or cow dung and deodar tree twigs. The following morning before the sunrise, the *Shivalinga* is circumambulated while holding a torch light made from goat wool *(laccham)*, tipped with butter. Apart from Shiva, people also worship the household deity *(kul devta)*, the village deity and other important deities like the *Nagaraja, Raja Ghephan* and the Goddess *Hidimba.*

Another feature of *Phagli* festival is the paying of respect and obeisance to the elders by the younger generations. The eldest man of the village is offered flowers by the villagers than he and other elders give their blessings to them in return. Also, gifts in the form of socks, flowers or money etc., are exchanged among family members and friends. This is followed by feasting and drinking *chhang.*

(iii) Chheshu : This is a festival celebrated in various monasteries of Lahoul in the month of May, June and July. People from all over the valley assemble in the gompa to witness the celebrations which involve a lot of drinking and dancing. Lama perform a specific worship in the morning and then perform the devil or *cham* dance. The performers wear colorful brocade costumes,dance to the music of drums and cymbals. The dance is accompanied by the chanting of occasional chorus.The monotony of the proceedings is relieved by the pantomime style of acting of a clown. The dance owes its origin to Tibet and signifies a fight between good and evil. In this ceremony king Langdarma of central Tibet who was severely opposed to Buddhism, is the victim of numerous pranks played by the devils.

(iv) Bumkhor : *It* is a religious festival of agriculture and is celebrated mainly in sTod valley. People accompanied by lamas walk in a procession through fields full of crops, carrying religious book *Kangyur* i.e. 108 texts.It is believed that this would lead to a bumper harvest.The ritual culminates in a *puja* performed by the lamas followed by sharing of *chhang* and food by the villagers concerned.

(v) Pori Fair : This three day fair is held in the month of August at Trilokinath Temple, in Patan valley. It attracts pilgrims from the entire western Himalayas viz. Ladakh, Zanskar and other places who come to pay homage to the deity of Trilokinath (*Lord Shiva or Avalokiteshwara)* in a famous temple located at a village of the same name. Every morning and evening during these three days people circumambulate the abode of the idol three or seven times, rotate the *manne* (prayer wheel), prostrate several times in front of the idol and light butter lamps and utter prayers. After the paying of homage on the first morning, the festival begins. The main attractions are the numerous stalls seeing, all kinds of momentous and traditional dances performed by the local people in the evenings. On the second day, the thakur of Trilokinath village, riding on a decorated horse, leads a traditional procession, which leads to the place where legend has it that seven angles appeared from seven springs, youngest of who is believed to be the idol of Lord Trilokinath. The procession of the Thakur then return to the fair grounds for more festivities which continue into the third day. The thakur of trilokinath presides over the proceedings of the festivals from the vantage point, which is the verandah of a two storied house.

Other than these major festivals, there are several small festivals also which are celebrated at the village or community level. And in contemporary society, there is a change in the practice of observing these festivals and associated customs.

(vi) Nang Dhon and Phi Dhon : The festivals of Tinan valley is the celebrations which lasts for three to four days. Close relatives gather to eat, drink and make merry. People cook special dishes to treat each other. Celebrated in the month of January immediately after *Halda,* it is a gesture of welcoming the new year.

Phi Dhon is also celebrated mainly in the Tinan valley and is similar to the *Nang Dhon* festivals. During the festival people mostly dance and enjoy. It is considered as the time of interaction among the people of all age groups.

(vii) Puna : In this festival people gather at a place and then proceed in a processions to nearby field accompanied with musical instrument and there they worship different gods and goddesses. After the worship, the imitations of a goat is sacrificed and then they return complimenting each other.

(viii) Gyalto: This festival is held towards the end of December when people bid farewell to the old year. This is celebrated before *Halda* or *Loser. Nyainay* is a birthday celebration of lama Chan Rizi and it takes place on the 14th of the first bhoti month. This is celebrated by feasting but few traditional people observe fast and silence for 36 hours prior to the celebrations.*Dachang* is the festival of arrows.In this a young healthy boy shoots one arrow from a roof top towards the river to symbolize the victory over all the evils and diseases.This is celebrated by the men only in the month of February in every village and continues for six days.

(ix) Yane: It is a festival in which god Trilokinath is worshipped by old men and women of the villages after fasting for a day. This is celebrated in the second week of June every year. All old men and women of the village assemble together and ask for forgiveness of the sins committed by them during the preceding year from the god Trilokinath.

4.1.9 Temples and Monasteries

In the region of Lahoul, as name itself indicates there are many temples and monasteries, as it is also know as abode of Gods.

Temple of Trilokinath : 'Trilokinath' means 'the lord of three worlds'. This is one of the very rare places in the world which is worshipped equally by two different religions.

Durga Temple of Margul

A few miles west of Trilokinath there is a village on the right bank of the Chenab river, near its junction with Mayard Nallah locally known as Margul. It is also called Udaipur after Udai Singh who was the Raja of Chamba in the 17th century when he annexed this area to Chamba (Bajpai,1987). This ancient temple of Kali lies on a hill top at the northwestern end of the village. At the entrance of the *mandap* there are two huge but crudely covered statue over six feet tall, standing as gatekeepers. There is a superstition that if one says "lets go" while leaving the temple, then two gatekeepers also came along which is considered to being some kind of misfortune.

Guru Ghantal Monastery

This is one of the ancient monastery of Lahoul and it is the only monastery for most of the Patan valley that performs true death or funeral ceremonies. Situated far above the confluence of the Chandra and Bhaga rivers it is believed to have been established in the 8 century by Padma Sambhav. The main idol in this monastery is a head only made of marble.

Kardang Monastery

Kardang monastery is one of the most famous centers of Tibetan Buddhism today. Dozens of monks and nuns residing in the monastery have denoted their entire lives to meditations and study of Buddhist scriptures in pursuit of Nirvāna. This monastery is believed to have established some time in the 11th or 12th century. Kardang monastery has many achievements in the field of Buddhist philosophy and spirituality. However it is said that the lamas in this monastery have mastered the technique of freeing their soul at the time of death, sitting in meditation with full control over the mind and body rather than being at there mercy of nature on their death beds losing their senses until the body is declared dead.

Shashur and other Monasteries

Shashur meaning red cedar, the name itself signifies the location of the monastery. In the midst of cedar forest on the Bhaga rivers right bank, the

Shashur monastery is situated a few miles up a hill above Keylong the district headquarter of Lahoul. The outer structure particularly the entrance of Shashur monastery, is typical of Tibetan monasteries with large door and pillars and architrave of carved wood full of paintings. Inside there are a few rooms full of busts and images of Buddha and famous lamas. The other monasteries in this area are Tayul Gompa, Lapchang Gompa and Pyuker Gompa.

4.1.10 Status of Women

The position of women in the society affects its social organization. Desire for a son may be a strong instinct among the parents, but birth of a female child is also important. Women has a great economic importance and is valuable asset to the household. A girl starts making contribution in the economy of the household at very early stage by looking after younger siblings, helping her mother in small household chores, grazing lambs and calves, collecting fuel wood etc. By the time she attains the age of 14 -15 years her contribution to the economy of household is considered equal to that of an adult. The nature of economy is such that they favour a girl in retaining her at home, unmarried, in the family. But, whether married or not, all women in the household share the workload equally.They do all laborious works, such as carrying loads, weeding and harvesting the crops, carrying water, fuel etc. In agricultural operations they do all the work. Her role in the family management is also very important, for she is responsible for cooking of meals, taking care of infants, bringing up the youngsters and carrying on other household chores. The dominance of females in the household over the males is well reasoned by the burden they share in the household work. In fact whole economy revolves around the female who cultivate, spin and weave and also look after and control all family expenditure.

Her participation in political activities is limited to casting votes. Though they show active participation in *Mahila Mandals* but their arena does not touch village politics much. Though sometimes females are also elected to act as *panch* or *pradhan* of the village but chances of reservations policy playing a major decisive role in their election are also there. Social restrictions and shy nature of Lahouli women are not the only factors which enforce them to restrict their domain to their home and its management and thus to keep them away from political activities. In fact, the responsibilities they share in their household, make them too busy to participate in such activities. The whole economy of the family or household revolves around females who are the main workers and managers of all agricultural operations. If they are elected as *panch* or *pradhan* of a village, it requires their precious time, which they afford to give only at the cost of time of their short agricultural season. Thus, shortage of time due to busy agricultural season lessens their participation in political activities. Lahouli women has restricted rights in property as inheritance is in the male line.

4.1.11 Kinship

Family or household is the basic unit of the social organisation. It is a corporate unit for its members. It fulfills all the basic needs of the individual such as social, economic, emotional, and psychological; the community gives more recognition to a household than to an individual. A household must own a dwelling place and landed property in order to have full membership. In an attempt to become a self-sufficient unit, and to be able to fight against the adversities of environment condition, all the members of the household act in unison. To become a self-sufficient unit every household tries for possession of largest possible stock in terms of material wealth and human resources. All social ideals and social organization are directed towards the achievement of basic objective of being a self – sufficient and self sustained unit. The extreme hardships faced by the people of Lahoul reflect well in their social ideals and social organisation. Larger the household in respect of wealth, landholdings etc. more prestigious it is. Although the size of the holding may give one better status but, rights and duties of each household towards the community is equal.

While determining the kinship organisation and kinship behaviour of the people of an area a number of factors come into play, viz., geographical situation, interclass relationship, seniority on age, etc. Cultural norms enjoin upon everybody that each one must address his senior in age by some appropriate relationship, term, by the other person related, known or not at all.

The word used in Lahoul for a clan or tribe is *'rus'*, which means 'bone' and is applied to a class, denotes those descended from a common ancestor. *Ruspa* is a large kin group whose association extends in whole of Lahoul. It is explicitly based on a uni-lineal rule of descent from male line, i.e., patrilineal, and any two persons belonging to the same *rus* are believed to have descended from a common forefather. Every family and every individual belong to one or other *rus* and each *rus* possesses a name. The tribes and castes in Lahoul distributed by race, religion and occupation, differ from each other in all these respects. At the top of the hierarchy come the Thakurs of the agricultural classes. There are Buddhists and Hindus the two religions being much mixed. There are nine *'rus'* or clans or *gotras* of Buddhists and five of

Hindus. A few of them are meaningful, as such they provide us with clue of their probable origin. Among the Buddhist, the clans are arranged in the following hierarchical pattern:

1. *Otsaldungyud* - gotra of Brahma, the highest God.
2. *Guramshingpa* - gotra of Buddh.'*Ishkhuakhu*' is the gotra of Buddha, '*Ishkhuakhu*' and '*Guramshingpa*' are synonymous.
3. *Lonchhenpa* -gotra of the king of western Tibet.
4. *Misherabpa* -'mi' means 'men, 'sherab' means 'superior'. Thus *misherabpa* means 'superior men'.
5. *Khingopa* - this is the gotra of a saint of eleventh century of Tibet called Milereppa.
6. *Chepapa* - these are agriculturists.
7. *Merupa* - these are traders by profession.
8. *Lang-tsi* - these are animal breeders by profession.
9. *Darpa* - These people make dairy products. 'Darpa' means '*chach*'.

In this hierarchy pattern, *Otsaldungyud* and *Guramshingpa* are at the same level and *Lang- tsi* and *Darpa* are at the same level.

Among Hindus, the clans or *'gotras'* are arranged in the following hierarchical pattern:

1. *Saraswat*
2. *Bharadwaj*
3. *Markande (pandit)*
4. *Gautam*
5. *Prashar*

Membership of a *rus* is acquired only through birth. It cannot be acquired or lost by marriage or through adoption. A woman retains her affiliation to the *rus* even after her marriage, till her death. A male person adopted into a household does not acquire the *rus* of the new household. Similarly *ghar jamai* does not acquire the *rus* of the new family. He validly passes on his *rus* to his offspring, for a *rus* can be transmitted only through male generation, as the society is patriarchal. Change of residence does not affect the *rus* of a person. A male or female changing residence upon marriage etc. retains his or her original *rus* name. Generally in Lahoul, female leaves her house to go to live in her husband's house after marriage indicating patrilocal or virilocal type of residence. Uxorilocal type of residence is also found in Lahoul where husband comes to stay with wife in her house and takes care of her property.

A *rus* is a strictly exogamous unit. No marriage can be performed if boy and girl belong to the same *rus* it comes under prohibited category of relationships. Even joking relationship is a taboo between the persons of the same *rus*. There is no connection between the name of household and *rus*. There are households having same name but belonging to different *rus*. Similarly there may be a number of households of the same *rus* but having different names of their household. The kinship system in Lahoul exhibits same distinguishing features peculiar to the area.

4.1.12 Kinship Terminology

A list of various relationship terms is given below. The generation are described with Roman figures I to V with generation III being that of ego. Terms of address are in many cases identical with the terms of references but where they differ the terms of address is given in the brackets. In the first tabulation ego is taken be male and the differences in the case of woman as ego are listed in a subsidiary tabulation.

I

Term of Reference	Term of Address
Father's father	*me-me*
Father's mother	*a-bi*
Mother's father	*me-me*
Mother's mother	*a-bi*

II

Father	*a-ba*
Mother	*a-ma*
Father's elder brother	*ba-ra*
Father's younger brother	*a-ku or a chun*
Father's sister	*a –ne*
Father's elder brother's wife	*a-ma-chhedmo*
Father's younger brother's wife	*a –ma chun*
Mother's brother	*a-zhang*
Mother's elder sister	*a-ma chhedmo*
Mother's younger sister	*a-ma chun*
Mother's brother 's wife	*mi –chug*
Father's elders brother's wife	*a-ma chhedmo*
Father's Younger brother's wife	*a-ma -chunngun*
Elder step mother	*a-ma chhedmo*
Younger step mother	*a-ma chunngun*
Father's sister's husband	*pi- chung*
Wife's father	*a-zhang*
Wife's mother	*a-ne*

III

Eldest brother (first son)	*a-cho*
Second elder brother	*cho-cho*
Younger brother (addressed by name)	*no*
Eldest sister (first daughter)	*a-chi*
Second elder sister	*a-pu*
Younger sister (addressed by)	*a-pu*
Wife(teknonymy)	*ane*
Brother's wife	*tsha -mo*
Sister's husband	*tsha-u*
Wife's husband	*shakpo*

IV

Son	*bu-tsha*
Daughter	*bu -mo*
Brother's son	*tsha-bo*
Brother's daughter	*tsha-mo-tsi*
Sister's son	*tsha-bo*
Sister's daughter	*tsha-mo-tsi*
Son's wife	*na-ma*
Daughter's husband	*mag-pand*

V

Son's son	*tsha-bo*
Son's daughter	*tsha-mo-tsi*
Daughter's son	*tsha-bo*
Daughter's daughter	*tsha-motsi*

Relationship terms used by a woman

I

Term of Reference	Term of Address
Husband's father mother	*a-ne*
Husband's father's father	*a-zhang*
Husband's mother's father	*a-zhang*
Husband's mother 's mother	*a-ne*

II

Husband's father	*a-zhang*
Husband's mother	*a-ne*

III

Husband's elder brother	*a-u*
Husband's sister	*ngyed-no*
Husband (teknonymy)	*a-u*

IV

Son's wife	*na-ma*
Daughter's husband	*magpa*

4.1.13 Family

The family structure in Lahoul has been more or less dictated by the circumstances and the economic conditions of the people living on the valley. Basically the joint family system is in practice. The one thing that keeps a joint family intact is the commonly own property, which is usually the land and income. In this system, living under one roof may not be the necessary criterion, instead common wealth is the foundation of a joint family. The joint family structure is maintained by keeping the ancestral property intact, without dividing and selling the shares, even when the brothers live apart. The ancestral property, which belongs to all the brothers equally, the parental home will always remain the nucleus for all of them.

For instance, there may be three brothers in a family. Out of these three only one may be living in the ancestral home, taking care of the ancestral property while the others may be in some service or job or attending to some business away from home. The family however, maintains joint family structure in the sense, which the common wealth belongs to all the brothers equally (Sahani, 1994). In few families not only father, sons and brothers, and sometimes also uncles and nephews of the same descent live under one roof, but also own property in common.

In Lahoul where agriculture is the main occupation and amount of landholdings influence the status of the family in their society, as such some members of the family must stay home to take care of property. Often, eldest brother turns out to be the one who stays at home and acts as the head of the family. But in cases when the elder brother is interested in pursuing his job, one of the younger brothers will stay at home and act as the head of the family. In a few cases younger brother of the father's generation may be chosen to act as the head of the family. 51.67 percent of families are joint. It is believed in Lahoul that the joint family system incorporates within itself many advantages. It checks further division of land and also provides better adaptation whereby only one or two members of the family need to take care of the land while others could pursue business or professional careers. All their income is pooled and the whole family is better off. The financial burden is, thus, shared by all the brothers.In addition to this, joint family system always gives a feeling of togetherness which provides them strength to live in this difficult region and face problems collectively. Nevertheless, a number of separation cases year after year indicate a tendency is developing among the people of Lahoul to live separately and in nuclear families as 48.33 percent are nuclear families. The type of residence is now showing a trend towards setting up of neo-local residence.

Polyandry is supposed to be practiced in Lahoul to provide a strong joint family bond and check further division of their land with the practice of polyandry now declining common wealth is now the criteria for maintaining joint family structure. The change of family structure from the rigid joint families to nuclear families in now visible which is mostly a result of the occupational change that has been taking place over the years.

Customary Laws of Inheritance

In Lahoul, equigeniture is the rule of inheritance. The ancestral property is divided equally among all the brothers, after the demise of the father, who remains the head of the family as long as he is alive. In the absence of sons, the daughter may inherit the land and other property. In case the daughter's husband comes to live with her then he is called *ghar jawai* and then he manages her property. But in case, the daughter goes out of the house after marrying somebody, then her father's property goes to his brothers or to his collaterals. If any of the brothers dies without any issue, his property is again divided amongst the living brothers. In case a person dies without issue his widow is the only legal heir and title endures for life., unless she forfeits it by remarriage. In the event of there being no widow or male issue, the property is inherited by the daughters. A stepson succeeds his natural father and has no right to succeed his stepfather. A stepfather cannot assign any share of ancestral property except for his acquired property to his stepson.

4.1.14 Marriage

In Lahoul, monogamy is the general rule, but polygamy is also practiced among the people of Lahoul. Fraternal polyandry and polygyny have been practiced in Lahoul since olden times.The instances of polyandry are more as compared to those of polygyny. The reasons for polygyny are however either the requirement of more working hands in the family unit or impotency of wife leading to sororate type of polygyny or any extra marital affair of the husband ending in a marriage. However, now practice of polyandry and polygyny has declined much as is discussed in the topic of 'polyandry'.

Bride wealth

In marriages in Lahoul groom's side give gifts or pay some price in the form either money, dress material, cattle, utensils, blankets, and rarely land. Anything that could be purchased with money can be given as bride price. If the land is given to the girl, then the yield or the money obtained from the produce of the land is of the girl. But generally, when after marriage she becomes a part of the family the land becomes a common property of the household. Whatever is given to the girl as bride wealth is meant only for her. The boy hardly gets anything out of it other than the girl. This is a tribal way of providing the economic security to the girl. Moreover this relieves the financial pressure on the girl's parents also.

Certain restrictions are observed in contracting the marriage proposal. In the Brahmin community of Patan Valley in Lahoul region, marriage with father's sister's daughter and mother's brother's daughter and mother's brother's daughter is prohibited by custom but in ali other valleys such marriages are not prohibited. Consanguineous marriages are practiced mainly among Buddhist. Hypergamy is not recognized. Gotra exogamy is practiced here and hence no one can marry within the same gotra. Children of hypergamous marriages are called *Mundro*. The children of *Swanglas* who marry with the *Bodhs* loose their *Swangla* status and are called *Garu*. Love marriages between Swanglas and Bodhs are common these days.

Child marriage is not practiced here but some rare cases are found. Widow remarriages are allowed. In the event of death of husband in a polyandrous family, the lady does not become widow as she has more than one husband. But in few cases of non polyandrous families, in the event of death of the husband, she is married to the younger brother of her husband (Levirate). Levirate and Sororate are also practiced in some of the cases. Remarriage of widower, widow and divorcee are permitted.

4.1.15 Polyandry

Polyandry, a system in that a lady is treated as the wife of all the brothers of a family, is a recognised institution in Lahoul. Under the system, only the eldest brother is ceremoniously married with the woman and there is an understanding between the other brothers and the common wife. The senior husband or the eldest brother is the most responsible person in a polyandrous family and the younger brothers hold a subordinate position.

The common wife commands a respectable position in the family as she controls all the household affairs. Sexual rights in a polyandrous alliance are exercised through a tacit understanding among the brother and the relationship between son and father is not difficult to establish. Normally, the practice is that all the husbands are recognised as the father of each child. For day to day use the eldest among the living brothers is spoken of as the father of all the children born to a polyandrous wife. In the case of the division of the joint family the wife names the fathers of her different children.(Ghosh, 1987)

It is believed that economic conditions of the people were the main driving force in accepting the polyandry system of marriage. Now in defense of the institution of polyandry people say that small landholdings and other properties are saved from division. The institution, further, serves as an effective population control. They also believe that it is impossible for two sisters-in – law, with separate husbands and families, to live together, whereas two or more brothers with common wife can agree. The system thus checks division of land in the successive generations. Few people even believe in the myth that the institution of polyandry in the region has its origin since the time when Pandavas spend their exile period in the region, with their wife Draupadi. However the institution of polyandry in the contemporary society is on a gradual decline.

Cause of Decline of the Institution of Polyandry

After the 1970s, the massive road building projects were undertaken which provided more exposure to the outside world. Further, providing employment to the people of Lahoul by government agencies created major problem for the institution of polyandry. It is believed that in earlier times, when polyandry was much practiced it was rarely that all the brothers were at home at one time, as they had to pool the resources from agriculture, animal husbandry, trade and commerce. But now since work is available close to home all brothers preferred having individual wives rather than sharing a common wife.

Further as the contact with the outside world grew, the institution of polyandry faced criticism from the outsiders. People from the plains looked down upon such an institution. The constant criticism made the local people feel ashamed of their tradition and gradually they started hiding it, and later on those who had options preferred to go in for monogamy. Today as per the empirical data collected, 91 percent of marriages has been found to be monogamous. Only 9 percent of marriages are polygamous. Out of 9 percent, 8 percent are polyandrous marriages and only 1 percent of marriages are polygynous. It is important to mention here that, all the cases of polygamous marriages are those who were married at least 30 years before from today. Now, the young generation do not prefer polygamous marriages.

However, this institution was highly advantageous in the past and a very suitable form of marriage in the old desert region of Lahoul and Spiti.The region is harsh in terms of climate and resources. As a result, only a limited population could be sustained in this environment. This was an effective means of keeping a check on the population of the region. Further, it prevented the fission of the small, arable holdings. Fertile land was, as it is, scarce in the region, and its fission would render it economically unviable. Now the system of polyandry is vanishing because of the advent of modern education and changes in lifestyles. Now –days, more and more people are opting for government jobs. Thus it is common to find at least two out of three sons staying away from home, in places where their jobs take them. However, one brother stays back and looks after the ancestral house and fields. After getting married all brothers set up their own household.

4.1.16 Customary Laws and Justice Seeking

Although there is the system of Police Administration in Lahoul, but even then people prefer to go to Panch instead of police. Since, Lahoul is a small, isolated group of people, so the feeling of brotherhood prevails here. Being a Scheduled Tribe, the people are governed by the customary laws more. They prefer to follow their customary laws instead of constitutional laws in case of justice seeking. If there is any dispute in the Lahouli society, regarding Land, Water, Cattle, Societal argument, Betrothal, Marriage and divorce, Bastardy, Minority, Guardianship and alienation of property, Succession, Alienation, Adoption or appointment of an heir, Ghar Jawai, Polyandry (plurality of husband), Polygyny (plurality of wife), Special rights of women (stridhan), Partition. In all these cases Lahoulis prefer to go to Panch instead of police.

4.1.17 Economy

The region of Lahoul valley, where the terrain is extremely rocky, climate unpredictable and inhospitable, rainfall merely four inches during rainy season and which remain snow bound for more than six month of the year, the economic resources can only be few. In Lahoul economic resources of the people depends upon the mercy of nature and the type of work they are indulged in changes with climatic vissitudes. The ecology must have played a most dominant part in the evolution of professions of the people. Agriculture is primary source of economy in Lahoul, thus sustaining the economy. The people have adopted a variety of activities to supplement their income. Various economic activities undertaken in the area are – agriculture, handicraft, business like shops, contractors and government jobs.

(A) Agriculture and Pastoralism

In Lahoul the primary source of income is agriculture. Since the region of Lahoul and Spiti is a cold desert and the amount of rainfall is highly insufficient for irrigating the fields, cultivation is very difficult. Still people have devised way to cultivate in such terrain within hospitable climate condition. The agricultural season in Lahoul begin in the month of May and end up in October every year as the valley remains under snow from the month of October to early April. Sowing normally begins in the month of May. Man alone does only ploughing and women do the rest of agricultural work including the thrashing of the crops. It is the single crop agriculture provide most of the area in Lahoul. Only in Patan valley two crops are raised in one season. The peculiar topography had compelled the people of Lahoul to device an elaborate system to irrigate their field called *kuhl* system. In this water from natural resources like spring snow or glacier fed *nallas* is carried through channels to the desired place. These *kuhls* are constructed and kept in repair entirely by the landholder of the village, which use them. They are considered therefore to be the property of the shareholders in the water, who casts lots every year to decide the rotation in which each man shall irrigate his fields. Each holding furnishes a man for repairs; fines are levied on absentees. The general opinion is that no outsider can get share of the water of a canal except from the body of old shareholders.

Crops: Lahoul had subsistence economy till 1950's and only one crop could be grown during the summer season. People use to grow barley and buckwheat (*kathu*) for the consumption of the family there was no cultivation of vegetables as such. *Moravian* missionaries were the first to introduce potato and some variety of vegetable at Keylong in 1857 (Bajpai, 1987). The cultivation of these crops, however, remained at the subsistence level in the region. So, the economic condition of the people was not good and people had to struggle very hard to meet the necessity of the life. For six months nothing could be grown due to heavy snowfall and extremely cold climatic conditions. This restricted the adoption of the cultivation as the source of income for the people of Lahoul. But today, people of Lahoul cultivate barley, buckwheat (*kathu*), mustard and vegetables like cauliflower, carrot, radish, tomato, etc. Cash crop like peas, potato, *kuth* and hops are also grown in Lahoul.

Kuth : *Kuth* (*Sausserea lappa*), a Himalayan herb, is grown in Lahoul for subsistence as well as for commercial purposes. *Kuth* cultivation was started in Lahoul in 1930's but it matured in 1950's and 1960's. Much of the credit for the prosperity of this valley goes to this crop as it promised them some monetary gains. But because the market of *kuth* remains quite uncertain and also because the people of Lahoul valley find growing seed potato and peas more profitable than cultivating *kuth,* this crop is rapidly disappearing from the fields of Lahoul.

Potato: Potato has become the main cash crop and very profitable produce of the Lahoul valley. Being introduced by the *Moravian* missionaries, its production picked after 1972, when the people took it as a cash crop. Potato grown here is of very good quality and used as seed in about every part of the country. From one *beigha* of land the yield gives an income of around rupees eight thousands. Besides being a cash crop, the potatoes grown here serve as one of the staple foods of the local people. Transporting and marketing the produce from the remote corners of the region and across Rohtang is rather a challenging task. Lahoul Potato Cooperative Society (LPS) plays a very important role in transporting and marketing the produce from the remote corners of the region and across Rohtang which is rather, a challenging task.

Peas: Peas (*Pisum sativum*) is the most profitable cash crop grown in Lahoul. Cultivation of peas requires more monetary gains. The produce from one *beigha* of land gives them an income of Rupees eleven thousand.

Hops: Hop plant (*Humulus lupulus*) is a creeper that produces green flowers, shaped somewhat like a solidly filled rose bud, but more rounded in shape. These flowers are used in bear as a bittering or flowering agent as well as preservative. This crop is cultivated mainly in Patan valley. But with more profitable cash crops like peas and potato being produced more, the cultivation of hops has reduced much. But still, they prefer growing hop every year to preserve it as seeds.

Apple Orchards: Off late, owing to global warming apple cultivation is also catching up. Most of the families in Lahoul have their own orchards, at Kullu and a few have maintained it in Lahoul too. During winter, when the whole Lahoul valley is covered with snow and no agricultural work could be done, most of Lahoul people migrate to places like Kullu, Manali, Bhunter etc. to look after their orchards. Now people have started growing orchards in Lahoul on commercial lines, in anticipation that once Rohtang tunnel would be made, these orchards would bring them good financial gains.

(B) Handicrafts

Woolens are the common craft that keep people busy during the long winters. Many people have their own handlooms. Some improved handlooms have also been introduced. People twist yarn with a twisting rod worked with hand or by a twisting wheel. They make very fine cloth for their own use. They also weave good coarse cloth from goat hair for use as mats and outer bed – cloth. Women knit high quality socks, gloves and pullovers. Since people wear woolen clothes almost round the year, the wool obtained from the sheep they rear, are just enough for their own consumption. All the processing of wool like carding, spinning, weaving and stitching are done at home. The whole processing of wool is done during winters when other farm work is not possible and people just confine themselves within their houses.

(C) Domestication of Animals

Animal husbandry is an integral part of economy which can be visualized from the fact that almost all tribal families have been rearing one livestock or the other. The common livestock in Lahoul are sheep, cow, bull, goat and little poultry. Besides, *Zo* and *Zomo* (male and female progeny of a cow and yak) are also domesticated. Almost all households in Lahoul domesticate animals like sheep and sometimes goat, for wool, cows for milk and bulls to plough the fields. During winter, cattle are fed at stud and kept indoors. The activities relating to animal husbandry have created a visible impact in the field to the extent that fresh milk, which was in short supply in the area, is readily available. The number of cattle and amount of land holding are the two major parameters that determine the status and degree of influence of the person. The cattle serve the multipurpose needs of the people of Lahoul. Besides providing milk meat, wool etc. they also provide manure. When dead, their hides are used as clothes, coats and mattresses. Every village keeps one or two stud yaks jointly for breeding purposes. The villagers engage one or two persons as the common herdsmen for grazing the livestock of the whole village during summer. To provide animal health and to improve quality of indigenous breeds of animals various institutions have been established in the region.

(D) Other Occupations

The environmental system constraints the people to adopt a variety of economic activities.

In addition to agriculture, which is their main occupation, Lahouli people are involved in various other occupations like teaching, government jobs, medicine, engineering, contractors, business, etc. Under the joint family system, some family members may be farmers while others may be engaged in business or in some service to supplement the family income. Present professional opportunities for young people range from medicine, engineering to other governmental jobs. Nevertheless, farming has been the backbone of the valley since time immemorial and today, those in different jobs are even seen to be engaged in work during agricultural season. These people have learned to be self-sufficient and self –reliant.

Thus in Lahoul mutual cooperation between family members, relatives and villagers is the key to their prospering economy. As agricultural demands large numbers of workers for each kind of operation in the agrarian society of Lahoul mutual cooperation and help is much necessary. Further, the cooperation between family members is required while seeking the occupation in which one wants to involve him. Thus, in Lahoul, as a positive sanction the economy sub serves to maintain the other key social institutions like, marriage and family type. The variety of economic activities undertaken by the household keeps each of the family members busy in his own work. This is perfectly compatible with the marriage system, family structure and changes there in with the passage of time. It may be noted here that in the existing state of technology everything is based on labour and there is least use of machine, or exploitation of one class by the another. This augmented by the geographical location, environmental conditions of the region and difficult terrain, the economic system of Lahouli people sets an example.

4.1.18 Social Transformation

The process of transformation that is undergoing today was much induced and caused by external agents and circumstances. The area is today undergoing through a transitive period. Rapid change in every aspect of the culture and social system is the common phenomenon. One cannot say specifically at what point of time the wheel was set in motion. Earlier, it was a self –sustaining and inward looking society. Various institutions had attained perfection in their function and utility as such they had become stability and unchangeable. The people had been leading a quite life for centuries and no one could expect a seed of transformation to germinate on such a hard rock. All their energy was engaged in struggling for existence in the inimical ecology of the high Himalayas. Isolation, inaccessibility remoteness and severe atmosphere, all these circumstance made possible to live undisturbed. The exposure of this isolated area to the outside was the result of development olicies introduced by the government after the independence of the country, and become perceptible from the sixties. Lahoul was linked with Kulu through motorable roads across Rohtang Pass. Borders with Tibet were closed in 1959. This struck at the root of economic and cultural framework.

(A) Economy

With the closing of borders of Tibet in 1959, the economy of the region received a temporary setback for the trading activity had to be stopped. Traditional agriculture was aimed at self sustenance. But agriculture alone was not able to sustain life. So, people during earlier days opted for other economic activities like trading. In a family with two or more brothers one of them used to leave the house for trading purposes. If, on the one hand trading activity of the people was checked, on the other hand, improvement in agriculture was brought about by the use of improved seeds, introduction of chemical fertilizers, and adopting cash crops like *Kuth* seed potato etc. Construction of motorable roads facilitated the people in the produce to sell their produce in the market outside the area and in return bring goods of their need like rice, wheat, and various kinds of other essential items. This also changed the food habits and dress material used by the people. In this way, the traditional economy was linked with market economy. Further, democratization and massive development of work done by the state and other social service organisation have opened vast avenues for the people.Besides, government service from the competitive All India Services down to class four cadre of employment which the tribal young may now try to enter, chances of semi official and non official employment have increased many times. As a whole, sources of earning of people have increased and are expected to continue in the future. Due to shifting of sizable population to other economic activities acute shortage of labour has arisen in agriculture. Presently those staying at home are mostly women, old men and men who remained uneducated and unemployed. No educated man or woman would willingly stay to live on agriculture. Agriculture, even though is more remunerative today, is a profession of compulsion.

(B) Education

Traditionally people study Bhoti language in order to enter the religious order. The lamas and nun were the only educated section in the society. But now with the widening of avenues and government providing infrastructure facilities there is some inclination among the people towards getting educated. Primary schools, middle schools, secondary schools, senior secondary schools, and also colleges and vocational training schools are available in the area. Education has opened up new opportunities of employment and helped in raising the economic standards of the people. Education has brought about the mobility among the people. No educated man or woman would willingly stay to live on agriculture. On getting some good job they move out of the village. Migration of the educated population from the area although temporary has created an intellectual vacuum. Education has shown its impact on the decreasing practicing of old traditions and customs, like system of polyandry, joint family system etc. An unceasing conflict has arisen between the old and the new generation in this regard. The parents want that all the sons, if there are more than one, should not leave the home and at least one of them should stay at home. Some families are trying to solve this problem by dropping one of their sons after some stage of schooling and retaining him at home.

(C) Marriage

Now when exposed by various external agencies they are less capable of maintaining the standards of old traditions and customs, and in giving new direction to the society by inculcating new values. The culture, as a result, is decaying and degenerating. The business of steering the society is left to be taken over by the persons among the residual population.

Various development programs have brought along a very large number in the population because of the influx of workers from the neighboring district and because of which further government spending is needed for development.

4.1 Ethnographic Live of Rural Population

The predominant population of rural area comprises mainly of Hindus, which constitutes Jat, Brahmin, Punjabis, Baniyas and Chamars. Jat and Brahmin constitutes the major percent of the population. As in the present study two populations namely Jat and Brahmin, of Sampla Block, District Rohtak, Haryana have been taken into consideration. These two populations have been pooled together as rural population. The ethnographic life of Jat and Brahmin are presented here and both the groups show almost the similar life but different caste systems.

Jat are well known in history for their strength and bravery. They are divided into about 300 *gotras*. Few important *gotras* are Dahiya, Ohlian, Ludda, Khatri etc. They follow clan and village exogamy (Singh, 1994).

Brahmin also constitute of several caste groups as Bhardwaj, Vashsist, Kaushik, Parashar, Gautam etc. Previously their occupation was restricted to priesthood and similar to priesthood jobs. The matrimonial alliances are restricted to caste endogamy and exogamy rule in the level of Sub-caste and village area. People of the area live a simple life, suiting to the economy of the district. Monogamy is the usual rule, incidence of divorce and second marriage is also observed.

4.2.1 Settlement Pattern

The block is characterized by the colonial settlement, as they tend to appear in cluster. Various houses do not have nucleated existence, rather they tend to appear in cluster. Houses are built of bricks and cement. The houses have generally flat roofs which are also utilized for drying grains and for the sun basking.Kitchen gardens are the common features and the seasonal vegetables are grown here along with large open land for keeping animals. Some houses are made up of mud and bricks while some have semi – *pucca* houses with rooms made with bricks and cement, with their front yard as *kuccha.* The whole area is provided with electricity and water supply.

4.2.2 Dress Pattern

The clothes worn by the two populations are not of very special kind. Men wear shirts, trousers and shoes. The old men wear *dhoti, kurta* or shirt and *pagdi* (turban) on their head. The women wear *salwar*, *kurta* and *dupatta* covering their head and during rituals or functions they wear saris.

4.2.3 Ornaments

Men generally do not wear any ornaments. Those who belong to better socio-economic strata wear gold rings and chain. Women however, wear small ornaments. Bracelets (kara or kangan), nose rings, chain etc are ornaments worn by the women.

4.2.4 Language

They usually speak Haryanvi language or Hindi.

4.2.5 Food Habits

Both the populations of this rural area are mostly vegetarian. All people whether going to field or to their shops or going to office in the morning eat *roti* of wheat or *bajra* along with vegetable. All types of vegetables like cabbage, cauliflower, brinjal, beans, capsicum, bitter gourd, potato, leafy vegetables, *gheea* etc constitutes their diet. Milk and milk products are a major constituent of their diet. Lunch is taken by few people and few takes just two meals in a day. In the night, they have dinner consisting of *roti* with dal or any vegetable along with *lassi* or milk. Consumption of rice is very less as compared to another cereal.

4.2.6 Festivals

They celebrate Holi, Raksha bandhan, Diwali, Shivratri, Dussera, Phag, Teej and Holi. Songs are some of the classic forms of rich tradition of the people of Haryana, ceremony and seasonal songs, folk dances are also performed on the specific occasions, seasons, festivals, ritual harvesting etc.

4.2.7 Rites de Passage

(A) Marriage Rituals: Marriage in this community is completely exogamous that is marriage between the same gotra is not permitted in both the groups. Following sequence is followed for the marriage of a girl or a boy:

1. **Lagan :** This is decided by Pandits after seeing the horoscope of proposed boy and the girl.In this ritual a letter is given to the boy's side by the girl's side deciding the day of the marriage. This is given nine, eleven or twenty one days before marriage.
2. **Baan :** In this, some drops of mustard oil are rubbed on the feet, knee, shoulders and forehead,in this order, with the help of grass. This ritual takes place five or seven days before marriage.
3. **Roti :** The groom's side offers food for villagers and relatives. This is done a day prior to the day of marriage. Food consists of rice, chapattis, pulses, sweets etc.
4. **Sehra Bandhai :** In this the 'Sehra' brought by the maternal uncle is tied on the head of the groom by the *nai* (barber). Elder people put turban, after *sehra bandhai*, the groom along with the relatives goes to the nearby temple to take the blessings from the God. This is named as *gurchari.* And then they all proceed to the bride's place.
5. **Swagat Milai :** Bride's elder sister carries out the *pooja* of groom and than only the barat can enter the house of the bride.
6. **Varmala and Fere :** In this both bride and groom put garland into each other's neck and then circumambulate for seven times. This is called *fere*. After this seven promises are vowed by groom and bride.
7. **Bhoj :** After the *fere*, all relatives are given food by the bride's side.
8. **Vidai :** After the food, all baratis and bride is given farewell by the bride side.
9. **Kangna Khelna :** When bride and groom come to house, aarti is done by the mother of the groom and than both bride and groom play a game of searching ring by dipping their hand in a big plate which has the mixture of milk, water, turmeric and grass.

(B) Divorce : Disharmony between the couple in the community is first tried to be resolved among the family members. In case of extreme situations the case is proceeded through the lawyers to the court.

4.2.8 Religion

Both the groups are Hindu by religion and are very religious and believe in the supernatural things. Besides believing in God and Goddesses, they also believe in spirits, evil eye etc.

4.2.9 Child Marriage

Child Marriages are rampant in the area. In rural areas around 50 percent and in urban areas around 20 percent girls are married before they attain the prescribed minimum age – in violation of the Child Marriage Restraint Act, 1978. Three percent of girls in the State are married in infancy (Menon, 2003).

4.2.10 Caste Panchayat

In the rural areas there is the most alarming development of the rise of *khap* panchayats or *gotra* panchayats caste panchayats. These are the illegal extra – constitutional medieval institutions. These institutions violate constitutional rights as well as the human rights of the people. They have their own notions and customary laws about who can marry whom. These panchayats issues *fatwa* to those couples who marry endogamously i.e. in the same caste. People not complying with fatwas are excommunicated.

4.3 Ethnographic Live of Urban Population

There are 147 communities and 28 scheduled tribes in Delhi (Singh, 1996). All these communities are in the process of modernization and westernization. In the present study the urban population constitute the various ethnic groups namely Agarwal, Punjabis, Brahmin, Sindhi, Bengalis, Kashmiri Pandits and heterogeneous sample of South Indians. All these populations have been grouped together as urban population. As we know each ethnic group has its own ethnographic back ground. It has been observed that in the process the original customs and culture has changed. Due to some reasons it is not possible to give the ethnographic account of all the ethnic groups separately, but tried to give an overall profile of urban population.

Right from ancient times and more so today, Delhi has been and remains a melting pot of varied peoples and cultures, giving it a truly cosmopolitan character. The demographic composition of Delhi consists first of all the original population of Delhi which was, and still is mainly Urdu–speaking and

Hindi speaking.The Muslim population of Delhi returns itself as Urdu–speaking. The Punjabi population has increased greatly after the Partition,and has thereafter made a definite impact on the city. The Bengali speaking population was introduced to Delhi in considerable numbers when the British shifted the capital from Calcutta to Delhi in 1912. Thereafter, they have multiplied and made their impact too. The Sindhis with their dialect have also made an impression especially with their business acumen, mainly after the Partition. The populations speaking other languages made their entrance rather late, but have subsequently proliferated here. Delhi also has a fair number of Anglo – Indians whose mother tongue is English.There are also some Chinese speaking people who are Indian citizens. Delhi, being the seat of power, has invited and attracted peoples of all hues and colours from all corners of India and even from outside.

4.3.1 Religion

The religions practiced in Delhi are mainly Hinduism, Islam, Christianity and Sikhism. The type of Hinduism impressively represented in Delhi is the North –Indian type, although the Eastern variety of Hinduism is also found. Other religions, represented to a lesser degree, are, in order of importance, Jainism, Buddhism, Bahaism and Judaism. All the sects of Hinduism, Islam, Christianity and Sikhism, have their due representation in Delhi, as also those of Jainism and Buddhism. Rural Delhi is markedly Hindu.

4.3.2 Settlement Pattern

Delhi has multiethnic, multi-caste, multilingual and multi-religious settlements. However, some of the colonies have come up on an ethnic basis. These colonies, however, though predominantly uni-ethnic, do not debar other ethnic communities from taking up residences. Rather, Delhi's settlements are more inclined to be divided or demarcated on economic and bureaucratic lines.

5

Socio-economic and Cultural Characteristics of Tribal, Rural and Urban Populations

This chapter discusses various socio-economic, socio-cultural and population characteristics of the Tribal, Rural and Urban Populations. Various indicators like land holding pattern, housing pattern, occupation, income, family types, marriage types, religion practiced, total population of the households, age and sex wise distribution, sex ratio, age at marriage, education etc have been analysed in the order of Tribal Population, Rural Population and than Urban Population. The reason for following this gradation is that it is generally observed that tribes are isolated, secluded groups of people living in remote ecological environment. Thus there educational level and awareness level is observed to be lowest, followed by rural and than urban population. The role and impact of mass media and other cultures is found to be least among tribals. Keeping this in mind all the three populations has been discussed in the order as mentioned above.

5.1 Socio – economic Characteristics

1 a. Tribal Population

The state of Himachal Pradesh situated in the north western part of India is a land of lush green forests, deep river valleys, beautiful plateaus and snow capped lofty mountains. It is bordered with Jammu & Kashmir in North, Punjab in the West and South – West, Haryana in the South, Uttaranchal in the South – East and with China in the East. The area as a whole is hilly, mountainous and the major part is inaccessible, physiograpically complex, snow covered and forest clad. The altitude varies from 450 to 6500 meters above the sea level in Himachal Pradesh.

For the present study, the Lahoul and Spiti District of the Himachal Pradesh has been selected. The district of Lahoul and Spiti lies between East longitude 76' 29" and 78' 41' 34" and North Latitude 31' 4' 57" and 32' 59' 57" at an average altitude of 10,050 ft ranging between 5480 m and 6400 m above sea level. The total geographical area of the district is 13,835 sq. km. The total population of the district is 33,224 people, out of which 18,413 are males and 14,811 are females. The entire population of the district is rural as there is no town.

The work in this area was initiated with the idea that 'Lahouli' is a scheduled tribe, but after conducting field work it was found that the tribe has caste hierarchy. The word 'Lahouli' is a blanket term. It is a broad generic term, including anybody who is a permanent denizen of this area. The people such as the Brahmins, Ranas, Thakurs (Rajputs, Kanets or Bhots (or Bodhs) and the schedule castes like Lohars (iron smiths); Dagis or Shipps (carpenters) are all broadly classified as Lahoulis. Anybody living in this geographical territory enjoys a scheduled tribe status as per the constitution (Gupta and Kapoor, 2004).

1A.1 Household Coverage and Total Population

The present study has been undertaken among the Scheduled Tribe of the Lahoul Block of the District Lahoul and Spiti. The Block is divided into five valleys. To have a representative sample of the universe of study, villages from all the five valleys – sTod, Tinan, Pattan, Mayard, Tindi have been selected. Keeping the district head quarter as an epicenter, villages from all the directions has been taken into consideration. The villages has been selected from the interior most towards the head quarters. In sTod valley the interior most village is Yoche which at an altitude of 11,500 ft and is 40 km from district head quarters. Towards Zanskar side, the interior most village is Chhika which is at the altitude of 10,550ft and is at the distance of 38 km from the district head quarters. In Mayard valley the interior most village is Khanjar which is at an altitude of 12,000 ft and is at an distance of 83 km from district head quarters. In other direction towards Tindi side, the last village in which work was done was Kurched which was at an altitude of 6900 ft and is at a distance of 86 km from Keylong. In the Tinan valley Shashan was the last village in which work was done. It is at an altitude of 10,196 ft and is 30 km from head quarters.

Table 5.1: Distribution of Households and Population Among the Tribal Population of District Lahoul and Spiti, Himachal Pradesh

S.No.	*Village*	*Households*	*Male*	*Percent*	*Female*	*Percent*	*Total*	*Percent*
1.	Agaher	14	40	4.75	25	3.37	65	4.10
2.	Chimrat	10	27	3.21	13	1.75	40	2.53
3.	Darcha	16	58	6.89	45	6.06	103	6.50
4.	Gondhla	15	30	3.56	26	3.50	56	3.54
5.	Gushal	21	54	6.41	55	7.41	109	6.88
6.	Jahalman	13	39	4.63	42	5.66	81	5.11
7.	Jispa	17	50	5.94	36	4.85	86	5.43
8.	Khangsar	23	81	9.62	65	8.76	146	9.22
9.	Khanjar	6	20	2.38	17	2.29	37	2.34
10.	Kolong	14	47	5.58	47	6.33	94	5.93
11.	Kurched	12	32	3.80	30	4.04	62	3.91
12.	Lohni	8	26	3.09	24	3.23	50	3.16

(Contd.)

(Contd.Table 5.1)

S.No.	Village	Households	Male	Percent	Female	Percent	Total	Percent
13.	Lote	14	29	3.44	45	6.06	74	4.67
14.	Rapey	5	24	2.85	13	1.75	37	2.34
15.	Rarik	21	41	4.87	49	6.60	90	5.68
16.	Rashel	6	21	2.49	10	1.35	31	1.96
17.	Shashan	11	24	2.85	24	3.23	48	3.03
18.	Sissu	10	27	3.21	22	2.96	49	3.09
19.	Tholong	12	33	3.92	27	3.64	60	3.79
20.	Tingret	10	36	4.28	34	4.58	70	4.42
21.	Trilokinath	10	19	2.26	23	3.10	42	2.65
22.	Urgos	10	31	3.68	24	3.23	55	3.47
23.	Yangla	9	29	3.44	21	2.83	50	3.16
24.	Yoche	13	24	2.85	25	3.37	49	3.09
	Total	300	842	100.00	742	100.00	1584	100.00

To have a complete representation of the whole block, all these five valleys were worked in. From each valley five to six villages were selected, keeping common criteria in mind. Out of these six villages, two villages were selected, which were the interior most of the valleys i.e. where there is no road link also. Then two villages towards the district head quarters and then finally two near the police station (if present in that valley) or in the middle. Data from households, from the villages under consideration has been collected, depending on the availability of the Lahoulis and the size of the village. The data collected from all the villages have been pooled together for the purpose of analysis.

Table 5.1 presents the distribution of households and population among the tribal population of District Lahoul and Spiti. A total sample of 300 households have been collected from 24 villages of Lahoul Block. Out of the total population of 1584, 53.16 percent are males and 46.84 percent are females.

1A.2 Land Holding Pattern

The land holding or the size of the land owned by the household is an indicator for estimation of overall economic condition and its potential role in determining the awareness level of the family. Due to the hilly terrain in Lahoul District, the main source of livelihood is land. Therefore the size of land owned is an indicative of relative economic status and resources.

Table 5.2: Land Holding Pattern Among the Tribal Population of District Lahoul and Spiti, Himachal Pradesh

Land Holdings (beigha)	*Households*	*Percent*
Land less	35	11.67
1-10	81	27.00
11-20	124	41.33
21-30	56	18.67
31-40	2	0.67
41-50	1	0.33
51-60	1	0.33
>70	-	-
Total	300	100.00

1 beigha = 880 sq. yards.

Table 5.2 shows the land holding pattern among the tribal population of District Lahoul and Spiti. It has been observed that 11.67 percent households have been found to be landless. These are the households who do not have individual land holdings and who does not either take the share from the income as they are in service. This also includes those Lahouli females who are widow and are living alone. Thus their land is yielded by their own family members. In return, essentials for subsistence are provided to them. 41.33 percent have 11-20 *beigha* of land. Only 1.33 percent have land above 30 *beigha*. These are the *Thakurs* of the area having huge amount of land. In Lahoul the land is not always hundred percent cultivable as around 30 percent of the area is always kept for growing grass for cattle. This grass is kept in reserve for the winter seasons for the cattle.

The average land holding of an household in Lahoul is 14.13 *beigha.*

1A.3 Main Fuel Used in Kitchen

None of the households are found to be mainly depending on the Liquid Petroleum Gas (LPG) as the fuel in the kitchen. The reason of this type of usage behaviour is that in Lahoul the roads are not present in every village, terrain is very rough, so the suppiy of gas cylinder is very limited. The trucks of filled cylinders reaches to only those villages which lie on the Manali – Ladakh highway. People living in far off villages reaches the main road to get their cylinders filled. In addition to this, the economic conditions also affect the consumption pattern.

The maximum consumption of the fuel in the kitchen is wood (94.67 percent). Wood as a fuel is available to people as a natural resource. But with the advancing time the availability of wood in the forests is decreasing, thus people have to buy wood from the government shops opened in the area. However, there is also certain degree of disobedience of the official order of not cutting trees. Consumption of wood as a fuel in the kitchen serves the double purpose of fuel and of providing heat also.

1A.4 System of Disposal of Human Waste

It has been found that 87.00 percent of people have their own pit. These are also known as dry toilets. The excreta collected in the room below the toilet is removed from time to time and is spread in the agricultural fields. It is believed that if the excreta of the family is spread in their own field than the yield will be good. Only 9.67 percent of the households are reported to have the flush type of toilet. However, a small percentage of 3.00 percent households have no toilets.These people defecate in open.

1A.5 Housing Conditions

It has been observed that, in the villages of Lahoul, the houses are predominantly wooden. 77.33 percent houses are made by using stone, wood and mud. The reason for high percentage of tribal population living in the wooden houses is the ecology of the area. Since Lahoul is a cold desert, the temperature falls down to minus 15°C in winters. In such less temperatures, only wooden houses would be warm enough to sustain life without centralized heating. 15.00 percent population stay in *Kuccha* house. Only 7.67 percent houses are *Pucca* or cemented. These houses have an asbestos or tin roof. Asbestos roof or tin roof is symbolic of richness in Lahoul. The richest in the village has a cemented house.

1A.6 Housing Floors

It have been found out that 64.67 percent of the households have houses having double storey. 27.67 percent houses have single storey and 7.67 percent houses have triple storey. Majority of Lahoulis prefer having double storey house as many rooms are used as store rooms for storing the ration for the 6-8 months of winter season.

1A.7 Number of Rooms

It has been observed that majority of people reside in houses with 4-6 rooms. 27.00 percent of houses have 1-3 rooms. Only a small percentage of 0.67 percent of houses has more than 15 rooms. These are the *Thakurs* of high economic status, who have inherited these houses from their ancestors.

1A.8 Ownership of House

63.67 percent of the tribal population have inherited the houses from their ancestors. 30.67 percent reported that they have constructed their own house. A small percentage of 5.67 percent Lahoulis do not have their own house. They are residing in the rented accommodation. These are the people who are living separately from their families, in different villages because of their jobs and thus hiring a room.

1A.9 Drainage System

It has been observed that the maximum of 98.33 percent households have open drains. Only 1.67 percent of households have closed drains. However no house has been reported to be found without any drain.

1A.10 Location of Water Supply

It reveals that maximum of 93.33 percent of the households have their source of water outside the house. Only a small percentage of 6.67 percent households have the source of water supply in their house. It is believed in Lahoul that those who have the source of water in their houses are economically better than those who go out of house to collect water. Water collection is mainly confined to the women in the family. It is the responsibility of the women to fetch water from the nearest available water source for household activities. Since Lahoul is a hilly area, the main source of water is the melting of the glacier. However, in winters, the people of Lahoul depend on the under ground water, pulled out with the help of hand pumps.

1A.11 Economic Characteristics

Economic characteristics are widely acknowledged to execute dominant influence in the person's life and often act as relative indicators of the level of socio- economic status. It is believed that attitude towards work and occupation, working condition and nature of work have always influence on awareness of the individual. Table 5.3 presents economic characteristics among the tribal population of District Lahoul and Spiti. It shows that among the total population 12.33 percent are inactive, 44.33 percent are agriculturists, 31.00 percent are in service. Among males, the majority 43.50 percent are in service, 27.68 percent are in agriculture, 11.86 percent are inactive. Among females the majority of 68.29 percent are into agriculture, 13.01 are in service and are inactive each. In the belt of Himachal Pradesh women are more laborious than men. They work more in agricultural fields than men as is shown by the Table below.

Table 5.3 : Economic Characteristics Among the Tribal Population of District Lahoul and Spiti, Himachal Pradesh

Occupation	*Male*	*Percent*	*Female*	*Percent*	*Total*	*Percent*
Agriculturist	49	27.68	84	68.29	133	44.33
Service	77	43.50	16	13.01	93	31.00
Daily Labour	3	1.69	-	-	3	1.00
Business	19	10.73	4	3.25	23	7.67
Animal Husbandry	8	4.52	3	2.44	11	3.67
Inactive	21	11.86	16	13.01	37	12.33
Total	177	100.00	123	00.00	300	100.00

Table 5.4 presents the data of the main occupation of 300 households among the tribal population of District Lahoul and Spiti. The occupation

which is the major source of income for the household is known as the main occupation. 72.33 percent of the households have agriculture as their main occupation. 25.00 percent households reported service as their main occupation. Only a small percentage of 2.67 percent households has business as their main occupation.

Table 5.4 : Main Occupation of the Households Among the Tribal Population of District Lahoul and Spiti, Himachal Pradesh

Occupation	*Households*	*Percent*
Agriculture	217	72.33
Service	75	25.00
Daily Labor	-	-
Business	8	2.67
Total	300	100.00

The occupation which is the source of highest amount of money after the main occupation is known as subsidiary occupation. 52.33 percent of the households have no subsidiary occupation. These are the households which have single source of income. 17.33 percent of the households have small business to support their main source of income. 15.00 percent of the households report that service is their subsidiary source of income. The 14.33 percent of households have agriculture as their subsidiary income.

1A.12 Household Income

Household income is an indicator of socio-economic status. It has been observed that the better is the income of the household, better are the facilities present like TV, radio, newspaper, magazines etc. The monthly household income distribution i.e. total money income received by all earning members of a household has been studied. Table 5.5 shows the monthly income of the households among the tribal population of District Lahoul and Spiti. It shows that the lowest income group has been reported by 15.00 percent of the households. The maximum of 36.67 percent of tribal population earn on an average between Rs. 5100 to Rs.15,000 per month. In the category of those earning more than Rs. 40,000 per month, only 2.33 percent households have been found. The average monthly income of Lahoulis is calculated to be Rs.15,222.

Table 5.5 : Monthly Income of the Households Among the Tribal Population of District Lahoul and Spiti, Himachal Pradesh

Income Slabs(Rs)	*Households*	*Percent*
0-5000	45	15.00
5100-10000	110	36.67
10100-15000	64	21.33
15100-20000	41	13.67
20100-25000	15	5.00
25100-30000	11	3.67
30100-35000	3	1.00
35100-40000	4	1.33
40100-45000	2	0.67
45100-50000	1	0.33
50100-55000	-	-
55100-60000	-	-
60100-65000	-	-
65100-70000	1	0.33
70100-75000	2	0.67
>75000	1	0.33
Total	300	100.00

1B. Rural Population

The State of Haryana is situated in the North –Western part of India between 27°39′ and 30°55′ north latitudes and between 74°28′ and 77°36′ east longitude. The area of the State is 44,212 square kilometer. According to Census of India, 2001, total population of Haryana is 210.83 Lac. This means that Haryana, which comprises 1.44 percent area of India, sustains 2.05 percent of the population of the country. Among the states and union territories in the country, Haryana ranks 16th in terms of population size.

Haryana as a state has two locational advantages which have promoted its rapid development. First, it borders Delhi, which provides a vast market for its goods and employment for its people. Second, people and goods to reach Punjab, Himachal Pradesh, Jammu & Kashmir, and the Union Territory of Chandigarh from the rest of the country need to pass through Haryana, which makes Haryana a prime transit state.

The state of Haryana is divided into 19 districts. For the present study, work was conducted in the District of Rohtak, as it is the closest district from Delhi, thus receiving the maximum influence of the neighborhood of the metropolitan city. The Rohtak District contributes 4.46 percent of the state population. This districts stands at 13th position in growth of population. The districts lies in the South–east of Haryana State between 28°19′ and 29°18′

Table 5.6 : Distribution of Households and Rural Population of District Rohtak, Haryana

Village	*Households*						*Population*		
	Jat	*Percent*	*Brahmin*	*Percent*	*Total*	*Percent*	*Male Percent*	*Female Percent*	*Total Percent*
Sampla	45	30.00	105	70.00	150	50.00	44.47	45.03	44.73
Naya Bans	75	100.00	-	-	75	25.00	23.46	24.91	24.14
Khedi	15	37.50	25	62.50	40	13.33	18.44	16.86	17.69
Gadi Gaon	35	100.00	-	-	35	11.67	13.63	13.21	13.43
Total	170	56.67	130	43.33	300	100.00	100.00	100.00	100.00

north latitude and 76°13′ and 77°13′ east longitude and is compact in shape. It is bounded by the Jind and Karnal Districts on the north, the Gurgoan and Mahendragarh districts on the south, the Union Territory of Delhi and the Meerut Districts (Uttar Pradesh) on the east and the districts of Jind and Hissar on the west.

The rural population comprised of Jat and Brahmin ethnic groups of Sampla Block, District Rohtak. These groups of people are found to be at a lower level of modernization and westernization. Rural population is characterized by predominant agriculturalism, a lesser density of population, homogeneity in racial and psycho-social traits of the rural communities, lesser differentiation and stratification of the society, direct relationship with nature and open farms.

1B.1 Households Coverage and Total Population

Table 5.6 presents the data on the distribution of the households and rural population of District Rohtak. It shows that maximum households have been collected from the village Sampla (50.00 percent), followed by Naya Bans (25.00 percent), Khedi (13.33 percent), Gadi Gaon (11.67 percent). Out of the total households, 56.67 percent households are of Jat and 43.33 percent households are of Brahmin.

Village Sampla contributed to 44.73 percent of the total population, 4.47 percent males and 45.03 percent females. Village Naya Bans shares the percentage with 24.14 percent population, followed by Khedi (17.69 percent population), Gadi Gaon (13.43 percent population).

1B.2 Land Holding Pattern

Table 5.7 presents the land holding pattern of the rural population of District Rohtak, Haryana. It shows that a total of 32.67 percent households have been found to be land less. These are the households who do not have individual land holdings and who do not either take the share from the income as they are in jobs. Among Jat 22.35 percent households are landless. The maximum of 50.59 percent households have land between one to ten *beigha.* Among Brahmin 46.15 percent households are found to be landless. The maximum of 23.85 percent households have land between 11 to 20 *beigha.* The average land holding of an household in Sampla Block is 9.1 *beigha.*

As Jat and Brahmin were showing similar frequency in various socio-cultural and economic characteristics, they were pooled up for the further analysis. The reason for this type of response could be the common geographical environment in which both the communities live. Thus getting a common conditioning and a common exposure.

Table 5.7 : Land Holding Pattern of Rural Population of District Rohtak, Haryana

Land Holdings (beigha)	*Number of Households*					
	Jat	*Percent*	*Brahmin*	*Percent*	*Total*	*Percent*
Land less	38	22.35	60	46.15	98	32.67
1-10	86	50.59	30	23.08	116	38.67
11-20	29	17.06	31	23.85	60	20.00
21-30	8	4.71	4	3.08	12	4.00
31-40	2	1.18	3	2.31	5	1.67
41-50	3	1.76	2	1.54	5	1.67
51-60	4	2.35	-	-	4	1.33
61-70	-	-	-	-	-	-
>70	-	-	-	-	-	-
Total	170	100.00	130	100.00	300	100.00

One beigha land = 880 sq. yards

1B.3 Main Fuel Used in Kitchen

It is found that in 65.33 percent of households the main fuel used in the kitchen is Liquid Petroleum Gas (LPG). The consumption of LPG is reported to be higher among the rural population than tribal population. The main reason is the easy availability of the gas cylinders. 19.67 percent of the households reports that the main fuel used is wood and in 11.67 percent of the households the main fuel used is cow dung. Only a small percentage of 3.33 percent of the households have coal as their main fuel in the kitchen.

1B.4 System of Disposal of Human Waste

It is reported that 88.33 percent of households have their own flush. 11.67 percent of households have no latrine as they cannot afford the expenditures involved in the construction of the flush toilet in their houses. Thus, they go in open fields for defecating. This type of behaviour is seen in the households belonging to low income group.

1B. 5 Housing Conditions

It has been observed that, in the villages of Sampla Block, the houses are predominantly *pucca* or cemented. 75.00 percent houses are cemented.

25.00 percent houses are *kuccha.* However none of the houses were made of wood. The reason for high percentage of rural population living in cemented house is that in geographically plain areas of Haryana, the concept of living in wooden houses in not very much in vogue. It is generally observed that houses in an area are constructed with the material available in the area. Economically very poor people would also live in cemented rooms.

1B. 6 Housing Floors

It has been observed that 70.00 percent of houses are single storeyed. 25.00 percent houses are double storeyed. However, the minimum of 5.00 percent houses are triple storeyed.

1B.7 Number of Rooms

It has been reported that majority of rural population (61.67 percent) resides in the houses with 4 to 6 rooms, followed by 20.00 percent of people living in the houses with 1 to 3 rooms. Only 1.33 percent of the houses have 13 to 15 rooms, thus belonging to a high strata in the society.

1B. 8 Ownership of House

It has been found that majority of the population i.e. 51.67 percent have inherited their houses from their ancestors. 40.00 percent of the population has constructed their houses. Only a small percentage of 8.33 percent population have reported to be residing in the rented accommodation. These are the people who are not the permanent residents of the villages in which work was conducted. These people have migrated from the interiors of more rural villages to the less rural villages because of relatively better educational and job opportunities.

1B. 9 Drainage System

It has been observed that open drains are pre-dominant in the area as 57.67 percent households have open drains.However, 42.33 percent houses have closed drains.At the Block Level, the Block Development and Panchayat Officer (BDPO) are responsible for sanctioning the money for the development of the block for, running all the development programmes. In the Sampla Block, at the village panchayat level, the job of maintenance of the village is allotted to the Sarpanch.This includes forwarding requests for making and maintaining drains, providing potable water to the villagers, converting *kucca* roads to *pucca* roads , organizing for village level celebrations like – *Ramlilla, Jagran, Kirtan, Bhandara* (open feast).

1B.10 Location of Water Supply

It has been observed that in the majority of the households i.e. 96.67 percent the source of water is within the boundaries of the houses.Only 3.33 percent of the households have to move out of their house boundaries to collect water. None of the household has reported to be going outside the village to collect water.

1B. 11 Economic Characteristics

Table 5.8 presents the economic characteristics of the rural population of the District Rohtak. It has been observed that 5.33 percent of respondents are inactive. They do not contribute to the Unit of production of the household. Agriculture as an occupation engages the majority of 35.33 percent among the economically active population. 31.33 percent are in service, 12.00 percent in business.Among males and females the maximum percentage has been observed as 36.07 percent and 34.19 percent respectively.

Table 5.8 : Economic Characteristics Among the Rural Population of District Rohtak, Haryana

Occupation	*Male*	*Percent*	*Female*	*Percent*	*Total*	*Percent*
Agriculture	66	36.07	40	34.19	106	35.33
Service	56	30.60	38	32.48	94	31.33
Daily Labour	16	8.74	-	-	16	5.33
Business	26	14.21	10	8.55	36	12.00
Animal Husbandry	10	5.46	22	18.80	32	10.67
Inactive	9	4.92	7	5.98	16	5.33
Total	183	100.00	117	100.00	300	100.00

Table 5.9 presents the main occupation of the rural population of District Rohtak. It shows that 45.33 percent of the households have agriculture as their main occupation. Thus, the major source of income of the rural population is agriculture. However, 36.00 percent of households are into service. The various types of services which people are doing varies from services in government sector and private sector. Most of those who are engaged in

service moves out to near by areas like Bahadurgarh, Rohtak, Delhi. Least of all is 3.36 percent for those who depend on live stock as their major source of income.

Table 5.9 : Main Occupation Among the Rural Population of District Rohtak, Haryana

Occupation	*Households*	*Percent*
Agriculture	136	45.33
Service	108	36.00
Daily Labour	25	8.33
Business	20	6.67
Animal Husbandry	11	3.67
Total	300	100.00

It reports that for 59.00 percent of households there is no subsidiary occupation and these households have only one source of income. 33.67 percent of households have agriculture as a subsidiary occupation. For 4.33 percent of households, service is the subsidiary occupation.

Only 1.67 percent of the household reports the occupation of business as their subsidiary occupation.

1B. 12 Household Income

Table 5.10 presents the monthly income of rural population of District Rohtak. It shows that the majority of the households i.e. 46.00 percent of rural population come under the slab Rs. 5000 as their monthly income. 38.00 percent of rural households earn on an average between Rs.5100 to Rs.10,000 per month. No households are found in the category of those earning more than Rs. 40,000 per month. The average monthly income of the rural population is calculated to be Rs. 5656.89.

Table 5.10 : Monthly Household Income of Rural Population of District Rohtak, Haryana

Income Slabs(Rs)	*Households*	*Percent*
0-5000	138	46.00
5100-10000	114	38.00
10100-15000	15	5.00

(Contd.)

(Contd. Table 5.10)

Income Slabs(Rs)	*Households*	*Percent*
15100-20000	20	6.67
20100-25000	4	1.33
25100-30000	7	2.33
30100-35000	-	-
35100-40000	2	0.67
40100-45000	-	-
45100-50000	-	-
50100-55000	-	-
55100-60000	-	-
60100-65000	-	-
65100-70000	-	-
70100-75000	-	-
>75000	-	-
Total	300	100.00

1 C. Urban Population

Delhi is situated on the right bank of the river Yamuna at the periphery of the Gangetic plains. It lies a little north of 28 N latitude and a little to the west of 78 Longitude. One of the seven Union Territories, Delhi enjoys the privilege of being the capital of the Indian 'Union of States'. Delhi is unique in several respects in India's history of politics and governance. Besides being a metropolitan city with a cosmopolitan population, it is seat of power of the Republic with the Central Government, The Indian Parliament and the Supreme Court located in its territory.It is also the seat of several other apex institutions such as the Supreme Court of India, the National Human Rights Commission, the National Commission for Scheduled Castes and Scheduled Tribes, the National Commission for Women, the National Commission for Minorities, the National Legal Service Authority and the Communal Harmony Foundation.

Population of various states of India is declared 'urban' according to the definition given by census of India. For the present study the urban population of Delhi was selected because, Delhi not only has urban population, it is also a metropolitan city, with a cosmopolitan (multi-ethnic) environment. Multinational corporations, metro rail, fat salaries, snazzy eateries, swanky cars, neon signs, highways, flyovers, trendy apparel, vast multi-storeyed markets, wide roads, sub-ways, indoor stadiums and multiplex cinema halls and many more which makes it Metropolitan zone (Kapoor and Kapoor, 2001).

The Provisional population of NCT of Delhi is 13.78 million, consisting of 7.57 million males and 6.21 million females. The population of Delhi accounts for 1.34 percent of the total population of the country. Out of the nine districts, the North-west District with 2.85 million population constitutes 20.66 percent of the population of Delhi and is thus the most populated district. New Delhi District with 1.72 million population shares only 1.25 percent of Delhi's area and is thus ranked last. Right from ancient times and more so today, Delhi has been and remains a melting pot of varied peoples and cultures, giving it a truly cosmopolitan character. The demographic composition of Delhi consists first of all of the original population of Delhi which was, and still is mainly Urdu – speaking and Hindi speaking. Delhi, being the seat of power, has invited and attracted peoples of all hues and colours from all corners of India and even from outside. Delhi has multiethnic, multi-caste, multilingual and multi-religious settlements.

1C. 1 Household Coverage and Total Population

Table 5.11 shows distribution of households and urban population of Delhi. A total sample of 300 households have been collected from 10 different urban colonies in Delhi. To have a representative sample of the universe of the study, areas from all the district of Delhi have been covered. Out of the total population of 1575, 49.07 percent are males and 50.92 percent are females.

1C.2 Main Fuel Used in the Kitchen

It has been observe that 100.00 percent of the population use LPG gas cylinders as the main fuel in the kitchen. No users of kerosene, coal, cow dung have been reported among the urban population.

IC.3 System of Disposal of Human Wastes

It shows that all the households have the toilet facility. None of the households are without latrine. Hundred percent of households have their own flush toilets.

1C. 4 Housing Condition

It has been observed that hundred percent of houses are cemented. None of the houses of the respondents were either *kùccha* or wooden.

1C. 5 Housing Floors

It has been observed that majority of households among the Urban population (84.00 percent) have single storeyed houses. 15.00 percent of the

Table 5:11 : Distribution of Households and Population of Urban Population, Delhi

District	Area	Households	Male	Percent	Female	Percent	Total	Percent
South West	Najafgarh	30	65	8.41	77	9.60	142	9.02
North West	Jain Nagar	25	73	9.44	79	9.85	152	9.65
	Rohini	30	69	8.93	80	9.98	149	9.46
East	Vasundhara Enclave	30	86	11.13	74	9.23	160	10.16
	Mayur Vihar	25	89	11.51	92	11.47	181	11.49
West	Vipin Garden	25	90	11.64	110	13.72	200	12.70
North East	Dilshad Garden	30	98	12.68	86	10.72	184	11.68
South	Pamposh Enclave	20	47	6.08	52	6.48	99	6.29
Central	Inderpuri	60	79	10.22	67	8.35	146	9.27
North	Shakti Nagar	25	77	9.96	85	10.60	162	10.29
	Total	300	773	100.00	802	100.00	1575	100.00

households have reported to have double storey. Only three households (1.00 percent) among the urban population has triple storey house.

1C. 6 Number of Rooms

It shows that 50.00 percent of the houses have 1 to 3 rooms. 43.67 percent of the respondents reside in the houses having 4 to 6 rooms. 4.00 percent houses have 7 to 9 rooms. Only 2.00 percent houses are reported to have 10 to 12 houses. Only one house (0.33 percent) has been found to have rooms between 13 to 15.

1C. 7 Ownership of House

Delhi is a metropolitan city. The property in terms of land is considered a valuable asset of the household. Land is believed to be the most costly in the National Capital Region of Delhi. However those who are the early residents of the city owns property in the capital. In today's time buying a property is extremely difficult, because of sky rising prices of the property.

It has been observed that 33.00 percent of the people are reported to have inherited the house from their ancestors. 43.33 percent of households are those who have constructed their house. A major percentage of 23.67 percent households are renting a house.

1C. 8 Drainage System

It has been observed that closed drains are pre-dominant as hundred percent households have reported to have closed drains. Urban population has maximum percent of households having closed drains in comparison to tribal and rural population.

1C. 9 Location of Water Supply

It shows that all the households have their source of water in the boundaries of their houses. None of the members of any household have to move out from their houses for the purpose of collection of water.

1C. 10 Economic Characteristic

Table 5.12 presents the economic characteristics among the urban population of Delhi. It shows that 61.00 percent of the urban population are retired from various services, 23.33 percent are in service, 15.33 percent are in business. Among males and females the majority of respondents are retired, 50.97 percent and 71.72 percent respectively.

Table 5.12 : Economic Characteristics Among the Urban Population, Delhi

Occupation	*Male*	*Percent*	*Female*	*Percent*	*Total*	*Percent*
Service	40	25.81	30	20.69	70	23.33
Daily Labour	-	-	1	0.69	1	0.33
Business	36	23.23	10	6.90	46	15.33
Animal Husbandry	-	-	-	-	-	-
Retired	79	50.97	104	71.72	183	61.00
Total	155	100.00	145	100.00	300	100.00

Table 5.13 shows the main occupation of the households among the urban population of Delhi. It has been observed that 91.67 percent of the urban households have service as their main occupation, as for these households service is the major source of income in the family, 7.00 percent households have business as their main occupation. However, it also shows that for 1.33 percent of the households there is no main source of occupation.

Table 5.13 : Main Occupation of the Households Among the Urban Population, Delhi

Occupation	*Households*	*Percent*
Service	275	91.67
Business	21	7.00
Retired	4	1.33
Total	300	100.00

Table 5.14 shows the subsidiary occupation of the households among the urban population of Delhi. These are the occupations which are the additional source of the income for the household, apart from the main income. The Table reports that for the 94.67 percent of households there is no subsidiary

Table 5.14 : Subsidiary Occupation of the Households Among the Urban Population, Delhi

Occupation	*Households*	*Percent*
Agriculture	-	-
Service	6	2.00
Daily Labour	-	-
Business	10	3.33
No Subsidiary Occupation	284	94.67
Total	300	100.00

occupation. Thus they have only one source of income. 3.33 percent of households have business as a subsidiary occupation. They either have income from their business or their own shops. Only 2 percent of the households have service as their subsidiary occupation.

1C.11 Household Income

Table 5.15 presents the monthly household income among the urban population of Delhi. It depicts that 12.33 percent of the urban population come under the slab of Rs.5000 as their monthly income. The maximum of 25.33 percent of households earn on an average between Rs. 5100 to Rs.10,000 per month. In the category of those earning more than Rs. 40,000 per month, only 8.33 percent of the households have been found. The urban population shows 4.33 percent of those earning more than Rs. 50,000 per month. The reason being Delhi is metropolitan city, which has various opportunities to offer to the people in terms of educational facilities and occupational opportunities. The average monthly income of the urban population is calculated to be Rs. 19,461.

Table 5.15 : Monthly Household Income Among the Urban Population, Delhi

Income Slabs (Rs)	*Households*	*Percent*
0-5000	37	12.33
5100-10000	76	25.33
10100-15000	47	15.67
15100-20000	32	10.67
20100-25000	33	11.00
25100-30000	25	8.33
30100-35000	9	3.00
35100-40000	16	5.33
40100-45000	8	2.67
45100-50000	4	1.33
50100-55000	2	0.67
55100-60000	5	1.67
60100-65000	2	0.67
65100-70000	-	-
70100-75000	-	-
>75000	4	1.33
Total	300	100.00

5.2 Socio – Cultural Characteristics

Socio-cultural characteristics are the indicators of any ethnic group which gives an insight of the cultural belief system of the group. Various indicators like family pattern, ways of organizing marriage in the society, prevalence of consanguineous marriages among the members of the community, religion followed etc gives an insight of the ethnic group. In this section few of the socio-cultural characteristics of tribal, rural, urban populations have been presented.

2A. Tribal Population

The tribal population of Lahoul and Spiti District have distinct cultural characteristics. The extreme hardships faced by the people of Lahoul reflect well in their social ideals and social organization. All social ideals and social organisation are directed towards the achievement of basic objective of being a self–sufficient and self sustained unit. Family or household is the basic unit of the social organisation. It is a corporate unit for its members. It fulfills all the basic needs of the individual such as social, economic, emotional, and psychological; the community gives more recognition to a household than to an individual.

2A.1 Type of Families

It shows that among the tribal population 48.33 percent families are reported to be nuclear and 51.67 percent are joint families. There is a consistent rise in the emergence of number of nuclear families. The rise in this trend can be attributed to the fact that newer generations are moving in order to have higher education.With the widening of avenues and government providing infrastructure facilities there is some inclination among the people towards getting educated. Primary schools, middle schools, secondary schools, senior secondary schools, and also colleges and vocational training schools are available in the area. Education has opened up new opportunities of employment and helped in raising the economic standards of the people. Education has brought about the mobility among the people. Once educated, they don't want to come back to the agricultural economy. Thus making their own nuclear family.

2A.2 Type of Marriages

It has been observed that in Lahoul, monogamy (91.00 percent) is the general rule, but polygamy is also practiced among the tribal population of Lahoul. Fraternal polyandry and polygyny have been practiced in Lahoul since olden times.The instances of polyandry (8.00 percent) are more as compared to those of polygyny (1.00 percent). The reasons for polygyny are however either the requirement of more working hands in the family unit or impotency of wife leading to sororate type of polygyny or any extra marital affair of the husband ending in a marriage. However, now practice of polyandry and polygyny has declined much.

2A.3. Crosscousin Marriages

It has been observed that the majority of tribals i.e. 70.33 percent said that cross cousin marriages are not a feature of their society. However, 29.67 percent tribal population endorsed the fact that these types of marriages are a common feature in their society. Even till date people marry among their cousin. Matrilineal Cross-Cousin Marriage (MLCC) is more prevalent than Patrilineal Cross- Cousin Marriage (PLCC).

It has been observed that there is difference of prevalence of cross cousin marriages with reference to Hinduism and Buddhism. In Hinduism, all respondents said that these marriages are not prevalent in their religion.However,, there is mix response among those who follow Buddhism. 51.74 percent said that these marriages are prevalent in their religion and 48.26 percent respondents said that cross cousin marriages do not happen in their religion.

2A.4 Religion Practiced

It has been observed that 42.67 percent people follow Hinduism and 57.33 percent tribal follows Buddhism, as Lahoul has been under the impact of Ladakh.

2A. 5 Reading News Paper

It has been observed that only 8.33 percent of the population reads news paper. Majority of people (91.67 percent) do not read new paper at all. There are various factors for this type of reading behavior. First is the lack of interest, education, non –availability of news paper, lack of time etc.

2B. RURAL POPULATION

2B.1 Type of Families

It reports that 48.00 percent families are of nuclear type. Majority of 52.00 percent are joint families. Rural population are majorly joint in nature. But the family patterns are changing fast in the area, owing to the reasons of occupation. People have started moving out of the area for the purpose of earning their livelihood as sustaining only on agriculture is becoming difficult in today's time.

2B.2 Type of Marriages

It reveals that in the rural population only monogamy is found. No instances of polyandry and polygyny have been found as in Hinduism only monogamy is permitted.

2B.3. Cross Cousin Marriages

It has been observed that cross-cousin marriages are absolutely non prevalent among the rural population as Hinduism does not permit cross cousin marriage.

2B. 4 Religion Practiced

It has been observed that the hundred percent religion of the population in the rural area is Hinduism as the majority of the population of Haryana follows Hinduism.

2B. 5 Reading News Paper

It shows that majority of 58.33 percent of respondents reads the news paper and 41.67 percent do not read news paper. Those who do not read news paper are either illiterate or do not have money or have no interest in reading newspaper. Rural population is found to be more in the habit of reading news paper than the tribal population.

2C. Urban Population

2C.1 Type of Families

It has been observed that 55.67 percent families are nuclear, where as 44.33 percent are joint families. Delhi is a place of opportunity, many people migrate from their native places to Delhi in search of job thus detaching from their own families and gradually settling in Delhi and forming their own nuclear family.

2C.2 Type of Marriages

It has been observed that hundred percent informants of urban population practice monogamy as the major religion found in the sample collected is Hinduism and the constitution does not allow the second marriage of husband or wife in the presence of either partner, under the Hindu Marriage Act.

2C.3 Cross Cousin Marriages

It has been observed that in the urban population the consanguineous marriages were totally absent as all the respondents are found to be following Hinduism which does not favour cross cousin marriage.

2C.4 Religion Practiced

It has been observed that all the urban population follows Hinduism as their religion.

2C. 5 Reading News Paper

It has been observed that majority of urban population (68.67 percent) reads news paper. However in the urban population there are 31.33 percent of the respondents who do not read news paper. The reasons are due to lack of interest, eye problems, scarcity of time etc.

5.3 Population Characteristics

The population characteristics is taken as the internal structure of an ethnic group with regards to one or more demographic traits such as age, sex, marital status and economic activities, education characteristics etc at a given period of time. It is believed that population characteristics plays an important role in increasing the awareness of a person. Modernizing influences such as education and exposure through occupation are also important catalysts for knowledge and awareness of a person. This section deals with demographic profile such as age and sex composition, marital status, age at marriage, educational status, occupational status, respondent's characteristics.

3A. Tribal Population

3A.1 Age Structure and Sex Ratio

The age composition or age structure is basic and important demographic characteristic of the population. The measure of age composition is the percent distribution of the population at various age categories simultaneously cross classified by sex. The present data on age is collected in terms of completed whole and full years. The age data has been further categorized into five years groups instead of year numbers.

Table 5.16 presents the age structure and sex ratio among the tribal population of District Lahoul and Spiti. It reports that the age distribution of the total population have shown 16.54 percent of population under 15 years and 14.27 percent in the age group of 60+. It shows that the proportion of child population (0 -15) and old population (above 60) is almost same. The next broad age group of 16-50 years, 57.07 percent population lies in this group thus observing the population at fertile and peak productive ages. In the total population, 53.16 percent (842) are males and 46.84 percent (742) are females. Among males, the maximum percent is in the age of 16 to 20 years and among females, the maximum percentage is in the age of 26 to 30 years.

Maximum Sex Ratio of 1315.79 is found in the age group of 66 to 70 years, where as the lowest sex ratio of 500 is found in the age group of 6 to 10 years. Average sex ratio of the sample collected is 881.24 which is found to be higher than at the District level (804) and lesser than State level (970) (Census, 2001). The

Table 5.16 : Age Structure and Sex Ratio Among the Tribal Population of Lahoul and Spiti District, Himachal Pradesh

Age (years)	*Male*	*Percent*	*Female*	*Percent*	*Total*	*Percent*	*Sex Ratio*
0-5	42	4.99	30	4.04	72	4.55	714.29
6--10	50	5.94	25	3.37	75	4.73	500.00
11--15	71	8.43	44	5.93	115	7.26	619.72
16-20	89	10.57	67	9.03	156	9.85	752.81
21-25	84	9.98	68	9.16	152	9.60	809.52
26-30	78	9.26	96	12.94	174	10.98	1230.77
31-35	54	6.41	56	7.55	110	6.94	1037.04
36-40	58	6.89	49	6.60	107	6.76	844.83
41-45	39	4.63	44	5.93	83	5.24	1128.21
46-50	62	7.36	60	8.09	122	7.70	967.74
51-55	63	7.48	55	7.41	118	7.45	873.02
56-60	33	3.92	41	5.53	74	4.67	1242.42
61-65	37	4.39	22	2.96	59	3.72	594.59
66-70	19	2.26	25	3.37	44	2.78	1315.79
>70	63	7.48	60	8.09	123	7.77	952.38
TOTAL	842	100.00	742	100.00	1584	100.00	881.24

sex ratio of the total population (881.24) is found to be lower than the sex ratio of Hamirpur (1102), Kangra (1027), Mandi (1014), Una (997), Bilaspur (992), Chamba (961), Kullu (928), Sirmaur (901), Shimla (898) and higher than Solan (853), Kinnaur (851) districts as shown in Table 5.17.

Table 5.17 : Sex Ratio of Various Districts of Himachal Pradesh

S.No.	*District*	*Sex Ratio*
1.	Hamirpur	1102
2.	Kangra	1027
3.	Mandi	1014
4.	Una	997
5.	Bilaspur	992
6.	Chamba	961
7.	Kullu	928
8.	Sirmaur	901
9.	Shimla	898
10.	Solan	853
11.	Kinnaur	851
12.	Lahoul and Spiti	804 (Census, 2001) 881.24 (Present Study)

3A. 2 Literacy Rate

Literacy rate express the number of literate persons in a population who are able to read and write with understanding in at least one language at a specified time. Table 5.18 presents the literacy rate among the tribal population of District Lahoul and Spiti. It shows that among the total population of illiterates maximum (40.27 percent) percentage is obtained in the age group of above 60 years. Thus it can be said that literacy in the earlier times was not in vogue. Earlier the educational infrastructure was lacking far behind as compared to contemporary situation. 1.77 percent of the population is illiterate which lies in the age group of 6-10 years, when all the children are expected to be literate. Among the illiterate males and females, the maximum proportion of illiterates are in the age group of above 70 years.

Among total population of literates the maximum percentage of literates is in the age group of 26 to 30 years. Only 3.89 percent of population above 60 years is literate. There is only 0.71 percent of literates in the age group of above 70 years. Thus, it can be said, with the advancing time, the younger generation is moving towards literacy. Among literate males, the maximum percentage of 12.98 percent is observed in the age group of 16 to 20 years. Literacy rate among males of the tribal population is 80.52 percent.

Table 5.18 : Literacy Rate Among the Tribal Population of District Lahoul and Spiti, Himachal Pradesh

	Illiterate			*Literate*		
Age (years)	*Male (Percent)*	*Female (Percent)*	*Total (Percent)*	*Male (Percent)*	*Female (Percent)*	*Total (Percent)*
0-5	25.61	10.07	15.71	-	-	-
6-10	3.05	1.04	1.77	6.64	4.85	5.92
11-15	1.22	-	0.44	10.18	9.69	9.98
16-20	0.61	-	0.22	12.98	14.76	13.69
21-25	0.61	2.43	1.77	12.24	13.66	12.81
26-30	-	2.43	1.55	11.50	19.60	14.75
31-35	0.61	3.13	2.21	7.82	10.35	8.83
36-40	1.83	6.25	4.65	8.11	6.83	7.60
41-45	3.05	5.90	4.87	5.01	5.95	5.39
46-50	5.49	11.46	9.29	7.82	5.95	7.07
51-55	5.49	12.85	10.18	7.96	3.96	6.36
56-60	3.66	9.03	7.08	3.98	3.30	3.71
61-65	9.15	6.60	7.52	3.24	0.66	2.21
66-70	5.49	8.33	7.30	1.47	0.22	0.97
>70	34.15	20.49	25.44	1.03	0.22	0.71
TOTAL	100.00	100.00	100.00	100.00	100.00	100.00

Among literate females the maximum percentage of 19.60 percent is found to be present in the age group of 26 to 30 years. Literacy rate among females of tribal population is 61.91 percent which is less than males because females get lesser opportunities of studies than males in Lahoul. Females are more laborious than males in Lahoul.

Literary Rate among total tribal population is 71.46 percent which is lower than the District Literacy Rate (73.17 percent) and State Literacy Rate (77.13 percent).The literacy rate calculated from the tribal population (71.46) is found to be lower than Hamirpur (83.16 percent), Una (81.09 percent), Kangra (80.68 percent), Shimla (79.68 percent), Bilaspur (78.80 percent), Solan (77.16 percent), Mandi (75.86 percent), Kullu (73.36 percent) and higher than Sirmaur (70.68 percent) and Chamba (63.73 percent) districts.

Table 5.19 shows that, the majority of 35.00 percent of the tribal respondents are graduates or above and 24.33 percent are illiterates. Among males the majority of 47.46 percent respondents are minimum graduates or above. Among females the majority of 41.46 percent are illiterates. Thus, illiteracy is reported to be higher among females and higher education is more among males and less among females. The reason for this type of trend of literacy among the Lahouli males and females is because of their agricultural economy. Young female child is preferably kept at home to take care of other siblings. Adult females, on the other hand, keep busy with the agricultural work. Males generally move out for continuing their higher studies or to do some business.

Table 5.19 : Educational Status Among the Tribal Population of District Lahoul and Spiti, Himachal Pradesh

Education	*Male*	*Percent*	*Female*	*Percent*	*Total*	*Percent*
Illiterate	22	12.43	51	41.46	73	24.33
Primary	10	5.65	23	18.70	33	11.00
Middle	27	15.25	12	9.76	39	13.00
10th passed	20	11.30	9	7.32	29	9.67
12th passed	14	7.91	7	5.69	21	7.00
Graduates and above	84	47.46	21	17.07	105	35.00
Total	177	100.00	123	100.00	300	100.00

Table 5.20 : Marital Status Among the Tribal Population of District Lahoul and Spiti, Himachal Pradesh

	Unmarried			*Married*			*Divorced / Widowed*		
Age (years)	*Male (Percent)*	*Female (Percent)*	*Total (Percent)*	*Male (Percent)*	*Female (Percent)*	*Total (Percent)*	*Male (Percent)*	*Female (Percent)*	*Total (Percent)*
0-5	10.12	9.58	9.89	-	-	-	-	-	-
6--10	12.05	7.99	10.30	-	-	-	-	-	-
11--15	17.11	14.06	15.80	-	-	-	-	-	-
16-20	21.45	21.41	21.43	-	-	-	-	-	-
21-25	17.59	15.65	16.76	2.88	5.16	4.00	-	-	-
26-30	10.36	12.46	11.26	9.16	15.22	12.13	-	1.64	0.94
31-35	2.65	3.19	2.88	11.26	12.50	11.87	-	-	-
36-40	3.13	3.51	3.30	11.52	10.05	10.80	2.22	1.64	1.89
41-45	0.96	2.56	1.65	8.90	9.24	9.07	2.22	3.28	2.83
46-50	1.45	4.47	2.75	14.14	11.41	12.80	4.44	6.56	5.66
51-55	0.96	1.28	1.10	14.40	12.77	13.60	8.89	6.56	7.55
56-60	0.48	1.60	0.96	7.85	8.70	8.27	2.22	6.56	4.72
61-65	0.24	0.96	0.55	7.33	3.80	5.60	17.78	8.20	12.26
66-70	0.00	0.32	0.14	3.93	4.62	4.27	8.89	11.48	10.38
>70	1.45	0.96	1.24	8.64	6.52	7.60	53.33	54.10	53.77
Total	100.00	100.00	100.00	100.00	100.00	100.00	100.00	100.00	100.00

3A.3 Marital Status

Table 5.20 presents the marital status among the tribal population of District Lahoul and Spiti. It shows that in the category of unmarried total population, the maximum percent of21.43 percent population is unmarried in the age group of 16 to 20 years. 11.68 percent of the total population is still unmarried which lies in the age group of above 35 years. This sheds light on one aspect of the society. In Lahoul, being unmarried for ever is not tabooed. Unmarried members of a family are not a burden on the household, as they are the most potential workers of the house. Since the unmarried members are free from the responsibilities of family and children, so they get involved in the unit of production by being an integral part of agricultural economy.

Among the married total population, the maximum percentage of 13.60 percent is found in the age group of 51 to 55 years. It is to be noted here that incidence of married population begins after the age of 20 years, thus indicating at a higher average age of marriage for males and females.

Among the divorced or widowed category, the maximum percentage of 53.77 percent is found in the age group of above 70 years.

3A. 4 Age at Marriage

Maximum number of males i.e. 15.93 percent, got married at the age of 25 years. Maximum percent of females i.e. 12.79 percent got married at the age of 20 and 23 years. In the category of males, no marriage is found to happen after 38 years and in the category of females, no marriage has happened after the age of 35 years. On the other hand 2.58 percent marriages of males has happened who are below 20 years and 6.51 percent of females are married who are below 18 years.

Average age at marriage for tribal population is 23.79 years. Average Age at marriage for males in the tribal population is 24.93 years. Average Age at marriage for females in the tribal population is 22.66 years. The reason for the high mean of marriage of males and females can be attributed to awareness about proper age of marriage, literacy and high status of women in the society.

3A.5 Respondent's Characteristics

It shows that out of total respondents, 59.00 percent are males and 41.00 percent are females. 69.67 percent of the total respondents are married, 21.67 percent are reported to be unmarried and 8.67 percent are divorced or widowed. Among males 75.14 percent are married and 20.34 percent are unmarried. Among females 61.79 percent are married and 23.58 percent are unmarried.

Table 5.21: Age Structure and Sex Ratio Among Rural Population of District Rohtak, Haryana

Age (years)	*Male*	*Percent*	*Female*	*Percent*	*Total*	*Percent*	*Sex Ratio*
0-5	75	8.38	50	6.29	125	7.40	666.67
6--10	70	7.82	54	6.79	124	7.34	771.43
11--15	85	9.50	54	6.79	139	8.22	635.29
16-20	114	12.74	105	13.21	219	12.96	921.05
21-25	101	11.28	94	11.82	195	11.54	930.69
26-30	67	7.49	62	7.80	129	7.63	925.37
31-35	61	6.82	58	7.30	119	7.04	950.82
36-40	69	7.71	56	7.04	125	7.40	811.59
41-45	40	4.47	55	6.92	95	5.62	1375.00
46-50	54	6.03	43	5.41	97	5.74	796.30
51-55	32	3.58	25	3.14	57	3.37	781.25
56-60	28	3.13	37	4.65	65	3.85	1321.43
61-65	36	4.02	21	2.64	57	3.37	583.33
66-70	21	2.35	30	3.77	51	3.02	1428.57
>70	42	4.69	51	6.42	93	5.50	1214.29
Total	895	100.00	795	100.00	1690	100.00	888.27

3B. Rural Population

3B.1 Age Structure and Sex Ratio

Table 5.21 shows the age structure and sex ratio among the rural population of District Rohtak. It reports the age distribution of the total population. 22.96 percent of the population is under 15 years of age and 11.89 percent of population is in the age group of 60+. It shows that the proportion of child population (0-15) is double to the old population (above 60 years). The next broad age group of 16-50 years, 57.93 percent population lies in this group thus observing the population at fertile and peak productive ages. In the total population, 52.96 percent (895) are males and 47.06 percent (795) are females. Among males and females, the maximum percent is in the age of 16 to 20 years.

Maximum sex ratio of 1428.57 is found in the age group of 66 to 70 years, where as the lowest sex ratio of 583.33 is found in the age group of 61 to 65 years. Average sex ratio of the sample collected is 888.27 which is found to be higher, than at the District level i.e. 847 females per 1000 males and also at State Level i.e. 867 females per 1000 males (Census, 2001). All India ratio of females per 1000 males is 949. In India Haryana is at 30th rank in this regard, while Kerala with sex ratio of 1058 ranks first in the country.

Table 5.22 :Sex Ratio of Various Districts in Haryana

S.No.	*District*	*Sex Ratio*
1.	Panchkula	823
2.	Ambala	869
3.	Yamunanagar	863
4.	Kurukshetra	866
5.	Kaithal	854
6.	Karnal	864
7.	Panipat	830
8.	Sonipat	839
9.	Jind	853
10.	Fatehabad	886
11.	Sirsa	882
12.	Hisar	852
13.	Bhiwani	880
14.	Jhajjar	848
15.	Mahendragarh	919
16.	Rewari	901
17.	Gurgaon	874
18.	Faridabad	839
19.	Rohtak	847 (Census, 2001) 888.27 (Present Study)

Table 5.22 shows that the sex ratio of the total population (888.27) is found to be lower than Mahendragarh (919), Rewari (901) and higher than rest of all other districts.

3B. 2 Literacy Rate

Table 5.23 presents the literacy rate among the rural population of District Rohtak. It shows that among the total population of illiterates, maximum (31.97 percent) percentage is obtained in the age group of above 60 years as all children were not send to school in the earlier times. A large percentage of 26.84 percent is found to be illiterate in the age category of 16 to 50 years. Among the illiterate males (18.14 percent) and females (14.08 percent), the maximum proportion of illiterates are in the age group of above 70 years. It is observed that illiteracy is found to be higher in the population of higher age group, as education in the earlier times was not considered important. Only a selected few could read and write.

Among total population of literates the maximum percentage (69.80 percent) of literates is in the age group of 16 to 50 years. Only 3.74 percent of population above 60 years is literate. Among literate males, the maximum percentage of 16.79 percent is observed in the age group of 16 to 20 years. Literacy rate among males of the rural population is 76.98 percent. Among literate females the maximum percentage of 19.77 percent is found to be present in the age group of 16 to 20 years. Literacy rate among females of rural population is 64.28 percent. Females have lesser literacy rate than males as females in Indian society are treated second to the males. They get lesser opportunities in terms of education as compared to males.

Literary Rate among total rural population is 71.12 percent which is higher than the district literacy rate (70.28 percent) and state literacy rate (67.9 percent). The literacy rate calculated from the rural population (71.12 percent) is found to be higher than Fatehabad (54.65), Kaithal (56.40), Sirsa (56.42), Jind (59.13), Hisar, (61.08), Karnal (63.57), Panipat (64.91), Yamunanagar (65.46), Bhiwani (65.94), Kurukshetra (66.00), Ambala (70.74) and Sonipat (71.08) and lower than rest of the districts.

Table 5.24 presents the educational status among the rural population of District Rohtak. It has been observed that, 28.88 percent of the total population are illiterate and 44.67 percent have studied till graduation or above. 10.24 percent of the sample have studied till graduation and above. Among males the majority of 60.66 percent are graduates or above, 20.77 percent are illiterate. The minimum of 2.73 percent of males are tenth passed. Among females the majority of 40.17 percent are illiterates, 24.79 percent are primary

Table 5.23 : Literacy Rate Among Rural Population of District Rohtak, Haryana

	Illiterate			*Literate*		
Age(Years)	*Male (Percent)*	*Female (Percent)*	*Total (Percent)*	*Male (Percent)*	*Female (Percent)*	*Total (Percent)*
0-5	35.78	17.25	25.00	-	-	-
6--10	6.86	2.82	4.51	7.67	10.18	8.74
11--15	-	-	-	12.16	12.33	12.23
16-20	-	-	-	16.79	19.77	18.05
21-25	0.49	2.82	1.84	13.02	14.48	13.64
26-30	0.98	3.17	2.25	9.12	11.35	10.07
31-35	3.92	5.63	4.92	8.39	8.22	8.32
36-40	3.43	6.69	5.33	9.41	7.05	8.40
41-45	4.41	8.10	6.56	4.78	6.46	5.49
46-50	4.41	7.04	5.94	6.66	4.70	5.82
51-55	3.92	6.69	5.53	3.62	1.17	2.58
56-60	2.94	8.45	6.15	2.89	2.94	2.91
61-65	7.84	7.04	7.38	2.89	0.20	1.75
66-70	6.86	10.21	8.81	1.01	0.20	0.67
>70	18.14	14.08	15.78	1.59	0.98	1.33
Total	100.00	100.00	100.00	100.00	100.00	100.00

passed and 19.66 percent are graduates or above. Thus, higher education is more among males and less among females, as the age of marriage of females (17.60 years) is lower than age of marriage of males (21.57 years). This prevents the females from getting higher education as compared to males.

Table 5.24 : Educational Status Among Rural Population of District Rohtak, Haryana

Education	*Male*	*Percent*	*Female*	*Percent*	*Total*	*Percent*
Illiterate	38	20.77	47	40.17	85	28.33
Primary	11	6.01	29	24.79	40	13.33
Middle	8	4.37	12	10.26	20	6.67
10th Passed	5	2.73	3	2.56	8	2.67
12th Passed	10	5.46	3	2.56	13	4.33
Graduates and Above	111	60.66	23	19.66	134	44.67
Total	183	100.00	117	100.00	300	100.00

3B.3 Marital Status

Table 5.25 shows the age and sex wise distribution of marital status among the rural population of District Rohtak. It is to be noted that in the category of total unmarried population, the maximum percentage of 26.36 percent lies in the age group of 16 to 20 years. 4.52 percent of the unmarried population lies in the age of above 35 years, thus showing a small incidence of late marriage. In the category of married population the maximum percentage of 13.30 percent lies in the age group of 31 to 35 years and 36 to 40 years each. However, 2.22 percent of married rural population belongs to 16 to 20 years, thus showing the early incidence of marriage. In the category of divorced, widowed or separated, 41.46 percent are found in the age group of above 70 years. In contrast to this, 1.22 percent of this category is found in the age group of 26 to 30 years, which means early divorce in the marriage.

3B.4 Age at Marriage

Table 5.26 presents the age at marriage of the married males and females among the rural population of District Rohtak. Maximum number of males i.e. 13.22 percent, got married at the age of 20 years. Maximum number of Jat males

Table 5.25 : Age and Sex wise Distribution of Marital Status Among Rural Population of District Rohtak, Haryana

	Unmarried			Married			D/W/S ·		
Age (Years)	*Male (Percent)*	*Female (Percent)*	*Total (Percent)*	*Male (Percent)*	*Female (Percent)*	*Total (Percent)*	*Male (Percent)*	*Female (Percent)*	*Total (Percent)*
-5	16.63	15.71	16.25	-	-	-	-	-	-
-10	15.26	19.23	16.91	-	-	-	-	-	-
1-15	19.13	20.19	19.57	-	-	-	-	-	-
6-20	25.51	27.56	26.36	0.93	3.53	2.22	-	-	-
1-25	14.12	8.33	11.72	6.71	13.18	9.92	-	-	-
6-30	4.56	1.92	3.46	10.42	14.12	12.25	-	1.72	1.22
1-35	1.37	0.96	1.20	13.89	12.71	13.30	-	1.72	1.22
6-40	1.37	1.28	1.33	15.05	11.53	13.30	4.17	3.45	3.66
1-45	0.68	1.28	0.93	9.03	11.76	10.39	-	3.45	2.44
6-50	0.46	1.60	0.93	11.81	7.76	9.80	8.33	10.34	9.76
1-55	-	0.64	0.27	7.64	4.94	6.30	-	3.45	2.44
6-60	0.23	0.64	0.40	5.32	7.76	6.53	8.33	6.90	7.32
1-65	-	0.32	0.13	7.18	4.00	5.60	20.83	5.17	9.76
6-70	-	-	-	3.70	4.24	3.97	20.83	20.69	20.73
70	0.68	0.32	0.53	8.33	4.47	6.42	37.50	43.10	41.46
otal	100.00	100.00	100.00	100.00	100.00	100.00	100.00	100.00	100.00

Table 5.26 : Age at Marriage Among Rural Population of District Rohtak, Haryana

	Male			Female			
Age (Years)	Jat (Percent)	Brahmin (Percent)	Total (Percent)	Jat (Percent)	Brahmin (Percent)	Total (Percent)	Total (Percent)
10	-	-	-	1.16	0.92	1.05	0.54
11	-	-	-	1.94	1.38	1.68	0.86
12	-	0.47	0.22	6.98	4.61	5.89	3.12
13	0.83	1.40	1.10	11.24	6.45	9.05	5.17
14	0.42	0.93	0.66	12.02	7.37	9.89	5.38
15	2.08	1.87	1.98	5.81	13.82	9.47	5.81
16	2.92	3.74	3.30	6.20	9.22	7.58	5.49
17	4.58	8.88	6.61	8.14	10.14	9.05	7.86
18	7.08	6.07	6.61	5.81	10.14	7.79	7.21
19	12.50	9.35	11.01	7.75	8.29	8.00	9.47
20	14.58	11.68	13.22	8.14	4.61	6.53	9.80
21	6.25	9.81	7.93	2.71	4.15	3.37	5.60
22	9.58	7.94	8.81	5.43	4.15	4.84	6.78

(Contd.)

(Contd. Table 5.26)

Age (Years)	Male			Female			
	Jat (Percent)	Brahmin (Percent)	Total (Percent)	Jat (Percent)	Brahmin (Percent)	Total (Percent)	Total (Percent)
23	8.33	3.74	6.17	8.14	3.69	6.11	6.14
24	8.75	9.35	9.03	2.33	5.07	3.58	6.24
25	8.75	5.61	7.27	3.10	2.30	2.74	4.95
26	3.75	7.01	5.29	1.94	1.38	1.68	3.44
27	3.33	4.21	3.74	0.78	0.46	0.63	2.15
28	3.33	5.14	4.19	0.00	0.46	0.21	2.15
29	1.67	1.40	1.54	0.39	0.92	0.63	1.08
30	0.42	0.93	0.66	-	-	-	0.32
32	-	-	-	-	0.46	0.21	0.11
34	-	0.47	0.22	-	-	-	0.11
35	0.83	-	0.44	-	-	-	0.22
Total	100.00	100.00	100.00	100.00	100.00	100.00	100.00

i.e. 14.58 percent and maximum number of Brahmin males i.e. 11.68 got married at the age of 20 years. In the category of males, no marriage is found to happen after 35 years, on the other hand, 31.49 percent marriages of males has happened who are below 20 years.

Maximum percent of females, i.e. 9.89 percent got married at the age of 14 years. Maximum number of Jat females i.e. 12.02 percent got married at the age of 14 years. Maximum number of Brahmin females got married at the age of 15 years. In the category of females, no marriage has happened after the age of 32 years and 43.66 percent of females are married who are below 18 years.

Average age at marriage for rural population is 19.54 years. Average age at marriage for rural males is 21.57 years. Average age of marriage of Jat males is 21.63 years and that of Brahmin males is 21.52 years. Average age at marriage for rural females is 17.60 years. Average age of marriage for Jat females is 17.50 years and that of Brahmin females is 17.71.Average age of marriage of females is less than males, as females in the rural settings of Haryana are not given enough educational opportunities and thus marry them at an early age.

3B. 5 Respondent's Characteristics

It has been observed that 61.00 percent are males (183) and 39.00 percent are females (117). 81.00 percent are married, 9.67 percent are unmarried and 9.33 percent are divorced, separated and widowed. Among males 80.87 percent are married , 10.93 percent males are unmarried, 8.20 percent males are divorced, separated and widowed. Among females 81.20 percent are married, 7.69 percent are unmarried and 11.11 percent are divorced, separated or widowed.

3C. Urban Population

3C.1 Age Structure and Sex Ratio

Table 5.27 shows the age structure and sex ratio among the urban population of Delhi. It reports that the 17.14 percent of population under 15 years and 15.94 percent in the age group of 60+. It shows that the proportion of child population (0-15) and old population(above 60) is almost same. The next broad age group of 16-50 years, 54.60 percent population lies in this group thus observing the population at fertile and peak productive ages. In the total population, 49.07 percent (773) are males and 50.92 percent (802) are females. Among males the maximum percent i.e. 10.09 percent is in the age of 30 to 34 years and among females, the maximum percentage i.e. 10.22 percent is in the age of 30 to 34 years.

Maximum Sex Ratio of 1195.12 is found in the age group of 0 to 4 years, where as the lowest sex ratio of 850.00 is found in the age group of 55 to 59

Table 5.27 : Age Structure and Sex Ratio Among the Urban Population, Delhi

Age (years)	*Male*	*Percent*	*Female*	*Percent*	*Total*	*Percent*	*Sex Ratio*
0-5	41	5.30	49	6.11	74	4.70	1195.12
6--10	49	6.34	58	7.23	107	6.79	1183.67
11--15	45	5.82	52	6.48	89	5.65	1155.56
16-20	51	6.60	60	7.48	111	7.05	1176.47
21-25	44	5.69	49	6.11	87	5.52	1113.64
26-30	64	8.28	72	8.98	136	8.63	1125.00
31-35	78	10.09	82	10.22	160	10.16	1051.28
36-40	69	8.93	71	8.85	140	8.89	1028.99
41-45	67	8.67	57	7.11	124	7.87	850.75
46-50	49	6.34	53	6.61	102	6.48	1081.63
51-55	45	5.82	39	4.86	73	4.63	866.67
56-60	40	5.17	34	4.24	79	5.02	850.00
61-65	34	4.40	35	4.36	63	4.00	1029.41
66-70	42	5.43	40	4.99	82	5.21	952.38
>70	55	7.12	51	6.36	106	6.73	927.27
Total	773	100.00	802	100.00	1575	100.00	1037.52

Table 5.28 : Literacy Rate Among the Urban Population, Delhi

	Illiterate			*Literate*		
Age(Years)	*Male (Percent)*	*Female (Percent)*	*Total (Percent)*	*Male (Percent)*	*Female (Percent)*	*Total (Percent)*
0-5	55.56	43.59	49.33	-	-	-
6--10	2.78	5.13	4.00	5.14	7.60	6.39
11--15	1.39	-	0.67	5.14	6.77	5.96
16-20	5.56	-	2.67	6.70	8.29	7.51
21-25	4.17	-	2.00	6.85	6.63	6.74
26-30	-	-	-	9.13	10.91	10.04
31-35	5.56	3.85	4.67	10.56	10.91	10.74
36-40	2.78	1.28	2.00	10.56	9.67	10.11
41-45	2.78	2.56	2.67	9.27	8.01	8.63
46-50	1.39	2.56	2.00	6.85	7.18	7.02
51-55	-	2.56	1.33	5.14	6.49	5.82
56-60	4.17	11.54	8.00	8.84	4.70	6.74
61-65	5.56	14.10	10.00	3.71	4.56	4.14
66-70	4.17	12.82	8.67	5.99	3.59	4.77
>70	4.17	-	2.00	6.13	4.70	5.40
Total	100.00	100.00	100.00	100.00	100.00	100.00

years. Average sex ratio of the urban population collected is 1037.52 which is found to be higher than the Sex Ratio of Delhi (821), West Bengal (934), Goa (960), Karnataka (964) and lower than Pondicherry (1001) and Kerala (1058).

3C. 2 Literacy Rate

Table 5.28 shows the literacy rate among the urban population of Delhi. It is found that among the total population of illiterates 20.67 percent of population is in the age group of above 60 years as the prevalence of education in the earlier times was not very emphatic.

25.34 percent of illiterate population lies in the age group of 16 to 60 years. Among total population of literates the maximum percentage (73.35 percent) of population is in the age group of 16 to 60 years. Literacy rate among the urban population is found to be 90.48 percent as the educational infrastructure in the urban metropolitan city of Delhi is very good.

Among Literate males, the maximum percentage of 10.56 percent is observed in the age group of 31 to 35 years and 36 to 40 years each . Literacy rate among males of the urban population is 90.64 percent which is again attributed to the fact that Delhi being the hub of all the educational opportunities provides excellent prospects of learning.

Among literate females the maximum percentage of 10.91 percent is found to be present in the age group of 26 to 30 years and 31 to 35 years each. Literacy rate among females of urban population is 90.32 percent. Males and females among urban population are exposed to an equal opportunity towards education.

Table 5.29 : Educational Status Among the Urban Population, Delhi

Education	*Male*	*Percent*	*Female*	*Percent*	*Total*	*Percent*
Illiterate	4	2.58	9	6.21	13	4.33
Primary	3	1.94	5	3.45	8	2.67
Middle	1	0.65	7	4.83	8	2.67
10th Passed	12	7.74	18	12.41	30	10.00
12th Passed	15	9.68	22	15.17	37	12.33
Graduate and Above	120	77.42	84	57.93	204	68.00
Total	155	100.00	145	100.00	300	100.00

Table 5.29 presents the educational status of the urban population of Delhi. It has been observed that, only 4.33 percent of the total respondents are illiterate. The majority of 68.00 percent are graduates and above. Among

Table 5.30 : Marital Status Among the Urban Population, Delhi

	Unmarried			Married			Divorced / Widowed		
Age (Years)	Male (Percent)	Female (Percent)	Total (Percent)	Male (Percent)	Female (Percent)	Total (Percent)	Male (Percent)	Female (Percent)	Total (Percent)
·5	14.14	17.19	15.65	-	-	-	-	-	-
-10	16.90	20.35	18.61	-	-	-	-	-	-
l--15	15.52	18.25	16.87	-	-	-	-	-	-
;-20	17.59	21.05	19.30	-	-	-	-	-	-
l-25	14.48	13.68	14.09	0.44	0.86	0.65	-	-	-
;-30	16.90	8.07	12.52	3.30	10.54	6.96	-	-	-
l-35	2.76	0.35	1.57	15.38	17.42	16.41	-	-	-
;-40	0.34	0.35	0.35	14.95	14.84	14.89	-	1.92	1.25
l-45	0.69	-	0.35	14.29	12.26	13.26	-	-	-
;-50	0.34	-	0.17	10.55	11.18	10.87	-	1.92	1.25
l-55	-	-	-	7.47	7.53	7.50	-	7.69	5.00
;-60	-		-	9.45	6.88	8.15	7.14	3.85	5.00
l-65	-	0.35	0.17	6.59	6.02	6.30	10.71	13.46	12.50
;-70	0.34	-	0.17	7.69	7.74	7.72	46.43	17.31	27.50
70	-	0.35	0.17	9.89	4.73	7.28	35.71	53.85	47.50
otal	100.00	100.00	100.00	100.00	100.00	100.00	100.00	100.00	100.00

males the maximum of 77.42 percent are graduates and above and the minimum of 0.65 percent are middle passed. Among females the maximum of 57.93 percent are graduates and minimum of 3.45 percent are primary passed. Percentage of illiterates among males and females is 2.58 percent and 6.21 percent respectively. Thus, illiteracy is higher among females. The reason for less percentage of illiterates among the urban population of Delhi is excellent infrastructure of education. Number of convent schools, government schools is far more than what is there in the rural or tribal areas.

3C.3 Marital Status

Table 5.30 presents the marital status of the urban population of Delhi. It is to be noted that in the category of total unmarried urban population, the maximum percentage of 19.30 percent lies in the age group of 16 to 20 years. 1.39 percent of the unmarried population lies in the age of above 35 years. In the category of married population the maximum percentage of 16.41 percent lies in the age group of 31 to 35 years. All the married population is above 20 years of age. In the category of divorced, widowed or separated, 87.50 percent are found in the age group of above 60 years, in which maximum are widowed.

3C.4 Age at Marriage

It is found that maximum number of males i.e. 13.96 percent, got married at the age of 28 years. Maximum number of females i.e. 11.73 percent got married at the age of 25 years

In the category of males, no marriage is found to happen after 41 years and in the category of females, no marriage has happened after the age of 33 years. On the other hand 6.04 percent marriages of males has happened who are below 21 years and 7.50 percent of females are married who are below 18 years.

Average age at marriage for the urban population is 24.44 years. Average age at marriage for urban males is 26.15 years. Average age at marriage for urban females is 22.87 years.

3C. 5 Respondent's Characteristics

Table 5.31 presents the respondents characteristics of the urban population of Delhi. It has been observed that 51.67 percent are males (155) and 48.33 percent are females (145). 79.00 percent are married, 12.00 percent are unmarried and 9.00 percent are divorced, separated and widowed. Among males 70.97 percent are married, 17.42 percent males are unmarried, 11.61 percent males are divorced, separated and widowed. Among females 87.59 percent are married, 6.21 percent are unmarried and divorced, separated or widowed each.

Table 5.31: Respondent's Characteristics Among the Urban Population, Delhi

Marital Status	*Male*	*Percent*	*Female*	*Percent*	*Total*	*Percent*
Married	110	70.97	127	87.59	237	79.00
Unmarried	27	17.42	9	6.21	36	12.00
D/W/S	18	11.61	9	6.21	27	9.00
Total	155	100.00	145	100.00	300	100.00

6

Jurisprudence and Customary Laws

Literally by 'Jurisprudence' we mean the science or philosophy of law or a system or body of law. The study of customs as laws or customary laws has brought about a new phase of evolution in the field of jurisprudential study. Many social scientists had conducted legal studies, which were focused mainly to differentiate customs, rules, norms, and sanctions that subsequently developed into customary laws. The socio-legal scientist, as they may be called, tries to focus on the sociological aspects of law, such as, the influence of family and kinspersons in the dispute settlement, the role of the judge and the process of law in the absence of written code. Besides the attitude of the litigants, the reaction of the society towards the erring person and his family are also studied. The socio-legal scientist covers those aspects which are not taken up by the lawyers and legal scientists, who mainly carry out studies of judgment delivered in accordance with the statutory legislation of the state. The legal scientist, usually follows a particular code of conduct that has already been written down. The mode of dispute settlement is usually based on the written codes.

The assumption that developed law is an achievement of the modern world is implicit in a great deal of English legal anthropological writing, explicit interest in legal evolution had fallen away by the 1920s. In North America, on the other hand, this interest was sustained in such works as Hoebel's *'Law of Primitive Man'* (1954), Redfield's influential essay on *'Primitive Law'* (1967) and Newman's *'Law and Economic Organization'* (1983). All the three works search through the ethnographic record for the pre-legal and the proto – legal, mapping out with anthropological findings the path along which law has evolved. All three works search through the ethnographic record for the pre-legal and the proto-legal, mapping out with anthropological findings the path along which law has evolved.

6.1 Evolution of Anthropology of Law

The establishment of customary courts have created an interest among scholars, social scientists and socio-legal scientists to study the customary laws. The study of customary law has evolved into a new field known as the anthropology of law or legal anthropology. This study begins with the work of Sir Henry Maine's Ancient Law (1861) in which he had treated third-party decision making as the basic means of resolving disputes across all known societies. He saw the mode of resolution as one of imposed decision.

From 1920s a second anthropology of law began to develop. Some new questions arose. It quickly became clear that many of these societies had no obvious centralized authority. These were the societies without 'kings' courts, and constables', as Malinowski (1934) put it and yet they were not the savage anarchies. How were the evident coherence and regularity of these groups to be explained? What held them together? Did these societies have 'law'? If so, what form did it take and what were its central attributes?

The 1950s saw the appearance of a number of major ethnographies built around case histories of 'dispute', and for a couple of decades this work became a central concern of leading anthropologists in Britain and North America. Gluckman (1955), Bohannan (1957), Pospisil (1958), Bailey (1960), Gulliver (1963, 1971) and Fallers (1969) and major figures in post-war social anthropology, all made or consolidated their reputations with such ethnographies. For the majority of the authors mentioned above ,a conscious decision to focus on disputes was also influenced by the example of an earlier work, *The Cheyenne Way* (1941). This book, on a North American Indian group, was the product of a collaboration between Karl Llewellyn, a law professor, and Adamson Hoebel, a social anthropologist . According to Llewellyn and Hoebel, it initially proved difficult to get their informants to understand what it was they wanted from the informants, but in the end, a series of 'trouble cases' was assembled, from which in truly lawyerly manner, the two researchers managed to extract what they saw as some fundamental principles of Cheyenne law.

6.2 Dispute Resolution

On the basis of the ethnographies of disputes which appeared in the 1950s and 1960s, it was emphasized on the presence and absence of third-party intervention. A measure of agreement also began to emerge as regards the essential range of variation which empirical studies disclosed. There are three basic forms which may be taken (Roberts, 1995) for dispute resolution :

6.2.1 Bilateral Negotiation : the disputants may feel their way towards a settlement through bilateral negotiation;

6.2.2 Neutral Mediator : they may try to resolve the matter with the help of a neutral mediator ;

6.2.3 Umpire Decision : they may submit the quarrel to an umpire for decision.

6.2.1 Bilateral Negotiation

Bilateral negotiations represents the least complex form of settlement process. Here the rival disputants approach each other without the intervention of third parties and try to bring the dispute to an end through discussion. No intermediaries or supporters are involved, the achievement of communication and the subsequent process of settlement lie in the hands of the two parties alone. A variation of this mode of settlement occurs when partisans align themselves in support of one or other of the disputants.

6.2.2 Neutral Mediator

In this mode of settlement this bilateral element is removed by the intervention of third parties in some intermediate position. Where this role is mediatory, the third party helps the disputants towards their own solution rather than imposing a solution upon them. The most limited form of mediation arises where the third party acts as a 'go-between'.His role is passive and he works as a messenger between the two parties. He enables the disputants to communicate with each other.

6.2.3 Umpire Decision

Under the third mode of settlement the neutral party seeks to resolve the dispute by making a decision, rather than by assisting the disputants towards their own solution. Within this broad category we can distinguish two types of umpires – arbitrator and adjudicator. The arbitrator derives his authority to decide the dispute from the invitation of the disputants themselves, who have voluntarily submitted to his decision. The adjudicator, by contrast, derives his authority from some office in the community, and intervenes to impose a decision by virtue of that office rather than by the invitation of the disputants.

6.3 Views on Customary Laws

The customary law governs and regulates the social norms and behaviour of the simple, developing societies where the law of the complex society is yet to be applied. According to Pospisil (1974), by customary law is meant a 'law that is internalized by a social group. A law is internalized when the majority of the group considers it to be binding as when it stands for the only proper behaviour in a given situation'. For him, the customary law may appear to be a differentiated form of general custom and the basis of both custom and customary law seem to be prevalent.

According to Malinowski (1926), custom is referred to as the totality of the socially acquired behaviour patterns which are supported by tradition and generally exhibited by the members of the society. The customs people follow are by the force of convention, whereas customary laws are enforceable by certain coercive power. In the Angami society, some of the customs have also been given a legislative recognition for regulating and administering the society.These customs have to be stringently followed by every member and the breach of these customs is regarded as a social offence. These 'enforced customs' were used to maintain the harmonious relationship between its members. It became a set mode of conduct and behaviour which was a kind of obligatory norms that later developed into customary practices and then evolved as a 'law' known as the customary law. (Shimray, 1985)

The customary laws are not codified and are flexible. It is merely a comfortable adjustment and adaptation of the customs of simple societies to modern complex societies. Whenever a different or unusual crime is committed a new form of law is created. Thus we may refer to Hoebel's theory (1954), which says that 'the more civilized man becomes, the greater is man's need for law, and the more law he creates'. Law is a response to social needs.The laws may be created in order to maintain equilibrium between man and society as man's needs increase.

Ranger (1983) says that 'the customary law which was recognized in colonial legislation, and developed and 'applied' in the newly established 'native' courts was a tendentious montage with only a superficial connection with the past, supportive of the projects of colonial rule, and entrenching the position of the elders over juniors, men over women. Some have called it an 'invented tradition'.

The customs enacted as the customary law have sparkled a discussion on whether customary laws need to be codified. The customary law, as the initial stage of law in simple societies , may be considered difficult to codify as it is flexible and keeps on changing and modifying as the society develops. A study conducted by Pathak (1991) on the Adis of Arunachal Pradesh found that the elite section were of opinion that codification of customary laws shall not take away its originality and charm. Whereas the *dobashis* (the term *dobashis* is an Assamese word, 'do' means 'two' and '*basha*' means 'language') of Kohima District in Nagaland say that codification is not possible for customary laws because every similar case is completely independent of the other, because for them the motives behind the crime and the statements given by litigants and witnesses become more important than the crime itself. Therefore same law cannot be applied to similar crime committed by different individuals, which happens as in the case of the statutory laws or codified laws.

Yet society and its laws do not stand still. Changes in population composition, patterns of residence, technology and value necessitate alteration in the existing law. Thus, arose a dilemma for the judicial oligarchy, how to adjust their law to the ever changing social conditions and still maintain the illusion of sacrosanct old and 'unchangeable' custom. Once law was deposited in legal codes, the unconscious change characteristic of the previous era ceased. Law had been fixed in the form of written language and to change it conscious efforts had to be exercised and special devices had to be designed. (Maine, 1861, Pospisil, 1971). Maine (1861) had also given that 'with the invention of writing, which thus originated the early legal codes which had little in common with modern legislation'. The local customs are codified or the traditional customs are slowly transformed by the activity of the local courts into a consistent set of rules, which becomes the common laws of the land. Therefore it can be said that the customary law is the earliest form of law which led to the development of codified statutory law in contemporary period to impart justice.

The use of the word 'law' to 'enforced customs' had motivated different individuals to conceptualize law in a varied form. Diamond (1935), a socio-legal scientist, was of the opinion that the development of law takes place along parallel lines with the advancement of the people.He attributes it to the advancement of material culture as clearly reflected in developing law.

Radcliffe-Brown (1952) draws a conclusion that the development of law is marked by an increase in complexity and heterogeneity, where the right of prosecution shifts from the individual and his kin groups to clearly define public officials. Here he emphasized that the judicial and executive powers extend beyond local groups.

Gluckman (1955), gives an elaborate idea of dispute settlement process in the Lozi village council *(kuta)*. Gluckman defines law 'as a set of rules accepted by all normal members of the society as defining right and reasonable ways in which a person ought to behave in relation to each other and things including ways of obtaining protection for one's right. He adds in contrasting law with morality that 'Law defines rights and reasonable ways of acting, the ways of morality are right and generous'. His focus was basically upon the Lozi relationship and their *kuta.* The *kutas* constitute the judicial, administrative, legislative, economic and executive functions. The judges in the *kuta* try to settle the disputes as amicably as possible so that the relationship among kinsmen and litigants are not broken. Thus, Gluckman's work on the Lozi *kuta* give us an extensive idea of the judicial process and the dispute settlement according to the customary practices and customary laws.

Nader (1969) studied law among the Zapotec community. She focused on the style of dispute settlement. She emphasized that ' a comparison of the style of dispute settlement may lead us to discover similarities that cross–cut institution (courts, moots, administrative agencies) structurally different modes of dispute settlement (negotiations, adjudication or mediation, arbitration), and the types of sanctions imposed (restitutes, repressive). Thus, for her the students of law in society should look into the social and cultural factors that determine the style of dispute proceedings.

Pospisil (1974) discusses that the term customary law is used in modern anthropological literature in a very vague and meaningless way connoting any type of non-legislated law in a tribal society. Since accounts of legislative innovations are usually utterly lacking, the term in practice stands for all tribal laws. He was also of the opinion that law implies regularity, order and an organized group of people to uphold orders and see that it is enforced on the individuals who are unwilling to conform.

Sims (1995), identified four relatively sequential periods, the evolutionary period, descriptive period, disputatory period and the directions of the study of law. According to Sims, 'the law is a tool of limited usefulness and that not all resolutions of disputes involve law.' The three main functions of legal institutions are law- making, adjudication and law enforcement.

Thus till 1954, the study of law was based on its concept and structure, and how it evolved from custom to law. By late 1960's, the focus shifted to the process of dispute settlement where negotiations between the disputants, the member of the community and the judges were brought into consensus, and how new rules or laws were adapted along the existing custom to settle dispute. During this period, emphasis was given to distinguish the customary laws from custom.During 1970's a comparative analysis of the different theories of law was undertaken. The prevalence of 'legal pluralism' or the existence of more than one legal system was brought in with the study of law.

Baxi (1986) has noted that the first major point of socio-legal research in India should include 'a rational comprehension of the role of legal systems in social stability and growth demands a more wide-ranging awareness of law as a social system' and that 'the normative and institutional regimes of the people's law vary according to the stage of social and economic development'. He has also furthered his discussion on the formal recognition of customary law in India by saying that, 'The tribal communities are not above the state law. But for all practical purposes they are governed by complex regimes of customary law, administered by community dispute institution'.

Nader (2002) has tried to give a distinction on the work on law by anthropologists and other social scientists. She has also dealt with the working relations between lawyers and anthropologists. Nader has collected the empirical data among the Rincon Zapotec people on the aspects of dispute settling processes. The importance of the anthropological studies of law has been highlighted in her latest work. The author has explored in her work :

(a) What did people fight and argue about?

(b) Who initiated disputes and what was the outcome for the individual well as for the society?

(c) Within what groups were disputes concentrated?

(d) How did disputes at one level of organization affect those at another?

(e) And what were the manifest and hidden jobs of laws and how were they related to the social structure?

The above literature shows that no work had been done which highlights the customary laws present among the tribal population of District Lahoul Spiti, Himachal Pradesh, rural population of District Rohtak, Haryana and urban population of National Capital Territory of Delhi. The present work is an attempt to show the degree of dilution of the magnitude of the customary laws as one moves from tribal population to rural population to urban population. Till now all works on customary laws focuses on the sanctions imposed on the members of the society, ways of dispute settlement, origin of customary laws etc. No work till date has highlighted the role of customary laws in settling the issues of human rights violation which its members experience. A focus is also made on the specific issues for which people follow customary laws and thus goes to village panchayat and on the issues for which they go for the constitutional provisions.

6.4 Customary Laws Among the Populations Under Study

For the present study, among the three populations – Tribal area of District Lahoul Spiti, Rural area of District Rohtak , Urban area of all the Districts of Delhi; data has been collected (where ever available) with reference to customary laws prevalent in the area.

6.4.1 Customary Laws Among Tribal Population

The present study is an attempt to understand the customary laws in the Lahouli society and the place of morals, beliefs, values and customs in the society and their role in the maintenance of the society. Data related to the customary laws prevalent in the area is collected from various informants while conducting the field work. Following are the laws which are considered for settling the disputes which are approached to the panchayat. Each section is presented in the question answers form for a better understanding of the topic.

Section I :	**Betrothal**
Question 1.	Who can make contract of betrothal ?
Answer 1.	The parents of an adult or minor contracts for his/her betrothal.
Question 2.	In the absence of parents or guardians what relations can enter into contracts of betrothal and in which order ?

Answer 2. In the absence of parents, the adult enters into the contract of betrothal himself or herself, or nearest relation in this order – Brother, Grandfather, Uncle, Paternal Uncle, Paternal Grandfather, Grand-mother and in their absence collaterals of the nearest degree. In case of a minor the betrothal is entered into by the relations given in the above order.

Question 3. Has a minor the powers to repudiate a betrothal on attaining majority?

Answer 3. Yes, a minor on attaining the age of majority can repudiate the betrothal.

Question 4. What formalities are observed on the occasion of a betrothal?

Answer 4. On the day fixed, the parents of the boy take to the parents of the girl, *sattu,* ghee, and *halwa* and a rupee in cash. The eatables are distributed amongst the relatives.

Question 5. On what grounds can a contract of betrothal be annulled? Whether impotency, blindness, epilepsy, insanity and immorality of either party are sufficient grounds for annulment of betrothal?

Answer 5. Impotency, leprosy, blindness, epilepsy and insanity are considered as good reasons justifying the annulment of such contracts. Immorality is not considered as sufficient ground for annulment of betrothal but if the girl becomes pregnant before marriage, the betrothal can be annulled.

Question 6. Is a man who has contracted a betrothal entitled to marry another women before he marries her to whom he was first betrothed or does priority in betrothal entitle the female to priority in marriage? Is the first women or her guardian entitled to annul the betrothal?

Answer 6. The girl first betrothed should be married before the man marries another wife. If he does not do so, the first betrothal is generally broken off. Priority of betrothal however, does not rigidly entitle a girl to priority in marriage. The boy can marry another girl with the consent of the betrothed girl, but he must marry the betrothed the girl also after he had married the other girl. If he fails to do so, he has to pay the compensation to the betrothed girl. The amount of the compensation is determined by the village panchayat.

Question 7. If the betrothal is annulled either at the request of the bridegroom or his family or at the request of the bride or her family or by mutual consent, are the expenses incurred payable to the person who discharged them?

Answer 7. In case the annulment is at the request of either party, the expenses incurred are repayable by the party at whose instance it is annulled. The amount of expenses is settled mutually. In case the betrothal is annulled by mutual consent there is no repayment of expenses, or the payment may be made if the parties so wish, and to the extent agreed upon.

Question 8. If either party to a contract of betrothal dies before marriage, are the heirs of the deceased entitled to the return of the gifts given at the betrothal?

Answer 8. In such a case where either of the partner of dies, the girl is married to the younger brother of her deceased husband. In case the girl dies her younger sister is married with the boy. In case of refusal by either, party, the expenses of betrothal are borne by the refusing party.

Section II : Marriage And Divorce

Question 9. With what relation is marriage prohibited under custom? Can a man marry either father's sister's daughter or mother's brother daughter or mother's sister's daughter?

Answer 9. Brahmins of Lahoul replied that marriage with father's sister's daughter, mother's sister's daughter and mother's brother's daughter's is prohibited by custom. However, amongst the Rajputs of Lahoul marriage with the father's sister's daughter and mother's brother's daughter is not prohibited while there is no custom to marry mother's sister's daughters.

Question 10. What physical defects are sufficient for the annulment of marriage? Are idiocy, lunacy, impotency, mutilation and change of religion sufficient causes? Is any distinction made if the time of marriage or if the defect arose subsequently?

Answer 10. Idiocy, lunacy, impotency ,mutilation and change of religion are considered sufficient causes for annulment of the marriage, if the girl does not want to stay with her husband.

Question 11. May a man marry his wife's sister during the life time of the former and with what relations of his wife is marriage unlawful?

Answer 11. A man may marry his wife's sister during the lifetime of the former. He cannot marry wife's mother, wife's sister's daughter, wife's father's sister and wife's niece.

Question 12. What is the age of majority for a boy and a girl for the purpose of contracting marriage?

Answer 12. The age of majority as stated in Lahoul is 18 years for boys and 16 years for girls.

Question 13. Whose consent is necessary to the validity of marriage?

Answer 13. Normally the marriage takes place when both the boy and girl had attained majority. In the case when either of them is under age than the consent of their parents or guardian is necessary to the validity of the marriage.

Question 14. Is divorce permitted by custom?

Answer 14. Custom permits divorce but by mutual consent.

Question 15. Can a husband divorce his wife and if so under what circumstances?

Answer 15. A husband can divorce his wife on account of immorality

Question 16. Can a wife divorce her husband? If so under what circumstances?

Answer 16. She can claim divorce on account of any of the reasons given in answer to question 10 or with the consent of her husband. Change of religion by a husband also entitles the wife to get a divorce.

Question 17. Can a man or a women remarry after getting divorced ?

Answer 17. Yes, a man and a women can get married after being divorced.

Question 18. Has the renounced or deserted wife any claim against her husband for maintenance?

Answer 18. A women cannot claim maintenance if renounced or expelled for immorality. She can claim maintenance if renounced on other grounds.

Question 19. Has a renounced or deserted wife the right to remarry in the life time of her husband?

Answer 19. A renounced or deserted wife has no right to remarry in the life time of her husband. She can remarry in case she got proper divorce.

Question 20. Does the cohabitation of a man and women constitute a marriage ? Does the production of offspring validate an illegal connection? Is there any distinction made if the woman is a widow or unmarried ?

Answer 20. Cohabitation without the performance of marriage ceremony does not constitute a valid marriage. The reproduction of an offspring also does not validate an illegal connection. No distinction is made between a widow or unmarried girl for this purpose.

Section III : Bastardy, Minority And Guardianship

Question 21. Where a marriage has taken place which was not permissible owing to the parties being within prohibited degrees of relationships or on account of difference of relationship or on account of some other prohibition imposed by custom, will the offspring of such union be considered legitimate or not?

Answer 21. Such offspring are not considered legitimate for the purpose of inheritance. They are called bastards.

Question 22. What will be the position of the children born from a concubine (a women cohabiting with a man, without marriage), from a widow living in her previous husband's house or from an unmarried women living in her father's house?

Answer 22. Children from a concubine will not be legitimatefor the purpose of inheritance. Except the children born posthumous, other children corn from a widow shall be considered legitimate for inheritance purposes.

Question 23. Are illegitimate children who do not inherit, entitled to maintenance?

Answer 23. The illegitimate children are entitled to maintenance from their father till they attain maturity and not there after.

Question 24. Upon whom does the guardianship of the person and property of a minor successively devolve, if no appointment be made by the father ?

Answer 24. Generally the mother is the natural guardian of the person of her minor son and she is also supposed to be his guardian as regards property. In the absence of mother, guardianship successively devolve on grandmother, brother m uncle and maternal uncle etc.

Question 25. If widow being the guardian of the minor child remarries, will the widow's right of guardianship cease? On her again becoming a widow will it revive?

Answer 25. All the tribes reply that generally a widow's remarriage deprive her of her right of guardianship over her children from her prior deceased husband. Theses rights do not revive on her again becoming a widow.

Question 26. To what extent under what conditions and for what purposes, can a guardian alienate the property, movables or immovable of his ward by sale, gift, exchange, mortgage or lease?

Answer 26. A guardian cannot alienate, sell or gift away the ancestral or self-acquired property of his ward but he can mortgage, lease out or exchange the property for the benefit of the ward in case of genuine and pressing necessity e.g. to liquidate the debts of ward's father or to meet the expenditure of education, marriage or maintenance of the ward.

Section IV: Succession

Question 27. If there be more sons than one by the same mother, will they take equal shares or in regard to the ages of the sons so that the eldest or the youngest son takes a greater or less share than his brothers?

Answer 27. There is no question of age. All sons share equally.

Question 28. If there be more sons than one by two or more wives, are the shares in the inheritance distributed according to the number of m others or according to the numbers of sons?

Answer 28. The share goes according to the number of sons and not of mothers.

Question 29. Can father in his lifetime nominate a particular son to take a larger share than his other brothers after the father's death? Can he exclude a particular son or sons as unfit to inherit? Is any distinction made between ancestral and acquired property?

Answer 29. The father cannot deprive any of his sons partially or wholly of the share in ancestral property nor can be allocate larger share of his ancestral property to any of his sons. He can do whatever he likes with the self-acquired property.

Question 30. Is a step-son entitled to maintenance from his step-father, and if so to what age ?

Answer 30. A step-son is not entitled to maintenance from his step-father.

Question 31. Does a widow succeed along with step-sons, and if so in what share? If she does not inherit, is she entitled to maintenance and in what manner?

Answer 31. A widow shares equally with her step-sons.

Question 32. Is the widow of a sonless son, who predeceased his father, entitled to succeed his share in the presence of other sons of the deceased or otherwise?

Answer 32. The widow of the predeceased son succeeds in the presence of other sons of the deceased to her deceased husband's share, provided the widow continues to reside in her deceased husband's house.

Question 33. If a man dies leaving no male descendants but a widow and a mother, what rights, if any, has the mother to succeed?

Answer 33. The mother and the widow succeed in the equal shares.

Question 34. Does an unchaste wife succeed to her husband?

Answer 34. An unchaste wife succeeds to her husband when she is living with him. But when she does not live with her husband she does not succeed.

Question 35. If a man marries two wives, one of whom receives some land as dowry or otherwise, from her father, will that land be distributed among the sons of both the wives ?

Answer 35. The land will go to the issues from the wife to whom it was given in dowry.

Question 36. Does a mother succeed? If so, in what circumstances is there any difference between a mother and a step-mother? Does she succeed if she has remarried before succession? If a man dies leaving a mother and a step-mother, do both the mothers succeed?

Answer 36. A mother succeed in the absence of a male lineal descendent, or widow. There is no difference between a mother and step-mother. She doesnot succeed if she has remarried before the succession.

Question 37. If a man has got two wives, one with male issue and the other with an unmarried daughter and the latter dies during the lifetime of her husband, will the daughter succeed with her step-brothers ? If so, to what extent?

Answer 37. An unmarried daughter does not succeed in Lahoul. She is maintained by her brothers till her marriage.

Question 38. Will daughter succeed to the estate of her father in preference to collaterals, where her father dies leaving no male issue, widows or widowed mother? What is the effect when she is unmarried? or when at the time of inheritance she is married?

Answer 38. The daughter if unmarried succeeds to the father in preference to collaterals but her interest is only till marriage. Married daughters cannot exclude collaterals.

Question 39. When a daughter succeeds what are her rights of alienation in the presence of collaterals of her father or in the absence of such collaterals?

Answer 39. She cannot alienate property in the presence of collaterals except for necessity as in the case of widow.. However in the absence of any such collaterals she has full rights.

Question 40. If a man dies leaving maternal grand daughters whose mothers have already died, how will they share in the ancestral or non-ancestral property of their maternal grandfather as compared to the collaterals?

Answer 40. They have no right in the preference to collaterals in ancestral or non-ancestral property. They will acquire right till lifetime or marriage in case the granddaughters of ghar – jowai.

Question 41. If a man dies leaving a daughter of the pre-deceased son, what will be her right to the ancestral or non-ancestral property of her grandfather as compared to the collaterals?

Answer 41. It was replied that she will exclude collaterals till her marriage if the girl is unmarried, otherwise not. No distinction is made between ancestral and non-ancestral property.

Question 42. Can sister or sister's son inherit the estate of their brothers in the presence of collaterals? Can they inherit when there are no collaterals?

Answer 42. The sister or sister's sons do not inherit in the presence of the collaterals. They can inherit in the absence of collaterals.

Question 43. If the sister succeed, can she alienate the property in the presence of collaterals of her brothers o r in the presence of such collaterals?

Answer 43. Sister had got the same rights as a daughter has.

Question 44. If a person voluntarily retires from the world and becomes a member of a religious order, what is the effect on his right to retain his own property?

Answer 44. If a man abandons the world, he retains his right over his property, though his heirs may continue to enjoy it in his name.

Question 45. If a man dies leaving no relations, will the property revert to the owners ?

Answer 45. In Lahoul the property of such a man reverts back to the village land ownership.

Section V : Alienation

Question 46. Where a widow, mother, step-mother, daughter, grand-daughter or a sister succeeds to immoveable property, can she mortgage, exchange or create occupancy rights in such property? If so, under what circumstances and to what extent?

Answer 46. Each one has a limited interest and in case the reversioners exist they cannot alienate the property except for very genuine needs such as marriage, education of children etc.

Question 45. Can a female alienate her property to a stranger in the absence of reversioners?

Answer 45. Yes, she is at liberty if she has no reversioners.

Question 46. Can a male proprietor sell, mortgage, exchange or create occupancy rights in the ancestral immoveable property ?

Answer 46. A male proprietor can sell mortgage, exchange and create occupancy rights in ancestral property for genuine pressing necessity.

Question 47. Can a male proprietor make a gift or will of his ancestral property in favour of one of his heirs to the exclusion of others, out of natural love and affection? If so, under what circumstances?

Answer 47. He cannot do so.

Section VI : Adoption or Appointment of An Heir

Question 48. Is it necessary that the person adopted should be a collateral of the adopter? Can a daughter's son, sister's son or a stranger be adopted?

Answer 48. Anybody can be adopted. There is no restriction except that the adoptee should be of the same tribe as the adopter.

Question 49. Can a man who has already adopted, adopt another person during the lifetime of the first? Hoe does the subsequent adoption effect the previous one ?

Answer 49. The system of such subsequent adoption in the lifetime of the Ist is not permitted by the local custom.

Question 50. Is an adopted son entitled to succeed to his natural father, in case the latter has no lineal issue. But in the presence of lineal issue he is excluded from succession?

Answer 50. He can succeed to his natural father, in case the latter has no lineal issue. But in the presence of lineal issue he is excluded from succession.

Question 51. What is the effect of the birth of a son after adoption ? Does the adopted son take an equal share with the natural son or less?

Answer 51. The son born after the adoption is entitled to an equal share with the adopted son.

Section VII : Ghar Jawai

Question 52. Does the custom of appointing a ghar jawai exist?

Answer 52. The custom of appointing a ghar jawai exists in Lahoul.

Question 53. What are the rights of a ghar jawai to inherit from his father and from his father-in –law?

Answer 53. Ghar jawai does not inherit from his father. He inherits from his father-in-law in the absence of his widow or children, the wife having died before his father-in-law.

Question 54. Does the ghar jawai succeed collaterally in the family of his father and in the family of his father-in-law?

Answer 54. The ghar jawai cannot succeed collaterally in father's family. He does not have any right to succeed in the family of his father –in-law.

Question 55. On the death of the proprietor, does the property go to the daughter herself or to the ghar jawai?

Answer 55. The property first devolves upon the daughter and then on her son with the ghar jawai and in their absence on the ghar jawai.

Question 56. On the death of daughter (wife of ghar jawai) leaving a husband and children, does the property go to the children or to the husband?

Answer 56. The property goes to the children.

Section VIII: Polyandry (Plurality of Husband)

Question 57. Is the custom of polyandry recognized?

Answer 57. In Lahoul this custom of polyandry is recognized.

Question 58. When a women has more than one husband, should they necessarily be the sons of the same father? Can they be amongst the collaterals or can they be strangers to each other?

Answer 58. If a women has more than one husband, they should not necessarily be the sons of the same father but should be cousins.

Question 59. In case of issues of a polyandrous marriage, how is the parentage determined?

Answer 59. The parentage is determined on the statement of the women. If it is disputed than the eldest son is considered to be the son of the eldest brother and so on.

Question 60. Supposing three brothers have a common wife. One dies without leaving any issue, would the property go to his wife as his widow or to his remaining brothers? In case, if on the above question the property goes to woman, would she succeed to the property of second husband in case he also dies issueless?

Answer 60. The property would go to the brothers and not to the woman in Lahoul.

Question 61. Supposing there are five brothers and three of them have a common wife and all the three husbands die issueless. Would the common wife as their widow exclude the other brothers from the deceased husband's own inheritance?

Answer 61. The common wife will get the share of the husband dying last.

Question 62. If three brothers have got a common wife and there are more brothers also and if there is one son from that woman, would that son succeed to the property of all husbands of his mother to the exclusion of the remaining brothers who were not husbands of that woman?

Answer 62. He will succeed only to the property of the husband who is entered as his father in the chawkidara register and not to the property of his other step-fathers.

Question 63. If a women is the common wife of three brothers and one of them dies leaving a daughter, will the daughter exclude her mother to inherit the property of her deceased father?

Answer 63. The daughter will succeed to the property of her deceased father in preference to mother.

Section IX: **Special Property of Women (Stridhan)**

Question 64. What is the special property of a women? Describe 'stridhan'? What are the different descriptions of property that come under this category?

Answer 64. The special property of a women is that which is given by her parents in the form of dowry on the occasion of her marriage. It can be moveable property, like ornaments and jewels or immoveable property such as houses and land. The property either landed or moveable which the parents of the boy give to the girl in return for marriage is also called 'stridhan'.

Question 65. Define the extent of power of the husband over the stridhan of the wife ? Can he make use of or alienate it by sale ,gift or mortgage? If so, under what circumstances?

Answer 65. The husband cannot alienate or otherwise put to use such property without the consent of his wife. In case the wife leaves the husband, the latter can claim back the 'stridhan' which he had given to her, in return for marriage.

Question 66. Can a married women or a widow alienate 'stridhan' by sale, gift or mortgage?

Answer 66. They have full rights for this.

Question 67. Upon whom the stridhan of a married women successively devolves?

Answer 67. When the women dies, her sons succeed to the stridhan and if there are no sons, then daughters. In the absence of a daughter the entire property devolves on the son. In the absence of both, the land goes to the husband and other immoveable property is given in alms to a gompa. In the absence of all of them, the moveable property is given in alms to a gompa and land is reverts to the father of the women or his collaterals.

Question 68. If a women acquires other property with the income of stridhan, would it be regarded as her absolute property or would it form a part of her husband's estate?

Answer 68. The property so acquired is required as her special property. It cannot form part of the property of her husband.

6.4.2 Case Studies on Customary Laws Among Tribal Population

Case Study 1

Annulment of Betrothal

Asha, 26, unmarried female, graduate, stays in Manali now. Prior she was staying in Lahoul. On asking why she is living in Manali, she says, "In Lahoul her engagement broke, so she is living in Manali now, as she doesn't like the place". Informant told she know a boy since her college. Both agreed to get married and so got engaged. But soon she came to know from somebody that boy has married some other girl. Knowing her rights of getting compensation, informant went to her village pradhan alone. There the whole matter was told to the pradhan. She went to that boy's place with pradhan. Pradhan told the boy that according to customary laws if the betrothal is annulled without any specific reason than the party who initiated the annulment will have to pay the penalty. But the boy refused to pay. Informant said to the boy that if you will not give the penalty then she will go to police. Listening this he agreed to pay the penalty fixed by Panchayat.

Case Study 2

Annulment of Marriage

Chering Rigzin, 28, male, 10th passed, agriculturist, married Uren, 25 of a village 6 km. away from his village. Chering found that his wife is having a liking for some other person from her village. After discovering this, Chering talked to his wife Uren regarding this matter. But Uren lied to him denying everything. After 2 months again, Cheirng caught his wife with her paramour. This time he warned her if she will continue this, than he will take the matter to panchayat and divorce her. Even after this, she kept meeting him. Than one day Chering went to panchayat and discussed his problem with the panch. Panch said that according to our customary laws, immorality is a sufficient reason for the annulment of the marriage. Later Chering divorced Uren on account of immorality.

Case Study 3

Remarriage of Renounced Wife

Dolma, 32, 10th passed ,wife of Tashi Angrup was renounced or deserted by her husband. Dolma soon remarried Niraml Chand of a near by village in the presence of the panchayat members. According to the customary laws a renounced or deserted wife has no right to remarry in the life-time of her husband. She can remarry in case she got proper divorce. Panch said that Dolma will have to pay compensation money to her first husband, Tashi Angrup as she was not properly divorced by him.

Case Study 4

Succession of a Widow

Phunchuk Lammo, 53, widowed, illiterate, lives in her deceased husband's house. She has no children. Lammo's husband's two other brothers also live in the same house. Lammo once realized that her brother-in-laws are planning for a partition. Then she asked for her share also. But they refused her the share and said that if their brother would have been alive they have divided the property in three shares. But now since their brother is dead so, she is also not entitled in the property. Informant went to panchayat and discussed the matter with him. Then he called informant's brother-in-laws and told them that according to the customary laws of Lahoul, a widow of a sonless son, who predeceased his father, is entitled to the share in the property, provided the widow continues to reside in her deceased husband's house. Listening this informant's both the brother-in-law agreed to give her an equal share in the property.

Case Study 5

Special Rights of Woman

Chetan Dolma, 49, illiterate, married, told that once her husband tried to sell the land which she acquired with the income from the land she got in *stridhan*. Her husband fixed the deal without telling her. She came to know about the whole conspiracy just before few days when the deal was to be finalized. Knowing all this she got raged up and asked him to cancel the deal as she does not want to sell that land. But her husband didn't listen to her. Than Chetan went to panchayat and told her problem there. Panch called her husband and told him that according to customary laws a husband cannot alienate or otherwise put to use the property acquired by the wife with the income of *stridhan* without the consent of his wife. In case the wife leaves the husband, than husband can claim back the land given as '*stridhan*' to his wife, in return for marriage. Panch said to her husband that if he will do this against the customary laws than he will be boycotted by the village members. Chetan told later her husband cancelled the deal.

Case Study 6

Inheritance of a Ghar -Jawai

Bir Singh, 39, Graduate, hotelier, has become the *ghar jawai.* He has started living with his wife's parents. Since informant's wife is the only child of her parents, so she will inherit all the property of her parents. Informant told that earlier he has no idea that he will have to surrender his father's property if he will become *ghar jawai.* When he claimed his property form his father's side, his brothers told him that he has no rights now in that property. Not satisfied, informant went to panchayat. There, panch told him that in Lahoul *ghar jawai* does not inherit from his father's property but inherits from his father-in-laws property in the absence of his widow or children, if the wife dies before his father-in-law.

Case Study 7

Bastardy

Bina Devi, 34, 8th passed, unmarried, has a son. Shivlal, the man who is the father of the child refused to marry her but promised to gave her the maintenance before the child birth. Later when informant gave birth to the child, the biological father of the child refused to pay her the maintenance. Informant's condition was from hand to mouth. She went to that man's house for asking monitary help, but he refused her. Than she went to panchayat, and told the panch whole story. Later panch called Shivlal and told him that according to customary laws the illegitimate offspring born out of a union not permitted by custom are entitled to maintenance from their father till they attain maturity and not there after. Listening this provision which is there in the societal law, informant agreed to pay the maintenance.

All the case studies given above prove the fact that in Lahoul, customary laws plays a central role in the lives of members of the society. People still give importance to customary laws and takes its resort. Lahoulis decide about the issues relating to succession, alienation, land fragmentation, marriage rules, cross-cousin marriages, mating pattern, dispute settlement and rights of women through their customary laws.

6.4.3 Customary Laws Among Rural and Urban Populations

In the rural and urban society, it has been observed that as we move from tribal to urban society, the level of impact of customary laws get diluted. In the tribal area, important decisions of inheritance, marriage, divorce, succession, alienation, polyandry, special rights of women etc are decided through panchayat following customary laws.

In the day to day life, the Lahoul tribal society appears similar to rural society of Haryana and urban society of Delhi. People in all these societies have same daily routine of going to work, work profiles may vary; they have same festivals with same implications, but different ways of expressing; they have universal situations in which they feel happy or sad, however the expression of these feelings may vary according to the respective material culture. But as soon as any issue to be resolved happens in the society, the difference in these societies become explicit. The role of customary laws which remain 'latent' otherwise come into play. It is at this juncture that the main difference between tribal, rural and urban society emerges. Unlike tribal society, rural and urban society does not have extensive customary laws. The implication of customary laws gets superficial from tribal community to urban community.

Rural and urban populations said that there are customary laws in their native places but in rural and urban society they don't follow the traditional rules and taboos because of impact of modernization in their families. In addition to this some said that younger generations are naive to all the traditions followed by their ancestors as these unwritten laws had not been communicated to them by their parents, which are the only source of these traditions.

Table 6.1: Knowledge and Practice of Customary Laws Among the Tribal, Rural and Urban Populations

Customary Laws	*Tribal n(%)*	*Rural n(%)*	*Urbann n(%)*	*Total n(%)*
Knowledge of Customary Laws	300 (100.00%)	119 (39.67%)	0 (0.00%)	419 (46.56%)

(Contd.)

(Contd. Table 6.1)

Customary Laws	Tribal n(%)	Rural n(%)	Urbann n(%)	Total n(%)
Practice of Customary Laws	244 (81.33%)	105 (35.00%)	0 (0.00%)	349 (38.78%)

Table 6.i shows the knowledge and practice of customary laws among the tribal, rural and urban populations under study. It shows that tribal population has the highest percentage of knowledge of customary laws in the society, followed by rural population and then urban population (100.00 percent > 39.67 percent > 0.00 percent). It is because of the fact that the customary laws are unwritten coded rules. Their knowledge passes through oral communication from one generation to another generation. All these rules governing the society are like intangible assets which parents pass on to their children in the form of stories or instances. In the tribal population all the members have the knowledge of their age old customary laws. It is found that generally the most elderly one is the repertoire of all the customary laws of the society. In the rural population, it is found that the knowledge of customary laws is less than the tribal population. Urban population is found to have nil knowledge about their customary laws, if at all. The reason for this is the modernization of the society and lack of time to tell all the ancestral stories to their children.

Practice of customary laws in all the three populations reduces from tribal to rural to urban society (81.33 percent > 35.00 percent > 0.00 percent). The major reason for this type of response is that the tribal population live in small, isolated society, where feeling of brotherhood dominates in their culture. So for any dispute settlement, people take the recourse of elderly people or panchayat. Panchayat follows the code of unwritten rules of customary laws to solve the dispute. In the rural population, practice of customary laws is decreasing with the passage of time and induction of modernity. In Haryana, the percentage of people practicing their customary laws by going to panchayat for dispute settlement is reducing. With the advancement of the education, people prefer going to police instead of panchayat. Where as in the urban population, none of the members would practice the customary laws. In the metropolitan city like Delhi people are all far away from practicing their customary laws as they don't have the knowledge of their respective customary laws, plus its difficult to operate the society if its members are a pool of numerous different cultural backgrounds, controlled by numerous different customary laws. So the only feasible solution is to follow a constitutional norms which would be common for all the people living in that area.

7

Populations, Police and Human Rights: An Interface Dimension

This chapter highlights various variables which has an affect on the population's knowledge, attitude and practice towards Human Rights and role of police in a cross cultural perspective, highlighting an interface dimension.

7.1 Police and Human Rights

The concept of Human Rights has been discussed from past many decades, majorly since independence in the Indian context. But till today no work has been done on the aspects of Human Rights keeping the focus on the attitude, knowledge and practice towards it, among three populations of different geographical set ups namely tribal, rural and urban areas from anthropological dimension. Effect of various variables like education, occupation, income, land, movement, source of awareness etc has been seen on the knowledge, attitude and practice towards human rights. An attempt has also been made to conceptualize the definition of crime and human rights among all the three populations in broader framework.

7.1.1. Police and Human Rights Among Tribal Population of District Lahoul and Spiti, Himachal Pradesh

1.A Knowledge of Crime

Knowledge or definition of crime is the people's perception of crime, their understanding of the term 'crime'. The perception of 'crime' is affected by the education and the occupation of the individual and gender. In the present study crime has been taken as 'an intentional act in violation of criminal law committed without justification and penalized by the State.' However, anthropologically crime would be the 'violation of criminal law that is a breach of contract code specially sanctioned by the state which through its legislature agency defines crimes and their penalties and through its administrative agencies, prosecutes offender and imposes and administers punishment.' Deviance is universally found but whether an act deserves to be called 'crime' depends on the sanctions attached to norms.

Out of 300 informants, 21.33 percent exhibited the raw knowledge about crime by saying that anything done with wrong intention of hurting others is called crime, where as 78.67 percent have the constitutional knowledge of crime as they said any act which is punishable by law like theft, murder, rape or hurting anybody is called crime. Tribal population defined crime as *"actions which emotionally hurt others like telling lie, deceiving, playing foul games, theft, murder, rape and grievous hurt"*.

Table 7.1 shows the education and knowledge of crime among the tribal population. It shows that among those who have exhibited the raw knowledge of crime, 67.19 percent are illiterate and 3.13 percent are graduates and above.

Table 7.1 : Education and Knowledge of Crime Among the Tribal Population of District Lahoul and Spiti, Himachal Pradesh

Education	*Raw Knowledge*	*Percent*	*Constitutional Knowledge*	*Percent*
Illiterate	43	67.19	30	12.71
Primary	11	17.19	22	9.32
Middle	5	7.81	34	14.41
10th passed	1	1.56	28	11.86
12th Passed	2	3.13	19	8.05
Graduate and above	2	3.13	103	43.64
Total	64	100.00	236	100.00

Respondents having the constitutional knowledge of crime, 43.64 percent are graduates and above, as with education people get various opportunities to learn more and more things. However 12.71 percent of those having the constitutional knowledge are illiterates.

Table 7.2 shows the occupation of those who exhibited raw knowledge and the constitutional knowledge. 64.06 percent of those who have raw knowledge of crime are agriculturists. 23.44 percent of the respondents are inactive thus contributing nothing in the unit of production of the

Table 7.2 : Occupation and Knowledge of Crime Among the Tribal Population of District Lahoul and Spiti, Himachal Pradesh

Occupation	*Raw Knowledge*	*Percent*	*Constitutional Knowledge*	*Percent*
Agriculture	41	64.06	92	38.98
Service	4	6.25	89	37.71
Daily Labour	1	1.56	2	0.85
Business	3	4.69	20	8.47
Animal Husbandry	-	-	11	4.66
Nothing (Inactive)	15	23.44	22	9.32
Total	64	100.00	236	100.00

household. Only 6.25 percent of them are in service. 38.98 percent of those having constitutional knowledge are in agriculture, 37.71 percent in service and 9.32 percent are inactive.

Table 7.3 : Awareness of Crime and Human Rights Violation Among the Tribal Population of District Lahoul and Spiti, Himachal Pradesh

Awareness	*Respondents*	*Percent*
Aware	155	51.67
Unaware	145	48.33
Total	300	100.00

Table 7.3 presents the awareness of crime and human rights violation among the tribal populations. It shows that 51.67 percent respondents are aware of crime going on in and around their surroundings and thus the violation of rights. 48.33 percent are totally unaware of the happenings.

Table 7.4 shows the impact of education on the awareness of crime and human rights among the tribal population. It is found that 59.35 percent of the aware respondents are graduates and above, 5.16 percent are illiterate. Among the unaware respondents 44.83 percent are illiterate and 8.97 percent are graduates and above.

Table 7.5 presents the gender wise impact on awareness of crime and human rights violation. It shows that among males 58.52 percent are graduates, 5.19 percent are illiterates who are aware about human rights violation and crimes. Among females 65.00 percent are graduates and 5.00 percent are illiterates. In the category of unawareness, 9.52 percent males have done graduation or above and the maximum of 38.10 percent are illiterates. Among the females, 47.57 percent are illiterates and 8.74 percent are graduates who are unaware about human rights violation and crime.

Table 7.4 : Education and Awareness of Crime and Human Rights Violation Among the Tribal Population of District Lahoul and Spiti, Himachal Pradesh

Education	*Aware*	*Percent*	*Unaware*	*Percent*
Illiterate	8	5.16	65	44.83
Primary	5	3.23	28	19.31
Middle	17	10.97	22	15.17
10th passed	19	12.26	10	6.90
12th Passed	14	9.03	7	4.83
Graduate and above	92	59.35	13	8.97
Total	155	100.00	145	100.00

1.B Source of Awareness of Crime and Human Rights Violation

Source of Awareness has an important role in the degree of awareness of crime and human rights violation. Various sources such as watching TV, listening to radio, reading news paper, meeting friends and people, movement outside one's area. Other important source of awareness is the occupation of the respondent- agriculture, service, business or any other. Self experience has also been found to be an important source of awareness of crime and human rights violation.

Table 7.6 presents the main source of crime awareness and human rights violation among the tribal population. It shows that for the maximum of the total respondents i.e. 30.97 percent of the tribal population, radio is the source of the awareness. 20.65 percent of the population relies upon their occupation type as the source of awareness. Only 5.16 percent of the respondents depend upon news paper as source. The other sources providing awareness are TV (14.19 percent), meeting people (7.74 percent), movement outside the area (9.03 percent). Among males (32.59 percent) radio is the major source of awareness. Among females (25.00 percent) meeting people acts as a major source of awareness.

Table 7.5: Gender and Awareness of Crime and Human Rights Violation Among the Tribal Population of District Lahoul and Spiti, Himachal Pradesh

Education	*Aware*				*Unaware*			
	Male	*Percent*	*Female*	*Percent*	*Male*	*Percent*	*Female*	*Percent*
Illiterate	7	5.19	1	5.00	16	38.10	49	47.57
Primary	4	2.96	1	5.00	6	14.29	22	21.36
Middle	16	11.85	1	5.00	11	26.19	11	10.68
10th Passed	18	13.33	1	5.00	2	4.76	8	7.77
12th Passed	11	8.15	3	15.00	3	7.14	4	3.88
Graduate	79	58.52	13	65.00	4	9.52	9	8.74
Total	135	100.00	20	100.00	42	100.00	103	100.00

Table 7.6: Main Sources of Crime Awareness and Human Rights Violation Among the Tribal Population of District Lahoul and Spiti, Himachal Pradesh

Sources of Awareness	*Male*	*Percent*	*Female*	*Percent*	*Total*	*Percent*
T.V.	20	14.81	2	10.00	22	14.19
Radio	44	32.59	4	20.00	48	30.97
News Paper	8	5.93	-	-	8	5.16
Meeting People	7	5.19	5	25.00	12	7.74
Movement Outside the Area	14	10.37	-	-	14	9.03
Occupation Type	26	19.26	6	30.00	32	20.65
Self Experience	16	11.85	3	15.00	19	12.26
Total	135	100.00	20	100.00	155	100.00

Table 7.7 : Personal Experience of Crime and Human Rights Violation Among the Tribal Population of District Lahoul and Spiti, Himachal Pradesh

Personal experience	*Respondents*	*Percent*
Experienced	19	6.33
Inexperienced	281	93.67
Total	300	100.00

Table 7.7 depicts the personal experience of crime and human rights violation among the tribal population. It is observed that 6.33 percent of the tribal population has experienced the violation of their human rights in one or the other way. The basic and mundane issues which infringes the peace of mind are seen as the causes of human rights violation by the tribal population of Lahoul. Issues like land fragmentation, irrigation of agricultural land, change of religion etc have been categories as the cases of human rights violation. All

these cases were separately interviewed and the case studies have been given at the end of the chapter.

1.C Knowledge and Attitude Towards Human Rights

In the tribal belt of Lahoul and Spiti district, it was very difficult to make the respondent comprehend the meaning of the word ' Human Rights'. It has been observed that, 46.33 percent could not explain at all the meaning of the word 'Human Rights', even after discussions, thus coming into the category of ' unaware', as shown in Table 7.9

Table 7.8 : Knowledge of Human Rights Among the Tribal Population of District Lahoul and Spiti, Himachal Pradesh

Level of Awareness	*Respondents*	*Percent*
Unaware	139	46.33
Partially aware	137	45.67
Fully aware	24	8.00
Total	300	100.00

Table 7.8 presents the knowledge of human rights among the tribal population. 45.67 percent are those who could explain the meaning by giving examples, thus being partially aware. Only 8 percent respondents were fully aware, who gave the definition with examples. *Thus the tribal population defined human right collectively as "Rights given to a person, being a human by the constitution are called human rights."*

Table 7.9: Education and Knowledge of Human Rights Among the Tribal Population of District Lahoul and Spiti, Himachal Pradesh

Education	*Unaware*	*Percent*	*Partially Aware*	*Percent*	*Fully Aware*	*Percent*
Illiterate	57	41.01	15	10.95	1	4.17
Primary	26	18.71	7	5.11	-	-
Middle	23	16.55	16	11.68	-	-
10th Passed	13	9.35	14	10.22	2	8.33
12th Passed	9	6.47	12	8.76	-	-
Graduate and Above	11	7.91	73	53.28	21	87.50
Total	139	100.00	137	100.00	24	100.00

Table 7.9 shows the role of education in the knowledge of human rights among the tribal population. It is found that among the unaware respondents, majority of the respondents (41.01 percent) are illiterate, 7.91 percent are graduates and above. Among partially aware, the maximum (53.28 percent) response came from those who are minimum graduates or above. Among those who are fully aware (according to the criteria given above), the majority of percentage (87.50 percent) of the respondents are graduates and above. However, a small percentage of (4.17 percent) are illiterates also.

Table 7.10: Reasons for Rights Framed Among the Tribal Population of District Lahoul and Spiti, Himachal Pradesh

Reasons for Framing Rights	*Respondents*	*Percent*
Unaware	162	54.00
Aware	138	46.00
Total	300	100.00

Table 7.10 presents the reasons which are present for the rights framed among the tribal population. It reports that 54.00 percent of the informants are unaware as they don't know why rights are framed in the society and 46.00 percent are aware as they gave various reasons which all meant similar that – "all would have equal opportunity, nobody would be weak in the society, all would be equal".

Table 7.11 : Education and Reasons for Rights Framed Among the Tribal Population of District Lahoul and Spiti, Himachal Pradesh

Education	*Unaware*	*Percent*	*Aware*	*Percent*
Illiterate	65	40.12	8	5.80
Primary	29	17.90	4	2.90
Middle	25	15.43	14	10.14
10th Passed	14	8.64	15	10.87
12th Passed	13	8.02	8	5.80
Graduate and above	16	9.88	89	64.49
Total	162	100.00	138	100.00

Table 7.11 shows educational level of the population which is aware and unaware of the reasons of the rights framed. 40.12 percent of illiterate

population is unaware of the reasons behind the rights framed. However, it is to be mentioned here that 9.88 percent of the unaware respondents are minimum graduates or above. A majority of 64.49 percent of the aware population is atleast graduate or above. It is to be noted in this category that 5.80 percent of the respondents are illiterate and even than aware of the reasons of the rights framed.

Table 7.12: Occupation and Reasons for Rights Framed Among the Tribal Population of District Lahoul and Spiti, Himachal Pradesh

Occupation	*Unaware*	*Percent*	*Aware*	*Percent*
Agriculture	99	61.11	34	24.64
Service	22	13.58	71	51.45
Daily Labour	1	0.62	2	1.45
Business	12	7.41	11	7.97
Animal Husbandry	4	2.47	7	5.07
Retired	24	14.81	13	9.42
Total	162	100.00	138	100.00

Table 7.12 presents the occupational level of the respondents who are aware and unaware among the tribal population. It shows that for 61.11 percent unaware respondents, agriculture is their occupation, Service (13.58 percent), leading a retired life (14.81 percent). In the category of aware respondents, the majority of 51.45 percent are in service, 24.64 percent are in agriculture, 7.97 percent have their own business.

Table 7.13 shows that the number of human rights told by the informants. Various rights have been framed by the Constitution of India. Legally, human rights are understood as the basic rights and freedoms to which all humans are entitled. Personal liberties that protect individuals and groups, against individual or state conduct prohibited by international law or custom are known as human rights. These are the freedoms established by custom or international agreement that impose standards of conduct on all nations.

Human rights and fundamental rights are the two faces of a coin. The end of the boundary of fundamental rights marks the beginning of the domain of human rights. A fundamental right is often referred to the rights, a person has according to a country's constitution. These fundamental rights are usually seen as natural human rights. Fundamental rights enumerated from Article 14 to 32 in Part III of the Indian constitution, whenever violated seeks help of human rights for enforcement. Universal Declaration of Human Rights declared in 1948 highlights various rights in articles from 1 to 30. For the present work following rights and freedoms have been considered (Anand, 2001) :

(i) Right to Life, Article 3
(ii) Freedom from Torture, Article 5
(iii) Freedom from Slavery, Article 4
(iv) Freedom from Arbitrary Arrest and Detention, Article 9
(v) Freedom of Movement, Article 13
(vi) Equality before Courts, Article 10
(vii) Equal Protection of Law, Article 7
(viii) Freedom of Thought, Article 18
(ix) Freedom of Religion, Article 2
(x) Freedom of Expression, Article 19(1) a
(xi) Freedom to Seek, Receive and Impart Information, Article 19
(xii) Right to Peaceful Assembly, Article 20
(xiii) Right to Marry, Article 16
(xiv) Right of Minorities to Enjoy their own Culture, Religion and Language, Article 27
(xv) Right to Work, Article 23
(xvi) Right to Social Security, Article 22
(xvii) Right to an Adequate Standard of Living, Article 25
(xviii) Right of Everyone to Education, Article 26
(xix) Right to take part in Cultural Life, Article 27

Out of the human rights outlined above, a majority of 47.33 percent respondents were found to be absolutely unaware as they couldn't tell even a single human right article. Only 2 percent of the respondents were fully aware as they could tell more than 10 human right article. These are the lawyers, civil servants, or police officials.

Table 7.13: Human Right Articles Awareness Among the Tribal Population of District Lahoul and Spiti, Himachal Pradesh

Awareness of Rights	*Respondents*	*Percent*
None	142	47.33
One - Two	31	10.33
Three - Four	71	23.67
Five-Six	31	10.33
Seven-Eight	9	3.00
Nine-Ten	10	3.33
Above Ten	6	2.00
Total	300	100.00

It can also be derived from the Table that if 47.33 percent respondents couldn't tell even a single human right, than 52.67 percent were those which include as less as single human right or as much as above 10.

Table 7.14 : Awareness About Categories of Human Rights (Articles) Among the Tribal Population of District Lahoul and Spiti, Himachal Pradesh

S.No.	*Category of Human Rights*	*158(n)*	*Percent*
1.	Right to Education	127	80.38
2.	Right to Work	126	79.75
3.	Freedom of Religion	99	62.66
4.	Right to Marry	79	50.00
5.	Right to Life	66	41.77
6.	Freedom of Movement	46	29.11
7.	Equality before Courts	37	23.42
8.	Freedom of Thought	35	22.15
9.	Equal Protection of Law	30	18.99
10.	Right of Minorities	16	9.49
11.	Freedom of Expression	15	10.13
12.	Freedom from Torture	16	9.49
13.	Right to Social Security	9	5.70
14.	Right to Adequate Standard of Living	5	3.16
15.	Freedom from Slavery	5	3.16
16.	Right to take part in Cultural Life	4	2.53
17.	Freedom from Arrest	4	2.53
18.	Right to Peaceful Assembly	4	2.53
19.	Freedom to Seek information	3	1.90

Table 7.14 shows a further analysis of these 158 respondents. 80.38 percent of respondents believed in right to education and 79.75 percent know about right to work. The reason for such type of response could be assign to the fact that since its a tribal belt, most of the people here are aware of their tribal status and thus the benefits. Children are given free education, plus other facilities. Moreover, educational programmes run in the district are a major source of motivation for people to get inclined towards education. Since Lahoul has an agricultural economy, so everybody in the area works. This could be the probable reason for their awareness of right to work.

The top five answers were right to education, right to work, freedom of religion, right to life and freedom of movement.Looking at this pattern of answers it can be generalized by saying that "*for the tribal population the basic meaning of human rights is very rustic and uncomplicated and is also away from the constitutional labyrinth of covenants, charters etc. All they understand and demand is as basic as right to education, work, life, movement and religion".*

Table 7.15 : Awareness About Rights of Arrested Person Among the Tribal Population of District Lahoul and Spiti, Himachal Pradesh

Rights of Arrested Person	*Respondents*	*Percent*
Phone call	16	5.33
Lawyer	1	0.33
Both	29	9.67
Don't know	254	84.67
Total	300	100.00

An arrested person has been granted two rights by the constitution – first, he has the right to make a phone call and second he has right to wait for his lawyer to come before he speaks anything which goes on record. Table 7.15 shows the awareness about the rights of arrested person among the tribal population. It reveals that 84.67 percent of informants are totally unaware of any of the rights. Only 9.67 percent of the total respondents could tell both the rights of the arrested person. These were the people who were either in police job, or lawyer, or were aware by virtue of their age and experience.

Table 7.16 shows the impact of education on the awareness of rights of arrested person among the tribal population. It clearly indicates that in the category of completely unaware respondents who said that they don't know any of the rights of the arrested person, the majority (28.74 percent) are illiterate. Those who are graduates and above (25.98 percent) are also found to be unaware of these rights. In the category of those who could tell both these rights, the majority (89.66 percent) are at least graduates or above.

Table 7.17 shows the effect of occupation of the respondents on the awareness about human rights among the tribal population. It is found that majority of the respondents who could not tell about the rights of the arrested person are agriculturists (51.18 percent). 23.23 percent of those who are in service could not tell any of the rights. The majority of those who could tell

Table 7.16 : Education and Awareness About Rights of Arrested Person Among the Tribal Population of District Lahoul and Spiti, Himachal Pradesh

Education	*Phone Call*	*Percent*	*Lawyer*	*Percent*	*Both*	*Percent*	*Don't Know*	*Percent*
Illiterate	-	-	-	-	-	-	73	28.74
Primary	-	-	-	-	-	-	33	12.99
Middle	1	6.25	-	-	1	3.45	37	14.57
10th Passed	1	6.25	1	100.00	1	3.45	26	10.24
12th Passed	1	6.25	-	-	1	3.45	19	7.48
Graduate and Above	13	81.25	-	-	26	89.66	66	25.98
Total	16	100.00	1	100.00	29	100.00	254	100.00

Table 7.17 : Occupation and Awareness About Rights of Arrested Person Among the Tribal Population of District Lahoul and Spiti, Himachal Pradesh

Occupation	*Phone Call*	*Percent*	*Lawyer*	*Percent*	*Both*	*Percent*	*Don't Know*	*Percent*
Agriculture	2	12.50	-	-	1	3.45	130	51.18
Service	12	75.00	1	100.00	21	72.41	59	23.23
Daily Labour	-	-	-	-	-	-	3	1.18
Business	-	-	-	-	1	3.45	22	8.66
Animal Husbandry	1	6.25	-	-	3	10.34	7	2.76
Nothing	1	6.25	-	-	3	10.34	33	12.99
Total	16	100.00	1	100.00	29	100.00	254	100.00

both the human rights of arrested person are in service (72.41 percent). However, 10.34 percent of those doing animal husbandry are also aware of both these rights. These are the families who either have any civil servant as their relative or they frequently move out of the valley for accruing various household ration.

Table 7.18 : Attitude Towards Violation of Rights Among the Tribal Population of District Lahoul and Spiti, Himachal Pradesh

Take the Injustice Done	*Respondents*	*Percent*
Take an Action	117	39.00
Leave it After Few Discussion	78	26.00
Never Bother	105	35.00
Total	300	100.00

Table 7.18 throws light on the attitude of the tribal population towards the violation of rights. It shows that 35.00 percent reply came from those who said they would not be bothered by the violation of their rights. Most of the informants in this category were either the elderly people or were the females. The majority of respondents (39.00 percent) said they would take an action against the unjust done to them. 26.00 percent said they would leave the issue after discussing it.

1.D Practice of Human Rights

Table 7.19 : Dispute Processing Institutions Among the Tribal Population of District Lahoul and Spiti, Himachal Pradesh

Dispute Processing Institution	*Respondents*	*Percent*
Elderly People	46	15.33
Panchayat	253	84.33
Police	1	0.33
Total	300	100.00

Table 7.19 shows the prevalence of dispute processing institution in the tribal society. 84.33 percent said that panchayat system is more prevalent in the society. 15.33 percent said that tribal population of Lahoul prefer to go to elderly people instead of the Panch. Only 0.33 percent said, people go to police for seeking justice.

Table 7.20 : Individual Justice Seeking Among the Tribal Population of District Lahoul and Spiti, Himachal Pradesh

Institution	*Respondents*	*Percent*
Elderly People	54	18.00
Panchayat	190	63.33
Police	56	18.67
Total	300	100.00

When the same question was asked with a specific emphasis that where will you go for justice seeking than the results were absolutely different. Table 7.20 shows the individual justice seeking behaviour of the tribal population. It shows that 63.33 percent said they would go to Panchayat. 18.00 percent said they would go to elderly people of village. Entirely different result came in for those who would take constitutional help. 18.67 percent, as against 0.33 percent of Table 7.19 said, they would go to police instead of Panchayat or elderly people of village, as they find this path of justice seeking more faster and emphatic unlike that of Panch or Pradhan system.

Table 7.21 presents the impact of education on the individual justice seeking behaviour among the tribal population. It shows that in the category of those who goes to elderly people for their individual justice seeking, the majority of the respondents (25.93 percent) are illiterate. Only 12.96 percent of graduates and above goes to elderly people. Among those who goes to panchayat, not much difference is observed in the response of the tribal population , as 31.05 percent of the illiterates, 26.84 percent of the graduates and above goes to panchayat. However, a stark difference is observed in the response of the individuals who goes to police for justice seeking. 83.93 percent of those who go to police station for justice seeking are graduates and above. No illiterate is reported to be going to police station.

Table 7.22 : Panchayat Among the Tribal Population of District Lahoul and Spiti, Himachal Pradesh

Panchayat Decides with help of Constitutional Laws	Respondents	Percent
Yes	10	3.33
No	141	47.00
Don't Know	149	49.67
Total	300	100.00

Table 7.21 : Education and Individual Justice Seeking Among the Tribal Population of District Lahoul and Spiti, Himachal Pradesh

Education	*Elderly*	*Percent*	*Panchayat*	*Percent*	*Police*	*Percent*
Illiterate	14	25.93	59	31.05	-	-
Primary	11	20.37	22	11.58	-	-
Middle	9	16.67	28	14.74	2	3.57
10th Passed	6	11.11	18	9.47	5	8.93
12th Passed	7	12.96	12	6.32	2	3.57
Graduate and Above	7	12.96	51	26.84	47	83.93
Total	54	100.00	190	100.00	56	100.00

Table 7.22 shows the awareness of the tribal population about the role of constitutional laws in the Panchayat system. It is shown that 3.33 percent said panchayat decides with the help of constitutional laws, 47.00 percent tribal population said it doesn't decide with the help of constitutional laws and 49.67 percent could not decide any of the way.

Table 7.23: Laws Prevalent in Society Among the Tribal Population of District Lahoul and Spiti, Himachal Pradesh

Laws Predominant in Society	*Respondents*	*Percent*
Constitutional Laws	-	-
Customary Laws	300	100.00
Total	300	100.00

Table 7.23 reveals that when asked about the prevalence of laws in tribal society, all reply came in favour of customary laws as no body said that constitutional laws are prevalent in society. It appears that the bonding of Lahouli is made on the basis of customary laws.

1.E Attitude Towards Police and Court

Table 7.24 shows the attitude of the tribal population towards the police in the area. When asked to rate police officials behaviour, the majority of 50.33 percent of respondents said it was satisfactory. Contradicting this result a small percentage of 2.33 percent also said its bad where as 32.33 percent of informants said its not social, as they are very rude and don't talk properly.

Table 7.24 : Attitude Towards Police Officials Among the Tribal Population of District Lahoul and Spiti, Himachal Pradesh

Rate Police Official's Behaviour	*Respondents*	*Percent*
Very good	3	1.00
Bad	7	2.33
Satisfactory	151	50.33
Not Social	97	32.33
Don't Know	42	14.00
Total	300	100.00

Table 7.25 shows the percentage of the tribal population who have ever visited the police station. 86.67 percent has never ever gone to police station. Only a small percentage of 13.33 percent has gone to station.

Table 7.25 : Visit to Police Station Among the Tribal Population of District Lahoul and Spiti, Himachal Pradesh

Visit Police Station	*Respondents*	*Percent*
Visited	40	13.33
Never Visited	260	86.67
Total	300	100.00

Table 7.26 relates the education with the visit to the police station. Majority of these who have visited the police station are graduates or above (55.00 percent). However, 7.50 percent of the illiterates have also gone to police station. In the category of those who have never visited the police station, 31.92 percent are graduates and 26.92 percent are illiterates.

Table 7.26 : Education and Visit to Police Station Among the Tribal Population of District Lahoul and Spiti, Himachal Pradesh

Education	*Visited*	*Percent*	*Never Visited*	*Percent*
Illiterate	3	7.50	70	26.92
Primary	3	7.50	30	11.54
Middle	5	12.50	34	13.08
10th Passed	2	5.00	27	10.38
12th Passed	5	12.50	16	6.15
Graduate and Above	22	55.00	83	31.92
Total	40	100.00	260	100.00

Table 7.27 shows the occupation of those who have visited the police station and those who have never visited the police station. It is reported that those who have gone to police station, majority of the population (45.00 percent) is in service. The only of 2.50 percent of the tribal population who works as a daily labour has also gone to police station.

Among those who have never visited the police station, 48.08 percent are agriculturists and 28.85 percent are into various services.

Table 7.27: Occupation and Visit to Police Station Among the Tribal Population of District Lahoul and Spiti, Himachal Pradesh

Occupation	*Visited*	*Percent*	*Never Visited*	*Percent*
Agriculture	8	20.00	125	48.08
Service	18	45.00	75	28.85
Daily Labour	1	2.50	2	0.77
Business	5	12.50	18	6.92
Animal Husbandry	6	15.00	5	1.92
Inactive (No Work)	2	5.00	35	13.46
Total	40	100.00	260	100.00

Table 7.28 shows the various reasons for going to police station which is not always justice seeking. Out of those who have gone to police station, 62.50 percent of the tribal population have gone to police station for lodging an FIR to get justice, 15.00 percent have gone to pay the 'chalan' (fine), 12.50 percent go to police station as they work in police station.

Table 7.28: Reason for Going to Police Station Among the Tribal Population of District Lahoul and Spiti, Himachal Pradesh

Reasons of Going to Police Station	*Respondents*	*Percent*
For Lodging an FIR to Get Justice	25	62.50
To Take the License	4	10.00
To Pay the *Chalan*	6	15.00
To Discuss / Mediation/ Negotiation	-	-
Job Requirement	5	12.50
Total	40	100.00

Table 7.29 presents the attitude of the tribal population about the police men. It reports that 87.50 percent said that the behaviour of the police men at the police station is co-operative, 2.50 percent said its non-cooperative and 10percent said its rude.

Table 7.30 sheds some light on the attitude of respondents towards local court. Only 6.67 percent of respondents have ever gone to court and the major percentage of 93.33 percent have never ever gone to local court.

Table 7.29 : Behaviour of Police Men At the Station Among the Tribal Population of District Lahoul and Spiti, Himachal Pradesh

Behaviour of Police Men At Station	*Respondent's Visited*	*Percent*
Co-operative	35	87.50
Non-cooperative	1	2.50
Rude	4	10.00
Total	40	100.00

Table 7.30 : Visited Court Among the Tribal Population of District Lahoul and Spiti, Himachal Pradesh

Visit a Local Court (at Keylong or Kullu)	*Respondents*	*Percent*
Visited	20	6.67
Never Visited	280	93.33
Total	300	100.00

Table 7.31 shows the awareness of the tribal population about the court procedure. Only 33.67 percent of respondents know about the proper channel of approaching the Supreme Court i.e. session court than high court than Supreme Court. 66.33 percent of informants are not at all aware of these procedural steps.

Table 7.31 : Awareness About Approach to Court Among the Tribal Population of District Lahoul and Spiti, Himachal Pradesh

Approach the Supreme Court	*Respondents*	*Percent*
Session Court - High Court - Supreme Court	101	33.67
Don't Know	199	66.33
Total	300	100.00

Table 7.32 presents the impact of education on the awareness about approach to court among the tribal population. It shows that among those who are aware of the proper channel to reach to the supreme court, the majority of population (70.30 percent) are graduates and above. Only 2.97 percent of the respondents who are reported to be aware are primary passed.

Table 7.32: Education and Awareness About Approach to Court Among the Tribal Population of District Lahoul and Spiti, Himachal Pradesh

Education	*Aware of Procedure*	*Percent*	*Unaware of*	*Percent Procedure*
Illiterate	-	-	73	36.68
Primary	3	2.97	30	15.08
Middle	11	10.89	28	14.07
10th Passed	11	10.89	18	9.05
12th Passed	5	4.95	16	8.04
Graduate and Above	71	70.30	34	17.09
Total	101	100.00	199	100.00

Among those who are unaware of the proper channel to reach supreme court, 36.68 percent are illiterate. However 17.09 percent respondents in this category have done graduation or above.

Table 7.33: Occupation and Awareness About Approach to Court Among the Tribal Population of District Lahoul and Spiti, Himachal Pradesh

Occupation	*Aware of Procedure*	*Percent*	*Unaware of Procedure*	*Percent*
Agriculture	20	19.80	113	56.78
Service	56	55.45	37	18.59
Daily Labour	2	1.98	1	0.50
Business	8	7.92	15	7.54
Animal Husbandry	6	5.94	5	2.51
Inactive (No Work)	9	8.91	28	14.07
Total	101	100.00	199	100.00

Table 7.33 presents the occupation of the respondents who are aware and unaware of the procedure to approach supreme court. Majority of the respondents who are reported to be aware are into service (55.45 percent), 19.80 percent are agriculturists. It is to be noted here that 1.98 percent of the aware respondents are daily labourers. In the category of unaware respondents, the majority of the tribal respondents are agriculturists (56.78 percent), 18.59 percent are into service and 14.07 percent are retired. It is generally believed

that people doing agriculture have least exposure as these people live in less urbanized areas, generally belong to low income groups, are generally less educated and are mostly found unbothered about the awareness of the surroundings.

Table 7.34 : Awareness About Procedure of Public Interest Litigation (PIL) Among the Tribal Population of District Lahoul and Spiti, Himachal Pradesh

Procedure of Public Interest Litigation	*Respondents*	*Percent*
Aware	6	2.00
Unaware	294	98.00
Total	300	100.00

On further delving at respondents knowledge of courts and police, when it was asked if they knew about the provision of Public Interest Litigation i.e. informing the supreme court about their violation through a post card than only 2.00 percent of respondents were aware of this provision provided by constitution to its people. Rest, 98.00 percent were absolutely unaware (Table 7.34).

1.F Awareness and Violation of Various Human Rights

There are almost as many theories of rights as there are rights theorists. It is said that the only true rights are legal rights. Other scholars argue for a broader view of rights which would encompass moral rights as well. For many philosophical writers, a 'right' is treated synonymously with a 'claim' (Feinberg, 1973). The 'Oxford English Dictionary' defines a right as a 'justifiable claim, on legal or moral grounds, to have or obtain something, or to act in a certain way.' Feinberg said to have a right is to have a claim to something and against someone, the recognition of which is called for by legal rules or, in the case of moral rights, by the principles of an enlightened conscience. What distinguishes a right from a demand is that it is justified, either by appeal to pre-existing legal rules or to morality. Thus a right is a valid claim. McCloskey prefers to define a right as an entitlement rather than a claim. (c.f. Renteln, 1988).

In the following section all those rights which are considered as the 'justifiable claims' or the 'entitlements' are discussed which includes Child Right ,Women's Right, Marriage Right, Educational Right, Reproductive Right,

Development Right, Right to Proper Medical Treatment, Reservation Right and Right to Religion. These rights are consecutively studied in the tribal ,rural and urban populations. Each of these human rights are defined in various articles as framed by the Constitution of India spread in various clauses. Justice to all clauses of an article framed is not possible. Only major clauses are considered for the present work.

(i) Child Right

A child means every human being who has not completed the age of sixteen years. Here in this study the focus is either on the infants or on the child till the middle school. Article 24 of the Universal Declaration of Human Rights provides the basic rights of a child as :

(a) Proper consistent mother's feed till at least 8-10 months.

(b) The child, by reason of his physical and mental immaturity, needs special safeguards and care.

(c) Primary socialization of the child done by his or her mother.

Table 7.35 : Basic Right of Child Among the Tribal Population of District Lahoul and Spiti, Himachal Pradesh

Child Fed For Months	*Respondents*	*Percent*
0-3 Months	29	30.85
4-6 Months	41	43.62
7-9 Months	12	12.77
10-12 Months	6	6.38
More Than One Year	6	6.38
Total	94	100.00

Table 7.35 presents the data on certain aspects of basic right of a child. It shows that out of 94 respondents of this question, 43.62 percent Lahouli mothers fed their children for 4-6 months. 30.85 percent Lahouli women said they fed their babies for 0-3 months. Only 12.77 percent women said they fed their child till 7-9 months. However, 6.38 percent responded that they fed their child for more than a year. These were the mothers who were not pre-occupied by agricultural work, as either they had no land or the land was leased out.

It has been observed that 74.47 percent of the tribal mothers are violating the rights of their child by feeding them less than 8-10 months. Only 25.53 percent comply with the human rights of child who breast feed their child for more than 8-9 months.

Table 7.36: Child Care Among the Tribal Population of District Lahoul and Spiti, Himachal Pradesh

Care Taker of The Child	*Respondents*	*Percent*
Elder Siblings	4	4.26
Father / Mother	17	18.09
Other Family Members	48	51.06
Takes Along to Field	6	6.38
No Body	19	20.21
Total	94	100.00

Table 7.36 shows the members who take care of the child. It is reported that 51.09 percent mothers said that the care of the child is done by other family members as joint family (Joint) system is prevalent in Lahoul. 18.09 percent said that the care of the child is done by his or her parents. 6.38 percent takes the child along with them to their field. These are all nuclear family. 11.56 percent said nobody takes care of the child when the parents are out in field. In such cases children take care of themselves or the elder sibling takes care of the younger ones. Although it doesn't make much difference if the child is taken care by his or her parents or other members. But the basic fact that more the quality time spend with the child, better will be the inculcation of values, ethics and principles which helps in making an all the more a better individual. And this duty and responsibility can be best dispensed by the child's mother only. Keeping this in view, it can be said that the protection of the child as its human rights has been violated by 24.47 percent of the tribal population, as these families would either leave their younger child with elder child or no body would take care of them.

(ii) Women's Right

Article 2 of the Universal Declaration of Human Rights says that everyone is entitled to all the rights and freedoms set forth in this Declaration without distinction of any kind, such as race, colour, sex, language, religion, political or other opinion, national or social origin, property, birth or other status. All the International Covenants recognize that women as men have an equal right to enjoy all economic, social and cultural rights which includes – Right to Economic Equality, Right to the Highest Attainable Standard of Health, Right to Education, Right to Food, Right to Housing, Right to Water, Right to Work, Cultural Rights and Women's Rights. The human rights of women and of the girl-child are an inalienable, integral and indivisible part of universal human rights. The full and equal participation of women in political, civil, economic, social and cultural life, at the national, regional and international levels, and the eradication of all forms of discrimination on grounds of sex are priority objectives of the international community.

In view of the above, it was noted while working in Lahoul, that women folk here, work day and night laboriously, even in the pregnant conditions, as shown in the Table 7.37. From the total 94 ever married females, 90 respondents has babies and 4 were newly married.58.89 percent of women are reported to have worked till the 9th month of pregnancy. 30 percent have worked till 7-8th month. Women who have miscarriage, attribute this factor of heavy and extensive working for their mis-happening. On the contrary, elderly women vote for working even in the last month of pregnancy as they say this makes the child birth easy as muscles becomes strong.

Table 7.37 : Work Done During Pregnancy Among the Tribal Population of District Lahoul and Spiti, Himachal Pradesh

Months	*Respondents*	*Percent*
3-4th Months	-	-
5-6 Months	10	11.11
7-8 Months	27	30.00
9th Months	53	58.89
Total	90	100.00

Table 7.38 presents the reasons for working during pregnancy. It reveals that all the women were not working in the field willfully. 63.41 percent of women said they work in their lands during pregnancy because of economic reasons. In a given condition, if the family has other workers they would surely put the work in abeyance during those months. However, 36.59 percent also responded by saying that in-laws also pressurize them to work. 8 are those women who worked initially only) 82+8=90

It can be said here that working during pregnancy because of the pressure from the family members is the violation of human rights of the women. 36.59 percent of the women revealed that their human right has been violated. If they work willfully during this state of motherhood because of some economic reasons, than it cannot be termed as the violation of human rights.

Table 7.38 : Reason for Working Among the Tribal Population of District Lahoul and Spiti, Himachal Pradesh

Reason for Working	*Respondents*	*Percent*
Family Members Forcing	30	36.59
Husband Forcing	-	-
Economic Reasons	52	63.41
Total	82	100.00

Taking a note of women's right in property in Lahoul, it was found that, women face discrimination in many aspects of housing, including housing policy development, control over household resources, and rights of inheritance and property ownership, through the application of gender-biased law, customary laws (as discussed earlier), tradition and dominant social attitudes. Each of these obstacles can prevent women from owning, inheriting, leasing, or renting housing, and makes women vulnerable to forced eviction. A woman's precarious relationship to her housing may make her more likely to experience physical or psychological harassment.

(iii) Marriage Right

Article 16 of the Universal Declaration of Human Rights says that "Men and women of full age, without any limitation due to race, nationality or religion, have the right to marry and to found a family. They are entitled to equal rights as to marriage, during marriage and its dissolution. Marriage shall be entered into only with the free and full consent of the intending spouses. The family is the natural and fundamental group unit of society and is entitled to protection by society and the state" Constitution has granted every adult male and female to choose his or her partner wishfully. Since, Lahoul is a tribal area, so customary laws are in prevalence here over the constitutional laws. As explained earlier in Ethnographic life, marriage by elopement is permitted in Lahoul, which if seen otherwise without the rubric of customary laws may appear to be marriage by kidnapping the girl.

Table 7.39 shows if the informant knew or was told about the elopement prior to the act, then 80.43 percent of respondents (including both the sexes) said they were eloped or they eloped their partner without giving prior information and 19.57 percent said they knew about the act of elopement which is going to happen.

Table 7.39 : Practice of Marriage Among the Tribal Population of District Lahoul and Spiti, Himachal Pradesh

Did You / Were You Told About Elopement	*Respondents*	*Percent*
Aware	46	19.57
Unaware	189	80.43
Total	235	100.00

It can be said that 80.43 percent of the respondents have experienced the violation of their human rights of marrying willfully and with full consent.

Table 7.40: Nature of Elopements Among the Tribal Population of District Lahoul and Spiti, Himachal Pradesh

Elopements Always Willful	*Respondents*	*Percent*
Willful	3	1.00
Not Willful	297	99.00
Total	300	100.00

Table 7.40 shows the nature of elopements if they are willful or not willful. The majority of the respondents said that elopements are not willful (99.00 percent) and only a negligible percent of the population said that elopement marriages are willful (1.00 percent).

It can be said that 99.00 percent of the Lahouli population have experienced the violation of their human rights of marrying willfully.

Table 7.41 : Attitude Towards Forceful Elopements Among the Tribal Population of District Lahoul and Spiti, Himachal Pradesh

Forcefully Eloped, What Will You Do	*Respondents*	*Percent*
Accept the Man	192	64.00
Come Back	19	6.33
Take Action	31	10.33
Report to Police	58	19.33
Total	300	100.00

Table 7.42 : Education and Attitude Towards Forceful Elopements Among the Tribal Population of District Lahoul and Spiti, Himachal Pradesh

Education	*Accept the Man*	*Percent*	*Come Back*	*Percent*	*Take Action*	*Percent*	*Report to Police*	*Percent*
Illiterate	70	36.46	-	-	2	6.45	1	1.72
Primary	29	15.10	2	10.53	-	-	2	3.45
Middle	34	17.71	2	10.53	1	3.23	2	3.45
10th Passed	18	9.38	2	10.53	5	16.13	4	6.90
12th Passed	13	6.77	2	10.53	-	-	6	10.34
Graduate and Above	28	14.58	11	57.89	23	74.19	43	74.14
Total	192	100.00	19	100.00	31	100.00	58	100.00

Table 7.41 shows the response of an hypothetical question asked to all the respondents. It was asked 'if forcefully eloped, what will you do ?'. 64.00 percent said they would accept the conditions, 6.33 percent said they will go back to parent's house, 10.33 percent said they will take an action and 19.33 percent said they will report the matter to police. This indicates that inspite of the protection given to the custom of marriage by elopement by the parapluie of customary laws, people have started going to police stations showing their ostracism towards this customary law of their society. Young men and women have formed association to abolish this marriage pattern by elopement. But the older generation keep believing and following these traditions, which are called as obsolete and orthodox laws by the young members of the same society.

It show that the attitude of the tribal population towards the violation of their human rights is of accepting the injustice, as 64.00 percent of the tribal population said they would accept the person with whom they would be married forcefully and without their knowledge.

Table 7.42 presents the impact of education on the attitude towards forceful elopements among the tribal population. It shows that in the category of those who responded by saying that they will accept the man in case forcefully eloped, the majority of 36.46 percent are illiterates, 15.10 percent have studied till primary class. However 14.58 percent respondents are graduates also. In the category of those who will take any action against such forceful elopements, 74.19 percent who will take an action are graduates. Those who will approach police are found majorly (74.14 percent) in the category of graduates as they get maximum exposure through education.

(iv) Educational Right

Article 26 of the Universal Declaration of Human Rights says that "Everyone has the right to education. Education shall be free, at least in the elementary and fundamental stages. Elementary education shall be compulsory. Technical and professional education shall be made generally available and higher education shall be equally accessible to all on the basis of merit." Education has been conceived as one of the most powerful instruments for socio-economic uplift of an individual and for bringing about socio-economic transformation on egalitarian lines. It was, therefore, quite appropriate that our Constitution framers incorporated specific Articles to ensure that the State took active part in promoting education amongst all and specifically amongst weaker sections of the population.

The Articles relating to educational safeguards are as follows:

Article 46 included among the Directive Principles of State Policy provides: "The State shall promote with special care the educational and economic interests of the weaker sections of the people, and in particular, of the Scheduled Castes and Scheduled Tribes, and shall protect them from social injustice and all forms of exploitation".

Article 15(4) empowers the state to make any special provisions for the advancement of any socially and educationally backward classes of citizens or for SC & ST. This provision was added to the Constitution through the Constitution (First Amendment) Act, 1951. It enabled the State to reserve seats for SC & ST in educational institutions including technical, 16(4) the term 'backward classes' is used as a generic term and comprises various categories of backward classes. Viz., Scheduled Castes, Scheduled Tribes, Other Backward Classes, Denotified Communities and Nomadic and Semi-nomadic Communities.

Article 29 (1) provides that "any section of the citizens residing in the territory of India or any part thereof having a distinct language, script or culture of its own shall have the right to conserve the same". This article has special significance for all the Scheduled Tribes. Santhals have a script of their own, viz., Olchiki.

Article 350 A reads: " It shall be the endeavor of every State and of every local authority within the State to provide adequate facilities for instructions in the mother tongue at the primary stage of education to children belonging to linguistic minority groups, and the President may issue such directions to any State as he considers necessary or proper for securing the provision of such facilities." Most of the tribal communities have their own languages or dialects which usually belong to a different family of languages than the one to which the State's official language belongs. Various expert commissions and committees have recommended that instruction should be imparted to tribal children in their mother tongue in primary schools, at least in classes I and II.

It was found during the field work that many Lahoulis wanted to study but due to one or other reasons, could not study or those who could start studying could not complete it.

Table 7.43 reports various reasons among the tribal population for not completing the studies. It shows that 26.67 percent respondents never got any opportunity to study. These were majorly those cases who were the eldest siblings of the house, who were to share the responsibility of the house and the other younger siblings. 1.47 percent were those where the girl's in-laws refused her to continue the studies. 4.04 percent were those cases, where the informants never got time from household work, thus sacrificing their studies.

Table 7.43 : Reasons for Not Completing Studies Among the Tribal Population of District Lahoul and Spiti, Himachal Pradesh

If no, why	*Respondents*	*Percent*
Never Interested	132	44.00
Never Got Opportunity	80	26.67
In -laws Refused	4	1.33
Parents Refused	2	0.67
Got a Job	71	23.67
No Time From Household Works	11	3.67
Total	300	100.00

It can be said that all the respondents who could not study because of lack of opportunity or refusal by in-laws or parents or busy with the work in the household have experienced the violation of their right to education.

(v) Reproductive Rights

Reproductive rights is a political term to refer to women's rights in areas of sexual reproduction, including the rights to reproduce (such as forced sterilization) as well as rights not to reproduce, (such as birth control and abortion). Reproductive rights are mutual in nature, acquired by both the partners of the couple. It's the duty and the right of both the partners to take care of each other's need but with mutual consent.

Table 7.44: Decision of Having a Child Among the Tribal Population of District Lahoul and Spiti, Himachal Pradesh

Decision of Having a Child	*Respondents*	*Percent*
Husband	82	34.89
Wife	-	-
Both	153	65.11
In-laws	-	-
Total	235	100.00

Table 7.44 shows the contribution of decision of husband and wife in having a child. It reports that 65.11 percent of the respondents said both the

partners take the decision together of having a child. But 34.89 percent also said husband takes the decision of having a child.

It can be said that 34.89 percent of the respondents experience the violation of the reproductive rights which are mutual in nature, as only one partner takes the decision of having a child.

Table 7.45: Role of Male/Female in Decision Making Among the Tribal Population of District Lahoul and Spiti, Himachal Pradesh

Not Interested	*Male*	*Percent*	Female	Percent
Succumb to Spouse's Desire	14	9.93	83	88.30
Stick to Your Own Wish	127	90.07	11	11.70
Total	141	100.00	94	100.00

Table 7.45 shows the role of male/females in have a child. It shows that, among males 90.07 percent of the respondents said that they would stick to their own wish. Only 9.93 percent of the respondents said that they would succumb to their spouse's desire of having a child. Among females the responses were opposite, as 88.30 percent of the respondents said they would succumb to their spouse's desire. Only 11.70 percent females said they would stick to their own wish of having or not having a child. This ostensibly shows that the reproductive rights which are equal for both – the husband and the wife and are also mutual in nature, as imputed in the constitution, are actually different in the reality. Males as husbands have more say than females as wives.

It can be said that violation of the human right of mutual consent for procreation of the family is majorly experienced by the females ,as 88.30 percent would succumb to their husband's desire.

(vi) Development Right

The Right to Development is an inalienable human right by virtue of which every human person and all peoples are entitled to participate in, contribute to, and enjoy economic, social, cultural and political development, in which all human rights and fundamental freedoms can be fully realized. Human beings are the central subject of development and should be the active participant and beneficiary of the right to development. This includes not only accepting but also rejecting any development programme run by the state. It includes the right to know and avail various development programmes run in the village.

Table 7.46 : Awareness of Right to Development Among the Tribal Population of District Lahoul and Spiti, Himachal Pradesh

Right to Development	*Respondents*	*Percent*
Aware	12	4.00
Unaware	288	96.00
Total	300	100.00

Table 7.46 reports the awareness of right to development among the tribal population. It shows that 96.00 percent of the respondents are absolutely unaware of their right to development and only 4.00 percent knew that its their right to accept or reject the development programme.

It can be said that 96.00 percent are experiencing the violation of their right to development because of their unawareness.

Table 7.47: Awareness of Development Programmes Among the Tribal Population of District Lahoul and Spiti, Himachal Pradesh

Development Programmes	*Respondents*	*Percent*
Aware	151	50.33
Unaware	149	49.67
Total	300	100.00

Table 7.47 shows that in yet another question, if the respondent is aware – 50.33 percent of the population is aware of the development programmes running in his or her village and 49.67 percent are unaware, showing their ignorance about these programmes. This ignorance may be because of two reasons – either the programmes are not well propagated or people are uninterested. Reason may be any, but the result is same. Inspite of huge calculations and massive investments in these programmes, desired results could never be achieved.

(vii) Right to Medical Treatment

Article 25 of the Universal Declaration of Human Rights says that "Everyone has the right to a standard of living adequate for the health and well being of himself and of his family, including food, clothing ,housing and medical care and necessary social services, and the right to security in the event of unemployment, sickness, disability, widowhood, old age or other lack of livelihood in circumstances beyond his control." Keeping this in mind respondents were asked about the medical facilities available.

Table 7.48 reports the conditions of the medical facilities available among the tribal population. It shows that 59.67 percent said the facilities are good and available, 9.67 percent said the facilities are good but are not available as all the cases are referred outside Lahoul, either to Manali or Chandigarh.

Table 7.48: Facilities Available Among the Tribal Population of District Lahoul and Spiti, Himachal Pradesh

Facilities for Treatment	*Respondents*	*Percent*
Good Available	179	59.67
Good not Available	29	9.67
Not Available	92	30.67
Total	300	100.00

So these respondents think that facilities are not provided to the patients deliberately 30.67 percent said facilities are not at all available. Health centers in Lahoul play the mere role of dispensing units.

It can be said that 40.34 percent of the tribal respondents are experiencing the violation of their human right to proper medical care as they are not getting facilities for the treatment of their ailment.

Table 7.49 reports the quality of doctors among the tribal population. It shows that 68.00 percent of respondents says that the doctors here are experienced and good where as 32.00 percent said that doctors are freshers and un-experienced, as all the major cases are referred out of Lahoul.

Table 7.50 : Quality of Doctors Among the Tribal Population of District Lahoul and Spiti, Himachal Pradesh

Quality of Doctors	*Respondents*	*Percent*
Experienced	204	68.00
Freshers and Inexperienced	96	32.00
Total	300	100.00

Table 7.50 presents the percent of population who have been given the wrong medicine among the tribal population. It shows that 97.65 percent of

respondents said doctors have never given any wrong medicines, but 2.35 percent said wrong medicines had been given by doctors. These were the respondents who think that their ailment was not cured because of doctor's mistreatment or wrong medicines.

Table 7.50: Wrong Medicines Given Among the Tribal Population of District Lahoul and Spiti, Himachal Pradesh

Wrong Medicine	*Respondents*	*Percent*
Yes	7	2.35
No	291	97.65
Total	298	100.00

It can be said that 2.35 percent of the respondents have experienced the violation of their right to proper medical treatment. They blame doctors saying they are all fresh and un-experienced. Infact when the patient's statements were verified with the doctor's, a different picture emerged. Doctors say its only the patients' negligence that the medicines do not work or react, as they don't follow the precautions as directed.

Table 7.51: Action Taken Among the Tribal Population of District Lahoul and Spiti, Himachal Pradesh

Action Taken by You	*Respondents*	*Percent*
Never Gone to That Doctor Again	3	42.86
Gone Back to Report Him and Ended in an Argument	4	57.14
Filed a Case Against Him	-	-
Total	7	100.00

Table 7.51 reports the action taken by the patient who have been mistreated by the doctor. It shows that out of those respondents who had been given wrong medicines, 57.14 percent have gone back to the doctor to report him about the wrong medicines given to him and have ended up in an argument. 42.86 percent reports that they have never gone to that doctor again once he has given the wrong medicine.

(viii) Reservation Right

These are the special reservations given by the government to the groups of people like Scheduled Tribes (as declared by constitution), Scheduled Castes, Other Backward Communities; at the job place, admissions in the educational institutions, at the village level official systems and in the political assemblies etc.

Table 7.52: Aware of Reservation Among the Tribal Population of District Lahoul and Spiti, Himachal Pradesh

Aware that Seats Reserved for Scheduled Tribes in Jobs, Political Assemblies	*Respondents*	*Percent*
Aware	156	52.00
Unaware	144	48.00
Total	300	100.00

Table 7.52, shows the awareness of the tribal population about the reservation for the scheduled tribes. It reports that 52.00 percent respondents are aware of the reservation at the job place and 48.00 percent are reported to be unaware.

Table 7.53 shows that 74.00 percent of the tribal population are aware that they have been categorised in the Scheduled Tribe status and 26.00 percent are found to be unaware of this categorization.

Table 7.53: Aware About the Category Status Among the Tribal Population of District Lahoul and Spiti, Himachal Pradesh

Aware that Categorised Under Tribal Status	*Respondents*	*Percent*
Aware	222	74
Unaware	78	26
Total	300	100

Table 7.54 reports the status of the benefits received by the tribal population. 36.67 percent said benefits are in reality, 26.67 percent said benefits are on paper only and 36.67 percent said they can't say if they are getting the

benefits. Those who said can't say means, they are not aware of benefits they are entitled to.

Table 7.54 : Benefits in Reality Among the Tribal Population of District Lahoul and Spiti, Himachal Pradesh

Benefits in Reality	*Respondents*	*Percent*
In Reality	110	36.67
On Paper	80	26.67
Can't Say	110	36.67
Total	300	100.00

Three different views on the basis of the quality of benefits are reported from those saying that benefits are in reality i.e. 36.67 percent (Table7.54). Table 7.55 shows that, 73.64 percent says the quality of the benefits provided is good and 20.00 percent says the quality of the benefits is awfully bad and 6.36 percent said its satisfactory.

Table 7.55 : Quality of Benefits Among the Tribal Population of District Lahoul and Spiti, Himachal Pradesh

Quality of Benefits	*Respondents*	*Percent*
Good	81	73.64
Bad	22	20.00
Satisfactory	7	6.36
Total	110	100.00

Benefits include subsidized ration, seeds, fertilizers, other eatables etc. Tribals say that the quality of the ration is not good so they prefer buying it from market, outside Lahoul. Only those households take these food items who cannot afford to buy them, rest take it from the subsidized Food and Supply Stores. Similarly, the quality of seeds is not good as it is either infected or do not give good yield.

Table 7.56 shows the awareness of the tribal population about NCSCST and NHRC. It shows that in the tribal population only 4.67 percent respondents are reported to be aware of National Commission for Scheduled Castes and Scheduled Tribes (NCSC ST).These are either lawyers who comes to Delhi

Table 7.56: Awareness About National Commission for Scheduled Castes and Scheduled Tribes (NCSCST) and National / State Human Rights Commission (NHRC/SHRC) Among the Tribal Population of District Lahoul and Spiti, Himachal Pradesh

Commission	*NCSCST*	*Percent*	*NHRC*	*Percent*
Aware	14	4.67	55	18.33
Unaware	286	95.33	245	81.67
Total	300	100.00	300	100.00

frequently. The majority of respondents (95.33 percent) are unaware of it. 18.33 percent are aware of the presence of the National or State Human Rights Commission. 81.67 percent are unaware of the presence.

(ix) Right to Religion

Right to Religion is protected in the constitution by saying that every individual is free to opt and practice his or her own religion. Keeping this in mind it was asked why or why not would you change your religion. Table 7.57 shows the reasons for which tribal population would want to change their religion. 52.67 percent said they wouldn't change their religion as they don't wish to do so. 15.67 percent said they would not change their religion as they want to die in the same religion they have spend their lives for.

Table 7.57 : Change of Religion Among the Tribal Population of District Lahoul and Spiti, Himachal Pradesh

Reason	*Respondents*	*Percent*
Don't Wish to Change	158	52.67
Want to Die With Religion in Which Born	47	15.67
Right to Practice Any Religion	93	31.00
Wanted to Change	2	0.67
Total	300	100.00

31.00 percent however, said that they wouldn't change their religion as it is their right to practice the religion of their wish. A negligent percentage of 0.67 percent is also worth mentioning here, as these are the respondents who would want to change their religion because of their spouse. This percentage of those aspiring to change indicates that the idea of religion transformation is not absolutely alien to this society.

7.1.2 Police and Human Rights Among Rural Population of District Rohtak, Haryana

2.A Knowledge of Crime

Table 7.58 shows the concept of crime among the rural population of Haryana. On being asked the meaning of 'crime', out of 300 informants, 18.33 percent respondents gave the raw definition of crime.Raw knowledge or definition in the rural context means that those who gave simple definition of crime. For the rural population the meaning of crime is all that behavior which is injurious to society. For those people who are religious minded, they see crime as belonging to the genre of sin. Some of the respondents also equated falsehood with crime and truth as the ultimate value.

Table 7.58 :Definition of Crime Among Rural Population of District Rohtak, Haryana

Definition of Crime	*Respondents*	*Percent*
Raw Definition	55	18.33
Constitutional Definition	245	81.67
Total	300	100.00

81.67 percent population gave the constitutional definition of crime as they said any act which is punishable by law like theft, murder, rape or hurting anybody is called crime. Rural population defined crime as *"the actions which are injurious to the society and belong to the genre of sin like falsehood and other constitutional crimes like murder, theft, rape or hurting others"*.

Table 7.59 shows the impact of education on the knowledge of crime among the rural population. It shows that among those who have exhibited the raw knowledge of crime, 94.55 percent are illiterate. However no graduates have been found in this category. Among respondents having the constitutional knowledge of crime, 54.69 percent are graduates and above. However 13.47 percent of those having the constitutional knowledge are illiterates.

Table 7.60 shows the occupation of those who exhibited raw knowledge and the constitutional knowledge. 58.18 percent of those who has raw knowledge of crime are agriculturists. 21.82 percent of the respondents are inactive thus contributing nothing in the unit of production of the household.

Table 7.59: Education and Knowledge of Crime Among Rural Population of District Rohtak, Haryana

Education	*Raw Knowledge*	*Percent*	*Constitutional Knowledge*	*Percent*
Illiterate	52	94.55	33	13.47
Primary	2	3.64	38	15.51
Middle	1	1.82	19	7.76
10th passed	-	-	8	3.27
12th Passed	-	-	13	5.31
Graduate and Above	-	-	134	54.69
Total	55	100.00	245	100.00

Table 7.60 : Occupation and Knowledge of Crime Among Rural Population of District Rohtak, Haryana

Occupation	*Raw Knowledge*	*Percent*	*Constitutional Knowledge*	*Percent*
Agriculture	32	58.18	74	30.20
Service	-	-	94	38.37
Daily Labour	7	12.73	9	3.67
Business	-	-	36	14.69
Animal Husbandry	4	7.27	12	4.90
Nothing	12	21.82	20	8.16
Total	55	100.00	245	100.00

The majority of 38.37 percent of those having constitutional knowledge are in various services and 14.69 percent of the respondents who have their own business.

Table 7.61 shows the awareness of crime and human rights among the rural population. It shows that 86.00 percent respondents are aware of crime going on in and around their surroundings and thus the violation of rights. 14.00 percent are totally unaware of the happenings.

Table 7.61 : Awareness of Crime and Human Rights Violation Among Rural Population of District Rohtak, Haryana

Awareness	*Respondents*	*Percent*
Aware	258	86.00
Unaware	42	14.00
Total	300	100.00

Table 7.62 : Education and Awareness of Crime and Human Rights Violation Among Rural Population of District Rohtak, Haryana

Education	*Aware*	*Percent*	*Unaware*	*Percent*
Illiterate	67	25.97	18	42.86
Primary	36	13.95	4	9.52
Middle	14	5.43	6	14.29
10th passed	6	2.33	2	4.76
12th Passed	9	3.49	4	9.52
Graduate and Above	126	48.84	8	19.05
Total	258	100.00	42	100.00

Table 7.62 reports the impact of education on the awareness of crime and human rights on the rural population. It shows that 48.84 percent of the aware respondents are graduates and above, 25.97 percent are illiterate. Among the unaware respondents 42.86 percent are illiterate and 19.05 percent are graduates and above.

Table 7.63 present gender and awareness of crime and human rights violation among the rural population of District Rohtak. It has been observed that 61.68 percent males are graduates and they are the maximum who are aware about crime and human rights violation. Those who are least aware belong to middle (2.99 percent), 10th passed (2.40 percent) and 12th passed (2.99 percent) of their educational level. It is interesting to note that 17.96 percent males who are illiterate are aware about crime and human rights violation. Males generally get more exposure of the world than females as they get more opportunity to interact with people. In the case of females, 25.27 percent female graduates are aware of crime and human rights violation. It is to be noted here that 40.66 percent females are illiterate and 17.58 percent are primary passed who are aware of crime and human rights violation. This could

Table 7.63: Gender and Awareness of Crime and Human Rights Violation Among Rural Population of District Rohtak, Haryana

Education	*Aware*				*Unaware*			
	Male	*Percent*	*Female*	*Percent*	*Male*	*Percent*	*Female*	*Percent*
Illiterate	30	17.96	37	40.66	10	62.50	8	30.77
Primary	20	11.98	16	17.58	1	6.25	3	11.54
Middle	5	2.99	9	9.89	2	12.50	4	15.38
10th Passed	4	2.40	2	2.20	-	-	2	7.69
12th Passed	5	2.99	4	4.40	1	6.25	3	11.54
Graduate	103	61.68	23	25.27	2	12.50	6	23.08
Total	167	100.00	91	100.00	16	100	26	100.00

be because of the fact that in rural population, women have also started moving out of their houses for doing jobs, thus getting exposure and opportunity.

In the category of unaware respondents it has been observed that 62.50 percent males are illiterates and they are the maximum who are unaware about the crime and human rights violation. It is interesting to note here that 12.50 percent males who are graduate are unaware of the crime and human rights violation. In the case of females, 30.77 percent of the females are illiterate who are unaware about the crime and human rights violation. 23.08 percent female graduates, 15.38 percent of middle passed females, 11.54 percent of 12th passed females are found to be unaware about the crime and human rights violation.

2.B Source of Awareness of Crime and Human Rights Violation

Table 7.64: Main Source of Crime Awareness and Human Rights Violation Among Rural Population of District Rohtak, Haryana

Sources of Awareness	*Male*	*Percent*	*Female*	*Percent*	*Total*	*Percent*
T.V.	25	14.97	23	25.27	48	18.60
Radio	4	2.40	5	5.49	9	3.49
News Paper	36	21.56	5	5.49	41	15.89
Meeting people	45	26.95	35	38.46	80	31.01
Movement outside the Area	18	10.78	4	4.40	22	8.53
Occupation type	14	8.38	5	5.49	19	7.36
Self exp	25	14.97	14	15.38	39	15.12
Total	167	100.00	91	100.00	258	100.00

Table 7.64 reveals the main source of crime awareness among the rural population. It shows that for the maximum of the total respondents i.e. 31.01 percent of the rural population, meeting people is their main source of the awareness. 18.60 percent of the population watching TV is the second major source of awareness. 15.89 percent of the respondents depend on news paper as a source. The other sources providing awareness are movement outside the area (8.53 percent), occupation type (7.36 percent), radio (3.49 percent). It has been observed that among males (21.56 percent) and females (38.46 percent) meeting people is their major source of their awareness.

Table 7.65 : Personal Experience of Crime and Human Rights Violation Among Rural Population of District Rohtak, Haryana

Personal Experience	*Respondents*	*Percent*
Experienced	39	13.00
Inexperienced	261	87.00
Total	300	100.00

Table 7.65 gives the percentage of those who have the personal experience of crime and human rights violation. It reports that 13.00 percent of the rural population has experienced the violation of their human rights in one or the other way.

2.C Knowledge and Attitude Towards Human Rights

Table 7.66 presents the knowledge of human rights among the rural population. It reports that 46.67 percent could not explain at all the meaning of the word 'Human Rights'.

Table 7.66 : Knowledge of Human Rights Among Rural Population of District Rohtak, Haryana

Level of Awareness	*Respondents*	*Percent*
Unaware	140	46.67
Partially Aware	110	36.67
Fully Aware	50	16.67
Total	300	100.00

36.67 percent are those who could explain the meaning by giving examples, thus being partially aware. 16.67 percent respondents were fully aware, who gave the definition with examples. *Thus the rural population defined human right collectively as "Fundamental claims of a man are called Human Rights."*

Table 7.67 shows the effect of education on the knowledge of human rights among the rural population. It shows that among the unaware respondents, majority of the respondents (60.71 percent) are illiterate. There are no graduates in this category. Among partially aware, the maximum (83.64 percent) response came from those who are minimum graduates or above.

Among those who are fully aware (according to the criteria given above), the majority of percentage 84.00 percent of the respondents are graduates and above. There is no illiterate among this category.

Table 7.67: Education and Knowledge of Human Rights Among Rural Population of District Rohtak, Haryana

Education	*Unaware*	*Percent*	*Partially Aware*	*Percent*	*Fully Aware*	*Percent*
Illiterate	85	60.71	-	-	-	-
Primary	40	28.57	-	-	-	-
Middle	10	7.14	6	5.45	4	8.00
10th Passed	3	2.14	4	3.64	1	2.00
12th Passed	2	1.43	8	7.27	3	6.00
Graduate and Above	-	-	92	83.64	42	84.00
Total	140	100.00	110	100.00	50	100.00

Table 7.68: Reasons for Right Framed Among Rural Population of District Rohtak, Haryana

Reasons for Framing Rights	*Respondents*	*Percent*
Unaware	83	27.67
Aware	217	72.33
Total	300	100.00

Table 7.68 reports the awareness of the rural population about the reasons of the right framed. 27.67 percent of the informants are unaware of the reason of rights framed in the society. The majority of respondents, 72.33 percent are aware of reasons of rights framed.

Table 7.69 shows educational level of the population which is aware and unaware of the reasons of the rights framed. 81.93 percent of illiterate population are unaware of the reasons behind the rights framed. None of the graduates are found in this category. A majority of 61.75 percent of the aware population are minimum graduate or above. It is to be noted in this category that 7.83 percent of the respondents are illiterate and even than aware of the reasons of the rights framed.

Table 7.69 : Education and Reasons for Rights Framed Among Rural Population of District Rohtak, Haryana

Education	*Unaware*	*Percent*	*Aware*	*Percent*
Illiterate	68	81.93	17	7.83
Primary	13	15.66	27	12.44
Middle	2	2.41	18	8.29
10th Passed	-	-	8	3.69
12th Passed	-	-	13	5.99
Graduate and Above	-	-	134	61.75
Total	83	100.00	217	100.00

Table 7.70 : Occupation and Reasons for Right Framed Among Rural Population of District Rohtak, Haryana

Occupation	*Unaware*	*Percent*	*Aware*	*Percent*
Agriculture	48	57.83	58	26.73
Service	-	-	94	43.32
Daily Labour	13	15.66	3	1.38
Business	-	-	36	16.59
Animal Husbandry	10	12.05	6	2.76
Retired	12	14.46	20	9.22
Total	83	100.00	217	100.00

Table 7.70 discusses the impact of occupation on the awareness of the reason for rights framed among the rural population. It shows that for 57.83 percent unaware respondents, agriculture is their occupation, daily labour (15.66 percent), leading a retired life (14.46 percent). None of the unaware respondents are reported to be in service. In the category of aware respondents, the majority of 43.32 percent are in service, 26.73 percent are in agriculture, 16.59 percent have their own business.

Table 7.71 shows that the number of human rights told by the rural population, where none stands for those who were absolutely unaware as they couldn't tell even single human right article out of nineteen and above ten category stands for fully aware i.e. who could tell more than ten human right articles out of nineteen. The various articles under which human rights have been declared by Universal Declaration of Human Rights have been detailed out previously.

Table 7.71 : Human Right Articles Awareness Among Rural Population of District Rohtak, Haryana

Awareness of Rights	*Respondents*	*Percent*
None	91	30.33
One - Two	45	15.00
Three - Four	106	35.33
Five-Six	28	9.33
Seven-Eight	21	7.00
Nine-Ten	-	-
Above Ten	9	3.00
Total	300	100.00

A majority of 35.33 percent respondents lie in third category, who could tell three to four human right articles. 30.33 percent of the respondents could tell none of the human right articles. Only 3.00 percent of the respondents could tell more than 10 human right articles. It can also be derived that if 30.33 percent respondents could not tell even a single human right article, than 69.67 percent are those which include as less as single human right article or as much as above ten.

Table 7.72 : Awareness About Categories of Human Rights (Articles) Among Rural Population of District Rohtak, Haryana

S.No.	*Category of Human Rights*	*209(n)*	*Percent*
1.	Right to Life	201	96.17
2.	Freedom from Torture	198	94.74
3.	Right to Education	195	93.30
4.	Right to Marry	80	38.28
5.	Equality before Courts	72	34.45
6.	Freedom of Movement	70	33.49
7.	Freedom of Religion	68	32.54
8.	Right to Work	65	31.10
9.	Freedom of Thought	55	26.32
10.	Equal Protection of Law	44	21.05
11.	Freedom from Slavery	38	18.18

(Contd.)

(Contd. Table 7.72)

S.No.	Category of Human Rights	209(n)	Percent
12.	Freedom of Expression	27	12.92
13.	Right to Social Security	22	10.53
14.	Right to Adequate Standard of Living	22	10.53
15.	Freedom from Arrest	19	9.09
16.	Right to Take Part in Cultural Life	19	9.09
17.	Right of Minorities	19	9.09
18.	Right to Peaceful Assembly	17	8.13
19.	Freedom to Seek Information	15	7.18

Table 7.72 reveals that of these 209 respondents, 96.17 percent of respondents are aware of Right to Life, 94.74 percent knows about Freedom from Torture, 93.30 percent respondent are aware of Right to Education. The top five responses, according to the score of the percentage goes for 'Right to Life', 'Freedom from Torture', 'Right to Education', 'Right to Marry' and 'Equality before Courts'. Looking at this pattern of answers, it can be said that *the response among the Rural Population is of the mix type. The awareness of the population is more than basic awareness and less than advanced awareness.*

Table 7.73 : Awareness About Rights of Arrested Person Among Rural Population of District Rohtak, Haryana

Rights of Arrested Person	Respondents	Percent
Phone Call	35	11.67
Lawyer	16	5.33
Both	37	12.33
Don't Know	212	70.67
Total	300	100.00

Table 7.73 presents the awareness about rights of arrested person in the rural population. It shows that 11.67 percent respondents are aware of the rights of arrested person of making a phone call. Only 5.33 percent are aware that the arrested person has the right to talk only in front of his or her lawyer. 12.33 percent of respondents are aware of both of these rights of arrested person. Major percentage of 70.67 percent of the informants are unaware of both these rights.

Table 7.74 : Education and Awareness About Rights of Arrested Among Rural Population of District Rohtak, Haryana

Education	*Phone Call*	*Percent*	*Lawyer*	*Percent*	*Both*	*Percent*	*Don't Know*	*Percent*
Illiterate	-	-	-	-	-	-	85	40.09
Primary	-	-	-	-	-	-	40	18.87
Middle	-	-	-	-	-	-	20	9.43
10th Passed	2	5.71	-	-	-	-	6	2.83
12th Passed	2	5.71	-	-	1	2.7	10	4.72
Graduate and above	31	88.57	16	100.00	36	97.3	51	24.06
Total	35	100.00	16	100.00	37	100.0	212	100.00

Table 7.75 : Occupation and Awareness About Rights of Arrested Person Among Rural Population of District Rohtak, Haryana

Occupation	*Phone Call*	*Percent*	*Lawyer*	*Percent*	*Both*	*Percent*	*Don't Know*	*Percent*
Agriculture	3	8.57	-	-	-	-	103	48.58
Service	25	71.43	16	100.00	35	94.59	18	8.49
Daily Labour	-	-	-	-	-	-	16	7.55
Business	4	11.43	-	-	-	5.41	30	14.15
Animal Husbandry	-	-	-	-	-	-	16	7.55
Nothing	3	8.57	-	-	-	-	29	13.68
Total	35	100.00	16	100.00	37	100.00	212	100.00

Table 7.74 shows the effect of education on the awareness about the rights of arrested person among the rural population. It clearly indicates that 88.57 percent of the graduates are aware of the rights of an arrested person of making a phone call. All the respondents who knew about the rights of talking in front of his or her lawyer are all graduates and above. Among those who were aware of both the rights of the arrested person, 97.3 percent are graduates and above. However a small percentage of 2.7 percent respondents are 12th passed also. Among those who are not aware of any of the rights of the arrested person, 40.09 percent are illiterates, 18.87 percent are 12th passed. Here it is worth mentioning that 24.06 percent respondents are those who are graduates and above.

Table 7.75 relates occupation and awareness about rights of arrested person among the rural population. It shows that majority of the respondents who could not tell about the rights of the arrested person are agriculturists (48.58 percent). 14.15 percent of those who have their own business. The majority of those who could tell both the human rights of arrested person are in service (94.59 percent). However, 5.41 percent of those having their own business.

Table 7.76 : Attitude Towards Violation of Rights Among Rural Population of District Rohtak, Haryana

Take the Injustice Done	*Respondents*	*Percent*
Take an Action	272	90.67
Leave it After Few Discussion	28	9.33
Never Bother	-	-
Total	300	100.00

Table 7.76 presents the attitude towards human rights and its violation. 90.67 percent said they would take an action against the injustice done to them. 9.33 percent would prefer to leave the whole issue after discussing it.

2.D Practice of Human Rights

Table 7.77 shows the prevalence of dispute processing institutions among rural population. It shows that none of the respondents said that they would go to elderly people for their justice seeking. This indicates that the age old medieval practice of going to elderly people for solving one's problem have vanished. 39.67 percent respondents voted for Panchayat system, that is they would go to *Panch* or *Sarpanch* first for solving their problem. 60.33 percent said, that they would go to police directly for seeking justice.

Table 7.77 : Dispute Processing Institutions Among Rural Population of District Rohtak, Haryana

Dispute Processing Institution	*Respondents*	*Percent*
Elderly	-	-
Panchayat	119	39.67
Police	181	60.33
Total	300	100.00

Table 7.78 shows that when the variable of justice seeking preference is compared with another variable of education, then it has been found that the illiterates and the graduates and above account for exactly the same percentage of voters for Panchayat system i.e. 35.29 percent in both the categories. In the category of those who would take help of constitution for their justice seeking, 50.83 percent are graduates.

Table 7.78 : Education and Justice Seeking Among Rural Population of District Rohtak, Haryana

Education	*Elderly*	*Percent*	*Panchayat*	*Percent*	*Police*	*Percent*
Illiterate	-	-	42	35.29	43	23.76
Primary	-	-	13	10.92	27	14.92
Middle	-	-	11	9.24	9	4.97
10th Passed	-	-	5	4.20	3	1.66
12th Passed	-	-	6	5.04	7	3.87
Graduate and Above	-	-	42	35.29	92	50.83
Total	-	-	119	100.00	181	100.00

This indicates that education plays an important role in transforming the individual mind set. However, it needs to be mentioned here that 23.76 percent of illiterates also go to police for justice seeking.

Table 7.79 : Involvement of Panchayat Among Rural Population of District Rohtak, Haryana

Panchayat Decides with Help of Constitutional Laws	*Respondents*	*Percent*
Yes	110	36.67
No	40	13.33
Don't know	150	50.00
Total	300	100.00

According to 36.67 percent respondents Panchayat decides with the help of constitutional laws i.e. the Panchayat keeps the police system involved and informed about the happenings in the village (Table 7.79). These respondents also think that Panchayat decides the cases forwarded to it in the same way as the police does. 13.33 percent said it doesn't decide with the help of constitutional laws.Panchayat has its own system of rendering justice to the people. It doesn't work like the police system. However, 50.00 percent respondents do not know if panchayat works independently or with the police system.

Table 7.80: Laws Prevalent In Society Among Rural Population of District Rohtak, Haryana

Laws Predominant in Society	*Respondents*	*Percent*
Constitutional Laws	195	65.00
Customary laws	105	35.00
Total	300	100.00

Table7.80 shows the prevalence of laws in the rural society. 65.00 percent respondents said that Constitutional laws are prevalent in their society, where as 35.00 percent said that Customary laws are prevalent. Customary Laws here means people follow the unwritten rules and laws made by the elderly people of the society. They would go to the panchayat for solving their problems. Panchayat just mediates between the two aggrieved parties and help in the negotiation of the matter.

2.E Attitude Towards Police and Court

Table 7.81 shows that the attitude of the rural population towards the police. People share a bad image about the police system, irrespective of their visit to the police station. None of the respondents are satisfied with the behaviour of the police in the area. Supporting this a huge percentage of 91.00 percent said their behaviour is bad. 9.00 percent said official's behaviour is not social, as they are very rude and don't talk properly.

Table7.81 : Attitude Towards Police Officials Among Rural Population of District Rohtak, Haryana

Rate Police Official's Behaviour	*Respondents*	*Percent*
Very good	-	-
Bad	273	91.00
Satisfactory	-	-
Not social	27	9.00
Don't know	-	-
Total	300	100.00

Table 7.82 shows the percentage of the rural population who has gone to police station. It shows that 45.33 percent of the rural respondents have gone to Police Station, where as 54.67 percent have never ever gone to station.

Table 7.82 : Visited Police Station Among Rural Population of District Rohtak, Haryana

Visit Police Station	*Respondents*	*Percent*
Visited	136	45.33
Never Visited	164	54.67
Total	300	100.00

Table 7.83 relates the education with the visit to the police station. Majority of these who have visited the police station are graduates or above (83.82 percent). However, 6.62 percent of the illiterates have also gone to police station. In the category of those who have never visited the police station,12.20 percent are graduates and 46.34 percent are illiterates.

Table 7.83 : Education and Visit to Police Station Among Rural Population of District Rohtak, Haryana

Education	*Visited*	*Percent*	*Never Visited*	*Percent*
Illiterate	9	6.62	76	46.34
Primary	1	0.74	39	23.78
Middle	4	2.94	16	9.76
10th Passed	3	2.21	5	3.05
12th Passed	5	3.68	8	4.88
Graduate and Above	114	83.82	20	12.20
Total	136	100.00	164	100.00

Table 7.84 shows the occupation of those who have visited the police station and those who have never visited the police station. It is reported that those who have gone to police station, majority of the population (54.41 percent) is in service. The minimum of 3.68 percent of the rural population who works as a daily labour has also gone to police station.

Table 7.84: Occupation and Visit to Police Station Among Rural Population of District Rohtak, Haryana

Occupation	*Visited*	*Percent*	*Never Visited*	*Percent*
Agriculture	28	20.59	78	47.56
Service	74	54.41	20	12.20
Daily Labour	5	3.68	11	6.71
Business	12	8.82	24	14.63
Animal Husbandry	7	5.15	9	5.49
Nothing	10	7.35	22	13.41
Total	136	100.00	164	100.00

Among those who have never visited the police station are 47.56 percent agriculturists and 12.20 percent are into services.

Table 7.85 shows the reasons for going to police station. 66.91 percent have gone to police station for lodging an FIR to get justice. 25.74 percent respondents are those who have gone to police station with the intension of lodging an FIR but their dispute had been settled without getting into legal complications. This has majorly been achieved by a mutual compromise between the two parties or by also payment of the loss experienced by the victim. A small percentage of 7.35 percent are of those who go to police station as it is their job requirement.

Table 7.85 : Reason for Going to Police Station Among Rural Population of District Rohtak, Haryana

Reasons of Going to Police Station	*Respondents*	*Percent*
For Lodging an FIR to Get Justice	91	66.91
To Take the License	-	-
To Pay the *Chalan*	-	-
To Discuss / Mediation/ Negotiation	35	25.74
Job Requirement	10	7.35
Total	136	100.00

Table 7.86 presents the behaviour of police man at the police station. According to 6.62 percent respondents the behaviour of the police men at the police station is co-operative, 66.18 percent said its non-cooperative and 27.21 percent said its rude.

Table 7.86 : Behaviour of Police Men at the Station Among Rural Population of District Rohtak, Haryana

Behaviour of Police Men At Station	*Respondent's Visited*	*Percent*
Co-Operative	9	6.62
Non-Cooperative	90	66.18
Rude	37	27.21
Total	136	100.00

Table 7.87 presents the visit to court by the rural population. It has been observed that 29.33 percent of respondents have ever gone to court and the majority of the respondents (70.67 percent) have never been to court.

Table 7.88 shows the awareness of the rural population about the court procedure. 44.33 percent of respondents know about the proper sequence of approaching the supreme court i.e. Session Court than High Court than Supreme court. 55.67 percent of informants are not at all aware of these procedural steps.

Table7.87 : Visit to Court Among Rural Population of District Rohtak, Haryana

Visit to Court	*Respondents*	*Percent*
Visited	88	29.33
Never Visited	212	70.67
Total	300	100.00

Table 7.88 : Awareness About Approach to Court Among Rural Population of District Rohtak, Haryana

Approach the Supreme Court	*Respondents*	*Percent*
Session Court - High Court - Supreme Court	133	44.33
Don't Know	167	55.67
Total	300	100.00

Table 7.89 shows that education plays a major role when the awareness about the court procedures comes. Among those who are aware about the procedures to approach the court, 84.96 percent of the respondents are graduates or above.However, in this category it is worth mentioning that 3.76 percent of the respondents are absolutely illiterate. Among the category of the unaware respondents, maximum percentage of 47.90 percent are illiterate. 12.57 percent respondents who are graduates and above are also found to be unaware about the procedure to approach the court.

Table 7.89 : Education and Awareness About Approach to Court Among Rural Population of District Rohtak, Haryana

Education	*Aware of Procedure*	*Percent*	*Unaware of Procedure*	*Percent*
Illiterate	5	3.76	80	47.90
Primary	2	1.50	38	22.75
Middle	7	5.26	13	7.78
10th Passed	1	0.75	7	4.19
12th Passed	5	3.76	8	4.79
Graduate and Above	113	84.96	21	12.57
Total	133	100.00	167	100.00

Table 7.90 presents the occupation of the respondents who are aware and unaware of the procedure to approach supreme court. Majority of the respondents who are reported to be aware are into service (60.15 percent), 18.80 percent are agriculturists. In the category of unaware respondents, 48.50 percent are agriculturists, 8.38 percent are into Service and 17.37 percent are retired.

Table 7.90 : Occupation and Awareness About Approach to Court Among Rural Population of District Rohtak, Haryana

Occupation	*Aware of Procedure*	*Percent*	*Unaware of Procedure*	*Percent*
Agriculture	25	18.80	81	48.50
Service	80	60.15	14	8.38
Daily Labour	-	-	16	9.58
Business	20	15.04	16	9.58
Animal Husbandry	5	3.76	11	6.59
Nothing	3	2.26	29	17.37
Total	133	100.00	167	100.00

Table 7.91 shows that ,on further delving at respondents knowledge of courts and police, only 13.67 percent said they know about the provision of Public Interest Litigation i.e. informing the supreme court about their violation of a right through a post card. Rest 86.33 percent are absolutely unaware about the procedure of Public Interest Litigation.

Table 7.91 : Awareness About Procedure of Public Interest Litigation (PIL)Among Rural Population of District Rohtak, Haryana

Procedure of Public Interest Litigation	*Respondents*	*Percent*
Aware	41	13.67
Unaware	259	86.33
Total	300	100.00

2.F Awareness and Violation of Various Human Rights

In the following section, rights like child right, women's right, marriage right, educational right, reproductive right, development right, right to proper medical treatment, reservation right and right to religion are discussed. Articles in which these rights have been laid down by the Constitution of India have been detailed out in the previous section of tribal population.

(i) Child Right

Table 7.92 : Basic Right of Child Among Rural Population of District Rohtak, Haryana

Child Fed For Months	*Respondents*	*Percent*
0-3 Months	32	29.63
4-6 Months	41	37.96
7-9 Months	28	25.93
10-12 Months	3	2.78
More Than One Year	4	3.70
Total	108	100.00

Table 7.92 shows the practice of basic rights of a child among the rural population. It reveals, the maximum percentage of 37.96 percent rural mothers fed their children for 4-6 months, 29.63 percent rural women said they fed their babies for 0-3 months, 25.93 percent women said they fed their child till 7-9 months. However, 3.70 percent responded that they fed their child for more than a year.

It can be said that among rural population a total of 67.59 percent of the rural mothers violate the basic right of their children by depriving them from prolonged breast feeding.

Table 7.93: Child Care Among Rural Population of District Rohtak, Haryana

Care Taker of the Child	*Respondents*	*Percent*
Elder Siblings	25	23.15
Father / Mother	36	33.33
Other Family Members	47	43.52
Takes Along to Work Area	-	-
No Body	-	-
Total	108	100.00

Table7.93 shows the percentage of the members who take care of a child among the rural population. It shows that 33.33 percent respondents

said care taker of their children are either of the parents. 43.52 percent said other family members also take care of their child. 23.15 percent said elder siblings take care of the younger ones.

It can be said that 23.15 percent of the parents violate the basic right of a child for protection as these children are taken care by their elder siblings, who can be children themselves.

(ii) Women's Right

Table 7.94 : Work Done During Pregnancy Among Rural Population of District Rohtak, Haryana

Months	*Respondents*	*Percent*
3-4th Month	-	-
5-6th Month	20	18.52
7-8th Month	49	45.37
9th Month	39	36.11
Total	108	100.00

Table7.94 shows the respondents who have worked during their pregnancies among the rural population. It reports that out of 108 respondents for this question, 36.11 percent of women have worked till the 9th month of pregnancy. 45.37 percent have worked till 7-8th month. 18.52 percent women worked till 5 to 6th month.

It can be said that the human right of the pregnant women for rest and safety has been violated for 81.48 percent of the rural women, as they worked in the eighth and ninth month of the pregnancy also.

Table7.95: Reason for Working Among Rural Population of District Rohtak, Haryana

The Reason for Working	*Respondents*	*Percent*
Family Members Forcing	40	37.04
Husband Forcing	-	-
Economic Reasons	68	62.96
Total	108	100.00

Table 7.95 shows the various reasons for which pregnant women works among the rural population. 62.96 percent of women said they work during

pregnancy because of economic reasons. In a given condition, if the family has other workers they would surely put the work in abeyance during those months. However, 37.04 percent also responded by saying that in-laws also pressurize them to work.

It can be said here that those women who have worked after coming under the pressure of any family member, than it's a violation of their human right. 37.04 percent of the pregnant rural women have experienced this violation.

(iii) Marriage Right

"In Haryana, a trend of marrying their children at an early age has been observed (as shown by mean age of marriage of males and females in Chapter V, Table 5.69).

Table 7.96 : Practice of Marriage Among Rural Population of District Rohtak, Haryana

Aware of Getting Married	*Respondents*	*Percent*
Aware	52	19.19
Unaware	219	80.81
Total	271	100.00

Table 7.96 shows that 80.81 percent of the married people were unaware of their marriage that is at the time when the marriage is fixed neither the girl nor the boy knew each other. Only a small percent of 19.19 percent knew with whom they are going to get married.

It can be said that 80.81 percent of rural population have faced the violation of their right to marry with consent, as they are reported to be unaware of their marrying partner.

Table 7.97 : Attitude Towards Forceful Marriage Among Rural Population of District Rohtak, Haryana

Forcefully Married, What Will You Do	*Respondents*	*Percent*
Accept the Man	225	75.00
Come Back	-	-
Take Action	-	-
Report to Police	75	25.00
Total	300	100.00

Table 7.98 : Education and Attitude Towards Forceful Elopements Among Rural Population of District Rohtak, Haryana

Education	*Accept the Man*	*Percent*	*Come back*	*Percent*	*Take action*	*Percent*	*Report to Police*	*Percent*
Illiterate	59	47.20	-	-	26	40.00	-	-
Primary	37	29.60	-	-	2	3.08	1	0.91
Middle	12	9.60	-	-	5	7.69	3	2.73
10th Passed	6	4.80	-	-	-	-	2	1.82
12th Passed	9	7.20	-	-	3	4.62	1	0.91
Graduate and Above	2	1.60	-	-	29	44.62	103	93.64
Total	125	100.00	-	-	65	100.00	110	100.00

Table 7.97 shows the respondents attitude towards the forceful marriage. It is shown that, if forcefully married, 75.00 percent respondents will accept the conditions, 25.00 percent said they will report the matter to police. This question was asked to all the respondents irrespective of their marital status.

It can be said that 75.00 percent of the rural population will accept the violation of their right to marry, as they said that they would accept the person with whom they would be forcefully married.

Table 7.98 presents the effect of education on the attitude of the rural population towards forceful elopements. It shows that in the category of those who responded by saying that they will accept the man in case forcefully married, the majority of 47.20 percent are illiterates, 29.60 percent have studied till primary class. However 1.60 percent respondents are graduates also. In the category of those who will take any action against such forceful marriages, 44.62 percent who will take an action are graduates. It is observed that police station is approached by majority of graduates and above (93.64 percent) as they are most confident to approach police station because of the exposure and knowledge they got through education. However action is taken only by those who are practicing their knowledge.

(iv) Educational Right

Constitution has protected the right to education for every body. It was found during the field work that many among the Rural population wanted to study but due to one or other reasons, could not study or those who could start studying could not complete it.

Table7.99: Reasons for Not Completing Studies Among Rural Population of District Rohtak, Haryana

If no, why	*Respondents*	*Percent*
Never Interested	110	36.67
Never Got Opportunity	90	30.00
In -Laws Refused	50	16.67
Parents Refused	5	1.67
Got a Job	20	6.67
No Time From Household Works	25	8.33
Total	300	100.00

Table 7.99 reports the reasons for not completing studies among the rural population. It shows that, 36.67 percent respondents had never been interested in completing their studies. 30.00 percent are those who never got any opportunity. These are majorly those cases who were the eldest siblings of the house, who were to share the responsibility of the house and the other younger siblings. 16.67 percent are those where the girl's in-laws refused her to continue the studies. 8.33 percent respondents kept busy in the household activities at the cost of their studies. Only a small percent of 1.67 percent are the cases where their parents refused to study further.

It can be said that a total of 56.67 percent of the rural population have experienced the violation of their human rights to education as these respondents didn't get the opportunity to study or were not granted permission by their family members or kept busy with the daily chores of the household.

(v) Reproductive Rights

Table 7.100 : Decision of Having a Child Among Rural Population of District Rohtak, Haryana

Decision of Having a Child	*Respondents*	*Percent*
Husband	181	66.79
Wife	15	5.54
Both	35	12.92
In-laws	40	14.76
Total	271	100.00

Table 7.100 shows that, a majority of 66.79 percent said only husband takes the decision of having a child, showing the high handedness of the males in the society. 14.76 percent respondents said parents –in-laws tell their married children to have babies. 12.92 percent said that both the partners take the decision of having a child.

Table 7.101 presents the role of male/female in decision making among the rural population.Among males cent percent respondents said that they would stick to their own wish regarding the decision for a child, indicating the dominance of males in decision making. Among females 93.52 percent said that they would succumb to their spouse's desire. However, 6.48 percent females also replied that they would stick to their own wish regarding the issue.It is observed that only females have responded in the category of succumbing to spouse's desire.Further out of the total of those who said they would stick to their wish, 94.67 percent (163/170) are males and 5.33 percent (7/170) are females

Table 7.101 : Role of Male/Female in Decision Making Among Rural Population of District Rohtak, Haryana

Not Interested	*Male*	*Percent*	*Female*	*Percent*	*Total*	*Percent*
Succumb to Spouse's Desire	-	-	101	93.52	101	37.27
Stick to Your Own Wish	163	100.00	7	6.48	170	62.73
Total	163	100.00	108	100.00	271	100.00

(vi) Development Right

Table 7.102 :Awareness of Right to Development Among Rural Population of District Rohtak, Haryana

Right to Development	*Respondents*	*Percent*
Aware	89	29.67
Unaware	211	70.33
Total	300	100.00

Table 7.102 shows the awareness of right to development among the rural populations. It reveals that 70.33 percent of the respondents are absolutely unaware of their right to development thus showing their awareness level and only 29.67 percent knew that its their right to accept or reject the development programme. These respondents are reported to be aware that the development programme cannot be enforced upon the citizens. They may accept or reject the scheme offered to them.

It can be said that 70.33 percent of the rural population are self violating their right to development because they are unaware of their right.

Table 7.103 shows the data on the respondents awareness of development programmes. 40.33 percent are aware of the development programmes run by the state or block, where as 59.67 percent are absolutely unaware of these programmes.

Table 7.103 : Awareness of Development Programmes Among Rural Population of District Rohtak, Haryana

Development Programs	*Respondents*	*Percent*
Aware	121	40.33
Unaware	179	59.67
Total	300	100.00

(vii) Right To Medical Treatment

Table 7.104 : Facilities Available Among Rural Population of District Rohtak, Haryana

Facilities for Treatment	*Respondents*	*Percent*
Good Available	100	33.33
Good Not Available	125	41.67
Not Available	75	25.00
Total	300	100.00

Table 7.104 shows the conditions of the facilities available among the rural population. It presents that 33.33 percent respondents said the medical facilities are good and at the same time available. 41.67 percent said that facilities are good but are not made available to the patients because of corruption in the system.Government hospitals take the grants from the government but do update their facilities for the patients. 25.00 percent said facilities are not at all available.

It can be said that total of 66.67 percent of the rural respondents feel that their right to proper medical treatment has been violated as treatment facilities are not available.

Table 7.105 : Quality of Doctors Among Rural Population of District Rohtak, Haryana

Quality of Doctors	*Respondents*	*Percent*
Experienced	300	100.00
Fresher and Inexperienced	-	-
Total	300	100.00

Table 7.105 shows that hundred percent of the respondents said that doctors are experienced and good. The medical doctors present in the hospital are reported to be good.

Table 7.106 Wrong Medicines Given Among Rural Population of District Rohtak, Haryana

Wrong Medicine	*Respondents*	*Percent*
Yes	59	19.67
No	241	80.33
Total	300	100.00

Table 7.106 presents the percent of the wrong medicines given to the patients among the rural populations. It shows that, 80.33 percent of the respondents said that doctors have never given any wrong medicines. However, 19.67 percent of the respondents are the victims of the mistreatment of the doctor. According to them, they have been given wrong medicines.

It can be said that 19.67 percent of the rural informants have experienced the violation of their human right to proper medical treatment as they have been given wrong medicines by the doctor.

Table 7.107 : Action Taken Among Rural Population of District Rohtak, Haryana

Action Taken	*Respondents*	*Percent*
Never Gone to That Doctor Again	14	23.73
Gone Back to Report Him and Ended in an Argument	30	50.85
Filed a Case Against Him	15	25.42
Total	59	100.00

Table 7.107 presents the types of action taken by the those who have been treated wrongly in the rural population. It shows that 80.33 percent of the respondents said that doctors have never given any wrong medicines. However, 19.67 percent of the respondents are the victims of the mistreatment of the doctor.

(viii) Reservation Right :

Table 7.108 : Aware of Reservation of Seats Among Rural Population of District Rohtak, Haryana

Aware That Seats Reserved for Scheduled Tribes in Jobs, Political Assemblies	*Respondents*	*Percent*
Aware	260	86.67
Unaware	40	13.33
Total	300	100.00

Table 7.108 shows the awareness of the reservation of seats for scheduled tribes and other backwards classes among the rural population. It shows that 86.67 percent respondents are aware of the reservation at the job place and 13.33 percent said they are not aware.

Table 7.109 : Awareness About National Commission for Scheduled Castes and Scheduled Tribes and National/State Human Rights Commission Among Rural Population of District Rohtak, Haryana

Commission	*NCSCST*	*Percent*	*NHRC/SHRC*	*Percent*
Aware	20	6.67	25	8.33
Unaware	280	93.33	275	91.67
Total	300	100.00	300	100.00

Table 7.109 shows the awareness of NCSCST and NHRC among the rural population. It reveals that only 6.67 percent of the informants are aware of the National Commission for Scheduled Castes and Scheduled Tribes (NCSC& ST).93.33 percent are absolutely unaware. 8.33 percent are aware of National or State Human Rights Commission (NHRC/SHRC) ; 91.67 percent are those who do not know anything about the existence of the Commission.

(ix) Right to Religion :

Right to religion is protected in the constitution by saying that every individual is free to opt and practice his or her own religion.

According to Table 7.110, 33.33 percent of the rural population is aware of their right to practice the religion of one's own choice. 25.00 percent said they don't wish to change their religion. 30.00 percent said they would not change their religion as they want to die in the same religion they had spend their lives. 11.67 percent respondents would want to change their religion if some benefits are involved.

Table7.110 : Change of Religion Among Rural Population of District Rohtak, Haryana

Reason	*Respondents*	*Percent*
Don't Wish to Change	75	25.00
Want to Die with Religion in Which Born	90	30.00
Right to Practice any Religion	100	33.33
Wanted to Change	35	11.67
Total	300	100.00

7.1.3 Police and Human Rights Among Urban Population of Delhi

3.A Knowledge of Crime

Table 7.111 : Definition of Crime Among the Urban Population of Delhi

Definition of Crime	*Urban Respondents*	*Percent*
Raw Definition	22	7.33
Constitutional Definition	278	92.67
Total	300	100.00

Table 7.111 shows that among the Urban Population, only 7.33 percent exhibited the raw knowledge or gave the raw definition about crime and 92.67 percent have the constitutional knowledge of crime.Urban population defined crime as *"any punishable offence written under the IPC, CrPC of the Indian Constitution."*

Table 7.112 shows that among those who have exhibited the raw knowledge of crime, 27.27 percent are illiterate and 36.36 percent are graduates and above. Among the respondents having the constitutional knowledge of crime, the majority of percentage 70.50 percent are graduates and above. Only a small percentage of 2.52 percent are illiterates.

Table 7.112 : Education and Knowledge of Crime Among the Urban Population of Delhi

Education	*Raw Knowledge*	*Percent*	*Constitutional knowledge*	*Percent*
Illiterate	6	27.27	7	2.52
Primary	3	13.64	5	1.80
Middle	-	-	8	2.88
10th Passed	3	13.64	27	9.71
12th Passed	2	9.09	35	12.59
Graduate and Above	8	36.36	196	70.50
Total	22	100.00	278	100.00

Table 7.113 : Occupation and Knowledge of Crime Among the Urban Population of Delhi

Occupation	*Raw Knowledge*	*Percent*	*Constitutional Knowledge*	*Percent*
Service	1	4.55	69	24.82
Daily Labour	-	-	1	0.36
Business	3	13.64	43	15.47
Retired	18	81.82	65	59.35
Total	22	100.00	278	100.00

Table 7.113 shows the occupation of those who exhibited raw knowledge and the constitutional knowledge. 4.55 percent of those who has raw knowledge of crime are in service. The maximum of 81.82 percent of the respondents are retired.24.82 percent of those having constitutional knowledge are in service. Here also, the maximum knowledge of the constitutional knowledge of crime is exhibited by the retired members of the population. The reason for obtaining this pattern of occupation and awareness i.e. maximum percentage of those exhibiting constitutional knowledge are retired can be explained by saying that retired people have no dearth of time. They pass their time either by reading newspaper or watching TV or listening radio or meeting people. Thus increasing their knowledge about the crime happening in and around their area.

Table 7.114 : Awareness of Crime and Human Rights Violation Among the Urban Population of Delhi

Awareness Level	*Respondents*	*Percent*
Aware	281	93.67
Unaware	19	6.33
Total	300	100.00

Table 7.114 shows that 93.67 percent respondents are aware of crime going on in and around their surroundings and thus the violation of rights. Only 6.33 percent are totally unaware of the happenings.The high percent of the aware respondents can be attributed to the fact that in the metropolitan culture, the impact of mass media is strongest as compared to any other settings. Communication of information through various means is most effective in urban areas.

Table 7.115 : Education and Awareness of Crime and Human Rights Violation Among the Urban Population of Delhi

Education	*Aware*	*Percent*	*Unaware*	*Percent*
Illiterate	8	2.85	5	26.32
Primary	7	2.49	1	5.26
Middle	8	2.85	-	-
10th Passed	28	9.96	2	10.53
12th Passed	34	12.10	3	15.79
Graduate and Above	196	69.75	8	42.11
Total	281	100.00	19	100.00

Table 7.115 shows that 69.75 percent of the aware respondents are graduates and above, only a small percentage of 2.85 percent are illiterate ,thus clearly indicating the impact of education on the awareness level. Among the unaware respondents 26.32 percent are illiterate and 42.11 percent are graduates and above. Majority of the unaware respondents are females who are either housewives or elderly.

Table 7.116 present gender and awareness of crime and human rights violation among the urban population of Delhi. It has been observed that 78.29 percent males are graduates and they are the maximum who are aware

Table 7.116: Gender and Awareness of Crime and Human Rights Violation Among the Urban Population of Delhi

Education	*Aware*				*Unaware*			
	Male	*Percent*	*Female*	*Percent*	*Male*	*Percent*	*Female*	*Percent*
Illiterate	2	1.32	6	4.65	2	66.67	3	18.75
Primary	3	1.97	4	3.10	-	-	1	6.25
Middle	1	0.66	7	5.43	-	-	-	-
10th Passed	12	7.89	16	12.40	-	-	2	12.50
12th Passed	15	9.87	19	14.73	-	-	3	18.75
Graduate and above	119	78.29	77	59.69	1	33.33	7	43.75
Total	152	100.00	129	100.00	3	100.00	16	100.00

about crime and human rights violation. Those who are least aware belong to middle (0.66 percent) ,primary (1.97 percent) and illiterate (1.32 percent) of their educational level. In the case of females, 59.69 percent females are graduates and aware of crime and human rights violation. Only 4.65 percent of illiterate females are also aware of crime and human rights violation.

In the category of unaware respondents, only three males have been reported. 66.67 percent of unaware males are illiterate. In the case of females, 18.75 percent of the females are illiterate who are unaware about the crime and human rights violation. However 43.75 percent of the females are graduate and above who are also unaware of the crime and human rights violation. This may be because of the fact that most of the females in this category are senior citizens, who generally pass their leisure in meditation or doing small households chores, thus restricting their routine to house only. This given them lesser opportunities to know about the advances happening in the world outside.

3.B Source of Awareness of Crime and Human Rights Violation

Table 7.117 : Main Source of Crime Awareness and Human Rights Violation Among the Urban Population of Delhi

Sources of Awareness	*Male*	*Percent*	*Female*	*Percent*	*Total*	*Percent*
T.V.	68	34.87	43	50.00	111	39.50
Radio	4	2.05	8	9.30	12	4.27
News Paper	89	45.64	8	9.30	97	34.52
Meeting People	10	5.13	12	13.95	22	7.83
Movement Outside the Area	-	-	-	-	-	-
Occupation	11	5.64	6	6.98	17	6.05
Self Experience	13	6.67	9	10.47	22	7.83
Total	195	100.00	86	100.00	281	100.00

Table 7.117 shows that for the maximum of the total respondents i.e. 39.50 percent of the urban population, T.V. is their source of the awareness. 34.52 percent of the population depend on newspaper as the source of awareness. The other sources providing awareness are meeting people (7.83 percent), self experience(7.83 percent), radio (4.27 percent). Among males the major source(45.64 percent) of awareness is newspaper. Among females the major source (50.00 percent) of awareness is watching TV.

Table 7.118 : Personal Experience of Crime and Human Rights Violation Among the Urban Population of Delhi

Personal Experience	*Respondents*	*Percent*
Experience Violation	22	7.33
Inexperienced	278	92.67
Total	300	100.00

Table 7.118 reports that 7.33 percent of the urban population have experienced the violation of their human rights in one or the other way. All these cases had been separately interviewed and the cases studies have been given separately at the end of the chapter.

3.C Knowledge and Attitude Towards Human Rights

In the urban area of Delhi it has been most convenient to make the respondent understand the meaning of the word 'Human Rights'. It has been observed in Table 7.119 that only 4.00 percent of the urban population is unaware of the meaning of human rights.

Table 7.119 : Knowledge of Human Rights Among the Urban Population of Delhi

Level Of Awareness	*Respondents*	*Percent*
Unaware	12	4.00
Partially Aware	178	59.33
Fully Aware	110	36.67
Total	300	100.00

59.33 percent of the respondents are partially aware and 36.67 percent are fully aware of the concept of human rights. *Thus urban population defined human right collectively as "those legal rules and valid claims framed by constitution for the members of its state."*

Table 7.120 shows that among the unaware respondents, majority of the respondents (41.67 percent) are illiterate. None of the graduates are found in the category of unaware respondents. Among partially aware, the maximum (60.11 percent) response come from those who are minimum graduates or above. Among those who are fully aware (according to the criteria given above), the majority of percentage 88.18 percent of the respondents are graduates and above. None of the illiterates are found to be fully aware among the urban population.

Table 7.120: Education and Knowledge of Human Rights Among the Urban Population of Delhi

Education	*Unaware*	*Percent aware*	*Partially*	*Percent aware*	*Fully*	*Percent*
Illiterate	5	41.67	8	4.49	-	-
Primary	3	25.00	3	1.69	2	1.82
Middle	1	8.33	7	3.93	-	-
10th Passed	2	16.67	23	12.92	5	4.55
12th Passed	1	8.33	30	16.85	6	5.45
Graduate and Above	-	-	107	60.11	97	88.18
Total	12	100.00	178	100.00	110	100.00

Table 7.121: Reasons for Right Framed Among the Urban Population of Delhi

Reasons for Framing Rights	*Respondents*	*Percent*
Unaware	34	11.33
Aware	266	88.67
Total	300	100.00

Table 7.121 reports that only 11.33 percent of the informants are unaware as they don't know why rights are framed in the society and the majority of percentage of 88.67 percent are aware as they gave various reasons which all meant similar that –all would have equal opportunity, nobody would be weak in the society, all would be equal.

Table 7.122 shows educational level of the population which is aware and unaware of the reasons of the rights framed. 32.35 percent of illiterate population is unaware of the reasons behind the rights framed. However, it is to be mentioned here that 14.71 percent of the unaware respondents are minimum graduates or above. A majority of 74.81 percent of the aware population is minimum graduate or above. It is to be noted in this category that a negligible percent (0.75 percent) of the respondents are illiterate and even than aware of the reasons of the rights framed.

Table 7.122 : Education and Reasons for Right Framed Among the Urban Population of Delhi

Education	*Unaware*	*Percent*	*Aware*	*Percent*
Illiterate	11	32.35	2	0.75
Primary	4	11.76	4	1.50
Middle	2	5.88	6	2.26
10th Passed	7	20.59	23	8.65
12th Passed	5	14.71	32	12.03
Graduate and Above	5	14.71	199	74.81
Total	34	100.00	266	100.00

Table 7.123: Occupation and Reasons for Right Framed Among the Urban Population of Delhi

Occupation	*Unaware*	*Percent*	*Aware*	*Percent*
Service	-	-	70	26.32
Daily Labour	-	-	1	0.38
Business	-	-	46	17.29
Retired	34	100.00	149	56.02
Total	34	100.00	266	100.00

Table 7.123 shows occupation and reasons for right framed among the urban population. It has been observed that in the urban population only four occupational categories have been found. In the category of unaware respondents cent percent response came from those who are leading a retired life. Contradicting this result, in the category of aware respondents the maximum response (56.02 percent) came from again from the retired respondents. 26.32 percent who are in service are aware and 17.29 percent who are in business are aware of the reasons of the rights framed.

Table 7.124 shows that the number of human right articles told by the informants. 7.67 percent of the population could not tell even a single human right article. 10.33 percent of the respondents could tell more than 10 human rights articles. However the maximum respondents (22.67 percent) could tell nine to ten human rights articles out of the list of nineteen.

Table 7.124 : Human Right Articles Awareness Among the Urban Population of Delhi

Rights Awareness	*Respondents*	*Percent*
None	23	7.67
One - Two	15	5.00
Three - Four	60	20.00
Five-Six	37	12.33
Seven-Eight	66	22.00
Nine-Ten	68	22.67
Above Ten	31	10.33
Total	300	100.00

It can also be derived that if 7.67 percent respondents couldn't tell even a single human rights article, than 92.33 percent are those which include as less as single human right article or as much as above 10.

Table 7.125 shows a further analysis with regard to awareness about human rights. Out of 277 respondents. 90.25 percent of respondents are aware of Equal Protection of Law and 88.81 percent knows about Equality before courts. Further, it has been observed that awareness about the basic and simpler human rights like Right to Work (35.74 percent), Right to Marry (33.94 percent), Right of Education (23.83 percent), Freedom of Movement (10.47 percent) are less.

The reason for such type of response could be assigned to the fact that Delhi being the national capital territory of the country, is the hub of all types of activity. The number of channels broadcasted in Delhi on T.V. and radio is much higher than the channels received in the near by rural and tribal areas. The number of newspapers in Delhi is much higher than the surrounding areas. So any activity happened, is immediately flashed in the city through various modes of transmission. This is the reason of awareness of the people of the urban set up. People are aware that law is for all. Everybody should be given equal protection of law. They are very well aware of the legal and the constitutional aspect of living in a society.

The top five responses, according to the score of the percentage goes for Equal Protection of Law, Equality before Courts, Right to Life, Right to Adequate Standard of Living and Freedom to Torture. Looking at this pattern of answers, it appears that the *Urban Population is very well aware of their Human Rights. They have the knowledge of the means to safe guard their interest and punish the wrong doer.*

Table 7.125 : Awareness About Categories of Human Rights (Articles) Among the Urban Population of Delhi

S.No.	*Category of Human Rights*	*N=277*	*Percent*
1.	Equal Protection of Law	250	90.25
2.	Equality Before Courts	246	88.81
3.	Right to Life	194	70.04
4.	Right to an Adequate Standard of Living	160	57.76
5.	Freedom to Torture	154	55.60
6.	Right to Social Security	152	54.87
7.	Freedom of Religion	137	49.46
8.	Freedom of Thought	105	37.91
9.	Right to Work	99	35.74
10.	Right to Marry	94	33.94
11.	Freedom from Arrest	91	32.85
12.	Right to Education	66	23.83
13.	Freedom of Movement	29	10.47
14.	Freedom of Expression	26	9.39
15.	Freedom from Slavery	24	8.66
16.	Freedom to Seek Information	15	5.42
17.	Right of Minorities	15	5.42
18.	Right to Take Part in Cultural Life	12	4.33
19.	Right of Peaceful Assembly	10	3.61

Table 7.126 : Awareness About Rights of Arrested Person Among the Urban Population of Delhi

Rights of Arrested Person	*Respondents*	*Percent*
Phone Call	30	10.00
Lawyer	1	0.33
Both	89	29.67
Don't Know	180	60.00
Total	300	100.00

Table 7.126 reveals that 60.00 percent of informants couldn't tell none of the rights of the arrested person although the unaware urban respondents are lesser than tribal and rural populations. Delhi being the centre of all trade

and activity is expected to show higher awareness pattern of its population. The reason for lower awareness of percentage could be the fact that people here are have superficial knowledge of their rights and freedoms. Only lawyers and police officials are found to be aware of the detailed knowledge of their rights. 29.67 percent of the total respondents could tell both the rights of the arrested person. These are the people who are well educated as shown in the next Table.

Table 7.127 : Education and Awareness About Rights of Arrested Person Among the Urban Population of Delhi

Education	*Phone call*	*Percent*	*Lawyer*	*Percent*	*Both*	*Percent*	*Don't know*	*Percent*
Illiterate	-	-	-	-	-	-	13	7.22
Primary	-	-	-	-	2	2.25	6	3.33
Middle	-	-	-	-	-	-	8	4.44
10th Passed	4	13.33	-	-	3	3.37	23	12.78
12th Passed	1	3.33	-	-	3	3.37	33	18.33
Graduate and Above	25	83.33	1	100.00	81	91.01	97	53.89
Total	30	100.00	1	100.00	89	100.00	180	100.00

It has been observed from Table 7.127 that the maximum percentage of the unaware respondents are atleast graduates in education. It can be justified in the manner that the rights of the arrested person comes in the technical rights category, so people are less aware of this provision provided to the arrested persons. 7.22 percent are illiterate in this category. Among those who could tell both the rights 91.01 are atleast graduates or above. None of the illiterates are reported in this category.

Table 7.128 shows that majority of the respondents who could not tell about the rights of the arrested person are retired (69.44 percent). 15.00 percent of those who are in service could not tell any of the right. It is contradictory here to note that the majority of those who could tell both the human rights of arrested person are retired (48.31 percent). 40.45 percent of respondents are in service, 11.24 percent are in business.

Table 7.128 : Occupation and Awareness About Rights of Arrested Person Among the Urban Population of Delhi

Occupation	*Phone call*	*Percent*	*Lawyer*	*Both*	*Both*	*Percent*	*Don't know*	*Percent*
Service	6	20.00	1	100.00	36	40.45	27	15.00
Daily Labour	-	-	-	-	-	-	1	0.56
Business	9	30.00	-	-	10	11.24	27	15.00
Retired	15	50.00	-		43	48.31	125	69.44
Total	30	100.00	1	100.00	89	100.00	180	100.00

Table 7.129 : Attitude Towards Violation of Rights Among the Urban Population of Delhi

Take the Injustice Done	*Respondents*	*Percent*
Take an Action	237	79.00
Leave it After Few Discussion	50	16.67
Never Bother	13	4.33
Total	300	100.00

Table 7.129 takes a note of attitude towards human rights and its violation, 4.33 percent said they would not be bothered by the violation of the rights. The majority of 79.00 percent said they would take an action against the unjust done to them. 16.67 percent said they would leave the issue after discussing it.

3.D Practice of Human Rights

Table 7.130 : Dispute Processing Institutions Among the Urban Population of Delhi

Punishment	*Respondents*	*Percent*
Elderly	-	-
Panchayat	-	-
Police	300	100.00
Total	300	100.00

Table 7.130 shows the prevalence of dispute processing institution in the society. Hundred percent of the respondents said they would go to police for their dispute settling.

Table 7.132: Laws Prevalent in Society Among the Urban Population of Delhi

Laws Predominant in Society	*Respondents*	*Percent*
Constitutional Laws	300	100.00
Customary laws	-	-
Total	300	100.00

Table 7.132 presents the prevalence of laws in the urban society. It reveals that when asked about the prevalence of laws in urban society, hundred percent reply came in favour of constitutional laws.

3.E Attitude Towards Police and Court

Table 7.132 shows the attitude of the urban population towards the police in the area. When asked to rate police officials behaviour, the majority of 85.33 percent of respondents said its bad. Contradicting this result only 14.67 percent said its satisfactory.

Table 7.132 : Attitude Towards Police Officials Among the Urban Population of Delhi

Rating of Behaviour	*Respondents*	*Percent*
Very good	-	-
Bad	256	85.33
Satisfactory	44	14.67
Not social	-	-
Don't Know	-	-
Total	300	100.00

Table 7.133 shows the percentage of the urban population who have ever visited the police station. 63.67 percent has never ever gone to police station whereas only 36.33 percent have gone to police station.

Table 7.133 : Visit to Police Station Among the Urban Population of Delhi

Visit Police Station	*Respondents*	*Percent*
Visited	109	36.33
Never Visited	191	63.67
Total	300	100.00

Table 7.134 relates the education with the visit to the police station. Majority of these who have visited the police station are graduates or above (75.23 percent). None of the illiterates are found to have gone to police station. Again in the category of those who have never visited the police station, 63.87 percent are graduates and above and 6.81 percent are illiterates.

Table 7.134 : Education and Visit to Police Station Among the Urban Population of Delhi

Education	*Visited*	*Percent*	*Never Visited*	*Percent*
Illiterate	-	-	13	6.81
Primary	2	1.83	6	3.14
Middle	-	-	8	4.19
10th Passed	10	9.17	20	10.47
12th Passed	15	13.76	22	11.52
Graduate and Above	82	75.23	122	63.87
Total	109	100.00	191	100.00

Table 7.135 shows the occupation of those who have visited the police station and those who have never visited the police station. It is reported that those who have gone to police station, majority of the population (40.37 percent) is retired, 29.36 percent are in service and 30.28 percent are in business.

Among those who have never visited the police station, 72.77 percent are retired and 19.90 percent are into service.

Table 7.136 shows the various reasons for going to police station. Out of those who have gone to police station, 70.64 percent have gone for lodging an FIR to get justice. 28.44 percent have gone with the intension of lodging a complaint but came back after discussing the matter with the police officials

Table 7.135 : Occupation and Visit to Police Station Among the Urban Population of Delhi

Occupation	*Visited*	*Percent*	*Never Visited*	*Percent*
Service	32	29.36	38	19.90
Daily Labour	-	-	1	0.52
Business	33	30.28	13	6.81
Retired	44	40.37	139	72.77
Total	109	100.00	191	100.00

Table 7.136 : Reason for Going to Police Station Among the Urban Population of Delhi

Reasons of going to Police Station	*Respondents*	*Percent*
For Lodging an FIR to Get Justice	77	70.64
To Take the License	-	-
To Pay the Chalan	-	-
To Discuss / mediation/ negotiation	31	28.44
Job Requirement	1	0.92
Total	109	100.00

Table 7.137 discusses the attitude of the urban population towards police. It reports that only 9.17 percent said that the behaviour of the police men at the police station is co-operative, 36.70 percent said its non-cooperative and the majority of 54.13 percent said its rude.

Table 7.137 : Behaviour of Police Men at the Station Among the Urban Population of Delhi

Behaviour of Police Men	*Respondents Visited*	*Percent*
Co-operative	10	9.17
Non-cooperative	40	36.70
Rude	59	54.13
Total	109	100.00

Table 7.138 sheds some light on the attitude of respondents towards court. 37.76 percent of respondents has ever gone to court and the major percentage of 62.33 percent has never ever gone to court.

Table7.138 : Visited Court Among the Urban Population of Delhi

Visit to Court	Respondents	Percent
Visited	113	37.67
Never Visited	187	62.33
Total	300	100.00

Table 7.139 shows the awareness of the urban population about the court procedure. A majority of 89.33 percent of respondents knew about the proper channel of approaching the supreme court i.e. session court than high court than supreme court.Only 10.67 percent of informants are not at all aware of these procedural steps.

Table 7.139 : Awareness About Approach to Court Among the Urban Population of Delhi

Approach to Supreme Court	*Respondents*	*Percent*
Session Court -High Court -Supreme Court	268	89.33
Don't Know	32	10.67
Total	300	100.00

Table 7.140 presents the education of those who have visited court. Among those who are aware of the proper channel to reach to the supreme court, the majority of population (76.12 percent) are graduates and above. Only 2.99 percent of the respondents who are reported to be aware are illiterates.

Table 7.140: Education and Awareness About Approach to Court Among the Urban Population of Delhi

Education	*Aware of Procedure*	*Percent*	*Unaware of Procedure*	*Percent*
Illiterate	8	2.99	5	15.63
Primary	2	0.75	6	18.75
Middle	3	1.12	5	15.63
10th Passed	21	7.84	9	28.13
12th Passed	30	11.19	7	21.88
Graduate and Above	204	76.12	-	-
Total	268	100.00	32	100.00

Among those who are unaware of the proper channel to reach supreme court, 15.63 percent are illiterate. None of the graduates are found to be reported in this category.

Table 7.141: Occupation and Awareness About Approach to Court Among the Urban Population of Delhi

Occupation	*Aware of Procedure*	*Percent*	*Unaware of* Procedure	*Percent*
Service	70	26.12	-	-
Daily Labour	-	-	1	3.13
Business	39	14.55	7	21.88
Retired	159	59.33	24	75.00
Total	268	100.00	32	100.00

Table 7.141 presents the occupation of the respondents who are aware and unaware of the procedure to approach supreme court. Majority of the respondents who are reported to be aware are retired (59.33 percent), 26.12 percent are into service and 14.55 percent have their own business. In the category of unaware respondents, 75.00 percent are retired, 21.88 percent have their own business and 3.13 percent are daily labourers.

Table 7.142 : Awareness About Procedure of Public Interest Litigation (PIL) Among the Urban Population of Delhi

Procedure of Public Interest Litigation	*Respondents*	*Percent*
Aware	99	33.00
Unaware	201	67.00
Total	300	100.00

Table 7.142, shows the awareness about PIL among the urban population. It shows that 33.00 percent of respondents are reported to be aware of the provision of Public Interest Litigation i.e. informing the supreme court about their violation through a post card and 67.00 percent are absolutely unaware.

3.F Awareness and Violation of Various Human Rights

(i) Child Right

Table 7.143 : Basic Right of Child Among the Urban Population of Delhi

Child Fed by Mother	*Respondents*	*Percent*
0-3 Months	50	36.76
4-6 Months	56	41.18
7-9 Months	28	20.59
10-12 Months	1	0.74
More Than One Year	1	0.74
Total	136	100.00

Table 7.143 presents the basic rights of a child as is observed among the urban population. It reveals, the maximum percentage of 41.18 percent urban mothers fed their children for 4-6 months, 36.76 percent urban women said they fed their babies for 0-3 months, 20.59 percent women said they fed their child till 7-9 months.Only a negligible percentage of 0.74 percent of the women have been reported to fed their child for more than a year. This may be because of the fact that in the urban setting, men and women work to meet their both ends. So the prolonged breast feeding is not practically possible in such circumstances which leads to alternative methods of feeding the child.

It can be said that 77.94 percent of the urban mothers violate the basic right of their child as they do not indulge in prolonged breast feeding.

Table 7.144 : Child Care Among the Urban Population of Delhi

Care Taker of the Child	*Respondents*	*Percent*
Elder Siblings	-	-
Father / Mother	98	72.06
Other Family Members	31	22.79
Takes Along to Field	-	-
No Body	7	5.15
Total	136	100.00

Table 7.144 shows the care taker of the children as is found among the urban population. It shows that the majority of 72.06 percent respondents said care taker of their children are either of the parents. 22.79 percent said

other family members take care of their child. Only a small percentage of 5.15 percent said they leave their child alone when they go for work.

It can be said that 5.15 percent of the urban parents are violating the basic right of protection of their children by leaving them on their own.

(ii) Women's Right

Table 7.145 : Work Done During Pregnancy Among the Urban Population of Delhi

Months	*Respondents*	*Percent*
3-4th Month	-	-
5-6th Month	37	27.21
7-8th Month	59	43.38
9th Month	40	29.41
Total	136	100.00

Table 7.145 presents the duration for which pregnant mothers have worked. It reports that out of 136 respondents for this question, 29.41 percent of women have worked till the 9th month of pregnancy. 43.38 percent have worked till 7-8th month. 27.21 percent women worked till 5 to 6th month.

It can be said that 72.79 percent of the urban women have experienced the violation of their right.

Table7.146 : Reason For Working Among the Urban Population of Delhi

The Reason for Working	*Respondents*	*Percent*
Family Members Forcing	65	47.79
Husband Forcing	-	-
Economic Reasons	71	52.21
Total	136	100.00

Table 7.146 shows various reasons for which pregnant women works. 52.21 percent of women said they work during pregnancy because of economic reasons. However, 47.79 percent also responded by saying that in-laws also pressurize them to work.

It can be said that 47.79 percent of the urban mothers have experienced the violation of theirhumanrights.

(iii) Marriage Right

Table 7.147 : Practice of Marriage Among the Urban Population of Delhi

Aware of Getting Married	*Respondents*	*Percent*
Aware	257	97.35
Unaware	7	2.65
Total	264	100.00

Table 7.147 shows that only 2.65 percent of the married people were unaware of their marriage i.e. at the time when the marriage is fixed neither the girl nor the boy knew each other. 97.35 percent knew with whom they are going to get married.

It can be said that only 2.65 percent of the urban population have experienced the violation of their wishful right to marriage.

Table 7.148 : Attitude Towards Forceful Marriage Among the Urban Population of Delhi

Forcefully Married, What Will You Do	*Respondents*	*Percent*
Accept the Man	48	16.00
Come Back	-	-
Take Action	-	-
Report to Police	252	84.00
Total	300	100.00

Table 7.148 reveals the attitude of the urban population towards forceful marriages. It shows that, if forcefully married, the majority of 84.00 percent respondents would take an action against the violation of their human right by reporting the matter to police. However, 16.00 percent said they would accept the conditions. This question was asked to all the respondents irrespective of their marital status.

Table 7.149 shows the reasons for not completing the studies among the urban population. It reports that, the maximum of 43.00 percent didn't complete their studies as they got a job. 35.00 percent had never been interested in completing their studies. 8.67 percent are those who never got any opportunity. These are majorly those cases who could not study in their age.3.00 percent are those where the girl's in-laws refused her to continue the

(iv) **Educational Right**

Table7.149 : Reasons for Not Completing Studies Among the Urban Population of Delhi

Reason	*Respondents*	*Percent*
Never Interested	105	35.00
Never Got Opportunity	26	8.67
In -laws Refused	9	3.00
Parents Refused	22	7.33
Got a Job	129	43.00
No Time From Household Works	9	3.00
Total	300	100.00

studies . 3.00 percent are those cases, where the informants never got time from household work, thus sacrificing their studies 7.33 percent are the cases where their parents refused to study further.

It can be said that 22.00percent of the urban population has experienced the violation of their right to education.

(v) **Reproductive Rights**

Table 7.150 : Decision of Having a Child Among the Urban Population of Delhi

Decision of Having Child	*Respondents*	*Percent*
Husband	118	44.70
Wife	-	-
Both	146	55.30
In-laws	-	-
Total	264	100.00

Table 7.150 shows that, a majority of 55.30 percent said both the partners take the decision of having a child. Whereas 44.70 percent said that only husband takes the decision of having a child.

Table 7.151 shows that, the role of husband/wife in decision making for a child. Among males the majority of 96.85 percent respondents said that they would stick to their own wish regarding the decision for a child, indicating the dominance of males in decision making. Only 3.15 percent of the males

Table 7.151 : Role of Male/Female in Decision Making Among the Urban Population of Delhi

Decision	*Male*	*Percent*	*Female*	*Percent*	*Total*	*Percent*
Succumb to Spouse's Desire	4	3.15	115	83.94	119	45.08
Stick to Your Own Wish	123	96.85	22	16.06	145	54.92
Total	127	100.00	137	100.00	264	100.00

responded by saying that they would succumb to their spouse's desire. Among females 83.94 percent said that they would succumb to their spouse's desire. However, 16.06 percent females also replied that they would stick to their own wish regarding the issue. Further out of the total of those who said they would stick to their wish, 84.83 percent (123/145) are males and 15.17 percent (22/145) are females.

It can be said that 83.94 percent of females and 3.15 percent of males experience the violation of their reproductive rights which are mutual in nature.

(vi) Development Right

Table 7.152 : Awareness of Right to Development Among the Urban Population of Delhi

Right to Development	*Respondents*	*Percent*
Aware	232	77.33
Unaware	68	22.67
Total	300	100.00

Table 7.152 presents the awareness of the urban population towards the right to development. It reveals that 22.67 percent of the respondents are absolutely unaware of their right to development thus showing their awareness level and the majority of 77.33 percent knew that its their right to accept or reject the development programme. These respondents are reported to be aware that the development programme cannot be enforced upon the citizens. They may accept or reject the scheme offered to them.

Table 7.153 presents the condition of the medical facilities available among the urban population of Delhi. It has been observed that medical

(vii) Right To Medical Treatment

Table 7.153 : Facilities Available Among the Urban Population of Delhi

Facilities for Treatment	*Respondents*	*Percent*
Good and Available	300	100.00
Good and not Available	-	-
Not Available	-	-
Total	300	100.00

facilities are extremely good and are available all throughout the time.

Table 7.154 : Quality of Doctors Among the Urban Population of Delhi

Quality of Doctors	*Respondents*	*Percent*
Experienced	300	100.00
Freshers and Inexperienced	-	-
Total	300	100.00

Table 7.154 reveals the quality of doctors available to the urban population. It has been observed that all experienced doctors are available to the urban population.

Table 7.155 : Wrong Medicines Given Among the Urban Population of Delhi

Wrong Medicine	*Respondents*	*Percent*
Yes	20	6.67
No	280	93.33
Total	300	100.00

Table 7.155 presents the percent of the respondents who have been given the wrong medicine among the urban population. It shows that, 93.33 percent of the respondents said that doctors have never given any wrong medicines. However, 6.67 percent of the respondents are the victims of the mistreatment of the doctor. According to them, they have been given wrong medicines.

It can be said that 6.67 percent of urban respondents have experienced the violation of their human right to proper medical treatment.

Table 7.156 : Action Taken Among the Urban Population of Delhi

Action Taken	*Respondents*	*Percent*
Never Gone to That Doctor Again	6	30.00
Gone Back to Report Him and Ended in an Argument	5	25.00
Filed a Case Against Him	9	45.00
Total	20	100.00

Table 7.156 reveals the action taken by those who have been treated wrong among the urban population. It shows that 30.00 percent have never gone to that doctor again. 25.00 percent of the victims of the mistreatment, have gone back to the doctor and reported him, and ended in an argument. 45.00 percent have filed a case against the doctor who has given wrong medicines.

(viii) Reservation Right :

Table 7.157 : Aware of Reservation of Seats Among the Urban Population of Delhi

Aware That Seats Reserved for Scheduled Tribes in Jobs, Political Assemblies	*Respondents*	*Percent*
Aware	279	93.00
Unaware	21	7.00
Total	300	100.00

Table 7.157 presents the awareness of the urban population about the reservation of seats. It shows that 93.00 percent respondents are aware of the reservation at the job place and 7.00 percent said they are not aware.

Table 7.158 presents the awareness of the urban population about NCSCST and NHRC. It shows that only 27.67 percent of the informants are aware of the National Commission for Scheduled Castes and Scheduled Tribes (NCSC& ST).72.33 percent are absolutely unaware. 32.67 percent are aware of National or State Human Rights Commission (NHRC/SHRC) and 67.33 percent

Table 7.158 : Awareness About National Commission for Scheduled Castes and Scheduled Tribes and National/State Human Rights Commission Among the Urban Population of Delhi

Commission	*NCSCST*	*Percent*	*NHRC/SHRC*	Percent
Aware	83	27.67	98	32.67
Unaware	217	72.33	202	67.33
Total	300	100.00	300	100.00

are those who do not know anything about the existence of the Commission. The reason for this type of less awareness about NCSCST and NHRC among the urban population is that people have superficial knowledge about the human rights. Their knowledge restricts to going to police to settle their issue of any dispute which causes the violation of their rights.

(ix) Right to Religion :

According to Table 7.159, the majority of 47.33 percent said that they wouldn't change their religion as it is their right to practice the religion of their wish. 32.00 percent said that they don't wish to change their religion. 17.00 percent said that they would not change their religion as they want to die in the same religion in which they are born.

Table 7.159 : Change of Religion Among the Urban Population of Delhi

Reason	*Respondents*	*Percent*
Don't Wish to Change	96	32.00
Want to Die with Religion in Which Born	51	17.00
Right to Practice any Religion	142	47.33
Wanted to Change	11	3.67
Total	300	100.00

3.67 percent is also worth mentioning here, as these are the respondents who would want to change their religion if some benefits are involved.

7.2 An Interface Dimension

An 'interface' means a border, an edge or a crossing point. In the reference of the present study, the term 'interface' is used to study the difference and change in the knowledge, attitude and practice of the population, while crossing from tribal to rural till urban. Its an important dimension in the present study as all the three populations are viewed simultaneously. Thus, in the present phase of the chapter all the data from tribal, rural and urban populations are tabulated comprehensively, to study the cross cultural dimension more closely.

Table 7.160 shows the comparison of socio-economic variables among tribal, rural and urban populations understudy. The least agricultural landless households are observed among the tribal population (11.67 percent). Lahoul dwells exclusively on agriculture.

Table 7.160: Comparison of Socio-Economic Variables in Tribal, Rural and Urban Populations Under Study

S.No.	*Socio-Economic Variables*	*Tribal %(n)*	*Rural %(n)*	*Urban %(n)*	*Total %(n)*
1.	Agricultural Landless Households	11.67(35)	32.67(98)	100.00(300)	48.11(433)
2.	Main Fuel Used In Kitchen				
(a)	LPG	-	65.33(196)	100.00(300)	55.11(496)
(b)	Kerosene	-	-	-	-
(c)	Coal	-	3.33(10)	-	1.11(10)
(d)	Cow Dung	5.33(16)	11.67(35)	-	5.67(51)
(e)	Wood	94.67(284)	19.67(59)	-	38.11(343)
	Total	100.00(300)	100.00(300)	100.00(300)	100.00(900)
3.	Drainage System				
(a)	Closed Drain	1.67(5)	42.33(127)	100.00(300)	48.00(432)
(b)	Open Drain	98.33(295)	57.67(173)	-	52.00(468)
	Total	100.00(300)	100.00(300)	100.00(300)	100.00(900)
4.	Sanitation Facility				
(a)	Flush Toilet	9.67(29)	88.33(265)	100.00(300)	66.00(594)
(b)	Pit Toilet	87.00(261)	-	-	29.00(261)
(c)	Community Latrine	0.33(1)	-	-	0.11(1)

(Contd.)

(Contd.Table 7.160)

S.No.	*Socio-Economic Variables*	*Tribal %(n)*	*Rural %(n)*	*Urban %(n)*	*Total %(n)*
(d)	No Latrine	3.00(9)	11.65(35)	-	4.89(44)
	Total	100.00(300)	100.00(300)	100.00(300)	100.00(900)
5.	Type of House				
(a)	Kuccha House	15.00(45)	25.00(75)	-	13.33(120)
(b)	Wooden House	77.33(232)	-	-	25.78(232)
(c)	Pucca/Cemented House	7.67(23)	75.00(225)	100.00(300)	60.89(548)
	Total	100.00(300)	100.00(300)	100.00(300)	100.00(900)
6.	Housing Floors	Tribal %(n)	Rural %(n)	Urban %(n)	Total %(n)
(a)	Single Storeyed	27.67(83)	70.00(210)	84.00(252)	60.56(545)
(b)	Double Storeyed	64.67(194)	25.00(75)	15.00(45)	34.89(314)
(c)	Triple Storeyed	7.67(23)	5.00(15)	1.00(3)	4.56(41)
	Total	100.00(300)	100.00(300)	100.00(300)	100.00(900)
7.	Number of Rooms				
(a)	1--3	27.00(81)	20.00(60)	50.00(150)	32.33(291)
(b)	4--6	53.67(161)	61.67(185)	43.67(131)	53.00(477)
(c)	7--9	12.67(38)	11.67(35)	4.00(12)	9.44(85)
(d)	10--12	4.67(14)	5.33(16)	2.00(6)	4.00(36)
(e)	13-15	1.33(4)	1.33(4)	0.33(1)	1.00(9)
(f)	>15	0.67(2)	-	-	0.22(2)
	Total	100.00(300)	100.00(300)	100.00(300)	100.00(900)
8.	Ownership of House				
(a)	Inherited	63.67(191)	51.67(155)	33.00(99)	49.44(445)
(b)	Self	30.67(92)	40.00(120)	43.33(130)	38.00(342)
(c)	Rented	5.67(17)	8.33(25)	23.67(71)	12.56(113)
	Total	100.00(300)	100.00(300)	100.00(300)	100.00(900)

(Contd.)

(Contd.Table 7.160)

S.No.	Socio-Economic Variables	Tribal %(n)	Rural %(n)	Urban %(n)	Total %(n)
9.	Location of Water Supply				
(a)	Within House	6.67(20)	96.67(290)	100.00(300)	67.78(610)
(b)	Outside House	93.33(280)	3.33(10)	-	32.22(290)
(c)	Outside Village	-	-	-	-
	Total	100.00(300)	100.00(300)	100.00(300)	100.00(900)
10.	Economic Characteristics				
(a)	Agriculture	44.33(133)	35.33(106)	-	26.56(239)
(b)	Service	31.00(93)	31.33(94)	23.33(70)	28.56(257)
(c)	Daily Labour	1.00(3)	5.33(16)	0.33(1)	2.22(20)
(d)	Business	7.67(23)	12.00(36)	15.33(46)	11.67(105)
(e)	Animal Husbandry	3.67(11)	10.67(32)	-	4.78(43)
(f)	Inactive	12.33(37)	5.33(16)	61.00(183)	26.22(236)
	Total	100.00(300)	100.00(300)	100.00(300)	100.00(900)
11.	Average Monthly Income				
(a)	0-5000	15.00(45)	46.00(138)	12.33(37)	24.44(220)
(b)	5100-20000	71.67(215)	49.67(149)	51.67(155)	57.67(519)
(c)	20100-40000	11.00(33)	4.33(13)	27.67(83)	14.33(129)
(d)	40100-60000	1.00(3)	-	6.33(19)	2.44(22)
(e)	>60000	1.33(4)	-	2.00(6)	1.11(10)
	Total	100.00(300)	100.00(300)	100.00(300)	100.00(900)

In tribal area, every household has certain amount of acquired or inherited land. Households which do not have any land are allotted the minimum of 8 *beighas* of land by the government to sustain their livelihood in Lahoul. Rural population has 32.67 percent of the households which have been reported to be landless at the time of field work. This trend is observed as the villages in which field work have been carried out are comparatively recent in their setup. Many households have sold their agricultural land to move towards comparatively less rural areas in the hope of better earning options, educational opportunities, development etc. Among the urban population, all females are found to be agricultural landless. In the total population representing three geographical areas 48.11 percent households are calculated to be landless.

The main fuel used in the tribal, rural and urban kitchen is wood (94.67), LPG (65.33), and LPG (100.00) respectively. Lahoul being a remote forest belt has as a natural source. People here use wood collected from forest or purchased from the subsidized governmental depot to burn it in their kitchens. This helps them in solving two purposes- one as a fuel for cooking and second as a source of heat. This practice of the people is however resulting into faster depletion of this natural resource. Rural areas of Haryana does not have enough forest reserves to support the need of the people. LPG is reported to be the main fuel in rural and urban population. In the total population also LPG (55.11 percent) is found to be the main fuel used.

Drainage system in the tribal area is 98.33 percent open, in the rural area, it is 57.67 percent open and in the urban area no open drains has been reported. In the total population 52.00 percent of the households have open drains.

Sanitation facility in the tribal area is very different than what is found in rural or urban areas. 87.00 percent of the tribal households has pit toilets, 88.33 percent of rural households and hundred percent of the urban households have flush toilets. In the total population 66.00 percent of the households have flush toilets.

Type of house in tribal area is predominantly wooden (77.33 percent). Only 7.67 percent of the houses are cemented in the area. In the rural area the majority of houses are cemented (75.00 percent). Where as in the urban areas hundred percent households are cemented. In the total population 60.89 percent of the houses are cemented.

Housing floors in the house indicates the level of socio economic status. More the number of floors constructed, better is the socio-economic status of the family. In the tribal area 64.67 percent of the houses has double storey in their houses. Ground floor is mostly used as a cattle shed. It serves double benefits to the tribal population, as it provides warmth in the severe winters and cattles are also safe in the vicinity of the house. In the rural and urban population the majority of houses 70.00 percent and 84.00 percent respectively has single storey construction. In the total population 60.56 percent houses had been found to have single storey in their houses.

Number of rooms in a house varies depending on the financial conditions, need and space available. In the tribal and rural area 53.67 percent and 61.67 percent of the houses respectively are reported to have 4 to 6 rooms. In the urban areas 50.00 percent houses has one to three rooms. In the total population 53.00 percent of the households are reported to have 4 to 6 rooms.

Ownership of house is also a direct indicator of socio-economic status. It is reported that among tribal population 63.67 percent of the respondents had inherited their houses. More the percent of inherited houses the older the village is. The villages in which work was conducted had settled some 500-600 years before. However, few settlements were recent in origin also. In the rural population 51.67 percent of the respondents inherited their houses from their ancestors. The percent of inherited houses is found to be lowest in the urban setup (33.00 percent). In the area of Delhi it has been observed that people are selling their land to contractors and thus making a building their.This trend has reduced the percentage of the inherited houses in Delhi.In the total population, 49.44 percent houses has been reported to be inherited by the ancestors of the family.

Location of water supply in the tribal area is found to be outside the house in 93.33 percent of the households. In the rural area 96.67 percent of the houses have their source of water within the premises of their house. In the urban areas cent percent houses have the water source in the house. Location of the source of water supply is a cultural indicator of the population. In the tribal area, where females go out to the common place to fill water for the daily needs, they exchange and communicate information, thus updating each other of the village issues and happenings. In the urban culture, lack of communication is major reason behind the unknowingness of the families living in the neighborhood. Here people don't talk, don't interfere in other person's life, thus restricting to their own niche.

Economic characteristics of the tribal population indicates that 44.33 percent of the households are into agriculture. In the rural population the trend is of the mix type as 35.33 percent of the households have agriculture as their economic characteristic and 31.33 percent of the households are into service. The reason for this shift in the trend in the economic characteristics can be attributed to the fact that returns from agriculture is reducing year after year. With more educational opportunities coming up, rural population has starting drifting away from the agriculture as their main source of income.

Average monthly income in all the three population is found to be maximum in the slab of Rs.5000/ to Rs.20000/, with 71.67 percent, 49.67 percent and 51.67 percent of the households in tribal, rural and urban populations respectively. 57.67 percent of the households in the total population lies in the slab of Rs 5000/ to Rs 20000/.

Table 7.161: Comparison of Socio-Cultural Variables in Tribal, Rural and Urban Populations

S.No.	*Socio-Cultural Variables*	*Tribal %(n)*	*Rural %(n)*	*Urban %(n)*	*Total %(n)*
1.	Type of Families				
	Nuclear	48.33(145)	48.00(144)	55.67(167)	50.67(456)
	Joint	51.67(155)	52.00(156)	44.33(133)	49.33(444)
	Total	100.00(300)	100.00(300)	100.00(300)	100.00(900)
2.	Type of Marriage				
(a)	Polygamous Marriage	9.00(27)	-	-	3.00(27)
(b)	Monogamous Marriage	91.00(273)	100.00(300)	100.00(300)	97.00(873)
(c)	Consanguineous Marriage	Present	Absent	Absent	-
	Total	100.00(300)	100.00(300)	100.00(300)	100.00(900)
3.	Religion				
(a)	Hinduism	42.67(128)	100.00(300)	100.00(300)	80.89(728)
(b)	Buddhism	57.33(172)	-	-	19.11(172)
(c)	Any Other	-	-	-	-
	Total	100.00(300)	100.00(300)	100.00(300)	100.00(900)
4.	Read News Paper				
(a)	Reads	8.33(25)	58.33(175)	68.67(206)	45.11(406)
(b)	Do Not Read	91.67(275)	41.67(125)	31.33(94)	54.89(494)
	Total	100.00(300)	100.00(300)	100.00(300)	100.00(900)

Table 7.161 shows the comparison of socio-cultural variables in tribal, rural and urban populations. Percentage of types of families in tribal and rural areas are almost similar. 48.33 percent and 48.00 percent among tribal and rural population respectively are joint families. The reason of higher percent of

joint families can be justified by the fact that with the changing time the trend of occupation is shifting from agriculture towards service. People have started migrating to different places in search of newer opportunities of job. In the urban population 55.67 percent of the households are nuclear. In the total population 50.67 percent of families are nuclear types.

Types of marriages found in the tribal population are majorly monogamous (91.00 percent). However, 9.00 percent of the marriages are reported to be of polygamous type. Lahoul being a remote belt of Himalayas have this tradition of sharing wives to prevent land fragmentation. But with times changing, this tradition has changed as people have stopped voting for this system of marriage. In rural and urban population hundred percent of the marriages were found to be of monogamous types. In the total population, 97.00 percent of the marriages are of monogamous types. Consanguineous marriages are completely absent in the rural and urban populations.

Religion plays a very important role in governing the lives of the people. Especially among the tribal people, where their daily actions are controlled by the religious beliefs. Majority of people are reported to be Buddhist (57.33 percent) in the tribal population. In the rural and urban population all the people are found to be following Hinduism. In the total population 80.89 percent of the people follow Hinduism.

Reading news paper is generally believed to be a major source of awareness. It is observed that the percent of people reading newspaper increases as we move from tribal to rural to urban population. Among the tribal population only 8.33 percent of the respondents are reported to be reading newspaper. This is because in Lahoul news paper do not come daily. It is atleast a day old till it reaches the district headquarters. The news paper gets older as it reaches to the interiors of the valley. This is the major reason for the lack of interest in tribal population to read news paper. Another reason for less readers of the news paper is the cost of the paper. News paper is found to be cheaper in the rural and urban areas as compared to tribal area of Lahoul, as the carriage cost of the news paper is also taken from the readers. In the rural population 58.33 percent are found to be reading news paper and the maximum readers are reported from the urban population (68.67 percent). Rural population and urban population have more opportunities to read news paper because of its easy availability, lesser cost. Urban population has highest percent of readers because in the urban way of life news paper plays a very vital role. It is a source of awareness for some, source of opportunities for some and a medium of expression for some. In the total population 45.11 percent of the respondents reads news paper.

Table 7.162: Comparison of Population Characteristics of Tribal, Rural and Urban Areas

S.No.	*Variables*	*Tribal %(n)*	*Rural %(n)*	*Urban %(n)*	*Total %(n)*
1.	Male Population	53.16(842)	52.96(895)	49.07(773)	51.76(2510)
2.	Female Population	46.84(742)	47.06(795)	50.92(802)	48.24(2339)
	Total	100.00(1584)	100.00(1690)	100.00(1575)	100.00(4849)
1.	Sex Ratio	881.24	888.27	1037.52	931.87
	Number of Literates				
1.	Literates	71.46(1132)	71.12(1202)	90.48 (1425)	77.52(3759)
2.	Illiterates	28.54(452)	28.88(488)	9.52(150)	22.48(1090)
	Total	100.00(1584)	100.00(1690)	100.00(1575)	100.00(4849)
	Literacy Rate				
1.	Total Literacy Rate	71.46	71.12	90.48	77.52
2.	Male Literacy Rate	80.52	76.98	90.69	82.47
3.	Female Literacy Rate	61.91	64.28	90.27	72.21
	Age at Marriage				
1.	Average Age at Marriage	23.79 years	19.54 years	24.41 years	22.61 years
2.	Male Average Age at Marriage	24.93 years	21.57 years	26.16 years	24.24 years
3.	Female Average Age at Marriage	22.66 years	17.60 years	22.94 years	21.05 years

Table 7.162 compares the population characteristics of tribal, rural and urban areas. Among tribal population 53.16 percent are males and 46.84 percent are females. Among the rural population, 52.96 percent are males and 47.06 percent are females. Among urban population, 49.00 percent are males and 50.92 percent are females. In the total population, 51.76 percent are males and 48.24 percent are females.

Sex ratio calculated among the population of Lahoul (881.24), Rohtak (888.27) and Delhi (1037.52). Sex ratio among the total population is calculated to be 931.87. Thus the lowest sex ratio is reported to be in the tribal area, than rural area and than urban area. The ratio available from the census of India, 2001 are in the order of Lahoul (804), Delhi (821) and Rohtak (847). It is to be observed here that the calculated sex ratio is higher than sex ratio in all the three populations as reported in the literature (Census, 2001). The reason for this type of result can be attributed to the fact that for the census, all the population which is staying in that area is considered for the purpose. It includes the migrant population also of the area. It is a known fact that among the migrant population, males dominate the population of females, thus reducing the sex ratio. For the present work, data had been collected only from those households which are permanent residents of the area- Lahoul Block, Sampla Block and Delhi thus increasing the sex ratio of the sample collected.

Number of literates and illiterates in any society reflects the educational status of the population. Among the tribal population, 71.46 percent of the population is found to be literate and 28.54 percent is found to be illiterate. Among rural population almost similar results are obtained as in tribal population. 71.12 percent and 28.88 percent are literates and illiterates among rural population. The percentages of literates and illiterates is not very low even in the tribal or the rural areas. The reason for this is, in Lahoul the prevalence of literacy programmes is observed to be high. The workers involved in the literacy mission are very motivated to work and reach to the interiors of the valley also to conduct the programme, thus motivating people to send their children to *aanganwadi* or primary school. In the urban population the percent of literates(90.48 percent) is obtained highest than the rest of the two populations. The main reason for this type of results is the fact that Delhi being the metropolitan city of India offers a lot of educational opportunities to people. In the total population, the percentages of literates and illiterates are 77.52 percent and 22.48 percent respectively.

Male literacy rate is found to be higher in all the three populations than the female literacy rate. Tribal males and females are at 80.52 percent and 61.91 percent of literacy. Rural males and females are at 76.98 percent and 64.28 percent of literacy. Urban males and females are at 82.47 percent and 72.21 percent of literacy. Females in all societies are the deprived gender who are given less opportunities in the educational aspects. Boys as compared to girls are promoted more to study. In the total population also male literacy (82.47 percent) is more than female literacy (72.21 percent).

Average age of marriage is found to be highest in the urban population (24.41 years), followed by tribal population (23.79 percent) and than rural population (19.54 years). It can be said here that among the urban population the higher literacy rate has postponed or delayed the age at marriage. In Lahoul the age of marriage is also calculated to be higher than the rural population as the status of women in this tribal area is better than the rural population. Women here are in the center of economy thus playing a role of major contributors in the unit of production in the society. Thus they are not considered as burden on the family as is the view among the rural population.

Table 7.163: Comparison of Police and Human Rights Among Tribal, Rural and Urban Populations

S.No	*Variables*	*Tribal %(n)*	*Rural %(n)*	*Urban %(n)*	*Total %(n)*
(A)	Definition of Crime				
1.	Raw Definition of Crime	21.33(64)	18.33(55)	7.33(22)	15.67(141)
2.	Constitutional Definition of Crime	78.67(236)	81.67(245)	92.67(278)	84.33(759)
	Total	100.00(300)	100.00(300)	100.00(300)	100.00(900)
(B)	Awareness About Crime and Rights Violation				
1.	Aware	51.67(155)	86.00(258)	93.67(281)	77.11(694)
2.	Unaware	48.33(145)	14.00(42)	6.33(19)	22.89(206)
	Total	100.00(300)	100.00(300)	100.00(300)	100.00(900)
(C)	Personal Experience of Violation	6.33(19)	13.00(39)	7.33(22)	8.89(80)
(D)	Knowledge of Human Rights				
1.	Unaware	46.33(139)	46.67(140)	4.00(12)	32.33(291)

(Contd.)

(Contd.Table 7.163)

S.No	Variables	Tribal %(n)	Rural %(n)	Urban %(n)	Total %(n)
2.	Partially Aware	45.67(137)	36.67(110)	59.33(178)	47.22(425)
3.	Fully	8.00(24)	16.67(50)	36.67(110)	20.44(184)
	Total	100.00(300)	100.00(300)	100.00(300)	100.00(900)
(E)	Dispute Processing Institution				
1.	Elderly	15.33(46)	-	-	5.11(46)
2.	Panchayat	84.33(253)	39.67(119)	-	41.33(372)
3.	Police	0.33(1)	60.33(181)	100.00(300)	53.56(482)
	Total	100.00(300)	100.00(300)	100.00(300)	100.00(900)
(F)	Attitude Towards Human Rights Violation	Tribal %(n)	Rural %(n)	Urban %(n)	Total %(n)
1.	Never Bother	35.00(105)	-	4.33(13)	13.11(118)
2.	Leave After Discussion	26.00(78)	9.33(28)	16.67(50)	17.33(156)
3.	Take an Action	39.00(117)	90.67(272)	79.00(237)	69.56(626)
	Total	100.00(300)	100.00(300)	100.00(300)	100.00(900)
(G)	Number of Human Rights Articles Told				
1.	None	47.33(142)	30.33(91)	7.67(23)	28.44(256)
2.	Above 10	2.00(6)	3.00(9)	10.33(31)	5.11(46)
(H)	Visited Police Station	13.33(40)	45.33(136)	36.33(109)	31.67(285)
(I)	Behavior of Police men	Tribal %(n)	Rural %(n)	Urban %(n)	Total %(n)

(Contd.)

(Contd.Table 7.163)

S.No	Variables	Tribal %(n)	Rural %(n)	Urban %(n)	Total %(n)
1.	Co-operative	87.50(35)	6.62(9)	9.17(10)	18.95(54)
2.	Non Co-operative	2.50(1)	66.18(90)	36.70(40)	145.96(131)
3.	Rude	10.00(4)	27.21(37)	45.87(59)	35.09(100)
	Total	100.00(40)	100.00(136)	100.00(109)	100.00(285)
(J)	Visited Court	6.67(20)	29.33(88)	37.67(!13)	24.56(221)
(K)	Awareness About Approach to Court	33.67(101)	44.33(133)	89.33(268)	55.78(502)
(L)	Awareness About Procedure of Public Interest Litigation	2.00(6)	13.67(41)	33.00(99)	16.22(146)

Table 7.163 shows the comparison of various variables of police and human rights among tribal, rural and urban populations. Definition of crime as is given, follows a pattern. The percentage of respondents who had given the raw definition of crime decreases from tribal to rural to urban population (21.33 percent to 18.33 percent to 7.33 percent) respectively. These definitions are the simpler forms of the complex issue of the society, law and constitution. Those respondents who have the raw concept of crime are more simple and uncomplicated at heart. This clearly indicates that simplicity decreases as we move from tribal population towards urban population. Similarly the response reflecting the constitutional definition of crime increases in the same order (78.67 percent to 81.67 percent to 92.67 percent). However, it is worth noting that even in the tribal belt of Lahoul, the constitutional definition of crime is given by majority of respondents, thus indicating at the induction effect from outside the valley. In the total population 15.67 percent give raw definition as most of the urban population and 84.33 percent give constitutional definition of crime.

The awareness about crime and rights violation increases from tribal population to rural population to urban population (51.67 percent to 86.00 percent to 93.67 percent) respectively. In the tribal area the sources of awareness are very limited. First and fore most reason is the inaccessibility of the area, thus keeping it cut off for almost seven to eight months from the rest of the whole world. This affects their knowledge about outer world. Media has very little impact on the lives of these people. TV, radio, newspaper are on the periphery of their lives. Where as in the rural population where the area is more accessible, people have more opportunities as compared to Lahoul, the sources of awareness is much more than what is available to tribal people. Urban population on the other hand is the most exposed lot of people. Delhi being the metropolitan city having metro rail, high ways, sub-ways, electronic parks, super malls and a hub of all information, government offices, police head quarters, parliament, supreme court, National Human Rights Commission, National Commission for Scheduled Tribes has given a lot of exposure to its residents. This is the reason for getting the highest percentage of aware respondents in Delhi, however their awareness is non-technical.In the total population 77.11 percent are aware of crime and human rights violation and 22.89 percent are unaware.

Personal experience of crime and human rights violation by the respondents are the case studies which had been collected during the field work. It is found that in all the three population, maximum number of violation of cases had been found in the rural population(13.00 percent) than in the urban population (7.33 percent) and least in tribal population (6.33 percent). Seeing at this trend it can be inferred that maximum violation of human rights is experienced by the rural population. It is observed that among the rural population the major issue of any type of argument or fight which later leads to the violation of human rights of any of the group involved, is the status of any group in the village. People fight for attaining a dominant status in the village. In the urban area people don't easily mess up with each other as they know everybody is aware of law and police. Here the type of violation is generally institutionalized, which means facing harassment at the hands of any office or government department, or complicated procedures etc. In the total population, 8.89 percent of the respondents have the persona; experience of crime and human rights violation.

Knowledge of human rights has a major link with the awareness pattern. It is observed here that the percentage of unaware respondents is almost same in the tribal and rural populations (46.33 percent and 46.67 percent) respectively. In the urban population, however this percentage has dropped many folds as only

4.00 percent respondents have been reported to be unaware of the human rights as in the urban area there are many means by which people living here get exposure. Moreover the National Capital Territory of India is the centre for all types to information, trade, educational and job opportunities and violations of human rights as compared to tribal population living in a remote area or rural population living in a less developed area. Similarly a trend is observed in the percentage of the fully aware respondents in all the three populations. The percentage goes almost double as we move from tribal to rural and than to urban population (8.00 percent to 16.67 percent to 36.67 percent) respectively. The highest level of awareness among the urban population can be attributed to the fact that among the urban population the network and role of media is very strong as contrast to tribal or rural population. Thus tribal area has least number of aware respondents and urban area has maximum number of aware respondents. In the total population, 32.33 percent of the respondents are unaware of the knowledge of human rights and 20.44 percent are fully aware.

Dispute processing institutions in any society reflect the level of modernity of the society. It is observed that Lahoul which is a tribal society is most remote among all the three populations. Here it is observed that 15.33 percent of the respondents would go to elderly people for their dispute resolution, 84.33 percent would go to Panchayat and only 0.33 percent would go to police. Among rural society, which is less remote than tribal society and more backward than urban society, 39.67 percent of the respondents would go to Panchayat and 60.33 percent would go to police. Here none of the respondents had been reported to go to elderly people for their dispute settlement. As we move towards an urban society, it is a known fact that in terms of modernity in material culture, urban societies are most advanced. Here all the respondents are reported to go to police for settlement of any kind of dispute. In the total population, 5.11 percent are reported to go to elderly people, 41.33 percent would go to Panchayat and 53.56 percent would go to police.

Attitude towards human rights violation indicates the practice of human rights knowledge. Respondents who said they would not be bothered about the violation of their rights could have two reasons for this type of response –either they are unaware about their human rights or they do not want to get into the complications of law to get it solved. However, in the tribal area of Lahoul the reason is unawareness. 35.00 percent of the respondents would never bother about their violations and 39.00 percent said they would take an action against the violator of their right. In the rural population, none of the respondents said that they would not bother about the violation of their rights. All the population is reported to take some action against the violation.

90.67 percent of the respondents said they would go to police to report about the violation. In the urban population 4.33 percent of the respondents said they would not be bothered about the violation. It is strange to get this type of response from the urban population ,which is considered to be the most aware than tribal and rural population. The reason which urban people give for avoiding the violation is that they don't want to get entangled in the complex police procedures.However, 79.00 percent of the urban people said that they would take an action against the violation of their human rights. It is to be observed here that rural population (90.67 percent) responded more than urban population (79.00), as those who would take an action against the violation. The reason behind this could be that, rural people have comparatively more leisure than urban people. In the villages, the major issue of disharmony is found to be the desire of attaining the status of the dominant group. Anybody making his or her own group becomes the cause of trouble for the dominant group thus leading towards the arguments and fights. So people take their small ego issues to the police. In the total population 13.11 percent said they would not bother about the violation and 69.56 percent said that they would take an action.

Number of human rights according to Articles told by the respondents clearly indicates their knowledge about human right articles. In the tribal population 47.33 percent respondents could not tell about any of the human rights articles. Only 2.00 percent could tell more than ten human rights articles. *For the tribal population the basic meaning of human rights is very rustic and uncomplicated and is also away from the constitutional labyrinth of covenants, charters etc. All they understand and demand is as basic as right to education, work, life, movement and religion.* Among the rural population 30.33 percent couldn't tell any of the human rights articles. Only 3.00 percent of the population could tell more than 10 human rights. *The response among the rural population is of the mix type. The awareness of the population is more than basic awareness and less than advanced awareness.* In the urban population, 7.67 percent could not tell about any of the human rights. 10.33 percent could tell above ten human right articles. It can be said that the *urban population is most aware of their Human Rights. They have the knowledge of the means to safe guard their interest and punish the wrong doer.* In the total population, 28.44 percent respondents couldn't tell about any of the human rights and 5.11 percent could tell more than 10 human right articles.

13.33 percent, 45.33 percent and 36.33 percent of the tribal, rural and urban respondents respectively have visited police station. It is to be observed here that rural population has gone to the police station more than urban population as the rural people would approach the police station even for small ego fights. Whereas the metropolitan population would think before going to police station as this procedure needs time. In the total population 31.67 percent of the respondents have gone to the police station.

The reverse order is seen when behavior is rated as rude among tribal, rural and urban (10.00 percent, 27.21 percent, 45.87 percent respectively) populations. In the total population 18.95 percent respondents rated the police behavior as cooperative and 35.09 percent rated it as rude.

Number of respondents who have gone to court increases from tribal to rural to urban population (6.67 percent to 29.33 percent to 37.67 percent) respectively. The reason for this could be the fact that in the tribal population the cases do not aggravate so much that they reach the court level. They are generally solved by the 'arbitrator decision' (as explained earlier) at the panchayat or at the most the police station level. Where as in the rural and urban population the 'adjudicator decision' is most vital for the case to be decided. 24.56 percent from the total population have ever gone to court.

Awareness about approach to court is found least among tribal population (33.67 percent), than in rural population (44.33 percent) and highest in urban population (89.33 percent). The reason for this could be the fact that since the tribal population goes less in the court so they are less aware of its procedure than rural or tribal population. Another reason could be the level of education and thus the general awareness about the procedures. 55.78 percent of the respondents from the total population could tell the proper procedure of approaching the court i.e. from session court to high court to supreme court.

Awareness about the Procedure of PIL (Public Interest Litigation) is found to be very less among the tribal population and the rural population (2.00 percent and 13.67 percent respectively). In the urban population, 33.00 percent of the respondents are reported to be aware of the provision of Public Interest Litigation i.e. informing the supreme court about their violation through a post card. Awareness about the procedure of PIL which is a constitutional clause and is considered as the 'strategic arm of the legal aid movement' is very less as it is a technical information (Bakshi, 2002). In the total population 16.22 percent are aware of PIL.

Table 7.164 presents the gender wise awareness of human rights in the tribal, rural and urban population. Raw definition of crime is given more by females in all the three populations in the decreasing order from tribal to rural to urban population (34.15 percent to 31.62 percent to 10.34 percent) respectively than males (12.43 percent to 9.84 percent to 4.52 percent)

Table 7.164: Gender and Human Rights Among Tribal, Rural and Urban Populations

S.No.	Variables	Tribal %(n) Male	Tribal %(n) Female	Rural%(n) Male	Rural%(n) Female	Urban%(n) Male	Urban%(n) Female	Total%(n) Male	Total%(n) Female
A.	Definition of Crime								
1.	Raw Definition of Crime	12.43(22)	34.15(42)	9.84(18)	31.62(37)	4.52(7)	10.34(15)	9.13(47)	24.42(94)
2.	Constitutional Definition of Crime	87.57(155)	65.85(81)	90.16(165)	68.38(80)	95.48(148)	89.66(130)	90.87(468)	75.58(291)
	Total	100.00(177)	100.00(123)	100.00(183)	100.00(117)	100.00(155)	100.00(145)	100.00(515)	100.00(385)
B.	Awareness About Crime and Rights Violation								
1.	Aware	76.27(135)	16.26(20)	91.26(167)	77.78(91)	98.06(152)	88.97(129)	88.16(454)	62.34(240)
2.	Unaware	23.73(42)	83.74(103)	8.74(16)	22.22(26)	1.94(3)	11.03(16)	11.84(61)	37.66(145)
	Total	100.00(177)	100.00(123)	100.00(183)	100.00(117)	100.00(155)	100.00(145)	100.00(515)	100.00(385)
C.	Personal Experience of Violation	84.21(16)	15.79(3)	64.10(25)	35.90(14)	59.09(13)	40.91(9)	67.50(54)	32.50(26)
D.	Knowledge of Human Rights Articles								

(Contd.)

(Contd.Table 7.164)

S.No.	Variables	Tribal %(n) Male	Female	Rural%(n) Male	Female	Urban%(n) Male	Female	Total%(n) Male	Female
	Articles								
1.	Unaware	22.60(40)	80.49(99)	43.72(80)	51.28(60)	-	8.28(12)	(23.30)120	44.42(171)
2.	Partially Aware	63.84(113)	19.51(24)	34.43(63)	40.17(47)	60.65(94)	57.93(84)	52.43(270)	40.26(155)
3.	Fully	13.56(24)	-	21.86(40)	8.55(10)	39.35(61)	33.79(49)	24.27(125)	15.32(59)
	Total	100.00(177)	100.00(123)	100.00(183)	100.00(117)	100.00(155)	100.00(145)	100.00(515)	100.00(385)
E.	Dispute Processing Institution								
1.	Elderly	11.30(20)	21.14(26)	-	-	-	-	3.88(20)	6.75(26)
2.	Panchayat	88.14(156)	78.86(97)	22.95(42)	65.81(77)	-	-	38.45(198)	45.19(174)
3.	Police	0.56 (1)	-	77.05(141)	34.19(40)	100.00(155)	100.00(145)	57.67(297)	48.05(185)
	Total	100.00(177)	100.00(123)	100.00(183)	100.00(117)	100.00(155)	100.00(145)	100.00(515)	100.00(385)
F.	Attitude Towards Human Rights Violation								
1.	Never Bother	33.90(60)	36.59(45)	-	-	1.94(3)	6.90(10)	12.33(63)	14.29(55)
2.	Leave After Discussion	19.77(35)	34.96(43)	3.83(7)	17.95(21)	12.90(20)	20.69(30)	12.04(62)	24.42(94)
3.	Take an Action	46.33(82)	28.46(35)	96.17(176)	82.05(96)	85.16(132)	72.41(105)	75.73(390)	61.30(236)
	Total	100.00(177)	100.00(123)	100.00(183)	100.00(117)	100.00(155)	100.00(145)	100.00(515)	100.00(385)

(Contd.)

(Contd.Table 7.164)

S.No.	Variables	Tribal %(n) Male	Female	Rural%(n) Male	Female	Urban%(n) Male	Female	Total%(n) Male	Female
G.	Number of Human Rights Told								
1.	None	42.25(60)	57.75(82)	24.18(22)	75.82(69)	39.13(9)	60.87(14)	35.55(91)	64.45(165)
2.	Above 10	100.00(6)	-	100.00(9)	-	64.52(20)	35.48(11)	76.09(35)	23.91(11)
H.	Visited Police Station	80.00(32)	20.00(8)	85.29(116)	14.71(20)	59.63(65)	40.37(44)	74.74(213)	25.26(72)
I.	Behaviour of Police men								
1.	Co-operative	93.75(30)	62.50(5)	1.74(2)	35.00(7)	4.62(3)	15.91(7)	16.43(35)	26.39(19)
2.	Non Co-operative	-	12.50(1)	74.14(86)	20.00(4)	41.54(27)	29.55(13)	53.05(113)	25.00(18)
3.	Rude	6.52(2)	25.00(2)	24.14(28)	45.00(9)	53.85(35)	54.55(24)	30.52(65)	48.61(35)
	Total	100.00(32)	100.00(8)	100.00(116)	100.00(20)	100.00(65)	100.00(44)	100.00(213)	100.00(72)
J.	Visited Court	100.00(20)	-	86.36(76)	13.64(12)	66.37(75)	33.63(38)	77.38(171)	22.62(50)
K.	Awareness About Approach to Court	95.05(96)	4.95(5)	84.96(113)	15.04(20)	53.73(144)	46.27(124)	70.32(353)	29.68(149)
L.	Awareness About Procedure of Public Interest Litigation	100.00(6)	-	100.00(41)	-	74.75(74)	25.55(25)	82.22(121)	17.12(25)

(Contd.)

respectively. This indicates two things- first that females are more simpler than males at heart and secondly the simplicity of females and males decreases as the complexity of the society increases from tribal society to rural society to urban society. In the total population 9.13 percent of males and 24.42 percent of females gave the raw definition. On the contrary, a reverse order is observed when the response for the constitutional definition is seen. Females have responded less (65.85 percent to 68.38 percent to 89.66 percent) than males (87.57 percent to 90.16 percent to 95.48 percent) in tribal, rural and urban societies respectively. But here the trend is increasing in both- females and males as we approach from tribal to urban. The reason for this could be that males get more exposure of the society as they move out more and meet different people as compared to females. Males get more opportunities to interact with people as compared to females who are house bound in most of the societies. In the total population 90.87 percent males and 75.58 percent females gave the constitutional definition of crime.

Awareness about crime and rights violation is found to be more in males than in females and that too in the increasing order in tribal, rural and urban population (76.27 percent to 91.26 percent to 98.06 percent) respectively. Males get more exposure than females through their occupation as they meet more number of people than females. This leads to their higher awareness about the crime and human rights violation. In the total population, males are 88.16 percent aware and females are 62.34 percent aware. However, unawareness about crime and human rights reduces among females as we go from tribal to rural to urban population (83.74 percent to 22.22 percent to 11.03 percent). Tribal females are found to be most unaware and urban females are most aware about the crime and violation of human rights. The reason for this could be that in the remote belt of Lahoul where already there is a dearth of information and opportunities, females who remain house bound or involved in agriculture has no source of exposure in their life. They lead their entire life in fulfilling their household liabilities, thus shunning their all sources of awareness. Rural or urban females on the other hand has better opportunities of exposure from the day to day life. In the total population 11.84 percent are unaware males and 37.66 percent are unaware females.

Personal experience of violation of human rights is found to be more among males (84.21 percent, 64.10 percent, 59.09 percent) in tribal, rural and urban societies respectively than females (15.79 percent, 35.90 percent, 40.91 percent). The reason for this type of response could be that since males mostly move out of their houses for their occupation and interact with other people so they come in contact of many persons who may try to exploit them.

Females who are generally house bound, do not get in touch with the unknown people in the same manner as the males get an opportunity. It is also observed that tribal males has experienced the maximum violation among the tribal, rural and urban males. The reason for this is that tribal males are relatively less aware than rural or urban males. In the total population 67.50 percent males and 32.50 percent females have experienced the violation of their rights.

Knowledge or awareness of human rights is found to be more in the males than in females. It is found that the percentage of fully aware males increases from tribal to rural to urban population(13.56 percent to 21.86 percent to 39.35 percent) respectively. It can be said that as the opportunities increases, so does the knowledge and awareness of human rights. None of the fully aware females are reported to be found among the tribal population. However rural and urban females contributed 8.55 percent and 33.79 percent to the fully aware category. In the total population 24.27 percent and 15.32 percent are fully aware males and females. In the category of unaware respondents, as slightly different trend is observed.The percentage of unaware male respondents first increases and than decreases as we move from tribal to rural to urban population (22.60 percent, 43.72 percent, 0.00 percent) respectively. In case of unaware females it continuously decreases from tribal- rural- urban females (80.49 percent to 51.28 percent to 8.28 percent) respectively. The reason for this could be that as the society modernizes, the general level of unawareness decreases. In the total population 23.30 percent and 44.42 percent are unaware males and females.

The tendency or the preference of going to elderly people or Panchayat is found to be more in females (6.75 percent, 45.19 percent respectively) than in males (3.88 percent, 38.45 percent respectively) in the total population. It is observed that in the tribal population males (11.30 percent) and females (21.14 percent) prefer going to elderly people of the village for their dispute settlement. This practice of going to elderly people for the dispute resolution is found to be restricted to the tribal population as none of the respondents from rural and urban population have been reported doing this. The reason for this could be that among all the societies ,the feeling of brotherhood is maximum in the tribal society. People give regard to the elders of the society. They hold a significant place in the decision making in the society. The percentage of respondents who would prefer approaching Panchayat decreases from tribal to rural population. In the tribal population males (88.14 percent) go more to Panchayat than females (78.86 percent) as males are found to be more vocal of their violation of rights in comparison to females whose silent self–sacrifice and self-denial has become their fortitude. In the rural population females

(65.81 percent) go more to Panchayat than males (22.95 percent). Here it could be explained by saying that females who find themselves unconfident of going to police station alone, prefers going to Panchayat. None of the urban respondents go to Panchayat for their dispute settlement as the institution of Panch and Panchayat does not exist in the urban society. In the tribal population only 0.56 percent of the male respondents would prefer going to police. Males prefer more than females to go to police station as they find the dispute settlement through police more assured. The percentage of males going to police station increases from tribal males to urban males (0.56 percent< 77.05 percent < 100.00 percent).This is because of decreasing importance of institutions like elderly people, Panchayat and police station from tribal to rural to urban population.

Attitude towards human rights and violation shows that percentage of females (14.29 percent) saying 'never bother' is more than males (12.33 percent) in the total population. It is to be observed here that none of the males and females are found to be saying 'never bother' in the rural population, thus showing their willingness to fight against the injustice. It is reconfirmed by the trend in the response of the population saying 'take an action'. The response increases than decreases in males (46.33 percent to 96.17 percent to 85.16 percent) and females (28.46 percent to 82.05 percent to 72.41 percent), in the order of tribal, rural and urban populations respectively. The reason for this type of response could be the combination of awareness and illiteracy which has lead to this increased response in rural males and females. In the total population 75.73 percent of the males and 61.30 percent of females would take an action against their violation of human rights.

In the tribal population, out of those who could not tell none of the human rights articles, 42.25 percent are males and 57.75 percent are females. In the rural population, out of those who could not tell any of the human rights articles, 24.18 percent are males and 75.82 percent are females. Similarly in the urban population, 39.13 percent are males and 60.87 percent are females. In the total population also, 35.55 percent are males and 64.45 percent are females. Thus, it is observed that females scores out than males, in those who could not tell even a single human right as female's are mostly restricted to household activity which restricts there knowledge and awareness also. Those who told above ten human rights articles are 100.00 percent males in the tribal and rural population. In the urban population however, 64.52 percent males and 35.48 percent females could tell more than ten human rights. In the total population 76.09 percent of males and 23.91 percent of females could tell more than ten human rights articles.

Out of those who have ever visited police station in the tribal population, 80.00 percent are males and 20.00 percent are fèmales. In the rural population, 85.29 percent are males and 14.71 percent are females. In the urban population, out of those who have ever gone to police station, 59.63 percent are males and 40.37 percent are females. Males are found to go to police station more than females as it is observed that females hesitate in going to police station alone in all the three societies, so they prefer not going. They will either go to elderly people of the society or to panchāyat but rarely to police station alone. In the total population, 74.74 percent are males and only 25.26 percent are females.

Behaviour of police men in the tribal population shows that 93.75 percent of males said it is cooperative and 6.52 percent said it is rude. Among females, 62.50 percent said its cooperative and 25.00 percent said its rude. In the rural population, the maximum percent of males (74.14 percent) responded by saying that the behaviour is non-cooperative and 45.00 percent females said that the behaviour is rude. In the urban population, maximum percent of males (53.85 percent) and females (54.55 percent) said the behaviour is rude. In the total population the maximum of males (53.05 percent) said the behaviour is non-cooperative and 48.61 percent females said that it is rude.

Among those who have visited court in the tribal population, 100.00 percent are males. In the rural population, 86.36 percent are males and 13.64 percent are females. In the urban population 66.37 percent are males and 33.63 percent are females. The reason for this type of restricted response from females could be the fact that females in all the three societies do not go to court alone without their male partners. In the total population of those who have ever visited court, 77.38 are males and 22.62 percent are females.

Out of those who have awareness about approach to court in the tribal population, 95.05 percent are males and 4.95 percent are females. In the rural population, 84.96 percent of males and 15.04 percent are females. In the urban population, however, the females share a good percentage unlike rural and tribal. 53.73 percent of urban males and 46.27 percent of urban females are aware of the procedure of approaching the court. In the total population70.32 percent males and 29.68 percent females are aware.

Out of those who are aware about the provision of public interest litigation, in the tribal and rural population, no aware females are found. In the urban population, 74.75 percent are aware males and 25.55 percent are aware females. The reason for more male awareness could be the fact that they get more exposure as they move out for their occupation, thus come across various people, as compared to females. In the total population only 17.12 percent of the females and 82.88 percent males are found to be aware.

Table 7.165: Ethnicity and Human Rights Among Tribal, Rural and Urban Populations

S.No.	Variables	Tribal%(n)		Rural%(n)		Urban%(n)					
(A)	*Definition of Crime*	*Swanglas*	*Bodhs*	*Jat*	*Brahmin*	*Agarwal*	*Kashmiri Pandit*	*Punjabi*	*S.Indian*	*Bengali*	*Sindhi*
1	Raw Definition of Crime	21.88(28)	20.93(36)	14.71(25)	23.08(30)	11.11(10)	0.00(0)	0.00(0)	26.92(7)	8.70(2)	20.00(3)
2	Constitutional Definition of Crime	78.13(100)	79.07(136)	85.29(145)	76.92(100)	88.89(80)	100.00(99)	100.00(47)	73.08(19)	91.30(12)	80.00(12)
	Total	100.00(128)	100.00(172)	100.00(170)	100.00(130)	100.00(90)	100.00(99)	100.00(47)	100.00(26)	100.00(23)	100.00(15)
(B)	Awareness About Crime and Rights Violation										
1	Aware	52.34(67)	51.16(88)	85.88(146)	86.15(112)	92.22(83)	100.00(99)	100.00(47)	84.62(22)	65.22(15)	100.00(15)
2	Unaware	47.66(61)	48.84(84)	14.12(24)	13.85(18)	7.78(7)	0.00(0)	0.00(0)	15.38(4)	34.78(8)	0.00(0)
	Total	100.00(128)	100.00(172)	100.00(170)	100.00(130)	100.00(90)	100.00(99)	100.00(47)	100.00(26)	100.00(23)	100.00(15)
(C)	Knowledge of Human Rights										
1	Unaware	56.25(72)	38.95(67)	38.24(65)	57.69(75)	4.44(4)	0.00(0)	2.13(1)	15.38(4)	13.04(3)	0.00(0)
2	Partially Aware	35.16(45)	53.49(92)	44.12(75)	26.92(35)	80.00(72)	39.39(39)	65.96(31)	61.54(16)	52.17(12)	53.33(8)

(Contd.)

(Contd. Table 7.165)

S.No.	Variables	Tribal%(n)		Rural%(n)		Urban%(n)					
3	Fully	8.59(11)	7.56(13)	17.65(30)	15.38(20)	15.56(14)	60.61(60)	31.91(15)	23.08(6)	34.78(8)	46.67(7)
	Total	100.00(128)	100.00(172)	100.00(170)	100.00(130)	100.00(90)	100.00(99)	100.00(47)	100.00(26)	100.00(23)	100.00(15)
(D)	Attitude Towards Human Rights Violation										
1	Never Bother	35.94(46)	34.30(59)	0.00(0)	0.00(0)	4.44(4)	0.00(0)	0.00(0)	15.38(4)	21.74(5)	0.00(0)
2	Leave After Discussion	13.28(17)	35.47(61)	8.82(15)	10.00(13)	21.11(19)	0.00(0)	6.38(3)	53.85(14)	56.52(13)	6.67(1)
3	Take an Action	50.78(65)	30.23(52)	91.18(155)	90.00(117)	74.44(67)	100.00(99)	93.62(44)	30.77(8)	21.74(5)	93.33(14)
	Total	100.00(128)	100.00(172)	100.00(170)	100.00(130)	100.00(90)	100.00(99)	100.00(47)	100.00(26)	100.00(23)	100.00(15)
(E)	Number of Human Rights Articles Told										
1	None	48.44(62)	46.51(80)	24.12(41)	38.46(50)	5.56(5)	0.00(0)	6.38(3)	23.08(6)	39.13(9)	0.00(0)
2	Above 10	3.13(4)	1.16(2)	2.35(4)	4.62(6)	5.56(5)	19.19(19)	4.26(2)	3.85(1)	4.35(1)	20.00(3)

Table 7.165 presents the awareness of human rights with reference to various ethnic groups which are taken into present study. These groups were pooled together to form a population as tribal, rural and urban population. Here each ethnic group has been separately taken (though the sample size is very small in some of the groups, even than it has been tried to focus on the ethnicity and human rights). An attempt has been made to highlight the ethnicity and human rights with reference to awareness.

It is to be observed here that among tribal population, two ethnic groups are found – one following Hinduism, known as Swanglas and other following Buddhism, known as Bodhs. Although not much difference is observed in both the ethnic groups. Among Swanglas, 21.88 percent of the population gave the raw definition of crime and 78.13 percent gave the constitutional definition. Among Bodhs, 20.93 percent gave the raw definition and 79.07 gave the constitutional definition. As it is observed here that among both the ethnic groups, not much difference is observed in the definitions given. In the rural population, two ethnic groups found are Jat and Brahmin. Among Jat, 14.71 percent gave the raw definition of crime and 85.29 percent gave the constitutional definition of crime. Among Brahmin, 23.08 percent gave the raw definition and 76.92 percent gave the constitutional definition. Among the urban population, six different ethnic groups are found- Agarwal, Kashmiri Pandit, Punjabi, South Indian(heterogeneous), Bengali and Sindhi. Among all these six ethnic groups of the urban population, South Indians gave the maximum percent of the raw definition (26.92 percent) followed by Sindhi (20.00 percent), Agarwal(11.11 percent), Bengali (8.70 percent). Ethnic group of Kashmiri Pandit and Punjabi did not gave any raw definition. Among those who gave the constitutional definition, hundred percent response is observed in the ethnic groups of Kashmiri Pandit and Punjabi populations, followed by Bengali population (91.30 percent), Agarwal community (88.89 percent), Sindhi group (80.00 percent) and South Indian heterogeneous group (73.08 percent). Ethnic group of Kashmiri Pandits and Punjabi gave the highest percent of constitutional definition. This could be because of the reason that both these ethnic groups have migrated to Delhi from the Jammu and Kashmir and Lahore respectively. These populations have suffered a lot of violation during the migration. Kashmiri Pandits have experienced a lot of trauma during the 1989-1990 riots, thus getting a first hand experience of crime.

Awareness of crime and rights violation among both the ethnic groups of the tribal population shows that Swanglas are 52.34 percent aware and 47.66 percent unaware and Bodhs are 51.16 percent aware and 48.84 percent unaware. It is again observed that not much difference is observed among the two ethnic groups of the tribal population. In the rural population, the awareness pattern of Jat (85.88 percent) and Brahmin(86.15 percent) is found to be almost similar, thus indicating that ethnicity is playing no role in increasing or decreasing the awareness. Among the urban population, the ethnic groups of Kashmiri Pandit, Sindhi and Punjabi have shown the hundred percent awareness about crime and human rights violation, followed by Agarwal (92.22 percent), South Indian (heterogeneous)(84.62 percent) and Bengali (65.22 percent) group. The reason for this higher percent of awareness among few ethnic groups is the type of experience they have under gone, which has acted as their source of getting awareness.

Knowledge of human rights among all the ethnic groups shows that, among Swanglas 8.59 percent and among Bodhs 7.56 percent are found to be fully aware of human rights. Among the rural population, both the ethnic groups of Jat(17.65 percent) and Brahmin(15.38 percent) showed similar results, thus indication that ethnicity did not effect the awareness of human rights among these populations. In the urban population, however, the awareness about the human rights is found to be maximum in the ethnic group of Kashmiri Pandit (60.61 percent) followed by Sindhi (46.67 percent), Bengali (34.78 percent), Punjabi (31.91 percent), South Indian (23.08 percent) and lowest in the Agarwal community (15.56 percent). Ethnic group of Kashmiri Pandit because of self experience of violation of human rights have highest knowledge of the same.

Attitude towards the human rights violation shows that in the tribal population, 50.78 percent of the Swanglas and 30.23 percent of the Bodhs would take an action against the violation of their human rights. Among the rural population, 91.18 percent of Jat and 90.00 percent of the Brahmin said they would take an action against the violation of their human right. Among the urban population, all the Kashmiri Pandit respondents said that they would take an action against the violation of their human rights.

Number of human rights articles told by the ethnic groups of tribal population shows that, only 3.13 percent of the Swanglas and 1.16 percent of the Bodhs could tell told human rights articles above ten. In the rural population, 2.35 percent of Jat and 4.62 percent of Brahmin could tell more than ten human rights articles. Among the urban population, 19.19 percent of population of the ethnic group of Kashmiri Pandit could tell more than ten human rights. The reason for this type of increased awareness among this ethnic group is their self experience of crime and human rights violation.

Table 7.166 Distance from Police Station and Awareness of Human Rights Among Tribal, Rural and Urban Populations

S.No.	*Variables*	*Tribal%(n)*		*Rural%(n)*		*Urban%(n)*		*Total%(n)*	
(A)	Definition of Crime	Near	Far	Near	Far	Near	Far	Near	Far
1.	Raw Definition of Crime	16.00(24)	26.67(40)	8.00(12)	28.67(43)	6.67(10)	8.00(12)	10.22(46)	21.11(95)
2.	Constitutional Definition of Crime	84.00(126)	73.33(110)	92.00(138)	71.33(107)	93.33(140)	92.00(138)	89.78(404)	78.89(355)
	Total	100.00(150)	100.00(150)	100.00(150)	100.00(150)	100.00(150)	100.00(150)	100.00(450)	100.00(450)
(B)	Awareness About Crime and Rights Violation								
1.	Aware	66.67(100)	36.67(55)	93.33(140)	78.67(118)	100.00(150)	87.33(131)	86.67(390)	67.56(304)

(Contd.)

(Contd. Table 7.166)

S.No.	Variables	Tribal%(n)		Rural%(n)		Urban%(n)		Total%(n)	
2.	Unaware	33.33(50)	63.33(95)	6.67(10)	21.33(32)	-	12.67(19)	13.33(60)	32.44(146)
	Total	100.00(150)	100.00(150)	100.00(150)	100.00(150)	100.00(150)	100.00(150)	100.00(450)	100.00(450)
(C)	Knowledge of Human Rights								
1.	Unaware	34.00(51)	58.67(88)	52.67(79)	40.67(61)	3.33(5)	4.67(7)	30.00(135)	34.67(156)
2.	Partially Aware	55.33(83)	36.00(54)	26.00(39)	47.33(71)	58.00(87)	60.67(91)	46.44(209)	48.00(216)
3.	Fully	10.67(16)	5.33(8)	21.33(32)	12.00(18)	38.67(58)	34.67(52)	23.56(106)	17.33(78)
	Total	100.00(150)	100.00(150)	100.00(150)	100.00(150)	100.00(150)	100.00(150)	100.00(450)	100.00(450)
(D)	Dispute Processing Institution								
1.	Elderly	13.33(20)	17.33(26)	-	-	-	-	4.44(20)	26(5.78(26)

(Contd.)

(Contd.Table 7.166)

S.No.	Variables	Tribal%(n)		Rural%(n)		Urban%(n)		Total%(n)	
2.	Panchayat	86.00(129)	82.67(124)	-	79.33(119)	-	-	28.67(129)	54.00(243)
3.	Police	0.67(1)	-	100.00(150)	20.67(31)	100.00(150)	100.00(150)	66.89(301)	40.22(181)
	Total	100.00(150)	100.00(150)	100.00(150)	100.00(150)	100.00(150)	100.00(150)	100.00(450)	100.00(450)
(E)	Number of Human Rights Told								
1.	None	4.00(6)	90.67(136)	12.00(18)	48.67(73)	6.67(10)	8.67(13)	7.56(34)	49.33(222)
2.	Above 10	4.00(6)	-	6.00(9)	-	10.67(16)	10.00(15)	6.89(31)	3.33(5)
(F)	Visited Police Station	11.67(35)	1.67(5)	32.67(98)	12.67(38)	18.67(56)	17.67(53)	42.00(189)	21.33(96)

(Contd.)

Table 7.166 shows the effect on the awareness of living near the police station among the tribal, rural and urban populations. It is observed here that in the tribal population, those living near the police station gave more constitutional definition of crime (84.00 percent) and less raw definition of crime (16.00 percent). Where as those living far from the police station gave comparatively more raw definition of crime (26.67 percent) and less constitutional definition of crime (73.33 percent) than those living near the police station. In the rural population also, the same pattern have been observed. Those living near the police station gave less of the raw definition (8.00 percent) and more of the constitutional definition (92.00 percent). Those living far from the police station gave comparatively more of the raw definition (28.67 percent) and less of the constitutional definition (92.00 percent) as compared to those living near the police station. The reason for this could be that in the tribal and rural areas, only few villages lie close to police station. All those living near the police station get an exposure regarding the cases which come in the police station where as those living far from the police station remain unaware of the cases with which people approach police station. In the urban population, however, it is found that there is not much difference in the response of those living near (6.67 percent) and far (8.00 percent) from the police station. It could be because of the fact that in the urban area police stations are in more frequency as is found in the tribal and rural areas. In addition to this, there are other major sources of awareness which plays a very vital role in increasing the awareness. In the total population 10.22 percent of those who gave raw definition lives near the police station and 21.11 percent lives away from the police station. 89.78 percent of those living near the police station and 78.89 percent of those living far from the police station gave the constitutional definition of the crime.

Awareness of crime and human rights violation in the tribal population is found to be more among those who live near (66.67 percent) the police station than those who live far from the police station (36.67 percent). Unawareness about crime and human rights is found to be less among those who live near the police station (33.33 percent) and more among those who live far from the police station(63.33 percent). In the rural population also, awareness about crime and human rights is found to be more among those who live near the police station (93.33 percent) than those who live far from the police station (78.67 percent). Unawareness is less among the population living near (6.67 percent) the police station and more among the population living far from the police station (21.33 percent). The reason for this is again the same that living near the police station gives a lot of exposure about the types of cases with which people approach the police station. Those living far away are deprived of this type of exposure. In the urban population however, the results are not very distinguishing. Hundred percent of those living near the police station are reported to be found aware of the crime and human rights violation. 87.33 percent of those living far from the police station are found aware. None of the respondents who live near the police station are reported to be unaware. Whereas, 12.67 percent of the respondents who live far from the police station are unaware of the crime and human rights violation. In the total population, 86.67 percent of those living near the police station and 67.56 percent of those living far from the police station are found to be aware of the crime and human rights violation. 13.33 percent of those living near and 32.44 percent of those living far from the police station are found to be unaware about the crime and human rights violation.

Knowledge of human rights is found to be more among those living near the police station. In the tribal population among those who are reported to be fully aware of the human rights, 10.67 percent of the population is found to be living near the police station and 5.33 percent away from the police station. In the rural population 21.33 percent of those who are found to be fully aware lives near the police station and 12.00 percent lives far from the police station. In the urban population, the responses of those living near (38.67 percent) the police station and far (34.67 percent) from it are not much different. In the total population 23.56 percent of the fully aware respondents live near the police station and 17.33 percent of those live far from the police station.

In the tribal population it is found that, only those who live near the police station have gone to them for their dispute settlement. None of those who live far away from the police station are found to go to police station. In the rural population, hundred percent of those living near the police station are reported to go to station for their dispute settlement, where as 20.67 percent of those who live away from the police station approach them for their dispute settlement. This can be explained by saying that in the tribal and rural areas, since many villages are far from the police stations, people do not prefer going to station for their dispute settlement. They prefer approaching the locally available and easily accessible institution for the same. In the urban population, hundred percent of the respondents would go to police station, as there is no other institution for dispute resolution. In the total population, 66.89 percent respondents living near the police station and 40.22 percent living away form the police station have gone to the station.

Number of human rights articles as told by the tribal and rural population living near the police station is 4.00 percent and 6.00 percent respectively.

None of the respondents living far from the police station are found to have told above ten human rights articles. In the urban population 10.67 percent of the those who answered above ten human rights articles live near to police station and 10.00 percent live far away from it. In the total population, 6.89 percent who told above ten human rights articles live near the police station and 3.33 percent live far from the police station.

In the tribal population, 11.67 percent of those who have visited the police station lives near the station. Only 1.67 percent of those living far from the police station have approached the station. In the rural population, 32.67 percent of those who have visited the police station lives near the police station. The reason for this is the easy accessibility of the police station. In the urban population, 18.67 percent of the population who have gone to police station lives near the police station. However those who live far(17.67 percent) from the police station also go to it. In the total population, 42.00 percent of the population which has gone to police station lives near it.

7.3 Case Studies

Supporting the above data case studies have been collected from tribal, rural and urban populations which are presented below :-

7.3.1 Case Studies Among Tribal Population

Following are the case studies which are collected from the field area which highlights the human rights violations written above:

Case Study 1

Violation to Right to Proper Medical Treatment

Phunchuk Dolma, 32, married female, a primary teacher by profession developed an infection in the finger of her hand. She went to the PHC. There doctor saw the infection and gave her medicine for 15 days. She started the course right away as her problem was increasing. By 10th day also there was no relief in her pain. She went again to doctor. Doctor changed her medicines and instructed the informant to take medicines for another one week. Then even after one week there was no improvement in the situation. She went third time to the doctor. By now, its been 18-20 days since she had been taking the medicines, but for no good. This time doctor shielded her for not taking medicines properly. Informant said than she decided that she will go to Manali hospital. There when doctor saw her finger and saw her previous prescription, he said that the earlier medicines were not good for your kind of problem.

Action Taken: Nothing

Case Study 2

Forceful Elopement

Chhimiangmo, 50, married female, middle passed house wife was married when she was 20 years old. She was forcefully picked up by a man. She didn't know, who is now her husband. She didn't resist also at that time, as she knows that this is the way to get married. Her husband was in a job, which required long touring. Few days after marriage he went over for a tour. When he was away, husband's younger brother, 22 (at that time) use to help her in field, in the household activity. Slowly they also became close and she had his first baby. When the elder brother came back from tour, he also didn't react to this relationship. He had always wanted a common wife for him and his brother as it negates land fragmentation. She had a total of 4 kids from both the brothers. Now the informant's elder husband has died. Forceful Elopement ended in unknown polyandry.

Action Taken: Nothing

Case Study 3

Violation of Right of Peaceful Assembly

Lal Chand, 50, married male, graduate B.Ed. teacher had gone to a Gotzi (Party) with friends. There after having *chhang*, he and one of his friends started arguing. Informant's friend had to give him Rs. 500/- back. When Lal Chand asked him to return his money, he started arguing with informant and suddenly hurt the informant on his back. He started bleeding profusely and fainted on the spot. He was than taken to doctor at that time, got stitches. In the morning when informant went to his friend's place to ask him to pay penalty, the other fellow refused. He didn't even was feeling sorry for hurting him and said he will give the informant's money later. Listening all this informant got angry and went to Panch. Then he again came with Panch. But the other fellow's reply was same. Then informant warned him that he will go to police and lodge an FIR. Soon the informant's friend was summoned to the Police Station, Keylong there when the police officials scolded him and warned him, he immediately agreed to return his money and pay the penalty of hurting his friend also. Informant's friend came back to village and met informant and returned his money and paid the penalty as fixed by Panchayat.

Action Taken: Justice Seeked

Case Study 4

Violation of Right to Education

Veena, 29, married female, Post Graduate in English, is a house wife. Informant was in the final year of her post graduation when she got married.

Before marriage she said to her parents that she wants to do her M. Phil. They said you can do it after marriage. So she agreed for marriage. After that she talked to her husband about her studies. Informant's husband said she should talk to his parents. When informant talked with her parents-in-law, they refused saying that what will you do after studying so much. Informant said she wants to do a job. But her parents-in-law refused saying they don't want their daughter-in-law to go out of house and work. She tried to convince them but of no good. When asked why don't she protest? Informant said she didn't want her family and marriage to break. So she dropped the idea of continuing her studies and is a house wife now. Informant agrees that this is violation of Human Rights to Education. But she says, a girl after marriage has to look up for various factors. She has to consider interests of all the family members and not only hers, even though it is a violation of Human Rights.

Action Taken : Nothing

Case Study 5

Violation of Right to Proper Medical Treatment

Padma Dolma, 38, illiterate house wife got her vasectomy done from District Hospital Keylong when she was 30 years old. After 8 years of operation, one day she came to know that she is pregnant. This sudden pregnancy had put the informant's life in danger. It was a very difficult pregnancy for her carry. She managed to survive. Informant never went to that doctor again to report back to him, as his posting has been changed.

Action taken : Nothing.

Case Study 6

Violation of Right to Freedom of Religion

Anil, 32, married male is a graduate, agriculturist by occupation. Informant changed his religion from Hinduism to Buddhism as he got impressed with the culture and ideas of Buddhism. As a result, after the change of religion, Anil lost his land, rights on his ancestral property. When he changed his religion, Panchayat summoned him and debarred him from his ancestral property. All the village members present in the Panchayat agreed with the decision. Informant has right over his self-acquired property only. He didn't protest the decision of the Panchayat, as he follows the customary laws. If the informant would have lodged an complaint in the Police Station saying that he has full right as a son on his father's property and he has full human right to change or follow any religion, then his case had an edge over the Panchayat decision.

Action Taken: Nothing

Case Study 7
Violation of Rights to Land

Gyan Chand, 48, married male, middle passed is an instructor in GREF(Ground Reserve Engineering Force). Informant's father had six *beigha* of land. He died without doing any land division. Informant asked his elder brother to do land division as Gyan Chand could guess his elder brother's intention of encroaching even his share in the land. But his elder brother refused saying informant has already have a job and so has no right on the land. Informant's brother said since he has no job so the whole land should go to him alone. Both the brothers had big fight. Informant than went to paanch, even then his elder brother didn't listen. Then he decided that he will go to police. He went to Keylong police station and registered an FIR saying that his elder brother has encroached his land. His brother was summoned to the police station. But his brother didn't listen even then and now their case is in Kullu court. In today's date both the brothers are living in different village. Gyan Chand had made a rocky land as his kitchen garden. His salary and the vegetables from the kitchen garden helps in running the house.

Action Taken : Case Filed

Case Study 8
Violation of Cultural and Social Rights

Chhawang Tashi, 41, married male, primary passed, is a *lamma* by profession and does agriculture also. Fields are irrigated by using the water supplied through *khoul* system. The water is given to each field by rotation. A neighbor of the informant once stole informant's chance to water. Informant ignored his mistake. Second time again he does the same thing, this time informant warned him to taking him to panchayat if he will repeat this thing. But he didn't listen stole for the third time. This time informant approached panchayat. Panchayat penalized him of money. After that he didn't do it again.

Action Taken : Justice Seeked

Case Study 9
Violation of Right to Social Security

Tanzin Sherap, 29 married male, primary passed is an agriculturist by profession. In his village, people of PWD were working. During the construction of the road, informant's some land was encroached by PWD. At that time informant didn't do anything as he thought that it's a government decision and no body can prevent his land from getting engulfed. Second time when GREF people were making metalled road in the village, some part of the field was again engulfed in the construction, as the informant's land was lying on the way through which the road was to be constructed. The road thus constructed would pass informant's field from the corner of his land. Tanzin said he applied for compensation but has never got it. He thinks that money must have been sanctioned for the compensation but inter-mediators must have taken all the money. On being asked why didn't he approach higher authorities, informant said he is not aware of the procedure and thus feels under confident to talk to higher authorities. He repents today saying that he would have got his money back, if he also might have studied till graduation ,as people also fears from those who is educated.

Action Taken : Nothing

Case Study 10
Violation of Women's Right

Sunita, 29 married female is middle passed and is a agriculturist by profession. Informant who was scared to say in the first meeting, confided in the second meeting by saying that she use to feel very weak during her pregnancy. Even than she use to work on the agricultural field. In the field because of her pregnancy many a times she had an increased heart rate. On being asked the reason of going in such a condition, she revealed that her in-laws use to force her to go and work on the field as it was the peak season of the agriculture. Informant said she use to go to the field only because of the fear factor of her in-laws. Sunita said during the pregnancy she use to fear that she might loss her child because of over exertion. But fortunately, nothing went wrong.

Action Taken : Nothing

Case Study 11
Violation of Right to Marry

Tashi Chering, 49, married male, middle passed is the up-pradhan of the village and has agriculture as his profession. Informant's eldest son married a girl from nearby village. The girl and the boy did court marriage. For this they'd gone to Mandi. The reason for going so far away from Lahoul was the insecurity from girl's parents side. They were behaving in a very raucous manner. They broke the window panes of the informant's house. Informant kept quite for quite some time thinking that it is her daughter-in-laws family. If they would be troubled, she would be troubled. He thought it would earn a bad name for the family also. But things were getting out of control. They abused them, threatened them. Informant made them understood that when both boy and girl are ready, than the parents should not create a fuss. But they didn't listen and again came one night and broke window panes of informant's house. In the morning Tashi went to paanch. Paanch intervened in the informant's daughter-in-law's family, but they didn't listen. Then informant went to Keylong police station for filing an FIR. In the police station, the police men directed him what to do. They came with the informant to his village which is 36 kms. away from the station, to see the crime scene i.e. broken window panes. Than later the case was send to CJM court. A date of hearing was also allotted to them. After the first hearing everything went fine and they became dormant.

Action Taken : Justice Seeked

Case Study 12

Violation of Child Right

Angdui, 34, married male, primary passed is an agriculturist by profession. Informant told that when he was a student than his father asked him to left his studies as at that time there were less workers in the field. The financial condition of the family was not strong enough to hire the help from outside. So informant left his studies. On being asked if he was forced to leave his studies, informant told that the stage of forcing never came, as for him it was a big thing that his father has asked him to do something. Informant neither refused him nor asked him the reason for doing so. Now when asked how does he feel about his decision, Angdui says that if he wouldn't have left his studies at that time than he might have completed his schooling at least. He says there is no saving and profit in agriculture as investment is equal to income. On asking the preference between job and agriculture, Angdui said he would prefer a job.

Action Taken : Nothing

Case Study 13

Violation of Right to Social Security

Tanzin Dolkar, 49 ,married female, illiterate and agriculturist by profession. Informant told that once in their field somebody's *zo* (ox) entered.It destroyed a lot of standing crop. When informant's husband went to ran him away, it hit him and he got a deep cut on his hand. He was taken immediately to the district hospital, 35 km away from their village. There doctor stitched his hand.After coming back to the village in the evening, Dolkar's husband went to the panch and reported him the whole issue. In the morning, the owner of the *zo* was summoned in the panchayat ghar. Panch told him to pay the penalty

as it was his *zo*. But the owner of the *zo* not only refused to pay the penalty he misbehaved and didn't say sorry also. All the elderly people sitting there said to him that even if you feel sorry and talk humbly, that would be enough. Than may be he understood his mistake and said sorry to Tanzin's husband. In all this hue and cry informant's husband has to bear the brunt of the situation.
Action Taken: Nothing

7.3.2 Remarks on Case Studies Among Tribal Population

All the case studies collected from the tribal area of Lahoul shows that all people seek help of a third party for their dispute resolution. This third party is the Panchayat of the village who intervenes between the disputants, sometimes on their invitation (arbitrator) and sometimes without invitation (adjudicator). When any one of the party of the disputants did not agree than the matter is proceeded to police, not before that.

7.3.3 Case Studies Among Rural Population

Case Study 1

Violation of Right to Adequate Standard of Living

Ram Dhaniya, 60, widowed male, is illiterate and retired from post of peon in the police department. Informant told that the water supply near his house was very dirty. The water could not be drunk. So he decided to complaint about the issue. He filled a bottle with a water and went to PHC to meet CMO of the hospital. There the CMO didn't pay any attention to the informant. On his regular requests also, the doctor didn't agree to pay a visit to the site. Informant warned the doctor that he will lodge a complaint against him for mis-behaving with him. Infuriated, informant went away from hospital to police station. There when he told the mohar constable that he wants to lodge a complaint against the doctor of PHC, they asked him to go and not get involved in the issue. Finally he decided that he will go to Rohtak and meet the CMO of the district. There that doctor asked him that why is it so that only you have come to complained about the dirty water and no body else? What is the proof that you have collected the water from the right place ? At this, informant asked the doctor to visit the site from which the water has been collected. When the doctor refused to go to that place, informant told the doctor that 'it is your duty to go to the site with the patient under clause 11G of your service paper'. The surgeon was shocked to see the informant's knowledge about the clause and immediately agreed to accompany him to the site. Reaching at the site from where the sample of water had been collected, the doctor realized the gravity of the conditions and within few days water supply was improved. It is only because of the informant's awareness about his right to proper living conditions that he could put in efforts to get what he deserved.

Action Taken : Justice Seeked

Case Study 2

Violation of Freedom from Arbitrary Arrest and Detention

Krishan Kumar, 24, unmarried graduate, searching a job, told that their neighbors had always have a tussle with their family. The neighbors reported falsely that the informant had hit and run their vehicle and lodged a complaint in the police station. Police came to Krishan's house and arrested him. On asking what is his mistake they said 'after reaching station you will come to know'. At that time informant's father who is in Delhi police was not at home. Using his absence as an opportunity, they took the informant to the station and talked to him in a very uncouth and boorish manner, trying to demoralize and scare him. Later in the evening when his father came, he brought him home, warning them not to repeat this again. On being asked if informant enquired the police officials about his crime, and the arrest warrant ,he said he was scared to ask about it from them as they may hit him. Informant says that it is very important to not get scared in front of police officials, as once they know that the person is getting scared, they scare him more. One should boldly ask about the issue of arresting the person and the warrant also.

Action Taken : Nothing

Case Study 3

Violation of Freedom from Torture

Mahender, 35, married male, tenth passed, is a private blue-line bus driver.Once an auto-rickshaw and informant's bus had an accident. Although with the help of immediate brakes, their was no loss of life, but the auto-rickshaw got damaged. The driver of the rickshaw demanded Rs.2000 from the informant for repairing his vehicle. At that time informant had no money so he refused to pay. Warning the informant, rickshaw driver went to the police station to lodge the complaint. There the police men on duty said he would not lodge the FIR if informant pays Rs.5000. Since than its been 10 years that he is going to magistrate's court to attend the summons issued. Mahender told that now it cannot be postponed any more. Till now he has spend Rs.20,000 in this whole process of hiring a lawyer, going to court etc. Now the magistrate is saying that if the informant gives him Rs.20,000 he will discard his case. Informant says that he can never think of giving this big money now. He repents that he should have given Rs.2000 at that time and get the whole case shut at that time only. Since than informant has made his rule that to make one's life easier give the money asked by police men.

Action Taken : Nothing

Case Study 4

Violation of Right of Equal Protection of Law

Basant Kumar, 32, married male, 10th passed is a peon in a government office in Bahadurgarh. Informant says that one of his friend in the village has encroached his one *beigha* of land gradually over the period of 6 months. Now when informant is asking back his land from him, he is refusing saying it is his land. The second fellow is at more influential position. He is warning the informant that if the informant goes to police than he will land up in trouble as the second fellow will put the informant behind bars in false case, as he has contacts with high police officials. Listening this bluntly and flatly informant got scared and decided to forgot about that one *beigha* of his land.

Action Taken : Nothing

Case Study 5

Violation of Right to Marry

Sharmila, 26 married female, is a housewife and has three kids. Informant told that she was married when she was in tenth class. She was 17 years old at that time. When she came to know from her mother that her father has settled her marriage, she refused initially to get married, saying she doesn't know the person and moreover she wants to study further, at least till graduation. But in the male dominating society of Haryana, her father got her married forcefully. Sharmila confided that earlier she didn't like her husband as the age gap of 10 years was too much for her to adjust. She resisted to begin the husband-wife relation. But her resistance was not accepted by her husband.

Action Taken : Nothing

Case Study 6

Violation of Social and Culture Rights

Murath Ram, 48, married male, illiterate agriculturist has 2.5 beigha of land. His financial condition is hand to mouth. His irrigational land is surrounded by big and rich land owners. Informant says that although water for irrigation is distributed by rotation system, even then informant has to maintain a humble requesting attitude towards those big land owners. Murath Ram says that if he will not do their pampering, those rich people may behave nasty and deprive his field of the water thus spoiling his yield. On asking if informant knows that it is his right to get water, he says there is no 'right' in front of money. One who has money, has power and one who has power has all the authority and control to violate or follow human rights.

Action Taken: Nothing

Case Study 7

Violations of Reproductive Rights

Beeta, 23, married female, 10th passed is a housewife by profession. She got married when she was 17 years old. Her husband works in a factory in Rohtak. In a very sensitive and confidential discussion, the informant told the researcher with choked voice that on the day after marriage she has been ravished by her husband. Repeated denial of his demand outraged him, than he had first beaten her and than forcefully mishandled her. On asking if she has told this incident to anybody, she says she doesn't want to trouble her parents by telling this. Her mother-in-law however, guessed it the next day seeing the informant but neither said nor did anything. Now its been seven years since Beeta is married to this man and nothing has changed for her.

Action Taken : Nothing

Case Study 8

Violation of Freedom from Torture

Ramashish, 38, married man, post graduate in arts, is a lecturer in Jat college. The informant told that, once he was surrounded by 10-12 boys of the college. All were graduate students. They stopped him and warned him to tell them the question paper of the internal exam. Informant refused to do that. Then gradually argument changed into a slight fight. Few of the boys tried to hit him but other boys stopped those boys and let him go. Infuriated by this incident informant went straight to the principal. Principal politely asked the informant to forget all this as those boys belong to influential families and no action can be taken against them. Feeling insulted and helpless, informant was still determined to approach police regarding the issue. But later when informant's father and wife made him understood and requested him to forget all this, he pacified. On asking about the violation of freedom from torture, informant says that in this big world definition of violation changes according to people and their money.

Action Taken : Nothing

Case Study 9

Violation of Land Right

Bhajan Lal, 48, married male, is section officer in a government department in Delhi. He has five *beigha* of agricultural land also, which his other family members yield. This time the owner of the neighboring land encroached the common area which is left for the purpose of making a pathway between two fields. The informant couldn't go to the field for few weeks together and in the mean time his neighbor encroached that area. Now when informant asks him to vacate the area he says he had spend so much of money in buying seeds, manure etc. for that area, so now he will not vacate it till the yield comes. Informant asked him to give at least the share of his land, but the second person refused it. Bhajan Lal went to panchayat and than panch and informant went to that field. Panch also asked that second person, to give informant his share, but he refused than also. Informant told that later the *kanungo* also came, but the second person gave him some money and the matter was settled. On being asked about human rights violation, informant said that there is nothing called human rights. These are all constitutional terminology. In real life they do not exist.

Action Taken: Tried But Failed

Case Number 10

Violation of Right to an Adequate Standard of Living

Daleep Singh, 51, graduate, working as a technical assistant in a government office in Delhi was teaching his daughter in the evening time. Suddenly his next door neighbor played music at a very loud volume., thus disturbing them. He and his daughter kept quite for some time. They closed their windows and doors. Seeing this their neighbor increased the volume further, thus clearly indicating that he wanted to disturb them. Informant told that their neighbor's are jealous of them. They think that informant's family is financially strong and are educated also. So he keeps trying to trap them in frivolous disputes. When the volume kept on increasing, than informant went to his house to ask him to decrease the volume. There the informant's neighbor ,as if waiting for him to come started shouting at him. He abused informant and his family in front of all other families present. Then the argument increased and informant pushed the other person slightly with his hands. The neighbor got infuriated at this and went to police station.There he lodged an complaint saying that Daleep Singh came to my house to hurt me. In the morning when informant came to know about the complaint, than he was shocked. On asking the relevance of human rights in the society, informant said there is nothing called human rights in the society. These are constitutional juglary framed by the lawyers and policy makers. Later a compromise had been achieved with mediation of police officials and the case was dismissed.

Action Taken : Matter Solved

7.3.4 Remarks on the Case Studies Among Rural Population

The case studies collected from the rural population indicates that people go to police for their dispute settlement. Here it is also observed that these people are illiterate but not unaware. They are aware of their right to going to police station. In the rural population it is felt that the small issues of land, water, neighborhood arguments have forced people to go to police. The role of Panchayat is limited only to the development aspects of the village.

7.3.5 Case Studies Among Urban Population

Case Study 1

Violation of Right to Social Security

Ashok, 53, married male, engineer by profession parked his car outside his house while coming back from office. Next day in the wee hours of morning he heard some voices outside his house and got up. When he came out, he saw few people were standing near his car. He got doubtful and asked them. Listening informant's voice, all ran away. In the mean time Ashok who lives on first floor came down to his car and saw that one of the wheel of the car was missing. Soon he found a big knife also near the car. In the morning he went to police station to submit that knife. Informant said, although we pay regularly to the watchman who gives duty in night, even than such instances happen. Nothing is safe on road. Crime has increased many folds now.

Action Taken : Went to Police Station

Case Study 2

Violation of Right to Life

Arpita, 25, unmarried female, research scholar in Jawahar Lal University was going on a Sunday to her exam center with her father. They were in auto-rickshaw. Suddenly out of nowhere a car came and hit the auto-rickshaw. The driver, informant and her father all fell down on road. The vehicle also tilted and fall down. Driver got lot of injury. Informant was also hurt. Soon she realized that she cannot stand up and has got a broken bone. Thankfully her father was there with her. So he took her to the near by hospital in emergency as her exam time was very near. Doctors x-rayed her and told her that she has got a hair line fracture in the ankle. Her ankle was plastered. With the plastered ankle and pain she reached her exam center. On asking what had happened to that car who hit them, she said it fled in front of their eyes. No body could do anything. The informant said in a wild metro like Delhi there is no concept of human rights. Everybody is running in a mad race. On being asked if awareness could decrease the level of human rights violation, she said only awareness is not enough for stopping the violation, practice of awareness is also very important.

Action Taken : Nothing

Case Study 3

Violation of Right to an Adequate Standard of Living

Shobit, 35, married male, engineer by profession lives in a housing society. He has just shifted to this society. He has booked the house three years ago. At that time he was told that their would be 24 hours water supply, cent percent back up of electricity, parking facility. Informant told that the reason why he has changed his housing society was because in the earlier housing complex, there was a lack of these facilities. In the hope that he and his family would get a better living environment, they paid extra money to attain those standards of living. Soon after shifting to this new house, informant realized that the conditions here are no better than previous apartments. Within two months there was water seepage patch in their drawing room. The bathroom of the people living in the above apartment had blocked. The power back up of the complex is also very poor. The parking space has also not been constructed completely. Informant asks that if this is the standard of living which he is getting after paying the price also, than it is a sure violation of human right. On being asked if he has taken any action to get the things corrected than informant said he tried getting hold of the mediator who helped the informant to get the house, but for no good.

Action Taken : Nothing Happened

Case Study 4

Violation of Right to Education

Namashree, 32, married female, graduate ,works in a bank. She has a daughter of 6 years. Informant told that she and her husband are into service and their combined salary is Rs. 32000 per month. Informant tried for her admission in various convent schools in Delhi. Her name came in the list of one of the convent schools. When informant and her husband went to the school for getting the procedure done, than they were asked to pay Rs. 25000 donation. Now informant asks that when my daughter has cleared the interview than why should we pay donation money. The candidate is fully eligible to get admission in the school. It is her right to get admission in the school. But if school authorities will charge exorbitant donations than it would be difficult for middle class parents to get admission of their child in the school. The school should keep donations only for business class families and not for job class families. They already have so little source of income that they cannot afford to pay huge donations. On asked that will she report about the school, informant said "who has got time to get into all these procedures? Moreover the story is same in all the good schools of Delhi. All those parents who want to give their children the best education should be prepared to give donation, forgetting the equal right to education.

Action Taken : Nothing

Case Study 5

Violation of Right to Social Security

Bala Narang, 59, married female, post graduate in political science is a retired post graduate teacher. Informant shared that living in society demands a lot of protection of one's self interest and rights. According to her, people in society are opportunist, who would grasp the opportunity of exploiting other person's interest, to fulfill one's own interest. Bala told that a house is being constructed in her neighborhood. She complains ,the whole day there is noise and disturbance from this house, which is a nuisance for her whole family. The front portion of their house is always occupied by the construction material which creates the problem in parking their car. Once the labours were pouring water on the cemented walls. They were doing in such a manner that water was coming in the informant's house also. Informant ignored this act, even though things which she had kept in her balcony got wet. Informant warned the contractor also to make their labours understand to work properly. Second time, labours were doing plastering of the wall with the cement. This time, whole cement was spilling on the clothes laid down in informant's balcony and on the car parked in front of the house. This time she got exasperated and called police saying the neighbors are a threat to our family.

Action Taken : Went to Police Station

Case Study 6

Violation of Right to an Adequate Standard of Living

Akriti, 35, married female, graduate, runs her own boutique in her house. Informant told that neighbors had not connected their drain pipe with the sewer line which runs in the colony. These people have a open drain. Every time they wash their clothes in the balcony, water gets filled in the front of informant's boutique, thus blocking the alleyway of entering in the boutique. Bunged up water creates other problems of hygiene in front of her house. Informant asks if something happens to her children because of insects and mosquitoes which dwell on the water, who will be responsible? She adds, the dirty water in the ambience of her boutique plunders the aesthetics of her shop, thus reducing the customers. Informant had requested many times to her neighbours to get their drain connected, but these people in order to save some money does not bother to get it done. Akriti had a major fight also one day with them. Although it began with small argument, but soon grew into heated up fight. Informant's husband was hit by the neighbor's husband. After this, informant and her husband called at police station and soon police came. Informant registered complaint saying that their neighbor came to hit the informant's husband to hurt him grievously. Later when the neighbor came and said sorry and got his drain connected, informant's husband took back his complaint.

Action Taken : Justice Seeked

Case Study 7

Violation of Right to Work

Seema, 27, newly married female, engineer by profession works in a computer center of a government office. Informant told that her work is not only a source of income for her, but is also a source of tension for her. On being asked, why is her work a source of tension, she revealed that there are two male colleagues in her office, who treat her as a female only and not as a colleague. Informant says that these people know also that she is married even though, this doesn't deter them from their advances. Seema says, that she was lucky enough to got this government job at this age, now she cannot leave this opportunity only because some body at work is creating trouble for her. Informant argues that why cannot a female work without any psychological tension at the work place. She also has full right to work in a tension free environment. Why is the right to work limited only to male members in the society? On being asked, if she has taken any corrective measures, informant says that she cannot do anything regarding this, except completely ignoring the whole issue and those who does it.

Action Taken : Nothing

Case Study 8

Violation of Right of Freedom from Torture

Brijesh Kumar, 56, married male, is a junior engineer in the water works department. Informant told that once his telephone bill came of Rs. 10,400 for a month. His normal bill ranges from Rs. 1500 -2000 per month. Informant claims that he has not used the services for this much bill. He was definite that there was some problem while the bill was generated. Looking at the escalated bill, informant who has already undergone angioplasty, got severely tensed, as it is out of question for him to pay the bill from his regular salary. Since, then till today its been 45 days, that informant's ordeal of getting his bill adjusted is continuing. This has been a constant source of torture for the informant. Every now and then m he has to go the MTNL office, leaving his own work. His phone has also been disconnected because of non-payment of the bill. After trying all the possibilities, informant went to consumer forum and filed a case there. When he reached to the MTNL office with the copy of the complaint, his problem was dealt on the top priority. Now he is hopeful that his bill would be adjusted soon.But during this whole process, he had undergone a lot of torture and harassment in the office. Brijesh says that his family members had started worrying about his health, looking at the tension in which he was.

Action Taken : Justice Seeked

7.3.6 Remarks on the Case Studies Among Urban Population

The case studies collected from the urban areas shows that people go to police for justice seeking. The types of cases ranges from simple to complicated ones. It can be said that for the urban population, police plays the same role as the panchayat plays for the tribal or rural population. People approach police taking their small and big problems as is shown in the cases collected. Many a times police help the complainant to reach to a compromise. Cases support the view that among the urban population, people are aware about the human rights. They would immediately approach police even for a small issue of parking problem. There is no idea of sitting down and discuss out the problem.

7.4 Focus Group Discussions Among all the Three Population Under Study

The strength of focus group discussions as an interview technique lies in the ability of the researcher to observe and collect data from group interaction on a topic. Efforts are made to bring into focus the area of interests in these group discussions, so as to gain insights in the areas of research. It was ensured that participants in each focus group discussions belong to same age, sex, education and occupation level. The groups for the focus group were not pre–selected but were randomly chosen. Care was taken such that any one member did not dominate the focus group. In Focus Group Discussions primary, open ended, stimulus questions were asked first followed by secondary, probing/ specific questions.

Following questions were administered to the participants of each group among all the population to gather the information regarding their views about the police system, role of police, knowledge of Human Rights :

Table 7.167: Focus Group Discussion Among the Tribal Population of District Lahoul and Spiti, Himachal Pradesh

Focus Group Number	*Gender of Participants*	*Age Group (years)*	*Number of Participants*	*Educational Qualification of Participants*	*Marital Status of Participants*	*Occupation of Participants*	*Time Consumed in the Discussion*	*Remarks*
Group 1.	Female	60-63	5	Illiterate	M	House Wives	35 min.	Do not know about police system Unaware about Human Rights Do not know if Police plays a role in violation of Human rights Would leave the person who would do unjust to them.
Group 2.	Female	21-24	5	Illiterate	UM	Agriculture	40 min.	Don't know about the police system Unaware about human rights Do not know if Police plays a role in violation of human rights Would not leave the person who would do unjust to them

(Contd.)

(Contd.Table 7.167)

Focus Group Number	*Gender of Participants*	*Age Group (years)*	*Number of Participants*	*Educational Qualification of Participants*	*Marital Status of Participants*	*Occupation of Participants*	*Time Consumed in the Discussion*	*Remarks*
Group 3.	Female	38-41	6	12th passed	M	House Wives	30 min.	Rated police system as satisfactory Unaware of Human rights Police has no role in violation. The criminal forces the police to become strict with them. Would not leave the person who would do unjust to them
Group 4.	Male	65-70	6	Illiterate	W	Nothing	50 min.	Rated police system as satisfactory Partially aware about human rights Police plays a role in violation of human rights Would not leave the person who would do unjust to them

(Contd.)

(Contd.Table 7.167)

Focus Group Number	*Gender of Participants*	*Age Group (years)*	*Number of Participants*	*Educational Qualification of Participants*	*Marital Status of Participants*	*Occupation of Participants*	*Time Consumed in the Discussion*	*Remarks*
Group 5.	Male	45-50	5	Middle	M	Agriculture	40 min.	Rated police system as good Partially aware about human rights Police plays role in violation of human rights Would not leave the person who would do unjust to them

(i) What do you understand by Human Rights ?

(ii) How would you take the injustice done against you ?

(iii) How is the behavior of the police men at the station?

(iv) Have you ever heard of misbehavior of police officials ?

(v) What do you think is the role of the police men in spreading the knowledge and awareness of Human Rights ?

(vi) Do you think that police plays a role in violating the Human Rights?

(vii) What would you suggest to a person who has been a victim of Human Rights violation ?

7.4.1 Focus Group Discussions Among the Tribal Population

A total of five Focus Group Discussions have been conducted among the tribal population in the study area:

1. Females of age between 60 to 63 years.
2. Females of age between 21-26 years.
3. Females of age between 38 to 41 years.
4. Males of age between 65 to 70 years.
5. Males of age between 45to 50 years

Out of five group discussions conducted, participants of two groups were absolutely unaware about the police system and human rights. Rest believe that police system is satisfactory. Participants had the view that human rights are not violated by police officials of Lahoul. Awareness about Human rights is found to be very less among the tribal population. Even though the awareness is less among the population under study, yet it is found that people respond to unjust done to them by taking an action against the wrong doer.

7.4.2 Focus Group Discussions Among the Rural Population

A total of six Focus Group Discussions have been conducted among the rural population in the study area :

1. Females of age between 40 to 45 years.
2. Females of age between 55 to 60 years.
3. Females of age between 20 to 25 years.
4. Males of age between 30 to 35 years.
5. Males of age between 65 to 70 years.
6. Males of age between 45 to 50 years

It can be broadly said, all most all the rural participants of the Focus Group Discussion, believe that police system is bad and most of the Human

Table 7.168 : Focus Group Discussion Among the Rural Population of District Rohtak, Haryana

Focus Group Number	*Gender of Participants*	*Age Group (years)*	*Number of Participants*	*Educational Qualification of Participants*	*Marital Status of Participants*	*Occupation of Participants*	*Time Consumed in the Discussion*	*Remarks*
Group 1.	Female	40-45	5	Middle	M	House Wives	30 min.	♦ Rated police system as bad ♦ Partially Aware about Human Rights ♦ Police plays a role in violation of Human rights ♦ Would not leave the person who would do unjust to them.
Group 2.	Female	55-60	5	Illiterate	M	House wives	40 min.	♦ Rated police system as bad ♦ Unaware about human rights ♦ Police plays a role in violation of human rights ♦ Would not leave the person who would do unjust to them

(Contd..)

(Contd.Table 7.168)

Focus Group Number	*Gender of Participants*	*Age Group (years)*	*Number of Participants*	*Educational Qualification of Participants*	*Marital Status of Participants*	*Occupation of Participants*	*Time Consumed in the Discussion*	*Remarks*
Group 3..	Female	20-25	6	12th passed	M	House Wives	30 min.	♦ Rated police system as satisfactory ♦ Unaware of Human rights ♦ Police has no role in violation. The criminal forces the police to become strict with them. ♦ Would not leave the person who would do unjust to them
Group 4.	Male	30-35	5	12th Passed	M	Service	45 min.	♦ Rated police system as bad ♦ Fully aware about human rights ♦ Police plays a role in violation of human rights ♦ Would not leave the person who would do unjust to them

(Contd..)

(Contd.Table 7.168)

Focus Group Number	*Gender of Participants*	*Age Group (years)*	*Number of Participants*	*Educational Qualification of Participants*	*Marital Status of Participants*	*Occupation of Participants*	*Time Consumed in the Discussion*	*Remarks*
Group 5.	Male	65-70	6	Illiterate	W	Nothing	50 min.	♦ Rated police system as bad ♦ Partially aware about human rights ♦ Police plays a role in violation of human rights ♦ Would not leave the person who would do unjust to them
Group 6.	Male	45-50	5	Middle	M	Agriculture	30 min.	♦ Rated police system as bad ♦ Fully aware about human rights ♦ Police plays a role in violation of human rights ♦ Would not leave the person who would do unjust to them

Rights are violated by police officials. Awareness about human rights is found to be very less among the rural population. Even though the awareness is less among the population under study, yet it is found that people respond to unjust done to them by taking an action against the wrong doer.

7.4.3 Focus Group Discussions Among the Urban Population

Five Focus Group Discussions has been conducted among the Urban population under study.

1. Males of age between 20 to 25 years.
2. Females of age between 25 to 30 years.
3. Males of age between 38 to 45 years.
4. Females of age between 45 to 55 years.
5. Males of age between 60 to 70 years.

It can be broadly concluded, all most all the participants of the focus group discussions believe that police system is bad and most of the human rights are violated by police officials.

7.4.4 Focus Group Discussion in the Police Station of Tribal, Rural and Urban Population

As part of the proposed plan, visit to the police station was conducted.Visits in the police stations of Lahoul block, Sampla block and Delhi had been conducted. Focus group discussions had been carried out in the Keylong police station, Sampla police station, Inderpuri police station, West Patel Nagar police station and Mukharjee Nagar police station. Police Officials of all the rank and the hierarchy were interviewed. The Station House Officer (SHO), of the rank of Inspector of Police, Additional SHO of Inspector rank, Sub –Inspectors, Assistant Sub – Inspectors, Head Constables and Constables were interviewed. Individual interviews were carried out with the officials of all grade. Male and female officials of all hierarchy have been interviewed in the police station. Discussions had been carried out on the aspects of :

6. Police official's definition of human rights?
7. Types of human rights?
8. Human rights of arrested person ?
9. Procedure adopted by them after an arrest is done?
10. Officials knowledge and practice of human rights?
11. Situations in which they are forced not to follow human rights?

Table 7.169 : Focus Group Discussion Among the Urban Population of Delhi

Focus Group Number	*Gender of Participants*	*Age Group (years)*	*Number of Participants*	*Educational Qualification of Participants*	*Marital Status of Participants*	*Occupation of Participants*	*Time Consumed*	*Remarks*
Group 1.	Male	20 - 25	5	Engineer	UM	Student	45 min.	◆ Rated police system as bad ◆ Partially Aware about Human Rights ◆ Police plays a role in violation of Human rights ◆ Would not leave the person who would do unjust to them.
Group 2.	Female	25 - 30	4	Post Graduate (Doing Ph.D.)	UM	Student	35 min.	◆ Rated police system as bad ◆ Fully aware about human rights ◆ Police plays a role in violation of human rights

(Contd..)

(Contd.Table 7.169)

Focus Group Number	*Gender of Participants*	*Age Group (years)*	*Number of Participants*	*Educational Qualification of Participants*	*Marital Status of Participants*	*Occupation of Participants*	*Time Consumed*	*Remarks*
Group 3.	Male	38 - 45	4	Graduation	M	Service	30 min.	◆ Would not leave the person who would do unjust to them ◆ Rated police system as bad ◆ Fully aware of Human rights ◆ Police plays a role in violation.
Group 4.	Female	45 - 55	6	Graduate	M	House wives	50 min.	◆ Would not leave the person who would do unjust to them ◆ Rated police system as bad ◆ Partially aware about human rights ◆ Police plays a role in violation of human rights ◆ Participants has different views

(Contd..)

(Contd.Table 7.169)

Focus Group Number	*Gender of Participants*	*Age Group (years)*	*Number of Participants*	*Educational Qualification of Participants*	*Marital Status of Participants*	*Occupation of Participants*	*Time Consumed*	*Remarks*
Group 5.	Male	60 - 70	5	Post Graduation	M	Retired	1 hour	♦ Rated police system as bad ♦ Fully aware about human rights ♦ Police plays a role in violation of human rights ♦ Would not leave the person who would do unjust to them

Table 7.170 : Focus Group Discussion in Keylong Police Station, Lahoul

Focus Group Number	*Gender of Participants*	*Age Group (years)*	*Number of Participants*	*Educational Qualification of Participants*	*Marital Status of Participants*	*Rank*	*Time Consumed in the Discussion*	*Remarks*
Group 1.	Female	27-32	5	12th Passed	M	Line Officer	35 min.	♦ Rated police system as satisfactory for women ♦ Partially aware about Human Rights ♦ Police doesn't plays a role in violation of Human rights ♦ Would not leave the person who would do unjust to them.
Group 2.	Male	36-40	4	12th Passed	M	Constable	40 min.	♦ Rated police system as satisfactory ♦ Aware about human rights ♦ Police plays a role in violation of human rights ♦ Would not leave the person who would do unjust to them

Table 7.171 : Focus Group Discussion in Sampla Police Station, Rohtak

Focus Group Number	*Gender of Participants*	*Age Group (years)*	*Number of Participants*	*Educational Qualification of Participants*	*Marital Status of Participants*	*Rank*	*Time Consumed in the Discussion*	*Remarks*
Group 1.	Male	35-39	4	Graduate	M	Assistant Sub Inspector	35 min.	◆ ◆ Rated police system as satisfactory. ◆ Fully aware about Human Rights ◆ Police plays a role in violation of Human rights ◆ Would not leave the person who would do unjust to them.
Group 2.	Male	39-41	5	12th Passed	M	Head Constable	40 min.	◆ Rated police system as satisfactory ◆ Fully aware about human rights ◆ Police plays a role in violation of human rights ◆ Would not leave the person who would do unjust to them

(A) Focus Discussion in Keylong, Lahoul Police Station

The group discussion done with the male and female police officials of the constabulary rank, and line officer in the Keylong police station shows that police officials rates the police system as satisfactory. They say that the role of police in Himachal Pradesh in general and Lahoul in specific is very satisfactory. The reason for this type of behaviour is that since Lahoul is a small area, the reported crime is very less here. So the work of the police official is not that burdened as it is there in other states. This reduced mental tension is reflected in their behaviour.

(B) Focus Group Discussion in Sampla Police Station, Rohtak

The group discussion done with the police officials of the rank of Assistant Sub-Inspector and Head constable, in the Sampla police station shows that police officials rates the police system as satisfactory as they themselves agree that police plays a role in the violation of human rights.

(C) Focus Group Discussion in Delhi Police Stations

Three police stations, which were lying nearest to the field area in Delhi were visited.

1. Inderpuri Police Station
2. West Patel Nagar Police Station
3. Mukharjee Nagar Police Station

Table 7.172: First Focus Group Discussion in Inderpuri Police Station, Delhi

S.No.	*Group Member*	*Gender*	*Age Group*	*Number of Participants*	*Education*	*Marital Status*	*Rank*
1.	Station House Officer	Male	43	1	Graduation	Married	Inspector
2.	Sub-Inspector	Male	38-45	5	Graduation	Married	Sub-Inspector
3.	Assistant Sub-Inspector	Male	30-35	3	Graduation	Married	ASI
		Female	32	1	Graduation	Married	ASI

Focus Group Discussions was also organized in each of the Police Station. Table 6.6 shows the details of first focus group discussion done in Inderpuri police stations.

Inderpuri Police Station

Remarks of Focus Group Discussion I

The participants of the first Focus Group Discussion, carried out in the Inderpuri Police Station are Inspector, Sub – Inspector, and Assistant Sub – Inspector. All the ten members of the group share a common view and awareness regarding Human Rights. The discussion was carried on for 25 minutes.

4. They all rated Delhi Police System as very efficient. Its one of the best police in the country. They all also agree that there are certainly few loop holes in the system, which is responsible for earning bad name for the department.
5. Fully aware about Human Rights.
6. Police plays a role in violation of Human Rights.
7. Would not leave the person who would do unjust to them.

Table 7.173 : Second Focus Group Discussion in Inderpuri Police Station, Delhi

S.No.	*Group Member*	*Gender*	*Age Group*	*Number of Participants*	*Education*	*Marital Status*	*Rank*
1.	Head Constable	Male	44-46	4	12th Passed	Married	Head Constable
		Female	38-42	2	12th passed	Married	Head Constable
2.	Constable	Male	50-55	2	10th passed	Married	Constable
		Female	48-50	3	8th passed	Married	Constable

Remarks of Focus Group Discussion II:

The participants of second Focus Group Discussion, carried out in the Inderpuri Police Station, are Head Constables and Constables. All the eleven members of the group share the same views regarding the human rights violation. The discussion was carried out for 45 minutes.

- Rated Police System as satisfactory.
- Fully aware about Human Rights.
- Police doesn't play a role in violation of Human Rights.
- Would not leave the person who would do unjust to them.

Mukharjee Nagar Police Station

Table 7.174: Focus Group Discussion in Mukharjee Nagar Police Station, Delhi

S.No.	*Ranks of Participants*	*Gender*	*Age Group*	*Number of Participants*	*Education*	*Marital Status*
1.	Assistant Sub-Inspector	Male	35-40	2	Post Graduation	Married
		Female	32-35	1	Graduation	Married
2.	Head Constable	Male	35-39	2	12th Passed	Married
		Female	32-35	4	12th Passed	Married
3.	Constable	Male	42-44	2	10th Passed	Married
		Female	39	1	10th Passed	Widow

Remarks of Focus Group Discussion :

The participants of this Focus Group Discussion, carried out in Mukharjee Nagar Police Station are Assistant Sub-Inspector, Head Constable and Constable. All the 12 participants has the following views regarding the Human Rights. The discussion was carried out for 35 minutes.

- Rated Police System as satisfactory.
- Fully aware about Human Rights.
- Police doesn't play a role in violation of Human Rights.
- Would not leave the person who would do unjust to them.

West Patel Nagar Police Station

Remarks of Focus Group Discussion I:

The participants of the first Focus Group Discussions, carried out in West Patel Nagar Police Station are Inspector, Sub – Inspector, and Assistant

Sub – Inspector. All the eleven members of the group share a common view and awareness regarding Human Rights. The discussion was carried on for 30 minutes.

- They all rated Delhi Police System as very efficient.
- Fully aware about Human Rights.
- Police also plays a role in violation of Human Rights.
- Would not leave the person who would do unjust to them.

Table 7.175 : First Focus Group Discussion in West Patel Nagar Police Station, Delhi

S.No	*Group Member*	*Gender*	*Age Group*	*Number of Participants*	*Education*	*Marital Status*	*Rank*
1.	Station House Officer	Male	49	1	Graduation	Married	Inspector
2.	Sub-Inspector	Male	35-39	4	Graduation	Married	Sub-Inspector
3.	Assistant Sub-Inspector	Male	36-40	4	Graduation	Married	ASI
		Female	37-38		Graduation	Married	ASI

Table 7.176: Second Focus Group Discussion in West Patel Nagar Police Station, Delhi

S.No.	*Group Member*	*Gender*	*Age Group*	*Number of Participants*	*Education*	*Marital Status*	*Rank*
1.	Head Constable	Male	49-51	3	12th Passed	Married	Head Constable
		Female	43-44	2	12th passed	Married	Head Constable
2.	Constable	Male	50-53		10th passed	Married	Constable
		Female	39-41	3	8th passed	Married	Constable

Remarks of Focus Group Discussion II:

The participants of second Focus Group Discussion, carried out in the West Patel Nagar Police Station are Head Constables and Constables. All the eleven members of the group share the same views regarding the human rights violation. The discussion was carried out for 40 minutes.

- Rated police system as satisfactory.
- Fully aware about human rights.
- Police plays a role in violation of human rights.
- Would not leave the person who would do unjust to them.

Keeping in view the above work, it can be said now that police and its various facets have an impact on the populations human rights. The police personnel's can either play as a catalyst to increase the awareness about human rights of the general public or they can act as the violators of the human rights. Some of the studies done till now highlights various nuances of police. Bayley (1969), in his landmark study provides many empirically grounded insights in diverse areas of police organization and operations including attitudes of the community towards the police, student-police relations and rural police. Sharma (1977) extends the analysis of Bayley in some respects.

Baxi (1982), analyses the legal framework of the Indian police organization and the status of a colonial minority it creates. Baxi contrasts the existing para-military model of police organization with models of participative management and argues that police accountability and efficiency can be maximized by the latter model. A special feature of his analysis is the examination of institutionalized recourse to torture as way of policing; he examines the diverse political contexts which creates this situation and examines the diverse political contexts which create this situation and examines some of its underlying 'justification'.

Chaturvedi (2006), has also talked about the administration of police and their *modus operandi* adopted in investigation of the crime. He has outlined the primary functions of the police as the prevention and detection of crime, the maintenance of law and order, the prevention of public nuisances, the apprehension of offenders, escorting and guarding of prisoners, treasure of private or public property of which they may be placed in charge, and the prosecution of criminals. This up-to-date and comprehensive book examines police administration investigation of crime from multiple perspectives. It contains a number of answers to various questions relating to the police. It is a comprehensive overview of all the present and future possible requirements of the police.

Dhillon (2005), has talked about the nexus of Indian police and politics, focusing on the colonial concepts and democratic compulsions. The book is a compendium on the Indian police. The work is a sequel to his earlier study of the Indian police, covering the period up to the end of the colonial era. It is ambitious in scope and seeks to deal with the crucial area of police and politics since 1947.The one stick with which the police in India are constantly beaten is that they are so much part of the political executive that they lack objectivity and neutrality, two qualities crucial to professionalism. This is the image that has stuck ever since the country attained independence. Dhillon cites many communal riots in free India to support his thesis that policing devoid of politics is a thing of the past. The post-Godhra riots have been dissected so clinically that there is a consensus now that any effort to ensure objectivity in crises like Gujarat cannot succeed without releasing the police from executive control.

Pandey (2001), in his study of human rights and laws in a tribal community says that the issue could be very varied as the concept of human rights is culturally relative. Related to specific requirement of the tribal people and sometimes the lexi local (customary laws or traditional laws) and sub-cultural norms come in conflict with the development programs and the framed human rights. The national scenario of development in general and tribal development in particular indicates that the mega-projects and plans of development have been implemented at the cost of tribal displacement, depopulation on the one hand and on the other they create environmental degradation and ecological imbalances by disturbing the natural flora and fauna, and cause erosion of hills, landslides and deforestation.

Ramachandran (2005), in her article has discussed the customary laws with the reference to constitution. She has explained how the unwed mothers are accepted in the Adiyan society in Kerala. Adiyan women are easily attracted to cheap cosmetics, modern dresses and loving behaviour of the visitors and thus get exploited wlth the same. The dynamic and flexible nature of the customary laws of the Adiyan society encourages another marriage of the unwed mother. Adiyan men are ready to marry even an unwed mother if she earns better than him. In this whole process the child born to the unwed mother becomes isolated as the mother leaves the house with her new husband. According to Ramachandran, the birth of an illegitimate child means the birth of a legitimate criminal.

Mishra (2005), sees police as law enforcers and the first line of defense for human rights. They are the guardians of the law, including human rights law. In order to protect human rights, police must first know and understand them. Furthermore, police officers must be familiar with the various international guidelines and bodies of principles, and be able to use them as tools in their everyday work. They must understand that international human rights standards concerning their work were developed to provide invaluable guidance for the performance of their crucial functions in a democratic society. The present publication provides information on international human rights standards relevant to the work of police. It aims to assist law enforcement agencies and individual law enforcement officials in providing effective policing through compliance with international human rights standards. The principal beneficiaries are police trainers and training institutions, national police officials, civilian police engaged in peace-keeping operations and all concerned.

Messer (1993), has talked about the role of anthropologist in studying human rights. The author promotes the view that anthropologists are best suited for the study of human rights as they can make greater use of the human rights framework in their theoretical, action-or policy oriented analyses of social transformations. They are the best suited to advocate the rights of indigenous people.

Anand (2001), has highlighted various articles covering human rights. He has also discussed a classic case of Chakma refugees from Bangladesh who have crossed the Bangladesh borders and entered into the States of Assam, Tripura and Arunachal Pradesh. In retaliation to this, the Arunachal Pradesh Students Union had launched a movement to expel Chakmas out of the State. They proposed that these Chakmas are infiltrators who willfully have entered the country stealthily from Bangladesh border and have become the citizens of India by hook or crook with the help of anti-national party politics. The students approached court saying that these people have no right under the refugees law to remain in India. They are criminals and the government is free to take appropriate action against them for their expulsion from the country. The government has every right to send them to their home countries because they have not entered the country due to fear or apprehension of any risk to their life and liberty in their country, and have entered as infiltrators in conspiracy with their governments. But Supreme Court rejected all these pleas of the Students Union and has laid down that the state of Arunachal Pradesh was under constitutional obligation of Article 21 of the Constitution of India to protect and safeguard the life, health and well being of the Chakmas. The court directed the state to take all the measures necessary for ensuring the life and personal liberty of the Chakmas.

It can be said in view of above that in the present dearth of literature the work stands out uniquely and inimitably. The unique focus of the present work i.e. to study the knowledge, attitude and practice of the human rights makes it more different in the current scenario.

It can be said that the out of all the hypothesis framed earlier, five have affirmative results-

1. There is affect of ecological settings on the knowledge, attitude and practice of human rights. The more remote the area, the lesser is the knowledge, attitude and practice of human rights.
2. Education plays a role in deciding the level of awareness about human rights.
3. Exposure to the outer environment reduces the level of unawareness about crime and human rights violation. Interaction with various people and impact of mass media increases the awareness about the human rights.
4. Police plays a role in spreading the awareness about human rights as well as in violating them.
5. Living near the vicinity of the police station affects the awareness of the human rights.

Two hypotheses which have negative results are:

1. All customary laws comply with the state laws.
2. Customary laws are followed by those who are educationally backward.

To conclude, it can be said that a person's knowledge, awareness and practice of human rights is affected by the cultural settings of the population. Every culture has its own ideas about morality, but these are usually not readily extended beyond its boundaries to other groups. A great number of human societies are in intimate contact in the modern world, and because of the diversity of their ways of life, the primary task is the applicability of the Universal Declaration to all human beings, and not be a statement of rights conceived only in terms of the values prevalent in the countries of Western Europe and America. With the expanding number of categories, and more specific content of human rights, both experts and policymakers accept the idea that human rights concepts are culturally relative. Human rights are an image of human value. The better the human values are kept, the lesser the human rights are violated. If the human value is 'truly' added to the concept of human rights than there is no need of executing agencies and systems in a state. Some of the points have been emerged from the study which are as follows :

1. As the education increases, so is the level and complexity of crime in the society. Tribal population is found to be most sincere and honest among the three populations. Ecology plays an important role behind this feeling of mutual concern and brotherhood. Tribal population is

found to be least potential of violating other's human rights as their relationship with the other members of the society is symbiotic. They are very well aware that if today they commit something wrong against anybody, than tomorrow it may be there own chance. In the rural and urban population this dependency decreases, thus making people free of the obligatory relationship, hence more violation of human rights.

2. People expect that they should be absolutely free to enjoy all kinds of rights at every time and place without restraint. It cannot be accepted because rights and duties are complementary. If a person has a right than he has a duty also to perform. If rights become duties and duties become rights, society will function in harmony. Rights and duties should be considered as flip sides of the same coin.
3. Loss of sense of affection of one human being towards other is the main ause of the violation of human rights.
4. All the three geographically different populations studied have different insight of meaning of 'crime' and 'human rights'.
5. All the societies, be it, tribal or rural or urban has their own modes of justice seeking. The institutions of dispute settlement varies with the control of customary laws, which are latent in all the societies but becomes explicit only when there is any violation of the norms of the society.
6. The institutions of dispute processing also varies depending on the cultural set-up, accessibility of the alternative institution, education and awareness of the society.
7. Customary laws formed once in the society does not always comply with the human rights standards.
8. Remote, isolated tribal societies face the 'unknown' or the 'latent' violation of their rights through the hands of their customary laws.
9. It is observed that if in a tribal society, people doesn't go to police for their justice seeking, than they are seen as 'unaware'. Whereas if in the urban society, people do not go to police station, than they are seen as 'wise' as they would not want to get entwined in the complexities of law.
10. It is observed that a combination of awareness with illiteracy is quite destructive. As is already shown that education is not the only source of awareness. Occupation, exposure to the outer world, TV, radio, newspaper etc various other sources. In the rural population it has been seen that literacy is low but comparatively awareness is more, this has lead to their 'hyper' behaviour towards justice. These people would

get instigated by petty talks and arguments and would approach the police to satisfy their marred ego. They are unable to anticipate the consequences of the fight they indulge in.

11. It is also a known fact that feelings are universal in this world, its only their degree of perception which changes from community to community and population to population. Women rights violated by the members of a family are generally ignored even by those females who are fully aware of their human rights. The only reason behind this type of silent self sacrifice and self denial is the priority of the peace in the family.

As the populations along with mass illiteracy is increasing alarmingly, it becomes the function of the 'social scientists and activists' to educate the masses about their rights and obligations to make the social justice a reality. When the government has failed in its endeavour the responsibility to create the awareness among the people must be shared by the people themselves with the assistance of the social activist.

References

Adams, R.M.(1966): 'The Evolution of Urban Society', Weidenfeld and Nicolson Co., London.

Adegbite, L. O. (1968): 'African Attitudes to the International Protection of Human Rights', *International Protection of Human Rights*, A. Eide and A. Schou (eds.), Interscience Publishers, New York.

Agarwala, V.S.(1963): 'The Thousand Syllabled Speech- Vision in Long Darkness', Banaras Hindu University Press, Banaras.

Akers, R.L. (1965): 'Toward a Comparative Definition of Law', *Journal of Criminal Law, Criminology and Police Science*, September,56: 301-06.

Alderson, J. (1984): 'Human Rights and the Police', Council of Europe, Europe.

Ali, H. A. (1967): 'The Meos of Mewat', IBH Publishing Company, Oxford.

Ali, S. A. (1990): 'The Incidence of Crime Among the Tribals of Madhya Pradesh', pp 404- 420, In: *Applied Anthropology in India*, L.P. Vidyarthi (ed.), Kitab Mahal , Allahabad.

Aluko, M.A.O. (2003): 'Sociological Dimensions of Human Rights Violations in Nigeria', *Journal of Social Science*, 7(3): 161-170.

Amnesty International (1994): 'Police and Human Rights- From Antagonist to Protagonist', Amnesty International, Brazil.

Anand, S.(1957) : 'A Genetic Survey of ABO Blood Group Among The Punjabis', *The Anthropologist*, 4(1-2) : 28-34.

Anand, V.K. (2001): Human Rights, Allahabad Law, Agency, Haryana.

Anjum, K. (1986) : 'Maqaddima', pp 30-57 In: *Russom-e-Delhi*, Saiyid Ahmad Delhi (ed.),Urdu Academy, Delhi.

Ann, P.H. (1965): 'An Approach to Urban Sociology', Routledge and Kegan Paul, New York.

Annual Report (2004-05): 'Ministry of Tribal Affairs', Government of India.

Ansari, M. A. (1987): 'Tribals in Criminal Web', Publication Scheme Jaipur, Indore.=

Aparajita, U.(1994) : 'Culture and Development- Dongrias of Niyamgiri', Inter India Publication, New Delhi.

Appadurai, A. (1984): 'How Moral is South Asia's Economy? A Review Article', *Journal of Asian Studies*, 43: 481-97.

Apple, D. (1956): 'The Social Structure of Grand Parenthood', *American Anthropologists*, 58: 656-63.

Arora, R.C. (1978): 'Industry and Rural Development', S. Chand and Company, New Delhi.

Atkinson, E. T. (1973): 'The Himalayan Gazetteer', Cosmo Publications, Delhi.

Aujla, G. S. (1998): 'Police Training- A Profile', New Printing Press, Ludhiana.

Awasty, I. (1982) : 'Rural Women of India', B.R. Publishers, Delhi.

Baden- Powell, B.H. (1896): 'The Indian Village Community', Longmans Green and Company, London.

Baehr, P. R. (2002): 'Human Rights- Universality in Practice', Antony Rowe Ltd., Wiltshire.

Bailey, F. G. (1960): 'Tribe, Caste and Nation', Manchester University Press, Manchester.

Bailey, T. G. (1975) : 'Linguistic Studies from the Himalayas', Asian Publication Service, New Delhi.

Baines, A. (1976): 'Ethnography', Concept Publishing Company, Delhi.

Bairathi, S. (1991): 'Tribal Culture, Economy and Health', Rawat Publication, New Delhi.

Bajpai, S. C. (1987): 'Lahaul- Spiti- A Forbidden Land in the Himalayas', Indus Publishing Company, New Delhi.

Bajwa, G. S. (1995): 'Human Rights in India- Implementation and Violation', Anmol Publication, New Delhi.

Bakshi, P.M. (2002): An Introduction to Systems- Law, Society and Legal System, Booklet Published by National Law School of India University, Bangalore.

Bali, R.S. and A.N. Murti (1965): 'Ability to Smell Solutions of Sodium Cyanide Among South and North Indians', *The Anthropologist*, 12 (1&2): 13-16.

Bandopadhayay, P. K. (1994): 'Importance of Customary Law', *Central Indian Law Quarterly*, VII: 91-98.

Banerjea, D. (2005): 'Criminal Justice India Series', Vol. XIV, Allied Publishers, Kolkata.

Banerjee, S. (1985): 'Assortive Mating for Colour in Indian Population', *Journal of Bio-Social Science*, 17: 205-209.

Banerjee, S. (2004): 'India's Human Rights Diplomacy- Crises and Transformation', In: *Human Rights and Comparative Foreign Policy*, David P. Forsythe (ed.), United Nations University Press, Tokyo.

Banerji, D. (1992): 'Rural Social Transformation and Changes in Health Behaviour', pp 218-243, In: *Rural Social Transformation*, S.K. Lal & U.R. Nahar (eds.), Rawat Publications, Jaipur.

Bara, J. (2002): 'Tribe- Beast or Man: Case for a New Concept of Tribe', *Social Action*, April- June, 51:121-221.

Baraik, V.K. and B.M.R. Lakra (2003) : 'Literacy of Scheduled Tribes in Jharkhand- Patterns and Disparities', 1991-2001, *Indian Journal of Adult Education*, 64 (3-4): 19-34.

Bardhan, P.K.(1984); 'Land, Labour and Rural Poverty' , Oxford University Press, Delhi.

Barfield, T. (1997): 'The Dictionary of Anthropology', Blackwell Publishers, Oxford.

Barnard, A. and Jonathan Spencer (1996): 'Encyclopedia of Social And Cultural Anthropology', pp 489-90, Routledge Publishers, London.

Barry, H. III; J. L. Child & M. K. Bacon (1959): 'Relation of Child Training to Subsistence Economy', *American Anthropologist*, 61: 51-53.

Basoi, M. (1978): 'Human Rights- Accountability and Development', *Indian Journal of International Law*, 18: 279-83.

Batra, T. S. (1979): 'Human Rights- A Critique', Parashar Printing Press, Delhi

Baxi, U. (1982): 'Crisis of the Indian Legal System', Vikas Publishers, Delhi.

Baxi, U. (1986): 'Towards a Sociology of Indian Law', Satavhan Publications, New Delhi.

Baxi, U. (1999): 'Voices of Suffering, Fragmented University, and the Future of Human Rights', In: *The Future of International Human Rights*, Burns H. Weston and Stephan P. Marks (eds.), Transitional Publishers, New York.

Bayley, D. H. (1969): 'Police and Political Development in India', Princeton University Press, New Jersey.

Behari, B.(1976) : 'Rural Industrialization in India', Vikas Publishers, New Delhi

Bello, E. (1981): 'Shared Legal Concepts Between African Customary Norms and International Conventions on Humanitarian Law', *Indian Journal of International Law*, 1 (2): 72-107.

Benerjee, B.G. (1988) : 'Tribal Demography of Gonds', Gian Publishing House, Delhi.

Berreman, G.D. (1962): 'Pahari Polyandry-A Comparison', *American Anthropologist*, 64(1): 60-75.

Beshers, J. (1962): 'Urban Social Structure', Free Press, New York.

Bhalla, V and S. Singh (1979): 'Skin Pigmentation and Tanning in Some North Indian Populations', *Journal of Indian Anthropological Society*, 14: 253-76.

Bhargava, B.S. (1949) : 'The Criminal Tribes- A Social and Economic Study of the Principal Criminal Tribes and Castes in North India', Ethnographic and Folk Culture Society, Lucknow.

Bhatnagar , J.K. (1986): 'Kayasthas Rule', In: *Kayastha Parivar* , R.C. Srivastav (ed.) Naresh Chand Publishers, New Delhi.

Bhiwani District Gazetteers (1982): 'Haryana Gazetteers Organization', Chandigarh.

Bhowmick, P.K. (1980): 'Some Aspects of Indian Anthropology', Subarnarekha Press , Calcutta.

Bhowmick, P.K. (1994): 'Primitive Tribe Groups in Eastern India- Welfare and Education', Gyan Publishing House, New Delhi.

Bhowmick, P.K. (1963): 'The Lodhas of West Bengal- A Socio- Economic Study', Punthi Pustak, Calcutta.

Biju, M. R. (2002): 'Human Rights- Evolution, Issues and Challenges', *South Asian Journal of Socio- Political Studies*, 3: 1, 32-41.

Bilder, R. B. (1969): 'Rethinking International Human Rights- Some Basic Questions', *Human Rights Journal*, 2: 557-608.

Bingley, A.H. (1984): 'History of Sikhs', Sumit Publications, New Delhi.

Bingley, A.H.(1904): 'History, Caste and Culture of Jats and Gujars', Revised by K.P. Bahadur (1978), Ess Publication, New Delhi.

Bishnoi, M.L. (1986): 'Prayavaran Santulan Aur Jambhoji', *Amar Jyoti*, 12: 13-18.

Biswas , R.K. and A.K. Kapoor (2003): 'Educational Profile of Kamar Tribe', *Indian Journal of Adult Education*, 64 (3-4): 35-41.

Biswas, P.C. (1960): 'The Ex-Criminal Tribes of Delhi State', Department of Anthropology, University of Delhi.

Blanton, L. (1976): 'Anthropological Study of Cities', *Annual Review of Anthropology*, 5 : 249-264.

Blunt, E.A.H (1969) : 'The Caste System of Northern India', S. Chand and Company, New Delhi.

Boas, Franz (1911): 'The Mind of Primitive Man', The Macmillan Company, USA.

Bohanan, P. (1957): 'Justice and Judgment among the Tiv', Oxford University Press for the International African Institute, London.

Bolch, H. A. (1962): 'Man, Crime and Society', Random House Publishers, New York.

Bopemagage, A. (1957): 'Delhi- A Study in Urban Sociology', Bombay University Press, Bombay.

Bose, A. (1970): 'Urbanization in India- An Inventory of Source Materials', Academic Book Publisher, New Delhi.

Bose, A. (1978); 'India's Urbanization, 1901-2001', Tata Mc Graw- Hill, New Delhi.

Bose, N.K. (1964): 'Integration of Tribes of Andhra Pradesh', *Man in India*, 44(1): 97-104.

Bowden, E. (1969): 'An Index of Socio- Cultural Development Applicable to Pre-Civilized Societies', *American Anthropologist*, 71: 454-61.

Brown, J. K. (1963): 'A Cross- Cultural Study of Female Initiation Rites', *American Anthropologist*, 65: 837-53.

Brunton, P. (1937): 'Hermit in The Himalayas', Rider Publishing Company, London.

Burks, A. W. (1985): 'Japan- The Bellwether of East Asian Human Rights?', *Human Rights in East Asia*, J. C. Hsiung, Paragon House Publishers, New York.

Burman, B. K. Roy (1994): 'The Indigenous People and the Problem of Human Rights', *The Administrator*, April- June, XXXIX: 13-30.

Castells, M. (1976): 'Is there an Urban Sociology', pp 33-59, In: *Urban Sociology – Critical Essays*, C.G. Pickvance (ed.), Tavistock Publishers, London.

Census of India (2001): Series 1, India, Paper I of 2001, Registrar General and Census Commissioner, New Delhi, India.

Census of India (2001): Series 1, India, Provisional Population Totals, Paper 1 of 2001, Registrar General and Census Commissioner, New Delhi, India.

Census of India (2001): Series 1, Primary Census Abstract, India Registrar General and Census Commissioner, India.

Census of India (2001): Series 3, Himachal Pradesh, Provisional Population Totals, Paper 1 of 2001, Director of Census Operations, Shimla.

Census of India (2001): Series 3, Himachal Pradesh, Provisional Population Totals, Paper 2 of 2001, Director of Census Operations, Shimla.

Census of India (2001): Series 3, Himachal Pradesh, Provisional Population Totals, Paper 3 of 2001, Director of Census Operations, Shimla.

Census of India (2001): Series 7, Haryana, Provisional Population Totals, Paper 2 of 2001, Director of Census Operations. Haryana, Chandigarh.

Chakraborty, D.K. (1990): 'The Great Andamanese: Struggle for Survival', Seagull Books, Calcutta.

Chambers, R.; Richard Longhurst & Arnold Pacay (1981): 'Seasonal Dimensions to Rural Poverty', Osmun Publishers, New Jersey.

Chandra, J. P. (1969): 'Delhi- A Political Study', Metropolitan Book Company, Delhi.

Chandra, M. (1969): 'Socio-Economic Change in the Tribes of Andhra', pp 199-221 In: *Trends of Socio- Economic Change in India*, M.K. Chaudhari (ed.), Indian Institute of Advanced Studies, Shimla.

Chandra, R. (1972) : 'Socio-Economic Study of Kinnaures of Himachal Pradesh', In: *Report Submitted to Anthropological* Survey of India, Calcutta.

Chandra, R. (1994) : 'Forest and Tribal Economy- Some Observations', pp 45-55 In : *Tribal Economy, Health and Wasteland Development*, Neeti Mahanti (ed.), Inter-India Publications, New Delhi.

Chandra, R. (1996): 'Contextual Need for Change in Santhal Customary Law of Inheritance', pp. 345-53, In: *Tribes in India- Ongoing Challenges*, R. S. Mann (ed.), M. D. Publishers, New Delhi.

Chaney, R. and Rogelio Ruiz Revilla (1969): 'Sampling Methods and Interpretation of Correlations- A Comparative Analysis of Seven Cross-Cultural Samples', *American Anthropologist*, 71: 597-633.

Channa, S. (1975): 'The Cultural Relations of an Occupation – A Dhobi Case', *Man in India*, 55.

Channa, V.C. (1979) : 'Caste- Identity and Continuity', B.R. Publishing Corporation, Delhi.

Chaturvedi, J.C. (2006): 'Police Administration and Investigation of Crime', Isha Book Publishers, Delhi.

Chaturvedi, S.K. (1984): 'Pathology of Police –Public Relationship- Causes and Cure', *The Indian Police Journal*, July- September, XXXI (3).

Chaturvedi, S.K. (1988) : 'Police and Emerging Challenges', B.R. Publishers, Delhi.

Chauhan, B. (1967): 'A Rajasthani Village', Vir Publishing House, New Delhi.

Chenoy, Kamal Mitra (2001): 'Human Rights Violations in Jammu and Kashmir- A Report', *Social Action*, April- June, 51: 192-209.

Chetwood, P. (1972): 'Kulu-The End of the Habitable World', J. Murray Publishers, London.

Claude, R. P. and Burns H, Weston (1992): 'Human Rights in the World Community', University if Pennsylvania Press, Pennsylvania.

Clift, R. E. (1970): 'A Guide to Modern Police Thinking', W. H. Anderson Company, Cincinnati.

Cobbah, J. A. M. (1987): 'African Values and the Human Rights Debate- The African Perspective', *Human Rights Quarterly*, 9: 309-331.

Cohen, R. (1989): 'Human Rights and Cultural Relativism- The Need for a New Approach', *American Anthropologist*, 91: 1014-17.

Colby, B. N. (1966): 'Ethnographic Semantics- A Preliminary Survey', *Current Anthropology*, 7: 3-32.

Cook, R. I. (1994): 'Human Rights of Women', University of Pennsylvania Press, Philadelphia.

Crahan, M. (1982): 'Human Rights And Basic Needs in the America', Georgetown University Press, Washington.

Cranston, M. (1973): 'What are Human Rights?', Bodley Head Press, London.

Crawshaw, D. and Williamson (1998): 'Human Rights and Policing', Kluwer Law International, Netherlands.

Crawshaw, R. (1998): 'Human Rights and the Theory and Practice of Policing', Frank Cass Journals, Netherlands.

Crawshaw, R. (1999): 'Police and Human Rights', Martinus Nijhoff Publishers, Netherlands.

Crime in India (2002): National Crime Records Bureau, Ministry of Home Affairs.

Crook, W. (1896): 'The Tribes and Castes of the North –Western India', Government Printing Press, Calcutta.

Culshaw, G.M. (1961) : 'Patterns of Religious Observances in Three Villages of Rajasthan', *Journal of Social Research*, Vol.4.

Cunningham, A. (1854): 'Ladakh-Physical, Statistical and Historical', W.H. Allen Publishers, London.

Cunningham, A. (1963): 'Coins of Ancient India', Indological Book House, Varanasi.

Cunningham, A. (1967) : 'Coins of Medieval India', Indological Book House, Varanasi.

Cunningham, A. (1975): 'Ancient Geography of India', Bhartiya Publication, Varanasi.

Cunninghan, J. (1918): 'A History of the Sikhs from the Origin of the Nation to the Battle of Satluj', Oxford University Press, Bombay.

Dahia , B.S.(1980): 'Jats-The Ancient Rulers', Sterling Publishers Pvt. Ltd., New Delhi.

Dalton, E.T. (1872) : 'Descriptive Ethnology of Bengal' (Reprinted 1960), Government of Bengal, Calcutta.

Dalvi, S. and Milind Bokil (2000): 'In Search of Justice- Tribal Committees and Land Rights in Coastal Maharashtra', *Economic and Political Weekly*, 35:2843-50.

Danda, D.G. (2000) : 'Transformation of Onge Women Through Development', *Indian Anthropologist*, 30(1&2) : 47-56.

Dange, J.P. (1991): 'Poverty, Inequality and Unemployment Solutions- Tribal View', *Tribal Research and Training Institute*, 13(1): 8-9.

Darrow, C. (1934): 'Crime- Causes and Punishment', University of Chicago Press, Chicago.

Das, D.K. (1987): 'Understanding Police Human Relations', Scarecrow Press, London.

Das, J. K. (2003): 'The Right of Self- Determination of Indigenous Peoples: Developing Dynamics of Human Rights', *Indian Journal of International Law*, 43: 705-28.

Dasgupta, K.K. (1974) : 'Tribal History of Ancient India', Nabbharat Publishers, Calcutta.

Datta, C.L. (1973): 'Ladakh and Western Himalayas', Munshiram Manoharlal Publications, New Delhi.

Datta, V.N. and H.A. Phadke(1985): 'History of Kurukshetra', Vishal Publications, Kurukshetra.

Davidson, S. (1993): 'Human Rights', Open University Press, USA.

Davies, A. (1960): 'Across the Inner Line, Women's Overland Himalayan Expedition 1958', *The Himalayan Journal*, 22: 85-94.

Davis, S. (1984): 'International Strategies for the Protection of Human Rights of Indigenous Peoples', *Cultural Survival Quarterly*, 8(4): 64-65.

Dayal, M. (1978): 'Alam Mein Intikhab- Dilli', Urdu Academy, Delhi.

Deb, P.C. (1975): 'Social Stratification and Mobility in Rural Setting', Researchco Publications, Delhi.

Dehlvi, S. A. (1986): 'Russome- Dilli', Urdu Academy, Delhi.

Deogaonkar, S.G. (1990): 'Tribal Exploitation- A Study of Victims of Crime and Bondedness', Inter-India Publications, New Delhi.

Desai, A.R. (1959): 'Rural Sociology in India', Indian Society of Agricultural Economics, Bombay.

Desai, A.R. (1990): 'Trends of Urban Development in India Since Independence- Its Social Implications', pp 430-444, In: *Slums and Urbanization*, A.R. Desai and S. Devadas Pillai (eds.), Popular Prakashan, Bombay.

Dev, R. (2004): 'Human Rights, Relativism and Minorities in North- East India', *Economic and Political Weekly*, October 23.

Development Block Indicators (2003): District Statistical Office, Keylong, Lahaul & Spiti District, Himachal Pradesh.

Dhillon, K. (2005) : 'Police and Politics in India- Colonial Concepts, Democratic Compulsions- India Police', Manohar Publishers, Delhi.

Dhillon, P.K. (1989): 'Occupational Stress and Job Satisfaction in Relation to Hierarchical Position- A Study of Police Personnel', *Journal of Social Science International*, 5(1-2): 32-41.

Diamond, A. S. (1993): 'Primitive Law', Waits Company, London.

Diaz, S.M. (1983): 'Public Expectations, Perceptions and Attitudes to Police in India', *Indian Journal of Criminology*, 17(1).

Dikshit, R.C. (2000): 'Police- The Human Face', Gyan Publishing House, New Delhi.

Dikshit, R.C. and Giriraj Shah (1993): 'Police and Community', Trishul Publications, Noida.

Dinstein, Y. (1976): 'Collective Human Rights of People And Minorities', *International and Comparative Law Quarterly*, 25: 102-20.

Directorate of Economics and Statistics (1974): 'An Evolution Study of Lahaul-Spiti', Shimla.

District Statistical Report (2003): District Statistical Office, Keylong, Lahaul Spiti District, Himachal Pradesh.

Diwan , P. (1978): 'Contemporary Laws (of Punjab and Haryana)', Publication Bureau, Punjab University, Chandigarh.

Diwan , P. (1985): 'Modern Hindu Law', Allahabad Law Agency, Allahabad.

Dixit, N.K. (2006): 'Racial Identity and Rights of Tribes and Tribals' , Vista International, Delhi.

Donnelly, J. (1985): 'The Concept of Human Rights', Croom Helm Press, New York.

Donnelly, J. (1989): 'Universal Human Rights in Theory and Practice', Cornell University, Ithaca.

Doughty, P. (1988): 'Crossroads for Anthropology- Human Rights in Latin America', In: *Human Rights And Anthropology*, T. E. Downing and G. Kushner (eds.) Mass Cultural Survival Publishers, Cambridge.

Douglas, W. O. (1952): 'Beyond High Himalayas', Doubleday Publishers, New York.

Downing, T.E.(1988): 'Human Rights Research: The Challenge for Anthropologists', Cultural Survival Mass Publishers, Cambridge.

Downing, T. E. and G. Kushner (1988): 'Human Rights and Anthropology', Cultural Survival Mass Publishers, Cambridge.

Driver, H.E. (1966): 'Geographical- Historical versus Psycho- Functional Explanations of Kin Avoidances', *Current Anthropology*, 7: 131-82.

Driver, H. E. and A. L. Kroeber (1970): 'Cross-Cultural Sampling and the Galton Problem', In: *A Handbook of Methods in Cultural Anthropology*, Raoul Naroll and Ronald Cohen (eds.), Natural History Press, New York.

Drummond, L.(1980) : 'The Cultural Continum- A Theory of Intersystems', *Man*, 15 : 352-74.

Dube, S.C. (1955): 'Indian Village', Cornell University Press, Ithaca.

Dube, S.C.(1992): 'Reflections on Rural Transformation- The Indian Context', pp 1-12, In: *Rural Social Transformation*, S.K. Lal & U.R. Nahar (eds.), Rawat Publications, Jaipur.

Dunne, T. and Wheeler, Nicholas J. (1999): 'Human Rights in Global Politics', Cambridge University Press, Cambridge.

Dunsheat, J. et. Al (1957): 'Abinger Himalaya Expedition of 1956 to Bara Shigri Glacier', *The Himalayan Journal*, 21: 104-111.

Dworkin, R. (1977): 'Taking Rights Seriously', Harvard University Press, Cambridge.

Eberhard, C. (2002): 'Human Rights and Intercultural Dialogue- An Anthropological Perspective', *Indian Socio- Legal Journal*, 28(1 & 2): 99-120.

Eggan, F. (1954): 'Social Anthropology and the Methods of Controlled Comparison', *American Anthropologist*, 56: 743-63.

Eisenstadt, S.N. and A. Shachar (1987): 'Society, Culture and Urbanization', Sage Publications, London.

Elliot and Merrill (1950): 'Social Disorganization', Harper and Bros. Publishers, New York.

Elliot, Sir Henry (1896): 'The North-West Provinces of India', London Press, London.

Elwin,V. (1939) : 'The Baiga', John Murray & Co., London.

Elwin,V. (1943): 'Maria Murder and Suicide', Oxford University Press, Bombay.

Elwin,V. (1947): 'The Muria and Their Ghotul', Oxford University Press, Geoggrery Camberlege.

Elwin,V. (1955): 'Religion of an Indian Tribe', Oxford University Press, London

Elwin,V. (1958): 'A Philosophy of NEFA', NEFA Administration.

Elwin,V. (1964): 'The Tribal World of Verrier Elwin- An Autobiography', Oxford University Press, Oxford.

Evans-Pritchard, E.E. (1940) : 'The Nuer', Clarendon Press, Oxford.

Evans-Wentz, W.Y. (1970) : 'The Tibetan Book of The Dead', Oxford University Press, New York.

Executive Board, American Anthropological Association (1947): 'Statement on Human Rights Submitted to the Commission Of Human Rights, United Nations', *American Anthropologist*, 49: 539-43.

Fallers, L. (1969): 'Law without Precedent', University of Chicago Press, Chicago.

Feinberg, J. (1973): 'Social Philosophy', Prentice-Hall Press, Englewood Cliffs

Fernandes, W. and S. Anthony Raj (1996): 'The New Economic Policy and GATT- Their Impact on the Tribals', pp 295-323, In: *Tribes in India*, R.S. Mann (ed.), MD Publication, New Delhi.

Field, P.B. (1962): 'A New Cross-Cultural Study of Drunkenness', In: *Society, Culture and Drinking Patterns*, D. J. Pittman and C. R. Snyder (eds.), Wiley Publishing Co., New York.

Fields, A. B. (2003): 'Rethinking Human Rights For the New Millennium', Palgrave Macmillan, New York.

Fisher, R. H. (1963) : 'The Himalayan Battle Ground', Pall Mall Press, London

Fox, R.G. (1977): 'Urban Anthropology- Cities in Their Cultural Settings', Englewood Cliffs, New Jersey.

Francke, A.H. (1972): 'Antiquities of Indian Tibet', S. Chand and Co., New Delhi.

Furer- Haimdendorf, C.V.(1945): 'The Tribal Population of Hyderabad', Hyderabad Revenue Department, Census.

Furer- Haimdendorf, C.V.(1962): 'The Apa-Tanis, Their Neighbours- A Primitive Civilization of the Eastern Himalaya', Routlodge and Kegan Paul, New York.

Furer- Haimdendorf, C.V.(1969): 'The Konyak Nagas', Oxford University Press, Oxford.

Furer-Haimendorf, C.V.(1943): 'The Chenchus – Jungle Folk of Deccan', Macmillan and Co., London.

Fyzee, A.A. (1974): 'Outlines of Mohan Madan Law', Oxford University Press, Bombay.

Gahlot, J.S. (1966) : 'Rajputana Ka Ithihas', Hindi Sahitya Mandir, Jodhpur.

Gaikwad, V.R. (1963): 'The Anglo-Indians', Asia Publishing House, New York.

Gait, E.A.(1902): 'The Gramya Devata', *Census of India*, 1901, Vol. 6, Calcutta

Gazetteer of Delhi District (1913): Vintage Books, Gurgaon.

Ghosh, S. K. and K. E. Rustamji (1993): 'Encyclopedia of Police in India', I:3, Ashish Publishing House, New Delhi.

Ghosh, T.K. (1987) : 'Persistence of Lahoul Polyandry and Decline', pp 54-61, In : *Polyandry in India*, M.K. Raha (ed.), Gian Publishing House , New Delhi.

Ghurye, G. S. (1959): 'The Scheduled Tribes', Popular Press, Bombay.

Gill, M.S. (1972): 'The Himalayan Wonderland', Vikas Publications, Delhi.

Giri, S. P. (1950): 'Adarsh Goswami Vesh Bhusha', *Gauravank*, 14(9): 539-544.

Gluckman, N. (1955): 'The Judicial Process Among the Barotse of Northern Rhodesia', Manchester University Press, Manchester.

Godbole, N.N. (1963) : 'Rigvedic Saravati', Government of Rajasthan, Jaipur.

Goel, P. (1991): 'Delli Ki Tahzib', In: *Dilli Ki Tahzib*, Intizar Mirza(ed.), Urdu Academy, New Delhi.

Gore, M.S.(1968): 'Urbanization and Family Change', Popular Prakashan, Bombay.

Gray, A. (2002): 'Indigenous Rights and Development- Self Determination in an Amazonian Community', Berghahan Book Publishers, New York.

Gregory, R. J. (2003): 'Tribes and Tribal Origin, Use and Future of the Concept', *Study of Tribes and Tribals*, 1 (1): 1-5.

Grenard, F. (1904): 'Tibet –The Country and Its Inhabitants', Hutchinson and Company, London.

Grierson, G.A. (1916): 'Linguistic Survey of India', Motilal Banarsidas Publishers, Delhi.

Grierson, G.A. (1968): 'Linguistic Survey of India', Vol. III, part I, Moti Lal Banarsi Dass, Delhi.

Grigson, W.V. (1938): 'The Maria Gonds of Bastar', Oxford University Publishers, London.

Guenther, H.V. (1977) : 'Tibetan Buddhism in Western Perspective', Dharma Publications, California.

Gulliver, P. H. (1963): 'Social Control in an African Society', Routledge and Kegan Paul Publishers, London.

Gulliver, P. H. (1971): 'Neighbors and Networks', University of California Press, Berkeley.

Gupt, B. (1997): 'What is Ethnic', *The Eastern Anthropologist*, 50(2): 139-146

Gupta, A.S. (1974): 'Crime and Police in India', Sahitya Bhawan ,Agra.

Gupta, S. and Shilpy Gupta (2005) : 'Development Fallacy or Reality : A Case of Birhor Tribes of Chotanagpur', pp 562-583, In: *Primitive Tribes of India*, P. Dash Sharma (ed.) ,Serial Publications, New Delhi.

Gupta, Shilpy (2005) : 'Human Rights and Primitive Tribes – An Anthropological Perspective', pp 17-34, In : *Primitive Tribes in Contemporary India*, S.K. Chaudhuri & S.S. Chaudhuri (eds.) , Mittal Publications, New Delhi.

Gupta, Shilpy and A. K. Kapoor (2004): 'Ethnicity and Social Variability Among Lahouli', In: *Tribal Cultures of India* , M.K. Raha (ed.), Calcutta(In Press).

Gupta, Shilpy and A.K. Kapoor (2003) : 'Development or Globalization for Scheduled Tribes- An Anthropological Perspective', pp 385-91, In : *Understanding People of India- Anthropological Insight*, A.K. Kalla and D.K. Bhattacharya (eds.), University of Delhi, Delhi.

Gupta, Shilpy and A.K. Kapoor (2005): 'Human Rights, Development and Tribe- A Study Among the Lahoulis of Himachal Pradesh', In: *Human Genetics, Health and Ethics in Research – Anthropological Perspective*, Krishan Sharma (ed.), Panjab University, Chandigarh (In Press).

Gupta, Shilpy and A.K. Kapoor (2006): 'Reported Crime and Actual Crime- A Mis Match – A Study Among the Lahoulis of Himachal Pradesh', *The Indian Police Journal* , 52(3): In Press.

Gupta, S. (2001): 'Right of the Child to Education in India', *Social Defense*, October, 52(105) : 25-41.

Gupta, V. K. (1994): 'Judicial Activism and State Accountability for Human Rights Violations by State Agencies', *The Administrator*, April- June, XXXIX: 31-37.

Gupta, Shilpy and Kapoor, A.K., 2006. Ethnicity and Social variability among Lahoulis. Man and Life, 32 (1 &2): 15-24.

Gupta, Shilpy; Arya, Ankita and Kapoor, A.K., 2006. Tribal Rights and Justice: A Study in Lahoul Spiti, Himachal Pradesh. Indian Journal of Human Rights and the Law, 3: 165-175.

Gupta, Shilpy and Kapoor, A.K. 2005. Reported Crime and Actual Crime: A Mis-match- A Study among the Lahoulis of Himachal Pradesh. The Indian Police Journal, 52 (3): 61-69.

Gupta, Shilpy and Kapoor, A.K., 2006. Ethnicity and Social variability among Lahoulis. Man and Life, 32 (1 &2): 15-24.

Gurgaon District Gazetteers (1983): 'Haryana Gazetteers Organization', Chandigarh.

Haider, S. (2000): 'Migrant Women and Urban Experience in Squatter Settlement', pp 29-50, In: *Delhi – Urban Space and Human Destinies*, Veronique Dupont, Emma Tarlo and Denis Vidal (eds.), Manohar Publishers, New Delhi.

Hamalengwa, M; C. Flinterman and E. V. O. Dankwa (1988): 'The International Law of Human Rights in Africa- Basic Documents and Annotated Bibliography', Martinus Vijhoff Publishers, Netherland.

Harcourt, A. F. P. (1874): 'The Himalayan Districts of Kooloo, Lahoul & Spiti', London.

Hart, H. L. A. (1979): 'Are There Any Natural Rights?', Wadsworth Publishing Company, Belmont.

Hasan, N. (1978): 'Pesh Lafz', In: *Alam-Main-Intikhab-Dilli*, Maheshwar Dayal (ed.), Urdu Academy, Delhi.

Henkin, L. (1990): 'The Age of Rights', Columbia University Press, Columbia.

Henrard, K. (2002): 'Minority Protection in Post- Apartheid South- Africa- Human Rights, Minority Rights and Self Determination', Greenwood Publishing Group, USA.

Heredia, R. C.(2002): 'Interrogating Integration- The Counter-Cultural Tribal Other', *Economic and Political Weekly*, December, XXXVII (52): 5174:78.

Herskovits, M. (1947): 'Statement on Human Rights', *American Anthropologists*, 49(4): 539-43.

Himachal Academy of Art, Culture and Languages (1917): 'Lahaul Spiti- Kangra District Gazetteers', Shimla.

Hodson, T.C. (1989): 'The Naga Tribe of Manipur', Low Price Publication, Delhi.

Hoebal, E.A. (1954): 'The Law of Primitive Man', Mass: Harvard University Press, Cambridge.

Holms, P. (1958) : 'Expedition to Ratang and Parvati Region, 1955 and 1956', *The Himalayan Journal*, 21: 78-87.

Honigmann, J. J. (1973): 'Hand Book of Social and Cultural Anthropology', Rand Mc Nally and Company, Chicago.

Howard, R. E. (1986): 'Human Rights in Commonwealth Africa', Rowman And Littlefiekld Publishers, Tatowa.

Howard, R.E. (1984): 'Evaluating Human Rights in Africa- Some Problems of Implicit Comparisons', *Human Rights Quarterly*, 6: 160-179.

Hsiung, J. C. (1985): 'Human Rights in East Asia- A Cultural Perspective', Paragon House Publishers, New York.

Hunter, W.W. (1908): 'Imperial Gazetteer of India', Vol. XVII, Oxford University Press, Bombay.

Hunter, W.W. (1987) : 'The Annals of Rural Bengal' (Reprinted from 1st edition, London, 1868), Cosmo Publication, Delhi.

Hutchison, J. and J. Vogel(1933): 'The History of Punjab Hill States', Punjab Government, Lahore.

Hutton, J. H. (1931): With Complete Survey of Tribal Life and System', In: *Census of India*, Vol. I, Gian Publishing House, Delhi.

Hutton, J.H. (1946): 'Castes in India- Its Nature, Function and Origins', Cambridge University Press, Cambridge.

Ibbeston, D. (1916) : 'Panjab Castes: Races, Castes and Tribes of the People of Panjab', Government Press, Lahore.

Imperial Gazetteer of India (1908): Vol XVI, Oxford Press, London.

Inagaki, R. (1986): 'Some Aspects of Human Rights in Japan', In: *UNESCO*, UNESCO, Paris.

Indian Institute of Public Administration (1978): 'Police', *Indian Journal of Public Administration* ,(Special Issue), 24(1).

Iswaran, K.(1968) : 'Shivapur- A South Indian Village', Routledge and Kegan Paul, London.

Iyer, V. R. K. (2002): 'Public Law of Human Rights', *South Asian Journal of Socio- Political Studies*, June, 3(1): 13-19.

Jain, A.K. (1994): 'The Citizen of Delhi', Managmare Publishing Company, New Delhi.

Jones, G. (1958) : 'A Trek in Lahoul, 1958', *The Himalayan Journal*, 21: 138-140

Jones, S. (1982): 'Rural Poverty and Agrarian Reform', Allied Publishers, New Delhi.

Joshi, H.; K. Raghavendra & S.K. Subharao & V.P. Sharma(1985): 'Distribution of Human Blood Group Polymorphic Systems in Two Haryana Villages', *Indian Journal of Medical Research*, 81:180-185.

Joshi, P.C. (1992): 'Mass Participation and Rural Development- Some Basic Issues', pp 13-21, In: *Rural Social Transformation*, S.K. Lal & U.R. Nahar (eds.), Rawat Publications, Jaipur.

Joshi, V.H. (1992): 'Politico- Economic Change and Social Transformation in Saurashtra', pp 210-217, In: *Rural Social Transformation*, S.K. Lal & U.R. Nahar (eds.), Rawat Publications, Jaipur.

Kaarthikeyan, D. R. (2005): 'Human Rights- Problems and Solutions', Gyan Publishing House, New Delhi.

Kadar, A. (2001): 'Police in Transition', Central European University Press, Hungary.

Kalekar, K. (1955): 'Report of the Backward Classes Commission', Vol. I, Government of India.

Kant, R. (1996): 'Police Administration', Omsons Publications, New Delhi.

Kapoor, A. K. (1999): 'Law and Scheduled Tribes- A Socio- Legal Perspective', pp. 175-82, In: *Backward Communities*, V. K. Pant and B. S. Bisht (eds.), Gyan Publishing House, Delhi.

Kapoor, A.K. (1990): 'Genetics and Tribals- An Anthropological Perspective', *South Asian Anthropologist*, 11:55-62.

Kapoor, A.K. (1996): 'A Plea for Socio-Economic Development of the Tribals of Central Himalayas' , pp 163-172, In : *Man and Development in the Himalayas*, A.K. Kapoor and D. Singh (eds.), Academic Foundation, Delhi.

Kapoor, A.K. (1998): 'Role of NGOs in Human Development-A Domain of Anthropology', *Journal of Indian Anthropological Society*, 33: 283-300.

Kapoor, A.K. (2000 a) : 'Environment , Man, Technology and Development in Western Himalayas: Role of Anthropologist Vs. NGOs', *Man and Life*, 34:1-7.

Kapoor, A.K. (2000 b): 'Environment , Health and Development in Sahariyas- A Primitive Tribe of Rajasthan', pp 105-134, In: *Environment , Health and Development-An Anthropological Perspective* , P. Dash Sharma (ed.), S.C. Roy Institute of Anthropological Studies, Ranchi.

Kapoor, A.K. (2000 c): 'Ecology and Religions Practices Among the Bhotias in Himalayas', pp 221-235, In: *Tribal Religion: Change and Continuity*, M.C. Behra (ed.), Common Wealth Publishers, New Delhi.

Kapoor, A.K. and Satwanti Kapoor (2001): 'Crimes Against Aged: Socio-Ecological Perspective', pp 159-182, In: *Advances in Forensic Sciences*,

M.K. Bhasin and Surinder Nath (eds.), Department of Anthropology , University of Delhi, Delhi.

Kapoor, S. K. (2002): 'International Law', Ajanta Offset Printers, Allahabad.

Karnal District Gazetteers (1976): 'Haryana Gazetteers Organization', Chandigarh.

Kaul, R. (2006): 'Women and Crime', Omega Publication, Delhi.

Kaur, I. (2003): 'Human Rights of the Children and their Realization', *Delhi Law Times*, 104: J10- J14.

Kaur, Harpreet and Kapoor, A.K. 2006, Social and Cultural Rights of Tribals - A Myth or Reality? Indian Journal of Human Rights and the Law, 3:1-20.

Kaushal, R.K. (1967): 'Himaliyon Ke Desh Main', National Publishing House, New Delhi.

Kessinger, T. G. (1974): 'Vilyatpur 1848-19689 Social and Economic Change in a North Indian Village', University of California Press, Berkley.

Khan, M. A. (1995): 'Human Rights and Dalits', Uppal Publications, New Delhi.

Khan, S.A. (1983): 'Power, Police and Public', Vishal Publication, Kurukshetra

Khanna, H. R. (1978): 'Future of Human Rights in Contemporary World', *Indian Journal of International Law*, 18: 133-38.

Khare, R. (1991): 'The Issue of Right to Food Among the Hindus- Notes and Comments, Human Rights to Food', Religious Promise and Practice Lecture Series, Brown University.

Khare, R.S. (1972): 'Indigenous Culture and Lawyers Law in India' , *Comparative Studies in Society and History*, 14(1): 71-96.

Khosla, G. D. (1956): 'Himalayan Circuit- The Story of a Journey in the Inner Himalayas', London.

Khushalani, Y. (1983): 'Human Rights in Asia and Africa', *Human Rights Law Journal*, 4(4): 403-42.

Knop, K. (2004): 'Gender and Human Rights', Oxford University Press, Oxford

Kohli, K. (2005): 'Police Sub-Culture –An Analysis of Police Behaviour', *Indian Journal of Criminology*, January &July, 33(1-2): 64-76.

Kolenda, P. (1984): 'Caste in Contemporary India- Beyond Organic Solidarity', Rawat Publications, Jaipur.

Kolenda, P. (1987): 'Regional Differences in Family Structures in India', Rawat Publications, Jaipur.

Koran, R. R. & Lloyad W. Mac Corkle (1959): 'Criminology and Penology', Holt- Rinehart- Winston Publishers, New York.

Kothari, C. R. (2004): 'Research Methodology- Methods and Techniques', New Age International Publishers, New Delhi.

Krishnaswamy, S.Y. (1947): 'Rural Problems in Madras', Madras Government Press, Madras.

Krueger, R. A. (1988): 'Focus Groups- A Practical Guide for Applied Research', Sage Publications, California.

Kshatriya, G.K. and A.K. Kapoor (2003) : 'Progressive Dhodias of South Gujarat- Marching Ahead with the Mainstream Population', pp 600-624 In: *Understanding People of India- Anthropological Insight*, A.K. Kalla and D. K. Bhattacharya(ed.),University of Delhi, Delhi.

Kshatriya, G.K. and A.K. Kapoor (2003): 'Population Characteristics of the Bhils of Rajasthan', *Indian Anthropologist*, 33(1): 1-5.

Kulke, E. (1974): 'The Parsees in India - A Minority as Agent of Social Change', Vikas Publishing House, Delhi.

Kumar, A.(2006): 'Delhi Police- History and Heritage', Delhi Police, New Delhi.

Kumar, R. (1997): 'Research Methodology- A Step by Step Guide for Beginners', Sage Publications, New Delhi.

Kumar, R. (1988): 'Ethnic Conflicts and Human Rights', United Nations University Press.

Kumar, S. (1981): 'Human Rights And Economic Development: The Indian Tradition', *Human Rights Quarterly*, 3: 47-55.

Lama, D. XIV (1975): 'The Buddhism of Tibet and Key to the Middle Way', George Allen and Unwin Ltd., London.

Lama, D. XIV (1977) : 'My Land My People', Potala Corporation, New York.

Laqueur, W. and Rubin Barry (1979): 'The Human Rights Reader', Temple University Press, Philadelphia.

Lee, M. (1985): 'North Korea and the Western Notion of Human Rights', In: *Human Rights in East Asia*, J.C. Hsiung (ed.) Paragon House Publishers, New York.

Levinson, D. and Ember Melvin (1997): 'Encyclopedia of Cultural Anthropology', Vol. II, Oxford University Press, Cambridge.

Lewis , O. (1958) : 'Village Life in Northern India', University of Illinois Press, Urbana.

Little, W. ; H. W. Fowler & J. Coulson (1959): 'The Shorter Oxford English Dictionary', II: 1546, The Standard Literature Company, Calcutta.

Llewellyn, K. N. and Hoebal, E. A. (1941): 'The Cheyenne Way', University of Oklahoma Press, Norman.

Loewenstein, L. K. (1971); 'Urban Studies-An Introductory Reader', Macmillan Publishers, London.

Lokur, B. N. (1965): 'The Report of the Advisory Committee on the Revision of the Lists of Scheduled Caste and Scheduled Tribes', Department of Social Security, Government of India.

Luard, E. (1967): 'The Origins of International Concern over Human Rights', In: *The International Protection Of Human Rights*, E. Loward (ed.), Praeger Publishers, New York.

Madan, G. R. and Tara Madan (1983): 'Village Development in India- A Sociological Approach', Allied Publishers, New Delhi.

Maheshwari, H.L.(1970): 'Jambhoj- Vishnoi Sampardaya Sahitya', B.R. Publications, Calcutta.

Maine, H. S. (1861): 'Ancient Law', John Murray, London.

Maine, H. S. (1889): 'Village- Communities in the East and West', Henry Holt and Company, New York.

Majumdar , R.C.(1972): 'The Antiquity and Importance of Kurukshetra', *Journal of Historical Society*, V (4).

Majumdar, D.N. (1958): 'Caste and Communication in an Indian Village', Asia Publishing House, Bombay.

Majumdar, N. (1960): 'Justice and Police in Bengal (1665-1693)- A Study of Nizamat in Decline' , Firma Publishers, Calcutta.

Malhotra, B.S.(1981) : 'Development of Irrigation and Drainage in Mewat', Haryana Review , Chandigarh.

Malinowski, B. (1934): 'Introduction', In: *Law and Order in Polynesia*, H. I. Hogbin (ed.), Harcourt Brace Publishers, New York.

Malinowski, B. (1936): 'Crime and Custom in Savage Society', Routledge & Regan Paul Ltd., London.

Mallick, S. (2002): 'Delivery of Service by the Police- Quality and Cost', *The Indian Police Journal*, October- December , lL (4): 84-85.

Mamgain, M. D. (1975): 'Himachal Pradesh District Gazetteers', Lahaul & Spiti.

Mandel, B. P. (1980): 'Report of the Backward Classes Commission', Vol. I & II, Government of India, New Delhi.

Mann, P. H. (1965): 'An Approach to Urban Sociology', Routledge and Kegan Paul, New York.

Mann, R.S. (1973): 'Jarwas of Andaman- An Analysis of Hostility', *Man in India*, 53 (2): 201-220.

Mann, R.S. and Bageshwar Singh (1992): 'Tribal Polity of Western India' ,In : *Tribal Development in India- Problems and Prospects*, Buddhadeb Chaudhuri (ed.), Inter India Publication, Delhi.

Marasinghe, L. (1984): 'Traditional Conceptions of Human Rights in Africa', In: *Human Rights and Developments in Africa*, C. E. Welch Jr. and R. J. Meltzer (eds.), State University of New York Press, Albany.

Marjorie, A. (2001): 'Women, Gender and Human Rights', Rutgers Publishers, New Jersey.

Mathew, G. (2003): 'Panchayati Raj Institutions and Human Rights in India', *Economic and Political Weekly*, January, 11 :155-61.

Mathur, K.M. (1991): 'Police in India- Problems and Perspectives', Gyan Publishing House, New Delhi.

Mathur, K.M. (1994): 'Indian Police, Role and Challenges', Gyan Publishers, New Delhi.

Mathur, K. (2004): 'Countering Gender Violence', Sage Publications, Delhi.

Mawby, R. J. (1999): 'Policing Across the World', Routledge Publishers, London.

Mccabe, S. and Wallington, P. (1988): 'The Police, Public Order and Civil Liberties', Routledge Publishers, London.

Mehra, A. K. (1985): 'Police in Changing India', Usha Publications, New Delhi.

Mellor, J.W.(1972) : 'Developing Rural India', Plan and Practice Co., Bombay.

Mendelsohn, O. and Upendra Baxi (1994): 'The Rights of Subordinated Peoples', Oxford University Press, Delhi.

Menon, N. R. M. (2002): 'Criminal Justice India Series', Vol. VII, National Capital Territory of Delhi, Allied Publishers, National University of Juridical Sciences, Kolkata.

Menon, N. R. M. (2003): 'Criminal Justice India Series', Vol. X, Haryana, Allied Publishers, National University of Juridical Sciences, Kolkata.

Meron, T. (1991): 'Human Rights and Humanitarian Norms as Customary Law', Oxford University Press, Oxford.

Messer, E. (1993a): 'Anthropology and Human Rights', *Annual Review of Anthropology*, 22: 221-42.

Messer, E. (1993): 'Anthropology, Human Rights and Social Transformation', In: *A Transforming World: Roles for Anthropologists*, E. Moran (ed.), Oxford University Press, London.

Messer, E.(1997): 'Pluralist Approach to Human Rights', *Journal of Anthropological Research*, 53 (Fall): 293-317.

Miller, J. (1973) : 'Small Party Exploring in Kulu and Lahoul', 1972, *The Himalayan Journal*, Vol. 32.

Minh, C. (1963) : 'Hsuan Tsang- The Pilgrim and Scholar', Vietnam Buddhist Institute, Nha- Trang.

Mishra, G. K. (2002): 'Human Rights of the Child v. Breast Feeding', *All India Reporter*, December, 89: 342-47.

Mishra, R.C. (2005a): 'Human Rights in a Developing Society', Mittal Publications, Delhi.

Mishra, R.C. (2005b): 'Human Rights and Policing', Authors Press, New Delhi

Mishra, R. and Samarendra Mohanty (1992): 'Police and Social Change in India', Ashish Publishers, New Delhi.

Misra, M. and Rajan Misra (2003): 'Are Human Rights Human', *PRP Journal of Human Rights*, April- June, 7(2): 15-16.

Misra, S. C. (1977): 'A Handbook on Police Organization and Administration', Bureau of Police Research and Development, Ministry of Home Affairs.

Mitra, A. (1970): 'Delhi-Capital City', Thompson Press, New Delhi.

Mitra, K. (1982): 'Human Rights in Hinduism', In: *Human Rights in Religious Traditions*, A. Swidler (ed.), Pilgrim Press, New York.

Mohan, H. (1975): 'The Parhaiya – A Study in Culture Change', Bihar Tribal Welfare Research Institute, Ranchi.

Mohan, K. (1998): 'Scheduled Population of Tribal Area in Himachal Pradesh- A Spatial Analysis', In: *Tribal Development; Appraisal and Alternatives*, S. K. Gupta, V. P. Sharma, N. K. Sharda (eds.), Indus Publishing House, Delhi.

Molyneux, M. and Shahra Razavi (2003): 'Gender, Justice, Development and Rights', Oxford University Press, Oxford.

Moorcroft, W. and Trebeck, G. (1971): 'Travels in Hindustan', Sagar Publications, New Delhi.

Moran, E.F. (1996): 'Transforming Societies, Transforming Anthropology', University of Michigan Press, Michigan.

Morris, R. (1968): 'Urban Sociology', Allen and Unwin Publishers, London.

Morris, W. (1980): 'The American Heritage Dictionary of the English Language', Houghton Miffin Company, Boston.

Mrunalini, F. (2002): 'Human Rights for Affected Kashmiris due to Terrorism', *Journal of the Institute of Human Rights*, June, 5: 162-64.

Mukherjee, B.N.; S.K. Das and B.R. Ghosh (1975): 'Study of Three Enzyme Group System- Phosphoglucomutase, Lactate and Malate Dehydrogenase in a Punjabi Population of Delhi', *Indian Journal of Physical Anthropology and Human Genetics*, 1(1) : 67-74.

Mullik, B. N. (1969): 'A Philosophy for the Police', Allied Publishers, New Delhi.

Munilal (1974): 'Haryana', Vikas Publishing House, Delhi.

Murray, J.C.A. (1882) : 'An Account of Three Months Tour from Shimla Through Bussahir Kunowar and Spiti to Lahoul', Thaker Spink and Company, Calcutta.

Murray, R. (2004): 'Human Rights in Africa', Cambridge University Press, Cambridge.

Nader, L. (1969): 'Law in Culture and Society', Aldive Publishing Company, Chicago.

Nader, L. (2002): 'Life of the Law- Anthropological Projects', University of California Press, California.

Narain, I.; K.C. Pande & Mohan Lal Sharma (1976): 'The Rural Elite in an Indian State', Manohar Book Service, Delhi.

Narwani, G.S. (2004): 'Tribal Law in India', Rawat Publications, New Delhi.

Nath, T. (1978): 'The Indian Police', Sterling Publishers, New Delhi.

Nath, V. (1986): 'Urbanization in India – Review and Prospects', *Economic and Political Weekly* , February, 8 :21.

National Law School (2002): Essential Human Rights Law, Booklet Published by National Institute of Human Rights, Bangalore.

Negi, T. S. (1998): 'Tribes of Himachal Pradesh- Past, Present and Future', In: *Tribal Development- Appraisal and Alternatives*, S. K. Gupta, V. P. Sharma, N. K. Sharda (eds.), Indus Publishing House, Delhi.

Negi, T.S. (1975): 'Himachal Pradesh', District Gazetteer of Chamba, Himachal Government, Simla.

Newman, K. (1983): 'Law and Economic Organization', Cambridge University Press, Cambridge.

Noorani, A. G. (2002): 'Human Rights in Kashmir', *Economic and Political Weekly*, 37: 1081-82.

Noorani, A. G. (2005): 'Right to Privacy', *Economic and Political Weekly*, February, 26: 802.

O'F Lynam, J.P. (1958): 'The Gyundi and Bara Shigri', *The Himalayan Journal*, 21:97-101.

O'F Lynam, J.P. (1961): 'Back to Bara Shigri', *The Himalayan Journal*, 23 : 56-61.

Oakley, E.S. (1905): 'Holy Himalaya' Oliphant, Anderson and Ferrier Publishers, Edinburgh.

Ogunbameru, O. A. (2003): 'Focus Groups- Issues and Approaches', *Anthropologist* 5(1): 1-8.

Padhy, K. and R. K. Chaudhary (2004): 'Practices and Attitude of Mothers in Initiation of Infant Feeding', *South Asian Anthropologist*, 4(2): 157-60.

Pal, R. M. (2001): 'Denial of the Right to Education- A Human Right's Violation', *Social Action*, April- June, 51: 151-66.

Pandey, P. N. (2001): 'Human Rights and Tribal Communities', *Social Defense,* 51(149):33-40.

Pandey, R. (1993): 'Development, Peace and Human Rights in South Asia', *Journal of Social Works*, 4: 4.

Pandeya, R. C. (1986): 'Human Rights- An Indian Perspective', In: *Philosophical Foundations of Human Rights*, UNESCO (ed.), UNESCO, Paris.

Panikar, P.G.K. (1970): 'Rural Savings in India', Somaiya Publishers, Bombay.

Panikkar, R. (1982): 'Is The Notion of Human Rights a Western Concept?', *Diogenes*, 120: 75-102.

Parekh, B. (1999): 'Non- Ethnocentric Universalism', In: *Human Rights in Global Politics*, Tim Dunne and Nicholas J. Wheeler (eds.), Cambridge University Press, Cambridge.

Parmar, V.A. (1991): 'Urbanization in the Third World Countries', *Social Change*, 21: 10-21.

Pathak, M. (1991): 'Crimes, Customs and Justice in Tribal India- A Teleological Study of Adis', Mittal Publications, Delhi.

Pathak, M. (2005): 'Tribal Customs, Law and Justice', Mittal Publications, New Delhi.

Pathy, J. (1992): 'The UN System and Rights of Tribal Peoples', pp 97-101, In: *Tribal Transformation in India*, Vol. 3, Buddhadeb Chaudhari (ed.), Inter- Indian Publications, Delhi.

Patra, P.K.; C. Dash and A.K. Kapoor (1997) : 'Role of Mass Media in Tribal Development', *Vanyajati*, 46 (2) : 11-16.

Patton, M. (1990): 'Qualitative Evaluation and Research Methods', Sage Publishers, California.

Petersen, W. and Renee Petersen (1986): 'Dictionary of Demography- Terms, Concepts and Institutions', pp 684, Greenwood Press, Connectiant.

Peund, R. (1963): 'The Spirit of the Common Law', Beacon Publishers, Boston.

Pike, M. (1985): 'The Principles of Policing', McMillan Publishers, London.

Pillai, K.N.S. (1984): 'The Chronology of the Early Tamils', Asian Education Services, New Delhi.

Pollock, J. M. (2003): 'Ethics in Crime and Justice- Dilemmas and Decisions', Wadsworth Publishers, Texas.

Pospisil, L. (1958): 'Kapauku Papuans and their Law', Yale University Publications in Anthropology no. 54, New Heaven.

Pospisil, L. (1972): 'The Ethnology of Law', In: *An Addission Wesley Module in Anthropology*, Addission- Wesley Publishing Company, Massachusets.

Pospisil, L. (1974): 'Anthropology of Law- A Comparative Theory', Harper and Row Publishers, New York.

Prasad, K.N. (1991): 'India's Rural Problems', Concept Publishing Company, New Delhi.

Prasad, R.N. and P. Chakraborty (2006): Administration of Justice in Mizoram, Mittal Publications, New Delhi.

Prasad, R.R. and A.K. Kapoor (1982): 'Obstetrical Practices Among the Bhotia Tribals', *Tribal Research Bulletin*, 4(2):7-8.

Preis, A. B. S. (1996): 'Human Rights as Cultural Practice- An Anthropological Critique', *Human Rights Quarterly*, May, 18: 286-315.

Prem, K.(1970): 'Gazetteer of India (Haryana) Rohtak', Government of Haryana, Chandigarh.

Punjab District Gazetteer (1910): Rohtak District, Vol. III A, Punjab Government, India.

Punjab Government (1897): 'Gazetteer of the Kangra District', Part II-IV, Kulu, Lahaul & Spiti, Indus Publishing Company, New Delhi.

Puntambekar, S. V. (1948): 'The Hindu Concept of Human Rights', In: *Human Rights*, UNESCO, Allan Wintage Publishers, London.

Puri, B.N. (1988): 'The Khatris- A Socio- Historical Study', B.N. Publishers, Delhi.

Quesada, F. M. (1986): 'Human Rights in Latin America', In: *UNESCO*, UNESCO, Paris.

Radcliffe- Brown, A.R. (1922) :'The Andaman Islanders- A Study in Social Anthropology', Cambridge University Press, Glencce.

Radcliffe- Brown, A. R. (1952): 'Structure and Function In Primitive Society', Cohen and West Publishers, London.

Rai, Rahul (2006): 'Globalization of Human Rights', Author's Press, New Delhi.

Rajawat, M. (2005): 'Human Rights and Dalits', Anmol Publishers, Delhi.

Ram, S. (2005): 'Hindu Customs', Common Wealth Publishers. Delhi.

Ram, S. (2005): 'Hindu Women and their Rights', Common Wealth Publishers, New Delhi.

Ramachandran, B. (2005): 'Between Customary Law and Constitution- A Note on Unwed Maternity Among Adiyans', *The PRP Journal of Human Rights*, October-December, 9(4): 67.

Ramaswamy, B.(2002): 'Transformation of Tribals', *Civil Services Chronicle*, December, 93.

Ramcharan, B. G. (1983): 'The Concept of Human Rights in Contemporary International Law', In: *Canadian Human Rights Yearbook*, pp. 267-81.

Randhawa, M.S. (1959): 'Farmers of India', *Indian Council of Agricultural Research*, 1:125-126.

Ranger, T. O. (1983): 'The Invention of Tradition in Colonial Africa', In: *The Invention of Tradition*, E. Hobsbawn and T. O. Ranger (eds.), Cambridge University Press, Cambridge.

Rao, M.S.A. (1977); 'Urban Sociology in India', Popular Prakashan, Bombay.

Rao, M. N. K. (1982): 'Report of the Backward Classes Commission', Secretariat, Hyderabad.

Rao, N. (2003): 'Jharkhand- Life and Livelihood in Santhal Parganas- Does the Right to Livelihood Really Exist?', *Economic and Political Weekly*, September- October, 38 (39): 4081-84.

Rao, S. (1974): 'Social Justice and Law', National Publishing House, New Delhi.

Rao, V.K.R.V. and P.B. Desai (1965): 'Greater Delhi – A Study in Urbanization', 1940-1957, Asia Publishing House Bombay.

Rawat, G. S. (2005): 'The Status of Dalit and Human Rights in India', Sumit Enterprises , Delhi.

Redfield, R. (1967): 'Primitive Law', In: *Law and Warfare*, P. Bohanan (ed.), Natural History Press, New York.

Reid, S. T. (1976): 'Crime and Criminology', CBS College Publishers, Chicago.

Renteln, A. D. (1988): 'Relativism and the Search for Human Rights', *American Anthropologist*, 90: 56-72.

Rentlen, A. D. (1988): 'The Concept of Human Rights', *Anthropos* , 83: 343-64

Rivers, W.H.R. (1906): 'The Todas', Mac Millan and Co., London.

Rizvi, S.H.M. (1987): 'Mina- The Ruling Tribe of Rajasthan', B.R. Publishing Corporation, Delhi.

Roberts, S. (1995): 'Law and Dispute Processes', In: *Comparison Encyclopedia of Anthropology, Humanity, Culture and Social Life*, pp. 962-81, Tim Ingold (ed.), Routledge Publishers, London.

Rohtak District Gazetteers (1970) : 'Haryana Gazetteers Organization', Chandigarh.

Rose, H.A. (1919): 'Glossary of the Tribes and Castes of the Punjab and N.W.F. Province', Civil and Military Gazette Press, Lahore.

Roy, B. (1961): 'Ethnographic Study of Soligas', In: *Census of India*, Part V-B, No.6, Monograph Series, Karnataka.

Roy, H.L.D. (1981): 'A Tribe in Transition –The Jaintias of Meghalaya', Cosmo Publication, New Delhi.

Roy, S.C. (1912): 'Mundas and their Country', City Book Society, Calcutta.

Roy, S.C. (1915): 'The Oraons of Chotanagpur', Author's Bar Library, Ranchi.

Roy, S.C. (1921): 'Anthropological Researches in India', *Man in India*, 1: 11-56.

Roy, S.C. (1928): 'Oraon Religion and Customs', Man in India Office, Ranchi.

Roy, S.C. (1935): 'The Hill Bhuinyas of Orissa', Man in India Office, Ranchi.

Roy, S.C. (1937): 'The Kharia', Vol. I and II (with R.C. Roy), Man in India Office, Ranchi.

Roy. S.C. (1925): 'The Birhor- A Little Known Jungle Tribe of Chhotanagpur', Man in India Office, Ranchi.

Rural Development Statistics (2001): 'National Institute of Rural Development', Rajendaranagar, Hyderabad.

Russell, R.V. and Hiralal (1916): 'The Tribes and Castes of the Central Provinces of India', Macmillan and Company, London.

Saboohi, A. (1989) : 'Dilli Ki Chand Ajeeb Hastiyan', Maktaba-E-Jamia Ltd., New Delhi.

Sachchidananda (1992) : 'Rural Social Transformation in Bihar', pp 169-183, In: *Rural Social Transformation*, S.K. Lal & U.R. Nahar (eds.), Rawat Publications, Jaipur.

Sahani, R. N. (1994): 'Lahoul- The Mystery Land in the Himalayas', Indus Publishing Company, New Delhi.

Sahay, B.N. (1981): 'Political Institutions and Tribal Development', pp 287-296, In : *Tribal Development and its Administration,* L.P. Vidyarthi (ed.), Concept Publishing Company, Delhi.

Sahu, C. (1995): 'Birhor Tribe', Sarup and Sons Publications, New Delhi.

Sahu,C. (1998): 'The Birjia- A Primitive Tribe of Bihar', pp 42-53, In; *Tribal Culture and Identity*, Chaturbhuj Sahu (ed.), Sarup and Sons Publications, New Delhi.

Saini, S. L. (1970): 'Shoor Saini Jati Ka Itihas', Haryana Saini Sabha, Delhi.

Saklani, G.(1984) : 'The Uprooted Tibetans in India', Cosmo Publications, Delhi.

Saksena, N. S. (1987): 'Law and Order in India', Abhinav Publications, New Delhi.

Sangave, V.A.(1980); 'Jaina Community -A Social Survey', Popular Prakashan, Bombay.

Sapir, E. (1954): 'Custom', In: *Encyclopedia of Social Sciences*, Vol. III, pp. 658, Edwin R. A. Seligman And Alvin Johnson (eds.), Macmillan Company, New York.

Sarangi, D.R. (2003): 'State, NGOs and Tribals', *Economic and Political Weekly*, January, XXXVIII (1): 84.

Sarkar, R.M. (1986): 'Regional Cults and Rural Traditions', Inter- India Publications, New Delhi.

Sarkar, S. (1998): 'Human Rights in a Developing Society', A.P.H. Publishing Corporation, New Delhi.

Sastri, K.A. N. (1963) : 'Culture and History of the Tamils', Mukhopadhyay Press, Calcutta.

Sastry, V.N.K.V.(1993): 'Chenchu Food Gatherers and Hunters of Nallamala Forests- Problems of Transition', *Man and Life*, 19(1&2): 83-96.

Saunders, P. (1981): 'Social Theory and the Urban Question', Hutchinson & Co., London.

Scarr, J. (1961) : 'Women's Kulu Expedition 1961', *The Himalayan Journal*, 23: 62-70.

Schur, E. M. (1969): 'Law and Society', Random Publishers, New York.

Seligmann, G.G. (1911): 'The Veddas of Ceylon', Cambridge University Press, Cambridge.

Sen, S. (2000): 'Police in Democratic Societies', Gyan Publishing House, New Delhi.

Sengupta, A. (2001): 'Right to Development as a Human Right', *Economic and Political Weekly*, June, 7: 2527-36.

Sengupta, A. (2003): 'Human Rights to Development', *Journal of the National Human Right Commission*, 2: 1-10.

Sengupta, N. C. (1914): 'Sources of Law And Society in Ancient India', Art Press, Calcutta.

Sengupta, S. (1970): 'Ladies Lahoul Expedition 1970', *The Himalayan Journal*, 30 :221-227.

Sethi, R. M. (1992) : 'Women and Rural Social Transformation', pp. 244-267, In: *Rural Social Transformation*, S.K. Lal & U.R. Nahar (eds.), Rawat Publications, Jaipur.

Sethi, S.S. (1985): 'A Glossary of the Tribes and Castes', Rima Publishing House, New Delhi.

Setty, E.D. (1988): 'The Valayar of South India Society and Religion', Inter India Publications, New Delhi.

Seymour- Smith, C. (1986): 'Macmillan Dictionary of Anthropology', pp. 248, Macmillan Press, London.

Shabbir, M. (2005): 'Quest For Human Rights', Rawat Publications, New Delhi.

Shah, A.M. (2003): 'The Tribes- So Called- of Gujarat – In the Perspective of Time', *Economic and Political Weekly*, January, XXXVIII (2): 95-97.

Shah, G. (1993): 'Image Makers- An Attitudinal Study of Indian Police', Abhinav, Publications, New Delhi.

Shah, S.M. (1977): 'Rural Development- Planning and Reform', Abhinav Publications, Delhi.

Shams, S. (1981): 'Marriage Customs Among Meos of India', *Journal of Indian Law Institute*, 2.

Sharda, B.D (1977) : 'Status Attainment in Rural India', Ajanta Publications, Delhi.

Sharma, A.N. (1994): 'The Bharias of Patalkot', M.K. Offset Printers, Bhopal.

Sharma, K.L. (1992): 'Dynamics of Social Transformation in Rural Rajasthan Since Independence', pp 184-209, In: *Rural Social Transformation*, S.K. Lal & U.R. Nahar (eds.), Rawat Publications, Jaipur.

Sharma, K.L.(1974); 'The Changing Rural Stratification System', Orient Longman Publishers, New Delhi.

Sharma, P. D. (1999): 'Police, Society and Law- Crises of Obsolescence', Research Publications, New Delhi.

Sharma, P. D. (1996) : 'The Parhaiyas of Palamau- An Ethnographic Study', Bihar Tribal Welfare Research Institute, Ranchi.

Sharma, P.D. (1981): 'Police, Polity and People in India', Uppal Publishing House, New Delhi .

Sharma, P.D. (1985a): 'Dilemmas and Dimensions of Police Reform in India', *Indian Journal of Public Administration*, July-September.

Sharma, P.D. (1985b): 'Police and Criminal Justice Administration in India', Uppal Publishers, Delhi.

Sharma, R. P. (2003): 'Human Rights- An Overview', *All India Reporter*, March, 90: J65- J67.

Sharma, S. C. (2002): 'Human Rights of the Indian Poor- Reason for the Poor Reach', *South- Asian Journal of Socio-Political Studies*, 3(1): 27-31.

Sharma, S.L.(1992); 'Rural Development in India- Changing Concerns, Strategies and Issues', pp 28-49, In: *Rural Social Transformation*, S.K. Lal & U.R. Nahar (eds.), Rawat Publications, Jaipur.

Sharma, S.P. and J.B. Sharma(1999): 'Tribal Demography', Radha Publications, Delhi.

Sharma, S. (2005): 'Human Rights-Perspectives and Critical Issues', *The Oriental Anthropologist*, 5(1): 69-77.

Sharma, T.R. (1979): 'Tribal Customary Law in India- A Preliminary Statement' , *Journal of Social Research,* XXII (II).

Sharma, Y.D. (1992) : 'Delhi and its Neighbourhood', Archaeological Survey of India, New Delhi.

Shering, C. A. (1906): 'Western Tibet and British Borderland', Arnold Publishers, London.

Sherring, M.A. (1879): 'Hindu Tribes and Castes', Cosmo Publications, Delhi.

Shimray, R.R. (1985): 'Origin and Culture of Nagas', Somsok Publications, New Delhi.

Shivananda, S. (1962): 'Mother Ganges', Vedanta Forest Academy, Rishikesh.

Shivji, J. G. (1989): 'The Concepts of Human Rights in Africa', Codresia Book Series, London.

Shukla, A. (2005): 'Indian Tribes- A Psycho-Social Perspective', Kanishka Publications, Delhi.

Sims, M. M. (1995): 'Old Roads and New Directions: Anthropology and the Law, *Dialectical Anthropology*, 20: 341-60.

Singh, A. M. (1976): 'Neighborhood and Social Networks in Urban India', Marwah Publications, New Delhi.

Singh, J. (2002): 'Inside Indian Police', Gyan Publishing House, New Delhi.

Singh, K. S. (1994): 'People of India- Haryana', Vol. XXIII, New Delhi.

Singh, K.S. (1996) : 'People of India , Delhi', Vol. XX, Anthropological Survey of India.

Singh, K.S. and R.S. Mann (1993): 'Ethnography of Haryana- A Preliminary Study', *Journal of the Anthropological Survey of India*, 42 : 18- 29.

Singh, K.S; V. Bhalla & V. Kaul (1994): 'The Biological Variation in Indian Population', Vol. X, Anthropological Survey of India, Calcutta.

Singh, P.K. (1996): 'From Simplicity to Organized Complexity- With Special Reference to Tribal Customary Laws', pp 355-365, In: *Tribes in India*, R.S. Mann (ed.), MD Publications, New Delhi.

Singh, R. (1989): 'Haryana- Its Land and People', Souvenir XIX, All India Sociological Conference, Hissar.

Singh, R. (1986): 'Ror Itihas Ki Jhalak', Pal Publishers, Yamunagar.

Singh, S. S. (2006): 'Crime in India', Vista International ,Delhi.

Singh, S. C. (2006) : 'Social Justice and Human Rights in India', Serials Publication, New Delhi.

Singh, S. C.(2002): 'Reproductive Rights- A Part of Human Rights', *Supreme Court Journal*, 3: 12-15.

Sinha, A. K. (2003): 'Customary Law and Primitive Tribes- A Comparative Study of Hill Korwa and Kamar of Chattisgarh', pp. 554-90, In: *Understanding People of India- Anthropological Insight*, A. K. Kalla and D. K. Bhattacharya (eds.), Department of Anthropology, University of Delhi, Delhi.

Sinha, A.P. (1981): 'Crime and Custom in the Tribal Society', pp. 297-311, In: *Tribal Development and its Administration* , L.P. Vidyarthi (ed.), Concept Publishing Company , New Delhi.

Sinha, S. P. (1978): 'Human Rights Philosophically', *Indian Journal of International Law*, 18: 139-59.

Sircar, J. (1974): 'The Himalayan Handbook', Vol. I, Bose Publishers, Calcutta.

Sleen, V. D. (1929): 'Four Months Camping in the Himalayas', pp 44-45, London

Smyth, A. J. M. (1956): 'The Expedition of Royal Airforce Mountaineering Association to Lahoul, June 1956', *The Himalayan Journal*, 19: 147-155.

Solari, F. (1958): 'Chamba Lahoul Expedition of 1958', *The Himalayan Journal*, 21: 122-125.

Som, S. (1995) : 'The Great Andamanese- An Islam Community of Strait Island in Andaman', *Man in India*, 75(4) : 393-399.

Soni, L. N. (1998): 'The Bhil', In: *Tribal Culture and Identity*, Chaturbhuj Sahu (ed.), Sarup and Sons Publications, New Delhi.

Sorokin, P.A. and C.C. Zimmermann (1929): 'Principles of Rural- Urban Sociology', New York Press, New York.

Srivastava, A. (1999): 'Role of Police in Changing Society', A. P. H. Publishing Corporation, New Delhi.

Srivastava, S.S. (2003): 'Scheduled Castes and Scheduled Tribes- The Law and its Evaluation in Contemporary perspective with reference to Protection of Civil Rights and Prevention of Atrocities', *Allahabad Law Journal*, August, 101: 89-92.

Srivastav, V.P. (2006): 'HIV/AIDS and Human Rights', Indian Publishers,Delhi

Statistical Abstracts of Haryana (2000-01): 'Economic and Statistical Organization', Government of Haryana, 2002, Chandigarh.

Statistical Pocket Books (2000): 'Central Statistical Organization', Ministry of Statistical and Programme Implementation, Government of India, India.

Subramanaian, K. S. (2001): 'Human Rights of the Tribal People- The Basic Issue in Tripura', *Mainstream*, 39 (6): 23-32.

Subramanayam, A.(2001): 'Human Rights- Indian Perspective', *PRP Journal of Human Rights*, July- September, 5: 3-8.

Subramaniam, S. (1997): 'Human Rights- International Challenges', Manus Publications, New Delhi.

Sutherland, E. H. (1960): 'Principles of Criminology', J. B. Lippincott Company, New York.

Sutherland, E.H. and Donald R. Cressey (1978): 'Criminology', J. B. Lippincott Company, Philadelphia.

Sutherland, E. A. (1949): 'White Collar Crime', Holt- Rinehart- Winston Publishers, New York.

Sutter, R. B. (1978): 'Human Rights in China', Congressional Research Service, Library of Congress, Washington.

Swami, G.P. (1979): 'Sabad Vani Jhambhsar', *Sabad,* 16;139.

Tai, H. (1985): 'Human Rights in Taiwan- Convergence of Two Political Cultures?', In: *Human Rights in East Asia*, J. C. Hsuing (ed.), Paragon House Publishers, New York.

Tappan, P. (1960): 'Crime, Justice and Correction', McGraw- Hill, New York.

Tewari, A. ; K.Gauba and A. Goyal (1996): 'Evaluation of Existing Status of Knowledge Practice and Attitude Towards Oral Health of Rural

Communities of Haryana State', In: *Journal of Indian Society of Pedodontics and Preventive Dentistry*, 14(1): 21-30.

Thapar, R. (1978): 'The Ramification of Human Rights', *Indian Journal of International Law*, 18: 274-78.

The Himalayan Club (1973): 'Expedition Notes', *The Himalayan Journal*, Vol. 32, London.

Tiwari, D.N. (1984) : 'Primitive Tribes of Madhya Pradesh', Tribal Development Division, Ministry of Home Affairs, Government of India, New Delhi .

Tobdan (1993): 'The People of the Upper Valley- The STodpas of Lahul in the Himalayas', Book India Publishing Company, India.

Totten, S. (2002): 'Teaching About Genocide- Issues, Approaches and Resources', Information Age Publishing, USA.

Tripathi, T. D. (1992): 'Human Rights and TADA', *Kanpur Law Journal*, Issue 8.

Trivedi, S. (2004): 'Human Rights Revisited', *Civil Services Chronicle*, January: 30-33.

Troganowicz, R. C. and Samuel I. Doxon (1974): 'Criminal Justice and the Community', Prentice- Hall Inc., Englewood Cliffs.

UNESCO (1987): 'Anthropology and Human Rights', *Human Rights Teaching*, 6.

Upadhayay, V. (2003): 'Customary Rights over Tanks', *Economic and Political. Weekly*, November, XXXVIII(44), 4643-45.

Vadackumchery, J.(2001): 'Police Enforcement-Crimes and Injustice', Gyan Publishing House, New Delhi.

Vairagi, P. (1978): 'Shiva Puran', Shiksha Granthar, Mathura.

Vashum, R. (2005): 'Nagas Right to Self Determination', Mittal Publication, New Delhi.

Verma, A. (2005): 'The Indian Police- A Critical Examination', Regency Publication, New Delhi.

Vidyarthi, L.P.(1963): 'The Maler –A Study in Nature –Man Spirit Complex in a Hill Tribe of Bihar', Book Land Pvt. Ltd. , Calcutta.

Vidyarthi, L.P.(1971): 'The Ranchi Tribals in Andaman and Nicobar Islands', *Journal of Social Research*, 14:50-59.

Vithal, C.P.(1992): 'Socio-Economic Transformation of the Primitive Tribal Group- A Study of Chenchus of Andhra Pradesh', *Man in India*, 72(2): 189-206.

Vitso, A. (2003): 'Customary Law and Women- The Chakhesang Nagas', Regency Publications, New Delhi.

Vijayakumar, V.(2006): 'Traditional Futures-Law and Custom in India's Lakshadweep Islands', Oxford University Press, New Delhi.

Vyas, V. S. (1992): 'Occupational Diversification in Rural Areas-An Aspect of Rural Social Transformation', pp 22-27, In: *Rural Social Transformation*, S.K. Lal & U.R. Nahar (eds.), Rawat Publications, Jaipur.

Wai, D. M. (1979): 'Human Rights in Sub-Saharan Africa', In: *Human Rights-Cultural And Ideological Perspectives*, A. Pollis and P. Schwab (eds.), Praeger Publishers, New York.

Walters, G. J. (2002): 'Human Rights in an Info Age', University of Toronto Press, Toronto.

War, J. (1994): 'Family Structures, Customary Laws and Religion- The Khasi Context', *The Administrator*, July-September ,XXXIX: 17-23.

Welch, C. E. and R. I. Meltzer (1984): 'Human Rights and Development in Africa', State University Of New York Press, Alabany.

Wilson, A. (1914): 'The Abode of Snow', William Blackwood and Sons, Edinburgh.

Wilson, C. (1985): 'The Dictionary of Demography', pp. 202, Roland Pressat Press, Glasgow.

Wilson, H.H. (1837): 'Travel in Himalayan Provinces', London.

Wilson, R. W. (1985): 'Rights in the People's Republic of China', In: *Human Rights in East Asia*, J. C. Hsuing (ed.), Paragon House Publishers, New York.

Woodroffe, J. (1974): 'The Garland of Letters', Ganesh and Company, Madras.

Wright, R. M. (1988): 'Anthropological Pre-suppositions of Indigenous Advocacy', *Annual Review of Anthropology*, 17: 365-90.

Yadav, K.C. (1977) : 'The Revolt of 1857 in Haryana', Manohar Book Service, New Delhi.

Yin, R. K. (1991): 'Case Study Research-Design and Method', Sage Publishers, California.

Young, P. V. (1988): 'Scientific Social Surveys and Research', Prentice Hall of India Private Ltd., New Delhi.

Index

D

E

F

I